TEMPLE
Reflections

INSIGHTS INTO THE
HOUSE OF THE LORD

ALONZO L. GASKILL
EDITOR

CFI
AN IMPRINT OF CEDAR FORT, INC.
SPRINGVILLE, UTAH

ISBN 13: 978-1-4621-1899-1

Published by CFI, an imprint of Cedar Fort, Inc.
2373 W. 700 S., Springville, UT 84663
Distributed by Cedar Fort, Inc., www.cedarfort.com

LIBRARY OF CONGRESS CATALOGING-IN-PUBLICATION DATA

Names: Gaskill, Alonzo L., author.
Title: Temple reflections : insights into the house of the Lord / Alonzo L.
  Gaskill.
Description: Springville, Utah : CFI, an imprint of Cedar Fort, Inc., [2016]
  | ©2016 | Includes bibliographical references.
Identifiers: LCCN 2016008194 (print) | LCCN 2016009731 (ebook) | ISBN
  9781462118991 (hardback w/dustjacket : alk. paper) | ISBN 9781462126811
  (epub, pdf, mobi)
Subjects: LCSH: Mormon temples. | Church of Jesus Christ of Latter-day
  Saints--Doctrines. | Mormon Church--Doctrines.
Classification: LCC BX8643.T4 G37 2016 (print) | LCC BX8643.T4 (ebook) | DDC
  246/.9589332--dc23
LC record available at http://lccn.loc.gov/2016008194

Cover design by Shawnda T. Craig
Cover design © 2016 by Cedar Fort, Inc.
Edited and typeset by Rebecca Bird

Printed in the United States of America

10 9 8 7 6 5 4 3 2 1

Printed on acid-free paper

In celebration of the dedication of the Payson Utah Temple, June 7, 2015;
A glorious gift from God, and a source of power to all who walk its halls.

CONTENTS

CONTENTS

ACKNOWLEDGMENTS

I offer my sincere gratitude to the numerous individuals who have helped in the research, development, and review of this project. I express appreciation to the fourteen "blind reviewers" of various chapters in this book who anonymously looked over sections and offered their insights and suggestions. In addition, I am appreciative of several others who performed "open reviews," reading various chapters, and offering their suggestions for improvement—chief among them Dr. Brent L. Top (dean of Religious Education at Brigham Young University), Elder Khumbulani Mdletshe (of the Seventy), Dr. Ed J. Pinegar (former President of the Manti Temple), Erica Bennion, Janice Esplin, Wendy C. Top, and Drs. Rachel Cope, Guy L. Dorius, Scott C. Esplin, Robert L. Millet, Richard G. Moore, and Dana M. Pike. I am grateful to each for their careful readings and helpful recommendations.

I also offer thanks to my various research assistants from over the years. Each has dedicated time and talents to help me in the process of researching the various subjects in this book.

As always, I express my heartfelt thanks to Jan Nyholm who, over the years, has dedicated countless hours to improving that which I write. Words cannot express my appreciation for her selfless sacrifices on my behalf.

ACKNOWLEDGMENTS

Finally, I offer my sincere appreciation to my son Keaten for drawing each of the original illustrations in this book. His gifts, freely shared, have greatly improved the chapters in which they appear.

I am indebted to each of the aforementioned individuals for their generous assistance and insightful suggestions. I feel so very blessed to be associated with such talented and generous souls.

INTRODUCTION

◇◇

In a 1976 BYU Devotional, one of our most prolific General Authorities said, "I appreciate that what the world does not need is another book. But I like to write because it forces me to think."[1] I resonate with that declaration and, thus, here I am writing another book. And while I'm not sure if anyone wants to read another book by me, I needed to write it. Why? Well, I suppose the answer to that question is to be found in the words of the Athenian statesman and poet, Solon (circa 638–558 BCE), who famously claimed that "each day [he] grew older, [he] learnt something new."[2] In that same spirit, Hugh Nibley once quipped, "I refuse to be held responsible for anything I wrote more than three years ago. For heaven's sake, I hope we are moving forward here!"[3] The simple truth is this—like Solon and Nibley, I keep learning new things and, thus, I feel the need to write.

As a fairly new member of the Church, I assumed that Nibley spoke largely in hyperbole when he said, "If I went to the Temple five times and nothing happened, I would stop going. But I've gone hundreds of times, and the high hopes of new knowledge with which I go up the hill [to the Provo Temple] each week are *never* disappointed."[4] Could it really be true that a man, then seventy-eight years of age, could still be regularly learning new things about the temple? In my gospel infancy, I doubted such was likely. But having attended the temple regularly now for some thirty years, I can testify that such is *absolutely* possible. Time and again I see new things—things I had never noticed before. I continue to be surprised at the Spirit's ability to reveal new layers to the ordinances and covenants of the house of the Lord. And, thus, I offer one more installment in my series of temple-related books.

Anyone who has entered the doors of the temple and participated in the rites therein knows that symbolism is the language of those ordinances. Speaking generally, I have worried that the Saints do not care much for symbolism—or, at the very least, don't "get it"—and, thus, may not grasp much of what the Lord is seeking to convey to us within the walls of His most holy sanctuaries. For this very reason I wrote my books, *The Lost Language of Symbolism* (2003), *Sacred Symbols* (2011), and *The Truth About Eden* (2013). And it is for this reason that I offer this most recent installment, *Temple Reflections: Insights into the House of the Lord*. Each of these four books was penned in the hope that others would see how incredibly meaningful and enduringly applicable the rites and rituals of the temple are to our daily lives.

This book is a compilation of temple-themed essays that I've written over the years: some new and only recently written, and others previously published in obscure sources or academic journals. Each chapter looks at some aspect of the temple, its symbolism, theology, or history. Each stands as a testament to the power and profundity of God's house. And each is, in its own way, a testimony to the depth and beauty of what God revealed through the Prophet Joseph Smith. In the words of the Prophet, "the things of God are of deep import; and time, and experience, and careful and ponderous and solemn thoughts can only find them out. Thy mind, O man! . . . must stretch as high as the utmost heavens, and search into and contemplate the darkest abyss, and the broad expanse of eternity—thou must commune with God."[5] May this be our quest; and may this little installment facilitate that kind of contemplation.

NOTES

1. Paul H. Dunn, "Put On Your Spiritual Clothes," December 7, 1976, BYU Devotional, Provo, Utah, 3.

2. Solon, cited by Plutarch, in *Plutarch: The Lives of the Noble Grecians and Romans*, Dryden translation (Chicago: Encyclopedia Britannica, Inc., 1982), 65.

3. Hugh Nibley, *An Approach to the Book of Abraham* (Provo, Utah: Foundation for Ancient Research and Mormon Studies, 2009), 494.

4. Hugh Nibley, "An Intellectual Autobiography," in *Nibley on the Timely and the Timeless: Classic Essays of Hugh W. Nibley* (Provo, Utah: Religious Studies Center, BYU,

1988), xxvii–xxviii. Throughout the book, the spelling, punctuation, and capitalization of the original quotes have been preserved.

5.   Joseph Smith, *Teachings of the Prophet Joseph Smith* (Salt Lake City: Deseret Book, 1976), 137. See also Joseph Smith, et al., letter "to the Church at Quincy, Illinois, 20 March, 1839," in Dean C. Jessee, compiler, *Personal Writings of Joseph Smith*, rev. ed. (Salt Lake City: Deseret Book, 2002), 436.

THE WOMAN AT THE VEIL

AN EXAMINATION OF THE HISTORY & SYMBOLIC MERIT
OF THE SALT LAKE TEMPLE'S MOST UNIQUE SYMBOL[1]

Alonzo L. Gaskill and Seth G. Soha[2]

The Salt Lake Temple has been called "the most important building of The Church of Jesus Christ of Latter-day Saints."[3] By all accounts, it is the Church's most unique, eclectic, and architecturally grand temple. If, as they say, the Prophet Joseph was "a prophet's prophet,"[4] then the Salt Lake Temple is certainly a "temple's temple." Of all of our buildings, it is the most universally recognized by those outside of our faith, and it is the quintessential symbol of temples among practicing Latter-day Saints.

So much of the symbolism of this nineteenth-century gift to God is unique, from the exterior walls and doorknobs to the interior murals and stained glass. No temple of the Restoration, before or since, has utilized such distinctive symbols as teaching tools for its patrons.

One of those matchless symbols is found on the west wall, above the veil in the celestial room: an imposing six-foot figure clasping a branch and flanked by two cherubs.

The origin and meaning of this conspicuously placed statue has caused no small amount of speculation. Rumors run rampant, yet documentation is difficult to come by. What follows, though not exhaustive, is representative of the many interpretations of this symbol and its source.

The statue above the veil of the Salt Lake Temple.

THE VIRGIN MARY

One of the most commonly circulated explanations for this statue is that it represents the Virgin Mary and was given as a gift to The Church of Jesus Christ of Latter-day Saints by the Roman Catholic Church. Not knowing where to put it, or what to do with it, the Brethren (according to this version of the story) placed it above the veil in the temple's celestial room. One Latter-day Saint blogger explained:

> In 1992 (or there about), I went to the Salt Lake temple. While waiting for the rest of my party to come into the Celestial Room, I turned around the way I had come so that I could see them when they came. Above the veil was a statue that I recognized as the Virgin Mary from my days growing up in New Mexico. I asked one of the temple workers about it. He said that when the temple was dedicated, the Catholic church gave the church the statue. The brethren thought that the most appropriate place for the statue was in the Celestial Room.[5]

5

Though research shows this to be a very common assumption—there is no support for the claim. First of all, if the statue were indeed intended as a representation of the Virgin Mary, she most likely would have been holding a singular child, per traditional Catholic iconography, rather than having been flanked by two cherubs.

Traditional Roman Catholic statues of Madonna and child.

In addition, in a conversation with the Temple Department of the Church, we were informed that (contrary to popular claims) the statue was *not* a gift from an outside source, but was part of the temple's original design.[6] This information is confirmed by the blueprints of the temple's interior, whereon we find a sketch of the statue.[7]

 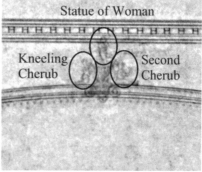

Original blueprint drawings of the celestial room view of the veil with the statuary above it.

The fact that the sketch of the three figures in the blueprint drawing is somewhat different than the final statue suggests that the idea for the three figures above the veil was present during the planning stages, but the decision as to the exact appearance of the figurines had yet to be decided when the original blueprints were drawn up. Additionally, since the drawings do not accurately reflect the statue, it seems evident that this could not have been a gift. It makes no sense for the person who drew the statues on the blueprints to draw them in a way dramatically different from the actual gifted statue. Thus, we can be certain this was not a surprise gift from the Roman Catholic Church, but, rather, something intended to be placed above the veil from the very planning stages of the project.

VENUS

Because of the shell-like design behind the central figure, some have assumed that the temple's statue is a depiction of the Roman goddess Venus or the Greek goddess Aphrodite. One LDS source states, "Inside the celestial room above the veil of the Salt Lake Temple is a female figure with child emerging from a seashell, which many associate with Venus. . . . Early Saints often had a good understanding of Venus symbolism."[8] Another suggested that "in the celestial room of the Salt Lake Temple" we find "Aphrodite (the goddess on a scalloped shell) . . . flanked by two cherubic figures. . . . The question is this: Why did . . . Brigham Young choose to include . . . pagan images that draw on . . . ancient traditions in [a temple] dedicated to the God of Israel?"[9]

The temple statue and a typical depiction of Venus.

Several things are curious about this claim. First of all, the aforementioned quote erroneously describes the statue in the temple. It is *not* of "a female figure with child." While there are two cherubs flanking the figure, she holds or coddles neither. In religious iconography, cherubs may look young or childlike, but they depict angels—not children. The reason for their youthful representation is because they symbolize "purity and innocence."[10] They are "guardians of the sacred and of the threshold"[11]—this statue, being strategically placed at the "threshold" of the celestial room, which is representative of God's abode.

A second concern with the Venus or Aphrodite interpretation is found in the fact that they are goddesses of love and fertility and are thus traditionally depicted nude—however, our temple statue is fully clothed.[12] One source on religious symbolism notes, "The prominent place of fertility in ancient symbol systems is . . . apparent from what archaeologists call Venus sculptures—small ivory or stone figures of large-breasted women. . . . These figures symbolized fertility in all its aspects, and were probably the forerunners of the earth-mother cults of early European civilization."[13] The likelihood that the Brethren would comfortably place a statue of a pagan fertility goddess in the celestial room of the temple seems very low—particularly if they *did* have "a good understanding of Venus symbolism"—as has been suggested.[14]

Finally, the symbol of the shell causes some problems for the Venus theory. The fluted shell is strongly associated with the goddess Venus in antiquity and in art. We know that the shell, from which she is customarily depicted as emerging, is a standard symbol for eroticism, fertility, or reproduction.[15] Again, it would be uncharacteristic for the presiding Brethren to employ such a symbol in the temple. Upon closer examination, one realizes that the design behind the woman is *not* a fluted shell. It *may* be nothing more than a classic design, but a close analysis suggests that it may also be a fan.

The temple statue's fan design and a scalloped shell.

Notice, for example, how the two extreme edges of the design, upon which the cherubs are perched, go out—unlike a shell (but like some feathered fans). Additionally, the bottom center of the design (just behind the woman's calves and feet) has slats in it, like a handheld feather fan, but unlike a shell. Thus the artistic representation is certainly not a shell. Again, while it *may* be nothing more than an aesthetically pleasing design, it may also be intended to represent a fan. From a symbolic perspective, fans are representative of that which is celestial.[16] They represent the Spirit and, thus, power.[17] They symbolize that which "wards off evil forces."[18] Fans represent the dignity of the one who possesses the device, thus being appropriately placed in the celestial room of the temple.[19] They are frequently associated with life—or, in this case, eternal life.[20] As one source notes, "The feathers" of a fan "stress the association with . . . celestial symbolism as a whole."[21]

Though we cannot be dogmatic about what the design behind the woman was intended to convey, we can say with a high degree of certainty that it is not a shell and that the woman is not the pagan goddess Venus.

HEAVENLY MOTHER

Some have proposed that the woman over the veil is a representation of Heavenly Mother.[22] While there is nothing in the statue and its evident symbolism that would necessarily challenge that view, as we shall shortly show, there are historical documents which *do* challenge the claim.

JESUS CHRIST

Though not a common theory, a few have proposed that the statue was intended to be a depiction of the Savior.[23] This seems problematic because a close examination of the statue leaves one with the distinct impression that the figure is a woman, not a man. The facial features in no way appear to be masculine. Additionally, the posturing of the figure does not fit traditional Christocentric iconography. Like the features of the face, the pose is rather feminine. One LDS author explained the obvious femininity of the figure this way: "It could be suggested that Christ has perfect balance with male and female qualities, between justice (male) and mercy (female), for example. In addition, companionship with a wife would further this balance, setting up an Elohim (plurality of gods)."[24]

The original 18-inch Carrera marble statue from which the 6-foot temple statue was modeled.

In other words, the source is suggesting that the figure is Jesus *because* its femininity represents Jesus's balance of justice and mercy, and because the statue could represent the idea that Christ has a wife. While we understand the author's point, it seems a great stretch; and, again, it seems unlikely that the Brethren would expect the Saints to pick up on such complex and non-traditional symbolism. Thus, we submit that this statue was not intended to be an image of Christ.

HISTORICAL ORIGINS

In scouring archives, books, articles, and the like for information regarding this statue and its origins, one quickly realizes how little has been formally written on the subject. While there is plenty of folklore and misinformation available, an accurate recitation of the statue's genesis has been elusive. Among the many theories as to the statue's identity and origins is this: "The statue was purchased out of a catalogue, as were many of the fixtures of the Salt Lake Temple. It doesn't represent anyone or anything. It is just an interesting figure common to the era."[25] While this explanation may serve to squelch the sizable amount of speculation that swirls around the statue's identity, it misrepresents the historical facts regarding its origins.

The head architect of the Salt Lake Temple was Truman O. Angell Sr. (1810–1887). He served in that capacity for thirty-four of the temple's forty years of construction.[26] Angell's successor was Joseph Don Carlos Young (1855–1938), son of President Brigham Young.

Don Carlos (as he was known) had been involved in the details of the temple prior to Angell's death, shouldering some of the burden during Angell's later years when his health prohibited him from fully functioning.

Joseph Don Carlos Young in 1891.

Within a few months after the death of Truman O. Angell, Sr., Joseph Don Carlos Young was appointed to be his successor. By the spring of 1888, he was already revising Angell's plans for the interior of the building. It was appropriate that one of Brigham Young's sons would be responsible for the completion of the Temple. Don Carlos' appointment marked a new era in which the Church would have available academically trained architects. Though he received a degree in engineering from Rensselaer Polytechnic Institute at Troy, New York, in 1879, he had always been interested in architecture. As the temple architect . . . Don Carlos' major contribution was redesigning Truman Angell, Jr.'s[27] plans for the interior of the Temple while maintaining his predecessor's basic layout and movement. . . . The result was a more aesthetically pleasing and unified design.[28]

The interior design of the Salt Lake Temple is largely the work and vision of Joseph Don Carlos Young. His handiwork is evident not only in the layout of the interior, but also in the original furnishings. Indeed, he is the individual responsible for the presence of "the woman at the veil," and his acquisition of the statue came through a rather fortuitous turn of events.[29] His grandson explained:

> Grandfather wanted to go to school in the east, along with his brother Feramorz (and others); and they asked their father if they could go. Well, one of Brigham's counselors had spoken in Conference recently and said that our young people should stay at home and shouldn't travel. They should stay here [in Utah] and build up the Kingdom. Well that was contrary to what [Joseph Don Carlos Young] wanted to do.
>
> So Brigham extracted a promise from [Don Carlos]: if he would let him go, when [Don Carlos] returned he would go to BYU and teach for three years. So [Don Carlos] went to Rensselaer Polytechnic, in Troy, New York. . . . They didn't have an architecture department. It was engineering [back then]. . . .
>
> [He] attended Rensselaer Polytechnic [from 1875 to 1879]. He came home [briefly] in '76. He didn't come home for his father's funeral in '77. He had asked his father permission to come home the summer of '77. And Brigham wrote him back and said "You and Feramorz could best utilize your time if you would go to Boston and put yourselves in the hands of Dudley Buck"—who was the greatest organist in the United States [at that time]. He said Brother [George] Careless [the conductor of the Tabernacle Choir] was not well and they would perhaps need [Don Carlos'] help when he came home. [Brigham was a] very practical man. . . . And he said, "If you spend your vacation in the way that I have intimated, it will be the best for you. But be sure [that you] do not study as to injure your health."

So, that summer—rather than coming home—[Don Carlos] went to Boston. Dudley Buck was in residence in New York City, so [upon learning this] he and Feramorz went to New York City. He had an interview with Dudley Buck [who] told him he did not have enough of the rudiments of the piano to start an organ career.

But while [Don Carlos] was in New York (in '77) they went down to the Italian district—down by the Battery [on the southern tip of Manhattan Island]—and [he] noticed these young boys sitting on the curb, carving Carrera marble. And he took a liking to this one [statue—the one that would eventually be placed above the veil of the temple] because it was nearly completed. And so he purchased it [along with the two busts of the cherubs]; not knowing what he would use it for—he just loved it![30]

Had Don Carlos not briefly pursued the possibility of learning the organ, he would not have been in New York City on the occasion of the carving of the statue and, therefore, would not, have acquired it.

Only a few years after his acquisition, Don Carlos found himself employed in helping to build the temple. Just over a decade after the purchase, he was the head architect. This facilitated "the woman at the veil's" placement in the temple. According to Don Carlos' son, "this angel and cherubs were taken to the temple by father as a model for the angel and cherubs that are over this arch coming into the Celestial Room."[31] From the eighteen-inch original, a "Utah sculptor" carved the six-foot high statue one sees today above the veil.[32] While we can't say for sure, speculation has been that the large-scale statue of the woman

The original three statues acquired by Joseph Don Carlos Young in New York.

and cherubs were the artistry of the non-LDS sculptor Cyrus E. Dallin.[33] Dallin also sculpted the statue of Moroni atop the Salt Lake Temple—he did so out of plaster[34]—the same medium used to sculpt the cherubs and woman in the celestial room. There is a remarkable resemblance between

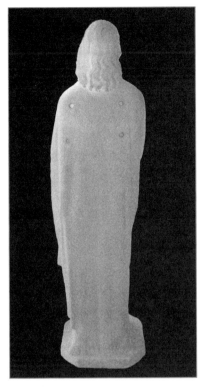

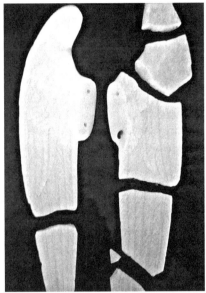

Left, the back of the original 18-inch statue with four holes visible where wings were once attached; right, original wings.

Dallin's known works and the cherubs of the Salt Lake Temple. We know for certain that Don Carlos and Cyrus Dallin knew each other[35] and, thus, Don Carlos may have selected him for the creation of this work, just as President Woodruff had selected him for the sculpting of the statue of Moroni.

Unlike what we see in the temple today, the original statue had wings and was named (possibly by the young boy who carved it) "the Angel of Peace." In his personal notes about the statue, Joseph Don Carlos Young penned this:

> About the middle of Fall one cold night as I was sitting with my feet enjoying the warmth of an open grate and my mind drowsily meditating on the power of the priesthood on earth as vested in a Prophet Seer and Revelator and the invisible power or influence that seems to accompany the Church of Christ as manifested everywhere, my eyes involuntarily raised to the mantel and my mind centered on a statue of the Angel of Peace by (   ) the original of which is in the ~~chathed~~ cathedral of (   ).[36] Those who have seen it or copies remember it represents the old Christian idea of heavenly beings and is presented

with a beautiful pair of wings carved in the most exquisite manner. Many times I have sat and admired this beautiful work but now something seemed to displease me. I thought what if Joseph, who had seen an angel should come here if he would admire this! or if Brigham or John would allow such as this to stand in a niche of our temple. The more my mind ran in this direction I felt impelled to remove the wings. Now I saw a smile and expression that I never saw before and I can now allow this . . . to be placed there again where the sculptor had placed them again.[37]

Out of concern that the Prophets—Joseph Smith, Brigham Young, or John Taylor—might be bothered by the wings on the original statue (and any replication of them on the copy made for the temple), Don Carlos removed them and felt that the improvement made the statue suitable to be placed in the house of the Lord.

The reverse of the eighteen-inch statue has four small holes where the wings were initially attached. The original marble figure and the six-foot plaster copy in the temple are, to this day, wingless, in accordance with Don Carlos' impressions that fall evening.

In its early days, the statue in the Salt Lake Temple was a pure white (like the marble original from which it was copied). Over time, however, portions were painted: starting with the palm branch and garland. Eventually, the entire statue was colorized. All of this was done after the death of Joseph Don Carlos Young. One of the Church's curators noted, "The current color scheme in the room was mostly done during the 1960s renovation by Edward Anderson. There were some slight color changes in about 1974 then again in 1982. Both of those were Emil Fetzer[38] managed projects."[39] Dave Horne, one of the painters involved in the remodel and the painting of the statue, indicated that it was in the 1960s that the majority of the colorization took place. He, along with Arnie Roneir and Alfred Nabrotski, changed the skin tone on the cherubs and woman, whereas previously only the palm branch and garland had been colorized.[40] As noted, none of this coloration was done during the life of Don Carlos, and there is reason to believe that he would not have been thrilled by the changes.[41]

SYMBOLIC MERIT

Though, based on the history, it is apparent that the statue is *not* the Virgin Mary, Venus, Aphrodite, Heavenly Mother, or Jesus, it would be misrepresentative to say that we know for certain what Joseph Don Carlos Young saw as the statue's ultimate symbolic meaning. Nor can we say that we know why its location over the veil was, for him, preferential to any other location in the temple. Don Carlos left us few clues. He did refer to the statue as "the Angel of Peace"—but it is unclear whether this was *his* name for the statue, or the name given it by the young boy in New York who carved it.[42] The only other piece of symbolic information Don Carlos left us was his statement that it symbolizes "heavenly beings" (in the plural).[43] Thus, what follows is but an examination of standard religious and scriptural symbolism, and how that relates to "the woman at the veil."

Keying off Joseph Don Carlos Young's statement that the statue is representative of "heavenly beings," we turn to John the Revelator's description of the bride of Christ. In the twelfth chapter of the book of Revelation John records, "And there appeared a great wonder in heaven; a woman clothed with the sun, and the moon under her feet, and upon her head a crown of twelve stars" (Revelation 12:1).[44] The "woman" is a standard scriptural symbol for the Church.[45] The fact that she is "clothed with the sun" represents her godly or celestial nature. Thus the woman described in the book of Revelation represents members of the Church who are keeping the commandments and are living pious lives.[46] She is a representation of all those who will receive exaltation in the celestial kingdom, thus becoming "heavenly beings."[47] The "crown" the woman (in John's vision) wears is significant. The Greek makes it clear that it is not a metal crown, like those worn by kings or rulers. Rather, it is a laurel wreath, symbolic of victory.[48] Thus she symbolizes those in the Church who overcome the world and are victorious against Satan.[49] Consequently, John describes those who were exalted through the blood of the Lamb as being "clothed with white robes, and [having] palms in their hands," crying "with a loud voice, saying, Salvation to our God which sitteth upon the throne, and unto the Lamb" (Revelation 7:9–10). In the woman, John sees all Saints who have faithfully endured and have thereby been exalted. The woman's white robe reminds us of her state of purity. The palm branch she holds is symbolic of her victory over Satan and the world! That being said, it seems "the woman at the veil" in the Salt Lake Temple is an ideal symbol for the bride of Christ—male and female—exalted in the celestial kingdom of God.[50] Clothed in a white robe, we understand her to have successfully utilized the Atonement of Christ to receive purity

Pictures of a palm branch, the statue's branch, and an olive branch.
Some have suggested that the woman at the veil is holding an olive branch.
However, a close inspection suggests that it is instead a palm branch.

through His blood. In her hands we see a palm branch, emblematic of her victory in the great test of mortality.

Joseph Don Carlos Young's explanation of the statue as a symbol of "heavenly beings" is perfectly in alignment with John's description of the bride of Christ, who symbolizes all Saints who become "heavenly" through their faith in the merits of Christ and through obedience to His word and will.

The cherubs who flank "the woman at the veil" are also instructive for temple patrons. President Brigham Young remarked, "Your *endowment* is, to receive all those ordinances in the House of the Lord, which are necessary for you, after you have departed this life, to enable you to walk back to the presence of the Father, passing the angels who stand as sentinels, being enabled to give them the key words, the signs and tokens, pertaining to the Holy Priesthood, and gain your eternal exaltation in spite of earth and hell."[51] The cherubs flanking the bride, placed at the threshold or entrance to the celestial room, appropriately mirror those "angels who stand as sentinels." As one source notes, they are "guardians of the sacred and of the threshold."[52] Their presence there suggests that all those on the celestial side of the veil have symbolically achieved their exaltation and are now worthy to dwell in God's holy presence. The garland, which they drape in front of the now-exalted bride of Christ, suggests her newfound access to the fruit of the tree of life, constituting every blessing available to, and to be enjoyed by, those who have received their exaltation.[53] As the Lord has promised the faithful, "all that my Father hath shall be given" unto them (D&C 84:38).

As for the fanlike figure behind the woman, upon which the cherubs perch, we simply remind the reader that this has traditionally been associated with the spiritual strength which comes from heeding the promptings of the Lord's Spirit. It represents the power had by the Spirit—directed over Satan and his influence. It is suggestive of the dignity that comes to those who are deified and reside for eternity in the presence of their God.[54]

CONCLUSION

The uniqueness of the Salt Lake Temple is a significant part of its appeal. While the ordinances offered therein are the same as those performed in other temples of the Church, Salt Lake's symbolic uniqueness makes it a "teaching temple" in ways that other temples of the Restoration are not. One small component of that is the "woman at the veil."

Truly, one of the beauties of symbols—whether scriptural, architectural, or otherwise—is that they can teach us many things, contingent upon our level of understanding, spiritual advancement, and attention to detail. As one commentator rightly pointed out,

> Symbols are the language of feeling, and as such it is not expected that everyone will perceive them in the same way. Like a beautifully cut diamond, they catch the light and then reflect its splendor in a variety of ways. As viewed at different times and from different positions, what is reflected will differ, yet the diamond and the light remain the same. Thus symbols, like words, gain richness in their variety of meanings and purposes, which range from revealing to concealing great gospel truths.[55]

What a blessing it is to be able to be taught from on high through a never-ending well of symbolic insights and ordinances. Truly, symbols are the language of God. He employed them throughout the scriptures; they are part of the process of making every covenant, and God utilizes them *everywhere* in the temple. To understand them is to find meaning. To misunderstand them is to court confusion. As we seek to learn the standard symbols of the scriptures and the Restoration, we find God teaching us about our place in His sacred plan. If, on the other hand, we neglect to educate ourselves in this divine language, we are more prone to confusion and erroneous ideas.

For all of the folklore that surrounds this wonderful statue, Don Carlos's "woman at the veil" is one of the Salt Lake Temple's most unique and edifying symbols. And while many have interpreted its symbolic purpose in unique ways, with Don Carlos we say it is, indeed, an "Angel of Peace" in that it can remind us—*the bride of Christ*—of the Lord's promise to all those who work in righteousness: "even peace in this world, and eternal life in the world to come" (D&C 59:23).[56]

NOTES

1.   A version of this article was originally published under the title "The Woman at the Veil: An Examination of the History and Symbolic Merit of one of the Salt Lake Temples Most Unique Symbols." See *An Eye of Faith*, ed. Kenneth L. Alford and Richard E. Bennett (Provo, Utah: Religious Studies Center, BYU, 2015), 90–111. This expanded version is republished here by permission.

2.   We wish to express our sincere appreciation to Richard W. Young, great-grandson of President Brigham Young and grandson of Joseph Don Carlos Young (the architect of the Salt Lake Temple's interior). Brother Young has been most helpful in facilitating our research, having opened his personal archives to us. We are deeply indebted to him for his kindness, support, and historical knowledge.

3.   C. Mark Hamilton, *The Salt Lake Temple: A Monument to a People*, 5th ed. (Salt Lake City: University Services Corporation, 1983), 8.

4.   Robert L. Millet, "Joseph Smith Among the Prophets," Ensign, June 1994, 19; see also Robert L. Millet, "Joseph Smith Among the Prophets," in Joseph Smith: The Prophet, The Man, ed. Susan Easton Black and Charles D. Tate Jr. (Provo, Utah: Religious Studies Center, BYU, 1993), 15.

5.   Comment posted by "Floyd the Wonderdog," May 31, 2008, http://www.bycommonconsent.com/2008/05/mary-and-judith-images-of-women-in-the-salt-lake-temple-1915/. See also http://forum.newordermormon.org/viewtopic.php?t=18892; http://thetrumpetstone.blogspot.com/2010/11/temple-statues-other-than-those-of.html; http://www.mormondialogue.org/topic/53525-temple-clamshellfan-design/.

6.   Richard Armstrong, Temple Department of The Church of Jesus Christ of Latter-day Saints, personal correspondence with the author, August 1, 2008.

7.   See Church Archives, call number: CR 679.13, folder 88, [n.d.]. While the earliest blueprint drawings we have of the Salt Lake Temple are dated February of 1853, these are of the exterior of the temple. Indeed, we have blueprint drawings of the exterior with dates as early as 1853 and as late as February 1891. Thus the blueprints were not all drawn up prior to beginning work on the temple. They developed and changed over the forty years it was under construction. While some of the interior blueprints do not have dates on them, a survey of interior drawings shows that the earliest interior blueprint was created in September of 1886. Most of the decisions as to the details of the

interior of the temple were made quite late in the construction process, and largely by Joseph Don Carlos Young rather than Truman O. Angell Sr.

8. Val Brinkerhoff, *The Day Star—Reading Sacred Architecture*, 3rd ed., 2 vols. (Salt Lake City: Digital Legends Press, 2012), 2:139. See also http://www.ldsfreedomforum .com/viewtopic.php?f=20&t=23547; http://thetrumpetstone.blogspot.com/2010/11/temple-statues-other -than-those-of.html; http://www.mormondialogue.org/topic/53525-temple-clamshellfan-design/; http://forum.newordermormon.org/viewtopic.php?f=2&t=18892&start=20.

9. Anthony E. Larson, http://grandpaenoch.blogspot.com/2009/03/artifacts-and-temple-3 -cherubim.html. See also http://www.ldsfreedomforum.com/viewtopic.php?f=20&t=23547.

10. See J. C. Cooper, *An Illustrated Encyclopaedia of Traditional Symbols* (London: Thames and Hudson, 1995), 34.

11. Ibid., 34.

12. See James Hall, *Dictionary of Subjects and Symbols in Art*, rev. ed. (New York: Harper & Row, 1974), 318–19.

13. David Fontana, *The Secret Language of Symbols: A Visual Key to Symbols and Their Meanings* (San Francisco: Chronicle Books, 1994), 25.

14. See Brinkerhoff, *The Day Star—Reading Sacred Architecture*, 2:137–39. This same source suggests that the brightness of the planet Venus symbolizes the brightness and glory of Christ. (See Brinkerhoff, *The Day Star—Reading Sacred Architecture*, 2:134–37.) Consequently, the woman (according to this theory) is really a representation of the goddess Venus, who symbolizes the planet Venus, which represents Christ incognito, per se. While a curious theory, there is nothing valid to support such an interpretation. Indeed, while the idea that the brightness of the planet Venus makes it a potential symbol of Christ is an interesting one, there is nothing to suggest that the early Brethren would have used a pagan symbol to represent Jesus. Nor does it make sense that they would expect Latter-day Saints standing in the celestial room to see the statue of a pagan goddess and then make the three-fold leap from that symbol to Christ.

15. See Jack Tresidder, *Symbols and Their Meanings* (London: Duncan Baird, 2000), 13. See also Fontana, *The Secret Language of Symbols*, 88; Hall, *Dictionary of Subjects and Symbols in Art*, 280.

16. J. E. Cirlot, *A Dictionary of Symbols*, 2nd ed. (New York: Philosophical Library, 1971), 101, s.v. "fan." See also Steven Olderr, *Symbolism: A Comprehensive Dictionary* (Jefferson, North Carolina: McFarland & Company, 1986), 47.

17. See Cooper, *An Illustrated Encyclopaedia of Traditional Symbols*, 64. See also G. A. Gaskell, *Dictionary of All Scriptures and Myths* (New York: Julian Press, 1960), 266.

18. See Cooper, *An Illustrated Encyclopaedia of Traditional Symbols*, 65. See also George Woolliscroft Rhead, *History of the Fan* (Philadelphia: J. B. Lippincott, 1910), 22, 88.

19. See Cooper, *An Illustrated Encyclopaedia of Traditional Symbols*, 64. See also *The Herder Symbol Dictionary: Symbols from Art, Archaeology, Mythology, Literature, and Religion*, trans. Boris Matthews (Wilmette, Illinois: Chiron Publications, 1986), 73, s.v. "fan"; and F. L. Cross, *The Oxford Dictionary of the Christian Church*, 2nd ed., ed. F. L. Cross and E. A. Livingstone (New York: Oxford University Press, 1990), 502, s.v. "fan."

20. Frederick Thomas Elworthy, *The Evil Eye: An Account of This Ancient & Widespread Superstition* (London: John Murray, 1895), 177. Elworthy goes on to explain, "The fan

is considered as a symbol of life" because "the rivet end is the starting point, and as the rays expand, so the road of life widens out." Ibid., 176–77. On a related note, elsewhere we learn that the fan "is a world-wide symbol of royalty . . . because it radiates like the sunbeams of the rising or setting sun." Harold Bayley, *The Lost Language of Symbolism*, 2 vols. (New York: Citadel Press, 1990), 2:162. Those who ultimately receive their exaltation will also "radiate like sunbeams," as the Prophet Joseph taught that the exalted dwell "in everlasting burnings." Joseph Smith, in *Wiford Woodruff's Journal: 1833–1898*, 9 vols., comp. Scott G. Kenney (Midvale, Utah: Signature Books, 1983), 2:384.

21. Cirlot, *A Dictionary of Symbols*, 101, s.v. "fan."

22. See Brinkerhoff, *The Day Star—Reading Sacred Architecture*, 2:139 and 175, n. 86; http://forum.newordermormon.org/viewtopic.php?t=18892; http://bycommonconsent.com/2008/05/30/mary-and-judith-images-of-women-in-the-salt-lake-temple-1915/.

23. See, for example, http://forum.newordermormon.org/viewtopic.php?t=18892; Brinkerhoff, *The Day Star—Reading Sacred Architecture*, 2:134–39.

24. Brinkerhoff, *The Day Star—Reading Sacred Architecture*, 2:137. One source on the Salt Lake Temple refers to the statue as "mother and children." See Hamilton, *The Salt Lake Temple*, 124. It is unclear if Hamilton is trying to suggest that this is "Heavenly Mother" and Her offspring, or generically a representation of all mothers with their children—though the latter explanation leaves one wondering why such a depiction would be appropriate or meaningful over the veil of the temple.

25. This was the claim of several we talked to at the Church Archives in Salt Lake City.

26. Truman started his work on the temple on January 22, 1853, and continued working on that edifice until his death on October 16, 1887. There was a period from 1861 until 1867 in which he was not able to work on the project due to severe illness. See Hamilton, *The Salt Lake Temple*, 50.

27. Truman Angell Jr., the son of Truman Sr., assisted his father and Joseph Don Carlos Young on the Salt Lake Temple starting in 1877—though much of the time (between 1877 and 1884) he was consumed with work on the Logan Temple, managing the construction of that edifice. The junior Angell was a draftsman and served in that capacity on the Salt Lake Temple. See Hamilton, *The Salt Lake Temple*, 58.

28. Hamilton, *The Salt Lake Temple*, 56–57. In the last year of the temple's construction, when they were pushing to get the interior done by the planned dedication in April, Joseph Don Carlos Young became ill. He "offered to resign, if doing so would hasten the completion of the work. President Woodruff refused and insisted that Young accomplish as much as he could and let others help." See Hamilton, *The Salt Lake Temple*, 56–57.

29. George Q. Cannon's journal, currently housed in the Church Archives, suggests that there was discussion about placing Alfred W. Lambourne's painting of Adam-ondi-Ahman over the veil (where the statue of the woman currently stands). Apparently not everyone involved in the decision-making process agreed on this, but ultimately Don Carlos' desire won the day, and the Lambourne painting was placed elsewhere in the temple.

30. Richard Wright Young, interview by the authors (Salt Lake City: October 9, 2012). See also George Cannon Young, George C. Young Oral History (unpublished manuscript: 1980), 13–14.

31. Young, Oral History, 13.

32. See Eugene Young, "Inside the New Mormon Temple," in Harper's Weekly (New York: Saturday, May 27, 1893), 510. It appears that the temple statue was most likely carved in 1892 (or possibly in early 1893), during the last year of the temple's construction.

33. Dallin, a Utah-born non-Mormon, initially turned down the invitation of President Wilford Woodruff to make the statue of the angel Moroni for the Salt Lake Temple. He told President Woodruff "that he was not a Mormon and 'didn't believe in angels.'" It was his opinion that "someone of greater spiritual capacity should be given the opportunity." With urging from his mother and the prophet, Dallin eventually "accepted the commission and began a study of Latter-day Saint scriptures and doctrine in an effort to truly interpret Moroni's character." Richard Neitzel Holzapfel, *Every Stone a Sermon* (Salt Lake City: Bookcraft, 1992), 48.

34. Young, interview.

35. We know that Dallin and Young met on July 21, 1891, to discuss the statue of the angel Moroni, and that the Moroni statue was not the only sculpture he created for the Church. See Matthew O. Richardson, "Voices of Warning: Ironies in the Life of Cyrus E. Dallin," in *Regional Studies in Latter-day Saint Church History: The New England States*, ed. Donald Q. Cannon, Arnold K. Garr, and Bruce A. Van Orden (Provo, Utah: Religious Studies Center, Brigham Young University, 2004), 211.

36. Don Carlos was trying to recall the name of the boy in New York who carved the original statue and the location of a similar statue that the boy had told him he had modeled his after, but to no avail. The blanks and strikeouts in this quote are in Don Carlos's original notebook.

37. Joseph Don Carlos Young, Private Notebook (no date; no pagination). This notebook is in the possession of Richard Wright Young, grandson of Joseph Don Carlos Young. Scans of the originals are in the possession of the authors.

38. In 1965, Emil B. Fetzer was called by President David O. McKay to serve as LDS Church architect, a position he held for twenty-one years. He designed more than twenty temples around the world, including the Provo, Jordan River, and original Ogden Temples, as well as the Mexico City, Freiberg Germany, and Tokyo Japan Temples. Fetzer also managed the remodel of a number of existing temples, including the Salt Lake Temple.

39. Emily Utt, historic site curator for The Church of Jesus Christ of Latter-day Saints, personal correspondence, October 16, 2012.

40. Conversation with Dave Horne, October 16, 2012. Horne was a subcontractor who worked on the Salt Lake Temple almost daily for seventeen years. Horne's brother, Dan (also a contractor), indicated that according to his recollection, Arnie Roneir was the one who actually painted the woman; and that took place in the early 1960s. Conversation with Dan Horne, October 24, 2012.

41. Don Carlos's son, George Cannon Young, noted in his oral history, "recently this marble statue replica has had color put on it—on the lips and other parts (flesh color)—which horrifies me. I can't imagine taking that replica of a marble statue and making [a] human out of it. To me that is almost sacrilegious and following the tradition of the sectarian world." Young, *Oral History*, 13. George added a family concern: "the time

will come . . . in the modernization of our temple buildings that this [statue] will be discarded." Young, *Oral History*, 14.

42. Young, *Private Notebook*; emphasis added. The fact that Don Carlos refers to it as "the Angel of Peace [carved] by . . ." seems to imply that the title was that of the sculptor, not Don Carlos. Young, *Private Notebook*.

43. See Young, *Private Notebook*.

44. The passage goes on to speak of the "woman" being in "travail" or labor. While some Roman Catholic commentators have taken this to mean that the "woman" must be Mary and the "baby" Jesus, LDS commentators have interpreted the "child" born to the "woman" as "the coming forth of the New Israel or the New Jerusalem." The baby is not Jesus but, rather, "the political kingdom of God whose laws will come forth from Zion." Richard D. Draper, *Opening the Seven Seals: The Visions of John the Revelator* (Salt Lake City: Deseret Book, 1991), 130. See also Jay A. Parry and Donald W. Parry, *Understanding the Book of Revelation* (Salt Lake City: Deseret Book, 1998), 148, 152.

45. See Draper, *Opening the Seven Seals*, 129; Parry and Parry, *Understanding the Book of Revelation*, 151; Bruce R. McConkie, *Doctrinal New Testament Commentary*, 3 vols. (Salt Lake City: Bookcraft, 1987–88), 3:516; Mick Smith, *The Book of Revelation, Plain, Pure, and Simple* (Salt Lake City: Bookcraft, 1998), 118; D. Kelly Ogden and Andrew Skinner, *Verse by Verse: Acts Through Revelation* (Salt Lake City: Deseret Book, 1998), 333; Leon Morris, *Tyndale New Testament Commentaries: Revelation*, rev. ed. (Grand Rapids, Michigan: Eerdmans, 1999), 152.

46. Parry and Parry, *Understanding the Book of Revelation*, 151; McConkie, *Doctrinal New Testament Commentary*, 3:516; Smith, *The Book of Revelation, Plain, Pure, and Simple*, 119.

47. Just as the sun is a symbol for things celestial, the moon reminds us of things that are terrestrial. The moon has no light of its own, but rather merely reflects the light of the sun. Thus John utilizes the image of the moon as a symbol for terrestrial churches or religions that only reflect some truth (revealed through the true Church)—but which are not the source of any of that truth themselves. It suggests that the religions symbolized by the moon are both less than the celestial woman and her truths, and also that they are (to some degree) in subjection to her. One text put it this way: "It may suggest that those of the Church who attain a celestial glory will have stewardship and ascendancy over those who attain a lesser glory." Parry and Parry, *Understanding the Book of Revelation*, 151. She can raise humans to a celestial level, because she is celestial herself. These other faiths—although valuable in making the world a better place and making lives more joyful and spiritual—can only raise people to a terrestrial level (as they have not God's authority, valid ordinances, keys, etc.). See McConkie, *Doctrinal New Testament Commentary*, 3:516.

48. Draper, *Opening the Seven Seals*, 129; *Theological Dictionary of the New Testament*, 10 vols., ed. Gerhard Friedrich (Grand Rapids, Michigan: Eerdmans, 1983), 7:620, s.v. "the games."

49. The "twelve stars" on the head of the woman/Church symbolized both the twelve Apostles that govern and also priesthood power or authority in general—as the number twelve is the number in Latter-day Saint symbology which denotes priesthood.

McConkie, *Doctrinal New Testament Commentary*, 3:517; Draper, *Opening the Seven Seals*, 129; Parry and Parry, *Understanding the Book of Revelation*, 151; Smith, *The Book of Revelation, Plain, Pure, and Simple*, 119; Ogden and Skinner, *Verse by Verse*, 333. See also Alonzo L. Gaskill, *The Lost Language of Symbolism* (Salt Lake City: Deseret Book, 2003), 134–36.

50.   Eugene Young was the grandson of President Brigham Young (through his oldest boy, Joseph Angell Young). Eugene's mother, having left the Church when Eugene was four years of age, reared him as a non-Mormon. However, because of his connections to the deceased prophet, and because he had an uncle that (in 1893) was serving in the Quorum of the Twelve, President Woodruff allowed Eugene to tour the interior of the Salt Lake Temple the night before it was dedicated. See Eugene Young, "The Mormon Temple—A Letter To A Friend," in *The Independent*, May 18, 1893, 669. After touring the soon-to-be-dedicated edifice, Young wrote an article in *Harper's Weekly* in which he discussed the various aspects of the interior and his general impressions of the temple. Though at times rather antagonistic in his public comments about the Church, in his "Inside the New Mormon Temple," (1893), Young seems rather touched by the building and his experience within. For example, in describing the celestial room, he notes, "If human art can present an idea of heaven, it must be presented in this part of the building, for an air of rest and comfort pervades the very atmosphere." (See 510.) Similarly, in his "Letter To A Friend," he penned this of the celestial room: "The only expression that I can find which will express my ideas of this room is, it is truly heavenly. To attempt to describe it would be folly; for there is nothing with which I can compare it; it is entirely original." Young, "The Mormon Temple," 669. Regarding the statue of "the woman at the veil," he wrote, "Over the arch [or veil] at the west end of the [celestial] room is a figure of the Virgin in white." Young, "Inside the New Mormon Temple," 510. Some have taken his comment about the "Virgin in white" to suggest that the statue was intended to be a representation of the Virgin Mary. It may well be that Young assumed that to be the case. He does not say that someone giving the tour told him this, but he does state rather matter-of-factly that that is what she represents. It is possible that he assumed this on his own, and it is also possible that someone else on the tour erroneously told him this. In addition, it is possible that someone explained to him that the statue represented the 144,000 who, in scripture, are referred to as "virgins" (Revelation 14:4) and he simply assumed that the reference was to the Virgin Mary instead of to those who have made their calling and election sure. We have no way of telling for sure. But we should be cautious about putting too much credence in Eugene Young's comment as (1) he was not a member of the Church and, therefore, may not have understood the lack of Mariology in Mormonism, (2) he gives no hint of where he developed the opinion that the statue represented the Virgin Mary, and (3) his claim contradicts what Joseph Don Carlos Young tells us about the statue—and, after all, Don Carlos is the person who placed the statue over the veil.

51.   Brigham Young, *The Complete Discourses of Brigham Young*, comp. Richard S. Van Wagoner, 5 vols. (Salt Lake City: The Smith-Pettit Foundation, 2009), 2:646.

52.   See Cooper, *An Illustrated Encyclopaedia of Traditional Symbols*, 34.

53. From Lehi's vision of the tree of life we read, "And it came to pass that I beheld a tree, whose fruit was desirable to make one happy. And it came to pass that I did go forth and partake of the fruit thereof; and I beheld that it was most sweet, above all that I ever before tasted. Yea, and I beheld that the fruit thereof was white, to exceed all the whiteness that I had ever seen. And as I partook of the fruit thereof it filled my soul with exceedingly great joy; wherefore, I began to be desirous that my family should partake of it also; for I knew that it was desirable above all other fruit" (1 Nephi 8:10–12). One commentator on these verses noted, "In his sermon to the outcast Zoramites (Alma 32–33), Alma identified fruit as the reward of a process. . . . Descriptive of the bounteous blessings of Christ's atonement, the fruit is most precious, sweet, white, and filling, leaving a disciple to no more hunger or thirst (Alma 32:42)." Camille Fronk, "Fruit," in *Book of Mormon Reference Companion*, ed. Dennis L. Largey (Salt Lake City: Deseret Book, 2003), 277. Elsewhere we are informed, "The fruit of the tree of life . . . ultimately is eternal life (1 Ne. 15:36; D&C 14:7)." Donald W. Parry and Jay A. Parry, *Symbols & Shadows: Unlocking a Deeper Understanding of the Atonement* (Salt Lake City: Deseret Book, 2009), 156. Elder Holland explained, "Christ is the seed, the tree, and the fruit of eternal life." Jeffrey R. Holland, Christ and the New Covenant (Salt Lake City: Deseret Book, 1997), 169.

54. See Cooper, *An Illustrated Encyclopaedia of Traditional Symbols*, 64–65; Cirlot, *A Dictionary of Symbols*, 101.

55. Joseph Fielding McConkie, *Gospel Symbolism* (Salt Lake City: Bookcraft, 1992), ix.

56. Nephi equated exaltation (or eternal life) with the receipt of peace. (See 1 Nephi 14:7.)

Chapter 2

GRACE AT THE VEIL

FINDING HOPE IN IMAGES OF THE JUDGMENT DAY

Alonzo L. Gaskill

In a rather public venue, an evangelical Christian friend of mine said to me, "Mormons simply do not believe that their salvation comes through the grace of Christ. They believe, instead, that salvation is something they earn through their works—through participating in ordinances and being obedient to commandments." While I was somewhat surprised by his willingness to publicly vocalize his disdain for Latter-day Saints and their doctrines, I suppose I was not shocked by the specifics of his claims, for I had heard this erroneous charge time and again during my thirty-plus years in the Church. Nevertheless, for a number of reasons I found his statement naïve and untrue.

First of all, my friend's comment seemed to call into question the fundamental reality that Jesus *did* give commandments: not suggestions—*commandments*.[1] In both the Old and New Testaments—in addition to latter-day scripture—Jesus *commands* those who consider themselves His disciples to obey, to follow, and to comply. For example, Matthew records, "And, behold, one came and said unto [Jesus], Good Master, what good thing shall I do, that I may have eternal life? And he said unto him, . . . if thou wilt enter into [eternal] life, keep the commandments" (Matthew 19:17). Additionally, Jesus ordered those who professed a belief in Him to "observe all things whatsoever I have commanded you" (Matthew 28:20). In giving the Ten Commandments, the Lord said, I will show "mercy unto . . . them that love me, and keep my commandments" (Exodus 20:6). In the book of Psalms we are commanded to "set" our "hope in God, and not forget the works of God, but keep his commandments" (Psalm 78:7). Hundreds of times in the standard works of the Church, the Lord (or His authorized representatives) "command" those who profess a belief in God to obey His laws and keep His commandments. Thus, whether Latter-day Saints believe they are saved by grace or by works, it seems evident that Jesus *commanded* us to do works; and to be dismissive of such commandments seems to be a violation of what it means to be a true Christian.

Aside from the fact that the scriptures are filled with directives given in the form of commandments, I was also uncomfortable with my friend's declaration that Mormons don't trust in the grace of Christ, because so many passages in the canon of Latter-day Saints speak of salvation by grace. Indeed, each and every book in the Latter-day Saint standard works teaches salvation by grace. For example, in the Old Testament, David sang to the Lord, "Have mercy upon me, O God, according to thy loving kindness: according unto the multitude of thy tender mercies blot out my transgressions. Wash me thoroughly from mine iniquity, and cleanse me from my sin" (Psalm 51:1–2).[2] In addition, in the New Testament the Apostle Paul taught, "For by grace are ye saved through faith; and that not of yourselves: it is the gift of God: Not of works, lest any man should boast" (Ephesians 2:8–9). In the Book of Mormon we read, "it is only in and through the grace of God that ye are saved" (2 Nephi 10:24). In the Pearl of Great Price we find Enoch declaring, "thou hast made me, and given unto me a right to thy throne, and not of myself, but through thine own grace" (Moses 7:58). And in the Doctrine and Covenants we are told, "my grace is sufficient for you, and you shall be lifted up at the last day" (D&C 17:8). While these are but a sampling of the plethora of passages teaching and testifying of salvation via grace, they are, nevertheless, sufficient to point out that the Saints have no scriptures in their canon that neglect this sacred truth.

So, having heard my friend's critical and inaccurate description of Latter-day Saint soteriology—and without getting into a bash by tossing around a bunch of scriptures, like those listed above—I simply bore witness to him that we *are* saved by grace; and that, with all the good we try to do, we will each *ever* be dependent upon Jesus's Atonement for our salvation and exaltation. None of us will *ever* merit salvation or exaltation based on our own works or faithfulness. After all we can do, it will yet be by grace that we will be saved (2 Nephi 25:23).[3] In response to my testimony, my friend matter-of-factly said, "I would love to see you in a cage match with Spencer W. Kimball or Bruce R. McConkie—because I'm pretty sure they would disagree with you!" Well, with that statement it had become evident that nothing I was going to say would change this good brother's perceptions of Latter-day Saint beliefs—including quotes to the contrary by President Kimball or Elder McConkie.[4] My evangelical friend "knew" what Latter-day Saints believed—regardless of what any of us taught or testified to. Any continued discussion ran the risk of becoming contentious, thereby grieving the Spirit of the Lord.

That being said, this rather disappointing exchange got me thinking about how clearly the doctrine of grace is taught in the restored gospel. In the process of my conversation with my Christian acquaintance, my mind was immediately drawn to the temple endowment and what we're taught there about grace and salvation. Permit me to explain.

In the temple, the narratives of the Creation and the Fall are juxtaposed.[5] One of the reasons they are placed side by side in the endowment is because therein they are used as teaching devices. As patrons view these ritual dramas, they are encouraged to see themselves as participants in the narratives being shared. Men and women are admonished to think of themselves in the place of Adam and Eve.[6] With that as background, the story of the Creation is one of idyllic beauty and perfection, and the story of the Fall is one of sorrow and disruption. In the Creation account, God makes all things in a state of paradisiacal perfection—and pronounces them "good" (Genesis 1:31; Moses 3:2). In the story of the Fall, humans disrupt that "goodness" and "perfection" by heeding the enticements of Satan. The ordinances of the temple (which are Christ-centered in nature) teach us how God offers a resolution to the predicament that we have created for ourselves. The temple endowment seeks to bring us full circle. It seeks to bring us back to paradise—to redeem us from the chaos that we have introduced into our lives and into this world (through our tendency to listen to the enticements of Satan).

So, what do the narratives of the Creation and Fall have to do with the question of whether Latter-day Saints are saved by grace or by works? I would summarize the application in this way: as terribly imperfect people (which we *all* are), one of the things which can help us with our feelings of inadequacy is to focus on God's grace, and to remember that our works and achievements are ultimately insignificant, token gestures, at best. We need to exhibit these outward behaviors, for they are fruits (and signs) of our devotion to, and love for, Him. However, owing to the degree to which we each sin, our level of "good works" does not come anywhere close to our level of "transgression" of God's laws.[7] Thus, as we move toward Judgment Day—conscious of our many imperfections—we may feel prone to worry about our ability to stand with confidence in the presence of God.[8] However, the temple offers hope.[9] President Boyd K. Packer taught that, at the end of our lives, "We shall approach the veil and there, with signs and tokens given, we will be extended the sublimest of all invitations: 'Enter into the joy of thy Lord.'"[10] Thus, at the conclusion of the endowment, as we symbolically encounter God, we act out our yet future judgment.[11] There we typologically communicate with our Heavenly Father. In the spirit of a Father's interview, He ascertains whether we have obtained and retained all that He offered and taught us during the holy endowment[12]—which is, itself, an emblematic depiction of our journey through mortality.[13] As we go through that symbolic judgment (or interview) we come to the realization that we have come up short.[14] We don't have what we need to be brought back into His presence.[15] Metaphorically speaking, our worst fears are suddenly realized.

Just as you and I may be prone to worry about whether we will be adequate before God on Judgment Day, we see symbolically depicted in the endowment that *we will not!*[16] And so, what is to be done? In symbolic language, we find our answer in the eighty-eighth section of the Doctrine and Covenants. There God says to His sons and daughters, "Draw near unto me and I will draw near unto you; seek me diligently and ye shall find me; ask, and ye shall receive; knock, and it shall be opened unto you" (D&C 88:63).[17] The Lord commands those who seek to commune with Him, to "draw near" to Him. Anciently we find depictions of God embracing the forgiven and redeemed at the Judgment Day. These depictions can expand our understanding of the council offered in section 88. Nibley noted that the "idea

Drawing of a fourteenth century BCE depiction from the north wall of the burial chamber of King Tut, depicting the Egyptian god Osiris (left) embracing King Tutankhamun (right) upon the latter's entrance into the next world.

of being embraced is . . . an expression for the Atonement."[18] Thus, any symbolic depiction of God "draw[ing] near to" someone—or embracing someone—can be viewed as representative of the divine intimacy, love, forgiveness, and acceptance that God has for His struggling yet striving children. The ritual act of embrace, which may be alluded to in the eighty-eighth section of the Doctrine and Covenants, implies that the Father loves and forgives—and that He can and will make up for what we do not have; for the areas in which we have fallen short. God has the ability—and the intent—to convey and provide what we are lacking in behavior, but *also* in knowledge, so long as we are sincerely striving to keep our covenants.[19] And, in the words of the Lord, "Because thou *knowest* these things ye are redeemed . . . ; therefore ye are *brought* back into my presence; therefore I show myself unto you" (Ether 3:13; emphasis added).[20] At the Judgment Day, when we have partaken of God's grace and, as President Packer has said, when we have "approach[ed] the veil and there, with signs and tokens given, [been] extended the sublimest of all invitations: 'Enter into the joy of thy Lord'"[21]—God will *draw us* into His presence: into the celestial kingdom.[22] It is grace. It is all about grace! You and I come up short and God looks past that; He covers[23] our shortcomings and saves us *in spite of* ourselves. He asks so little. And why? Because, as William Slone Coffin once said, "there is more mercy in God than [there is] sin in us."[24] *Of this I testify!* So long as you think all of this is about *you*, you'll feel overwhelmed, guilty, and unworthy. When you begin to sense how very much this is about *Him* and *His* love for you, the Atonement becomes real and you begin to be able to rely upon it, because you know you aren't able to do this yourself. But Jesus can *and will!*

So, while my evangelical Christian friend may believe that Latter-day Saints think they save themselves, those who have received their endowment in the holy temple know otherwise. The most sacred of our rites—the most holy of our sanctuaries—offers a message that is loud and clear. After all we can do, it will yet be by the grace of God that we will enter into His presence and enjoy the blessings He has in store for those who love and serve Him.

NOTES

1.   I am convinced that, more often than not, we misplace the emphasis when quoting 2 Nephi 25:23. The passage states, "for we know that it is by grace that we are saved, after all we can do." The traditional reading of this is "You must do everything you can, and

then grace will kick in—helping to save you." But I think that interpretation is the opposite of what this verse is saying. I firmly believe that Nephi's intended meaning was "After all you can do, you will still need God's grace to be saved." In explaining this passage, Stephen E. Robinson writes, "In my opinion some of the blame for our misapplication of gospel superlatives and other similarly obsessive reasoning comes from a misunderstanding of 2 Nephi 25:23: "For we labor diligently to write, to persuade our children, and also our brethren, to believe in Christ, and to be reconciled to God; for we know that it is by grace that we are saved, after all we can do." (Italics added.) At first glance at this scripture, we might think that grace is offered to us only chronologically after we have completed doing all we can do, but this is demonstrably false, for we have already received many manifestations of God's grace before we even come to this point. By his grace, we live and breathe. . . . I understand the preposition "after" in 2 Nephi 25:23 to be a preposition of separation rather than a preposition of time. It denotes logical separateness rather than temporal sequence. We are saved by grace "apart from all we can do," or "all we can do notwithstanding," or even "regardless of all we can do." Another acceptable paraphrase of the sense of the verse might read, "We are still saved by grace, after all is said and done." In addition, even the phrase "all we can do" is susceptible to a sinister interpretation as meaning every single good deed we could conceivably have ever done. This is nonsense. If grace could operate only in such cases, no one could ever be saved, not even the best among us. It is precisely because we don't always do everything we could have done that we need a savior in the first place, so obviously we can't make doing everything we could have done a condition for receiving grace and being saved! I believe the emphasis in 2 Nephi 25:23 is meant to fall on the word we ("all we can do," as opposed to all He can do). Moreover, "all we can do" here should probably be understood in the sense of "everything we can do," or even "whatever we can do." Thus, the correct sense of 2 Nephi 25:23 would be that we are ultimately saved by grace apart from whatever we manage to do. Grace is not merely a decorative touch or a finishing bit of trim to top off our own efforts—it is God's participation in the process of our salvation from its beginning to its end. Though I must be intimately involved in the process of my salvation, in the long run the success of that venture is utterly dependent upon the grace of Christ." Stephen E. Robinson, *Believing Christ* (Salt Lake City: Deseret Book, 1992), 90–92.

2.   Bruce R. McConkie, "What Think ye of Salvation by Grace," BYU Devotional, January 10, 1984. At this devotional, Elder McConkie taught, "Now, there is a true doctrine of salvation by grace—a salvation by grace alone and without works, as the scriptures say" (page 4). Similarly, as an example of President Spencer W. Kimball's understanding of the place of grace in salvation, note the following comment by him: "There can be no real and true Christianity, even with good works, unless we are deeply and personally committed to the reality of Jesus Christ as the Only Begotten Son of the Father, who bought us, who purchased us in the great act of atonement." Spencer W. Kimball, *The Teachings of Spencer W. Kimball*, ed. Edward L. Kimball (Salt Lake City: Bookcraft, 1998), 68. While it is true that both of these authorities spoke of the importance of works as "evidence" of true conversion to Christ, it would be misrepresentative to say that these two men bearing the prophetic mantle did not teach reliance upon the Atonement and grace of Christ as the ultimate means of salvation.

3.   See Immo Luschin, "Temples: Latter-day Saint Temple Worship and Activity," in *Encyclopedia of Mormonism*, 4 vols., ed. Daniel H. Ludlow (New York: Macmillan, 1992), 4:1447.

4.   It is generally understood that Adam and Eve were typological symbols for the human race. They serve as representations of each of us, and our own personal fall from grace. Indeed, President Gordon B. Hinckley, in speaking of the holy temple and the story taught therein, stated that "we have sketched before us the odyssey of man's eternal journey from premortal existence through this life to the life beyond." Gordon B. Hinckley, *Teachings of Gordon B. Hinckley* (Salt Lake City: Deseret Book, 1997), 636. See also Rex E. Cooper, "Symbols, Cultural and Artistic," in *Encyclopedia of Mormonism*, 4 vols., ed. Daniel H. Ludlow (New York: Macmillan, 1992), 3:1430–1431; Elaine Pagels, *Adam, Eve, and the Serpent* (New York: Vintage Books, 1989), xx–xxi, xxiv.

5.   Likewise, Elder Bruce C. Hafen expressed the following: "The experience of Adam and Eve is an ideal prototype for our own mortal experience. Their story is our story. The complete cycle of their fall from innocence and their ultimate return to God typifies a general human pattern." Bruce C. Hafen, *The Broken Heart* (Salt Lake City: Deseret Book, 1989), 37. (See also pages 33 and 50.) Hugh Nibley wrote this: "The Mormon endowment . . . is frankly a model, a presentation in figurative terms. . . . It does not attempt to be a picture of reality, but only a model . . . setting forth the pattern of man's life on earth with its fundamental whys and wherefores." Hugh Nibley, *The Message of the Joseph Smith Papyri: An Egyptian Endowment* (Salt Lake City: Deseret Book, 1975), xiii. Nibley added, "My story," and yours, "begins with Adam and Eve, the archetypal man and woman, in whom each of us is represented." Hugh Nibley, *Old Testament and Related Studies* (Provo, Utah: Foundation for Ancient Research and Mormon Studies, 1986), 87. Joseph Fielding McConkie and Donald W. Parry wrote, "Adam, a Hebrew name which means 'man' or 'mankind,' is a type for all men and for all mankind" (1 Corinthians 15:21–22; Romans 5:12–21). Joseph Fielding McConkie and Donald W. Parry, *A Guide To Scriptural Symbols* (Salt Lake City: Bookcraft, 1990), 12. Echoing the sentiments of these aforementioned brethren, another Latter-day Saint scholar has written, "What, then . . . of the Eden story? . . . A rehearsal of the key events of Eden brings the realization that we too are privileged to leave the lone and dreary world and enter the sacred sanctuaries of the Lord, where we participate in essentially the same experiences known to our first parents before the Fall. The temple is to us as Eden was to Adam and Eve. . . . The story of Eden, in fact, [is] a light that reveals the path all must travel to return to the divine presence." Joseph Fielding McConkie, "The Mystery of Eden," in *The Man Adam*, ed. Joseph Fielding McConkie and Robert L. Millet (Salt Lake City: Bookcraft, 1990), 29, 30, 23. Similarly, in an LDS publication dedicated to an examination of the life of Father Adam, one author informed his readers, "In the mind of first-century Jews and Christians, what Adam was, we are; what Adam could become, we can become." Stephen E. Robinson, "The Book of Adam in Judaism and Early Christianity," in *The Man Adam*, 128. Indeed, it is generally held within Mormonism that Adam and Eve "are symbolic representations of all men and women." Jolene Edmunds Rockwood, "The Redemption of Eve," in *Sisters in Spirit*, ed. Maureen Usenbach Beecher and Lavina Fielding Anderson (Chicago: University of Illinois Press, 1992), 18. Even when in sacred precincts, Latter-day Saints are instructed that, when

contemplating the Fall, they should substitute themselves for the persons of Adam and Eve. Clearly their story is our story. The message of the Fall is about us.

6.   This concept is not unique to Latter-day Saints. Even non-LDS scholars and theologians acknowledge that the scriptural story of the Fall is primarily designed to teach us about ourselves. As one noted, "Adam . . . is the Representative of the human race. . . . This story must be taken seriously but not literally. . . . It is a [scriptural story] that accurately reveals the existential situation in which man finds himself in the world. . . . While it is anchored in history, its significance is not limited to a particular history. . . . The language or terminology employed is, for the most part, symbolic. . . . To affirm that there are [figurative and symbolic] elements in Scripture is not to detract from its divine inspiration nor from its historical basis but to attest that the Holy Spirit has made use of various kinds of language and imagery to convey divine truth. . . . The tale in Genesis concerns not only a first fall and first man, but a universal fall and universal man. Adam is not so much a private person as the head of the human race. He is a generic as well as first man. He is Everyman and therefore Representative Man. He is the representative of both our original parents and of all humankind." Donald G. Bloesch, *Essentials of Evangelical Theology*, 2 vols. (Peabody, Massachusetts: Price Press, 2001), 1:104–6. See also Pagels, Adam, Eve, and the Serpent, xxi and 74. *Dictionary of Biblical Imagery* notes that Adam "is the prototypical human figure." He is the "true archetype of humankind" whose "reaching for the forbidden fruit epitomizes the irrationality and recklessness" of humans when they place themselves under the "power of sin." See Leland Ryken, James C. Wilhoit, and Tremper Longman III, eds., *Dictionary of Biblical Imagery* (Downers Grove, Illinois: InterVarsity Press, 1998), 9–10. Similarly, the prolific Jacob Neusner noted that in marriage and life, the man is symbolically living out the role of Adam, and the woman that of Eve. Jacob Neusner, *The Enchantments of Judaism* (Atlanta: Scholars Press, 1991), 53–65. Our first parents are symbols for the whole of "Israel" or "the children of Zion." See Neusner, *The Enchantments of Judaism*, 62. See also Jacob Neusner, *The Genesis Rabbah: The Judaic Commentary to the Book of Genesis* (Atlanta: Scholars Press, 1985), 174, 208, 209, 211, 213, 224, 230; Bruce Vawter, *On Genesis: A New Reading* (New York: Doubleday, 1977), 81, 90. When a man and woman marry, they adopt the roles of Adam and Eve; and hope that their home can become a new Eden or, better put, a temple. Neusner, *The Enchantments of Judaism*, 62. See also Beverly Campbell, *Eve and the Choice Made in Eden* (Salt Lake City: Deseret Book, 2003), 57.

7.   This does not mean that they are unimportant. But, in the scope of all that we do wrong, the small things we do as acts of faith are hardly sufficient to pay for our mistakes—and they are absolutely not sufficient to earn us any measure of salvation or exaltation.

8.   President Brigham Young taught, "God dwells in eternal burnings, [and] puts his hand through the veil. . . . Any person that goes through these ordinances, unless they cleanse their hearts and sanctify themselves, . . . it will burn them." Brigham Young, discourse given December 28, 1845, in *The Complete Discourses of Brigham Young*, 5 vols., ed. Richard S. Van Wagoner (Salt Lake City: The Smith-Pettit Foundation, 2009), 1:115.

9. The *Encyclopedia of Mormonism* points out that, as part of the endowment, we act out in a "figurative" way "how one may come to dwell again in God's presence." Luschin, "Temples: Latter-day Saint Temple Worship and Activity," 4:1447.

10. Boyd K. Packer, *Our Father's Plan*, rev. ed. (Salt Lake City: Deseret Book, 1994), 46. Nibley wrote, "He will receive you personally, take your hand, and give you the signs and tokens himself when you come, as he did to the Nephites." Hugh Nibley, *Teachings of the Book of Mormon*, 4 vols. (Provo, Utah: Foundation for Ancient Research and Mormon Studies, 2004), 1:204. (See also 1:242.) My citations of Nibley in this chapter are not for apologetic reasons. I seek to "prove" nothing here. I have freely cited Dr. Nibley throughout this chapter because he spoke and wrote frequently about the temple, and I wish to establish for the reader that the contents of this chapter have been discussed in print by those who have gone before me—both authorities of the Church (such as Boyd K. Packer) and scholars (like Nibley).

11. See Packer, *Our Father's Plan*, 46. The *Encyclopedia of Mormonism* explains, "In the Endowment, God alone is the judge." Kenneth W. Godfrey, "Freemasonry and the Temple," in *Encyclopedia of Mormonism*, 2:529. The *Encyclopedia of Mormonism* also states, "At the conclusion of the temple service, those participating in the Endowment ceremony pass from the terrestrial room to the celestial room through a veil, which symbolizes the transition from time into eternity." See Todd Compton, "Symbolism," in *Encyclopedia of Mormonism*, 3:1430.

12. Elder John A. Widtsoe wrote, "The candidate for the temple service is . . . instructed in the things that he should know. . . . At last, tests are given him, whereby those who are entitled to know may determine whether the man has properly learned the lesson." See John A Widtsoe, "Symbolism in the Temple," in *Saviors on Mount Zion*, ed. Archibald F. Bennett (Salt Lake City: Deseret Sunday School Union Board, 1950), 166. Elder Widtsoe also penned this regarding our temple experience: "Those who receive" their endowment must, at a certain point, "prove the possession of divine knowledge and religious works. It is a very beautiful, logical, and inspiring series of ceremonies." John A. Widtsoe, *A Rational Theology*, 7th ed. (Salt Lake City: Deseret Book, 1966), 125–26.

13. Hinckley, *Teachings of Gordon B. Hinckley*, 635.

14. Matthew Brown explained, "Some biblical scholars believe that Psalms 15 and 24 contain elements of an entrance liturgy. This 'sacred rite' supposedly took place at the gate leading into the temple courtyard, involved the priests and those desiring entry, and was in a question and answer format. Those who approached the gate evidently requested to pass through it (see Psalm 118:19–20) and were then required to answer the questions posed by the gatekeepers. One of the answers included the pronunciation of the sacred name of God which served as 'the password.' There was then a confirmation that the supplicants were 'qualified to ascend.'" See Matthew B. Brown, *The Gate of Heaven: Insights on the Doctrines and Symbols of the Temple* (American Fork, Utah: Covenant Communications, 1999), 93, n. 24. Of the Egyptian endowment, Nibley wrote, "The final and concluding rite of the ancient initiation . . . consist[ed] of a summary of what has gone before, taking the form of an exchange of formulas which are 'at the same time' a statement of 'creeds, liturgical formulas, and passwords,' all befitting of an ultimate rite de passage. It was an exchange of 'symbols,' a 'Question and a Response . . . probably spoken in an undertone [or whisper]

both by the priest and the initiand, perhaps . . . at the door of the Holiest.'" Hugh Nibley, *The Message of the Joseph Smith Papyri—An Egyptian Endowment*, 2nd ed. (Provo, Utah: Foundation for Ancient Research and Mormon Studies, 2005), 456. Drawing on another ancient document with temple parallels, Nibley added, "We are allowed to see what is behind the veil, and 'we enter into it in our weakness, through signs and tokens which the world despises." (Nibley, *The Message of the Joseph Smith Papyri*, 444. Nibley is quoting the Coptic-Christian "Gospel of Philip.")

15. President Brigham Young taught, "We have . . . the key words and tokens to take us through the veil into the celestial world and lead us to the throne of God." Brigham Young, discourse given July 6, 1851, in *The Complete Discourses of Brigham Young*, 1:441. Similarly, Nibley wrote, "God sits behind a series (taxis) of veils, which are 'drawn before the great king' and which can be approached only by passing tests at preliminary gates; hence the only way by which one can enter into the presence of the Father is 'to pass through the veil.'" Nibley, *The Message of the Joseph Smith Papyri*, 443.

16. Nibley pointed out that "'only the initiated free of guilt may pass through [the veil].' For it leads to another world and a higher state of being." Nibley, *The Message of the Joseph Smith Papyri*, 436.

17. In Jacob 6:5, the encouragement is found to "cleave unto God as he cleaveth unto you. And while his arm of mercy is extended towards you . . . harden not your hearts."

18. Nibley continues, "'Behold, he sendeth an invitation unto all men, for the arms of mercy are extended towards them, and he saith: Repent, and I will receive you.' This is the embrace; he is willing to take you. . . . And in 2 Nephi 1:15 we have it where he says, 'But behold, the Lord hath redeemed my soul from hell; I have beheld his glory, and I am encircled about eternally in the arms of his love.' That's what got us started here. It's the embrace he is in." According to Nibley, to "embrace is the idea [that] you cover a person." He added: "*kafata* [is] the same word as the Latin *capto*, which means 'to embrace, to capture, to hug around.' It's quite universal—our word cover and the rest. And the Jews go into various interpretations. As I said, it means all these things. The basic meaning is 'to arch over; to bend over; to cover; therefore, to cover your sins, to wipe them out, to forget them; to pass over with the palm of the hand, hence to wipe over; to cleanse; to expiate; therefore, to forgive, to renounce, to deny, to be found.' Then the basic meaning goes to encircle again, such as encircling a city, a town, a person, or anything else." Hugh Nibley, *Teachings of the Book of Mormon*, 4 vols. (Provo, Utah: Foundation for Ancient Research and Mormon Studies, 2004), 1:200, 198, 199.

19. In Helaman 5:29–30, we read of God's voice being as a whisper: "And it came to pass that there came a voice . . . , and beheld . . . it was not a voice of thunder, neither was it a voice of a great tumultuous noise, but behold, it was a still voice of perfect mildness, as if it had been a whisper, and it did pierce even to the very soul—" Elder Maxwell wrote that "God whispers to us in our pleasures." And so he does! And could there be a greater "pleasure" than to know that the Father has covered your sins and shortcomings; that the Father forgives and embraces His fallen and weak sons and daughters when they reach for him? See Neal A. Maxwell, *We Will Prove Them Herewith* (Salt Lake City: Deseret Book, 1982), 123. Elder Maxwell is quoting C. S. Lewis, *The Problem of Pain* (New York: Simon & Schuster Touchstone Books, 1996), 83.

20. Brigham Young made a rather interesting comment about the Lord taking "us through the veil and into the celestial world." See Brigham Young, in *The Complete Discourses of Brigham Young*, 5 vols., ed. Richard S. Van Wagoner (Salt Lake City: The Smith-Pettit Foundation, 2009), 1:441. See also Wilford Woodruff, "July 6, 1851," *Wilford Woodruff's Journal*, 9 vols., ed. Scott G. Kenney (Midvale, Utah: Signature Books, 1983), 4:45.

21. Boyd K. Packer, *Our Father's Plan*, rev. ed. (Salt Lake City: Deseret Book, 1994), 46. Nibley wrote: "He will receive you personally, take your hand, and give you the signs and tokens himself when you come, as he did to the Nephites." Hugh Nibley, *Teachings of the Book of Mormon*, 4 vols. (Provo, Utah: Foundation for Ancient Research and Mormon Studies, 2004), 1:204. See also 1:242.

22. Nibley noted: "The word for palm of the hand in all Semitic languages is *kāp*. It means 'to cover, hence to grasp by the hand; to wipe over, hence to cleanse, to expiate, to forgive, to renounce, to deny, to be found, to encircle.'" Nibley, *The Message of the Joseph Smith Papyri*, 1:198. The *Encyclopedia of Mormonism* reminds us that "a veil symbolically divides the terrestrial room from the celestial room." "The celestial room" symbolically "suggests through furnishings and décor the peace, beauty, and glory of the highest degree of heaven." (Luschin, in *Encyclopedia of Mormonism*, 4:1447). The scriptures emphasize that we are "brought" into God's presence, rather than having a right to enter it. Mormon 9:13 informs us, "And because of the redemption of man, which came by Jesus Christ, they are brought back into the presence of the Lord." Similarly, in 2 Nephi 32:4 we read: "Wherefore, now after I have spoken these words, if ye cannot understand them it will be because ye ask not, neither do ye knock; wherefore, ye are not brought into the light, but must perish in the dark."

23. Of course, the Hebrew word for atone/atonement means literally to "cover"— because the Atonement "covers" our sins, failings, shortcomings, and imperfections. Nibley offers this rather loose translation of the Hebrew: "Yom Kippur means embrace. It means enfolding or hugging a person. And . . . when the priest goes to the door to be received by the Lord, they embrace each other. There are interesting old Jewish pictures of the Lord's hand coming through the door of the tent and Moses taking the hand. . . . Kippur means atonement, and it also means embrace, the literal act of hugging." Nibley, *Teachings of the Book of Mormon*, 215. He added, "This idea of being embraced is very strong in the Book of Mormon as an expression for the Atonement." Nibley, *Teachings of the Book of Mormon*, 200. See, for example, 2 Nephi 1:15, Alma 5:7 & 33. Finally, Nibley pointed out that God "is the keeper of the gate, and he employs no servant there. We are talking about the Atonement when he greets you. This is the embrace we are talking about[.] That's the Jewish kpr, which is the embrace at the veil, the kapporeth of the tabernacle." Nibley, *Teachings of the Book of Mormon,* 243.

24. See William Sloane Coffin, in *The Riverside Preachers*, ed. Paul Sherry (New York: The Pilgrims Press, 1978), 163. See also William Sloane Coffin, *Credo* (Louisville, Kentucky: Westminster John Knox Press, 2004), 172. Coffin also said, "God has more grace and mercy than you and I have sins." See William Sloane Coffin, "Sermon," delivered March 12, 2001, in the Memorial Church at Stanford University, on the occasion of the installation of the Reverend Scotty McLennan as Dean of Religious Life at Stanford University.

Chapter 3

"CLOTHED UPON WITH GLORY"

SACRED UNDERWEAR AND THE CONSECRATED LIFE[1]

Alonzo L. Gaskill

There are three ritual acts that premodern religions traditionally have in common: eating, washing, and clothing. Ancient peoples engaged in rites of communion, wherein covenants with God and/or man were made and renewed through the partaking of food. Similarly, among most of the ancients, ceremonial washing was a requisite rite of passage with salvific connotations. The ritual act of clothing, receiving clothes, or being clothed has also held a sacral place in the faith of many of our predecessors.[2] While each of these acts is sacred and symbolic, our attention here will be on the latter of the three—the idea of clothing as a symbol of consecration.

"The transforming effect of clothes," one source informs us, "has always given them considerable emblematic power."[3] The significant role played by clothing in ancient society is particularly apparent in the Bible, where prophets used clothing metaphorically to make ethical exhortations, send theological messages, or to show the status or character of significant figures.[4] The importance of apparel in scripture and ceremony can be physical, economic, social, moral, or spiritual.[5]

Priestly or religious clothing is often intended to represent "the garb of God," and dressing in "special clothing" can denote a change in role or status.[6] The changing of one's clothes has long been a sign of consecration and preparation for "spiritual duties."[7] Thus, in the fourth century, Cyril of Jerusalem explained this about the Christian act of clothing: "As soon, then, as ye entered [the inner chamber or sanctuary], ye put off your tunic; and this was an image of *putting off the old man with his deeds.*" Cyril then added, "May the soul which has once put him off [i.e., the 'old man, which waxeth corrupt in the lusts of deceit'], never again put him on."[8] Thus, the sense for early Christians was that donning religious articles implied that one was a new person, committed and consecrated to his or her God. In many cultures, sacred garments are seen as a representation of the wearer's moral and spiritual qualities—qualities developed largely because the wearer has faith in and devotion toward his or her God. Obviously not all clothing, in scripture or in life, is symbolic. Much of it is nothing more than practical. Nevertheless, literal and figurative meanings are intertwined in nearly every category of clothing.[9] The apparel we wear speaks as loudly about who we are, what we desire, and what we will become, as does perhaps anything else.

A SUBJECT OF RIDICULE

While members of The Church of Jesus Christ of Latter-day Saints do not publicize the fact that they wear covenantal clothing—sacred, symbolic undergarments—it is no great secret either. Adult Latter-day Saints enter into one of their temples to receive an "endowment" or "gift" from God as one of their most hallowed and significant rites of passage. As part of that covenant-making process, Mormons receive a symbolic garment, which is worn as a reminder of the covenants entered into—somewhat like a Roman Catholic priest and the clerical clothing he dons once he has taken holy orders. Catholic priests wear their clerical collars on the outside; Mormons wear their garments underneath their clothing—but the concept is not dramatically different.

As it relates to their symbolic value, beyond representing the wearer's promises to God, for many Latter-day Saints the temple garments are also a symbol of the flesh of Christ and the need for the wearer to seek to live a life of holiness (Hebrews 10:19–20).[10] As faithful and consecrated living requires always keeping such truths at the forefront of one's mind, Latter-day Saints feel it important to wear the garments every day. In the minds of LDS-Christians, what is sacred is not the underwear itself, but what the underwear symbolizes. Thus, there is nothing "magic" about these items of covenantal clothing. They are simply a sacred reminder of one's promise to try to be better, to be more holy in his or her daily walk. If one endows them with meaning—with sacred significance—then they have power to protect the wearer. If not, they are nothing more than underwear. It is up to the wearer to determine the power of the garments.

While sacred covenantal underclothing is not unique to Latter-day Saints, our use of such apparel tends to be misunderstood, as is similar clothing worn by practicers of Judaism, Zoroastrianism, Sikhism, and Eastern Orthodoxy. As a singular example, on August 24, 2012, NBC's "Rock Center" (with Brian Williams) aired a segment entitled "Mormons in America." A portion of the program probed regarding the fact that temple endowed members of The Church of Jesus Christ of Latter-day Saints wear special underwear. As part of the program, interviewers probed members of the Church regarding the purpose of the garment and then, in an apparent effort to inform the audience, a man and woman were shown wearing nothing but a pair of LDS temple garments. Whether intentional or not, the NBC segment presented the concept of religious underwear (common to many ancient and modern religions) in such a way so as to make the practice of wearing such clothing seem not sacred, but somewhat weird—even cultish. In all probability, the producers of the NBC piece were unaware of the fact that millions upon millions of people today—whether Jew or Gentile—wear symbolic undergarments to remind them of the covenants they have entered into. Thus, though sometimes misunderstood or even mocked, the practice is foundational to many traditions—and serves as a powerful means of consecrating and focusing the life of the wearer.

PRIESTS OF THE ANCIENT JEWISH TEMPLE CULT

As attested in the Hebrew Bible, the priests and high priest who served in the ancient Israelite temple wore various articles of ritual clothing. It is widely accepted that one of those items of sacred apparel was a "special undergarment" in the form of "linen breeches" or underpants.[11] One text refers to these as "femoralia" or "drawers."[12] The books of Exodus (28:42) and Leviticus (6:10) both tell us that the priests were to wear these "linen breeches," which extended "from the loins even unto the thighs" (Exodus 28:42). In addition to the linen

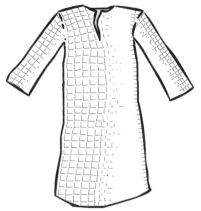

underpants, the priests also wore a "coat" or "shirt" on the upper half of their bodies, beneath their other liturgical vestments.[13] In AV Exodus 28:39 we read, "And thou shalt embroider the coat of fine linen." One source suggested that this coat or shirt was worn next to the skin and had sleeves. While scholars are not in complete agreement as to whether this sleeved shirt extended just slightly past the hips (like the Roman tunic), or perhaps all the way to the ankles (like the Greek *chitōn*),[14] what *is* evident is that it was an undergarment of sacred significance.

The biblical text itself makes it clear that this priestly underwear was received as part of a process of consecration and induction into the holy priesthood. And while the scriptural text does not elaborate on their symbolic meaning, scholars almost universally hold that these garments were not simply practical: there was some emblematic meaning to the various articles donned by the temple priest.[15] One text interprets the meaning of this holy underwear as follows: "The subject of holiness . . . is seen typified in each of the garments made of the fine twined linen, giving us an appreciation of the term 'Holy Garments'. The coat [or undershirt] that clad his person would signify an holiness of the heart that beat beneath it . . . whilst these linen breeches [or underpants] that covered his nakedness declare an holiness of the flesh" or "desires and passions." This same source adds that "the white coat" worn as an undergarment was "the emblem of righteousness."[16] One text on rites of passage noted that exchanging things or receiving gifts—including the receipt of ritual garments—binds the receiver to the giver. The receipt (or exchanging) of such items is equivalent to "pronouncing an oath" or entering into a covenant.[17]

Since these ancient priestly garments apparently carried the invitation to the wearer to keep his heart holy and his desires in harmony with the divine, Latter-day Saint Christians can also see in these ancient undergarments an invitation to self-assess. Do our own garments remind us to do the same? If not, are we failing to endow them with the meaning necessary to provoke the power and protection we desire from them?

ORTHODOX JUDAISM

Drawing on their own scriptural tradition and liturgical heritage, modern male Orthodox and Ultra-Orthodox Jews also wear an undergarment required of the faithful men in Hebrew Bible times.[18] In Deuteronomy 22:12 we read, "Thou shalt make thee fringes upon the four quarters of thy vesture, wherewith thou coverest thyself."[19] The garment of contemporary Orthodox and Ultra-Orthodox Jewry is not the "breeches" of the Levitical priest, but, rather an undershirt, of sorts, which they call *tallit katan*—sometimes translated "small tallit" or "little covering."[20] This holy article has the appearance of a small poncho-like shirt, and is worn under the outermost clothing by pious Jewish men.[21] On its four corners are twisted and knotted tassels called *zizit* (or *tzitzit*)—meaning "fringes." The 613 knots in the four tassels or cords are symbolic of the 613 commandments in the Law of Moses—commandments that Orthodox Jews seek to live each day.

While the wearing of this sacred undergarment is related to the Torah, Jewish tradition also explains how and why God commanded the Jews to wear special underwear—different from that found among their non-Jewish neighbors.

> The sin of the Sabbath-breaker was the occasion that gave rise to God's commandment of *zizit* to Israel. For He said to Moses, "Dost thou know how it came to pass that this man broke the Sabbath?" Moses: "I do not know." God: "On week days he wore phylacteries on his head and phylacteries on his arm to remind him of his duties, but on the Sabbath day, on which no phylacteries may be worn, he had nothing to call his duties to his mind, and he broke the Sabbath. Go now, Moses, and find for Israel a commandment the observance of which is not limited to week days only, but which will influence them on Sabbath days and on holy days as well." Moses selected the commandment of *zizit*, the sight of which will recall to the Israelites all the other commandments of God.[22]

Thus, according to this traditional account, for Jews who wear the *tallit katan*, it is a gift from God. It is a daily reminder of the covenants, promises, and obligations the wearer is under. It is a constant reminder of what God expects of him, and what he has promised his God he will seek to be. As the *Encyclopaedia Judaica* states, "strictly observant Jews wear the *tallit katan* under their upper garment the whole day, so as constantly to fulfill the biblical commandment of *zizit* (Numbers 15:39), a reminder to observe all the commandments of the Torah."[23]

For many of the most faithful, this undergarment has powers—powers by which the wearer can be protected.[24] Illustrative of this is the following story from the *Babylonian Talmud*.

> There was a man who was very careful in his observance of the *mitzvah* (the Law). He was ever found wearing the *tallit katan*, as the God of Israel had commanded. One day he heard of a prostitute in a far-off city and determined to make a visit. As the moment of his indiscretion arrived, now wearing nothing but his sacred undergarment, a miracle took place. The four knotted cords of his garment "struck him across the face," thereby awakening him to the sinful choice he was about to make. Stunned by the miraculous occurrence, he and the prostitute dropped to the floor to contemplate what they had just witnessed. As the man explained to the harlot about how his fringes had testified of his evil desires, she was spiritually moved. She left her life of sin, followed him home, earnestly studied the Torah, converted, married him, and they lived happily ever after.[25]

While Latter-day Saints will find such a story fanciful at best, it actually offers a meaningful message to those who wear the garments of God. As a singular example, years ago I was sitting in my living room, watching the national news when the excommunication of a prominent Latter-day Saint was announced. (This individual was *not* a general authority—but was well known in the media and, thus, his excommunication was of national interest.) When I heard that this man had been excommunicated for adultery, the first thought that went through my mind was this: "But what about his garments?!" In other words, I wondered how one who had entered into covenants—and who constantly wore a garment symbolic of those covenants—could reach the point of adultery without having to make a conscious decision to remove the garment. While our covenantal clothing is not going to literally "strike us across the face," if it has been endowed by us with meaning, it can metaphorically do just that when we are tempted to sin. But, again, the power of the garment to so do is contingent upon whether the wearer is contemplative about the underwear and what it symbolizes.

The Jewish undergarments (*tallit katan*) are not only a powerful symbol of the covenant relationship of the Jew with his God, they are also a gift from that God to protect and deliver the wearer from sin, temptation, and, therefore, damnation. As one source notes, "to be enfolded by the *tallit* is regarded as being enveloped by the holiness of the commandments of the Torah, denoting a symbolic subjection to the Divine Will."[26] The *zizit*, or "tassels" attached to the four corners of the sacred undergarment serve as a "talisman" or "amulet" for many who wear it. For the faithful, they function "as a protection against immoral conduct (an interpretation derived from Numbers 15:39)."[27] Let that be a lesson to *us*.

Unique in our day, and different from the underwear of his neighbors, the Modern-Orthodox and Ultra-Orthodox Jewish man wears his *tallit katan* as a symbol and reminder of his commitment to live a holy, faithful, and obedient life, and as a help in so doing. As one encyclopedia points out, "The rabbis regarded the *zizit* as a reminder to the Jew to observe the religious duties."[28]

ZOROASTRIANISM

Like Orthodox Jews, faithful Zoroastrians also have a sacred undergarment that is worn throughout one's adult life as a representation of the wearer's commitment to *Ahura Mazda* (God) and the ways of the Parsee tradition. Unlike in Judaism, however, in Zoroastrianism, the garment is worn by men *and* women.[29]

Somewhere between a child's seventh and fifteenth year,[30] he or she 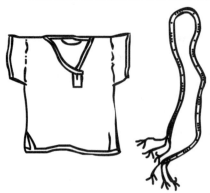 participates in the *Navjote* (or *Naojot*) initiation rite.[31] During that rite, the youth is washed and endowed with a rather plain white "sacred undershirt" which is to be worn next to the skin the remainder of the Zoroastrian's life. This undergarment, known as a *sudreh* (meaning "protection" or "advantageous path"), has a small pocket on the front side, in the center and right at the neckline. This pocket is called the *gireh-bân* (meaning "purse" or "bag of righteousness"), and the wearer is to metaphorically fill it with good works, good thoughts, and good deeds each day of his or her life. It is a reminder to the wearer that while he or she is free to pursue wealth, seeking personal righteousness is even more important.[32] It is a "symbol of the necessity of (a) obedience to God, (b) closing up the door against sin, and (c) breaking up the power of destruction."[33] Consequently, one text states that the wearer "makes his 'sudreh' an armor, a protection against which all attacks of demon or evil forces become futile. Thus he becomes the real conqueror of evil powers."[34] For Zoroastrians, then, this garment is a gift that provides the wearer with protection when it is utilized as God intended.

In addition to the sacred undershirt, initiates also receive a belt of sorts to be worn over the *sudreh*. This cord/belt is called the *kusti* (meaning "boundary" or "limit"—as it divides the upper body from the lower regions). Symbolically speaking, it is a reminder to the wearer of the need to nurture the body's "higher characteristics" (the things of the heart and brain), while controlling (and, in some cases, suppressing) the "lower characteristics" or physical appetites (greed, lust, and so on).[35] One Zoroastrian text informs us that "it is incumbent on all those of the good religion, women and men, every one [*sic*] who attains to fifteen years [of age], to wear the *sacred thread* girdle." By this "girdle" it is believed "the whole of demons and fiends" are "made extinct."[36] Because the "sacred thread girdle" or *kusti* has traditionally been made out of wool, it represents to the wearer the need for innocence and purity. The seventy-two threads with which it is woven are symbols of the seventy-two chapters of the sacred Zoroastrian scriptural text known as the *Yasna*. During his daily prayers, the wearer of the *kusti* unties and reties the knots of the "sacred girdle." This ritual serves to "cement" the wearer's "commitment to the faith"[37] and protect him from sins.[38]

While Latter-day Saints do not have as part of their sacred underclothing a belt that divides the lower portion of the body from the upper portion, the principle of separating the upper (higher) and lower (base) desires is indeed implied by the covenant associated with the garment—as entered into during the initiatory ordinances of the temple. If protection is to be found in the garments, such a principle must be contemplated and applied—as must be the principle of daily doing good to all. Certainly a garment that symbolizes the flesh of Christ—as the LDS garment does—calls us to this same kind of behavior each and every day of our lives.

For practitioners of the Parsee faith, wearing this garment serves to remind them of their covenantal responsibilities to their God (*Ahura Mazda*). As they daily untie and retie the *kusti* (while reciting their prayers), their obligations to live a holy life are brought to their remembrance, as is their promise to fill the *gireh-bân* with good things—holy things. In Zoroastrian belief, God had twin sons: one "beneficent" and one "hostile." The good son sought for good things; the bad son for that which was evil. Just as these two sons chose different paths, each Zoroastrian has two paths presented to him or her—the good and the evil. The sacred undergarments of the Zoroastrians (the *sudreh* and *kusti*) are a protection from evil, helping the practicer to focus on the path of God, and to not be seduced by the path of sin.

SIKHISM

In the year 1699, the last of the mortal Gurus—*Gobind Singh*—founded the Khālsā; an initiated body of believers who had participated in the *Amrit Sanchar* (a rite of initiation appearing much like a Christian baptismal ritual). These initiated members of the order served as members of the eighteenth-century Sikh military.[39] As part of their formation, *Gobind Singh* introduced the "Five Ks," five articles worn by members of the Khālsā as a statement to the world about who they are, and as a reminder to the wearer as to what he or she was obligated by covenant to be. From that time forward, Sikhs who have been initiated into this "castless fraternity" stood out, because of their unique appearance.[40] The "Five Ks" consist of:

- *Kesh*[41]—Uncut hair. This is a symbol for naturalness before God. For some Sikhs, it represents the need to accept who you are and the way God has made you; to accept God's will, even if it *seems* to be different from your own.
- *Kangha*—A comb, more symbolic than functional.[42] It highlights the need for the faithful practicer to exercise "mental order"; to control the mind and, thereby, control the body; to exercise "controlled spirituality" (to consciously live a spiritually centered life).
- *Kirpan*—A steel dagger, sometimes worn in the form of an actual knife, and other times worn as a pin or brooch. This is

emblematic of the Sikh's willingness to stand up for the truth and to push back on aggression toward their faith.[43] When a brooch made of two crossed swords is worn, it is sometimes seen as a symbol for the combination of political and religious authority—acknowledging that man would do better if his civil laws were God's laws, rather than trying to create his own.

- *Kara*—A steel bracelet, typically worn on the right wrist. This is representative of the need to be disciplined in one's actions, thereby developing unity with God. It implies that what one does or pursues should be in accordance with God's will and wants. Consequently, the bracelet also denotes the human who seeks to develop the attributes of the divine by living in harmony with the divine.
- *Kach*—Knee-length, baggy, white underpants. These stress the need to have "moral strength" and a chaste life. They are a representation of the Sikh commitment to not have sexual relations outside the bonds of marriage.[44]

While each of these items was originally associated solely with the Khālsā, today the "Five Ks" are commonly worn by many Sikhs—and by both sexes. One scholar noted, "Not all Sikhs have been members of the Khālsā. Nevertheless, the institution has come to define the image of the Sikh to outsiders and to be regarded by many within the community as the orthodox expression of its identity."[45] Elsewhere we read:

Those Sikhs who elect to take initiation as members of the Khalsa must swear when they undergo the *pāhul* ceremony always to observe the Five Ks. Women as well as men can undergo this ceremony and the women who do so must also promise to wear the Five Ks. These are the Amrit-dhari Sikhs (those who have drunk the amrit of initiation), as opposed to the Kes-dhari (those who [simply] maintain the Kes [or uncut hair]). All Amrit-dhari Sikhs are also Kes-dhari, but only a small proportion of Kes-dhari are Amrit-dhari, for only a small proportion of Sikhs take initiation. No one knows precisely just what that proportion is. . . .

Are those who are not Amrit-dhari Sikhs therefore freed from observing the Five Ks? In theory they may be released, but the strict variety of Sikh thinking certainly does not agree. According to this strict view every Sikh, whether formally a member of the Khalsa order or not, is bound to observe the Five Ks.[46]

Technically, therefore, the "Five Ks" are marks of a particular order of Sikhs. However, a significant number of Sikhs who have never been initiated into the Khālsā wear them.

Though these commonly recognized marks of Sikhism are a unit—worn together—our concern here is the *kach*; the sacred underpants of Sikhism. While the other five "marks" are largely worn openly, for all to observe—like the priestly garments of ancient Israel, the *tallit katan* of Ultra-Orthodox and Modern-Orthodox Judaism, the *sudreh* of Zoroastrianism, LDS Temple garments, and the phylakton *savanon* of Eastern Orthodoxy (which we shall discuss below)—the Sikh *kach* is worn beneath the clothing, concealing it from view. It is an inward sign of an inward commitment. In outward behaviors, the wearer's commitment is manifest. But the garment, itself, is not shown. The "moral strength"[47]

and "chastity"[48] it symbolizes is on public display (in the life of the practicer), but the symbol, the reminder of the covenant made to God ("One True Name"), is hidden from all but the one who has covenanted. As with each of the faiths we have discussed in this chapter, the undergarment is ultimately a private symbol of a consecrated life. It dramatically affects the public behaviors of the wearer, just as the LDS garment should dramatically affect the outward and public actions and activities of its wearers. Are the standards of your hidden garment evident in your public practices? Is it having that kind of influence upon your day-to-day behaviors (beyond simply the way you dress)?

EASTERN ORTHODOXY

During the consecration of the altar of a new Greek Orthodox church, the holy table is prepared to be the "place of the sacraments" by being ceremonially washed, anointed, clothed with an altar cloth, and then consecrated. For Eastern Orthodox Christians, the altar represents the tomb of Christ. Thus, metaphorically, His body lies therein. Consequently, the Orthodox hold that the altar must undergo its own ordinances akin to what an Orthodox Christian would participate in. Accordingly, the altar participates in a "baptism" (or washing), "chrismation" (or anointing), "clothing" in an altar cover (the newly baptized initiate typically receives a white garment to wear after his/her baptism), and the "receipt of the emblems of Christ's flesh and blood" (newly baptized children receive of the sacrament of the Lord's Supper).[49]

In conjunction with this ritual baptism of the altar, there is a practice in the Eastern Orthodox Church that mirrors much of what we have been discussing. Before washing and anointing the Altar Table, the Bishop puts on a white linen garment called the *savanon* or *sratchítza*.[50] The garment is worn in addition to the bishop or archbishop's liturgical vestments, and throughout the majority of the rite of consecrating the altar.[51] Near the conclusion of the consecration, at the point when the "vigil light" is placed upon the altar, the Bishop removes the aforementioned white garment.[52] The *savanon* is then cut up into small pieces and each person who attended the consecration is given a square of the

white cloth to be used as a phylakton—"a blessed object worn by an Orthodox Christian as a protection against evil."[53] It functions as a sort of amulet or talisman for the faithful Orthodox Christian.

Certainly not all members of the Eastern Orthodox faith subscribe to the use of a phylakton; though the Greek Orthodox congregation in which I was reared did.[54] For believers, the encouragement is to pin or sew this piece of blessed white cloth—this piece of the archbishop's vestment—to one's underclothing, thereby ensuring "protection against evil."[55]

In a sort of tangential use, but with related undertones, it has been common for families emigrating from Greece to send their sons to the "new country" to get established and to prepare a place for the rest of the family. These pioneer boys would often bring with them a phylakton as a source of protection and luck. One text notes that one of the family's "most important [parting gifts to their emigrating sons] was an amulet around their necks, a small cloth square enclosing a pinch of Greek earth."[56] The homeland "was holy to the Greeks."[57] Like the phylakton given to those who attend the consecration of an Orthodox altar, this version of the phylakton is also seen as something that can serve as a shield and protection to the wearer. The Greeks held that there were four "dangerous hours" in one's life—times when divine protection was more urgently needed; times which caused great anxiety for families. These were between birth and baptism, between engagement and marriage, the first forty days after a woman gave birth, and during the period of later life when an elderly person lost his or her vitality. During these times, as well as in times of travel, Greeks would commonly use a phylakton. One source notes that they would sew little squares of white cloth, "enclosing in them a piece of holy scripture or a sliver of the True Cross . . . to withstand the Evil Eye." They then pinned these phylakton to their shirts or underclothing "for protection against evil."[58] Because the original use of these Greek amulets appears to be liturgical, it seems likely that the cultural use among newborns, the engaged, new mothers, the elderly, and emigrants stems from the religious use that preceded it.

While the Eastern Orthodox practice is, in many ways, different from the other traditions discussed above, nevertheless, at its core, the principle is similar: a white garment, worn in a way so as to not be visible, blessed and holy, to be used by the faithful as a shield and protection against evil and sin. The *savanon*, once distributed as a phylakton, becomes a symbol of a faith's covenants and relationship with their God—and of their God's promise to intervene, shield, and protect. The disbeliever will scoff, but the wearer knows better—and so it is for faithful Latter-day Saints.

CONCLUSION

Though the wearing of "sacred underwear" may seem strange at best to most Westerners, this ritual behavior is clearly ancient in origin, and common in practice.[59]

Additionally, there is a manifest similarity in the meaning of the garments in each of the faiths we have discussed. While there are nuances in the implications and symbolism, generally speaking, the sacred undergarments of the ancient temple priests, the Modern-Orthodox Jew, the practicers of Zoroastrianism and Sikhism, the Latter-day Saints, and even the phylakton of Eastern Orthodoxy, represent covenants and consecration. They are reminders to the wearers of the sacred things God has done *for* them, and the promises He has made *to* them. Though worn discreetly, they encourage the wearer to live his or her religion faithfully and openly.[60] Latter-day Saints who have made covenants with God in the holy temple should periodically ask themselves in a reflective manner whether they are keeping those covenants. As noted, the garments only have as much power as the meaning we endow them with. If we are not contemplative about what they symbolize, they—and their associated covenants—will have little influence in our lives.

NOTES

1.   A version of this article was originally published in *The Journal of Inter-Religious Dialogue*, no. 12 (Spring 2013): 9–22. Republished here by permission.

2.   Curiously, the Evangelical movement (developing in modernity) has largely rejected all three of these. For many within that tradition, while the sacrament of the Lord's Supper has a place, it is not a requisite rite or a salvific ordinance. Baptism, though practiced by some Evangelicals, is also seen as more of an outward symbol but not a saving rite. Consequently, a high percentage of those who consider themselves Evangelical Christians feel no need to be baptized. Finally, while many Christian denominations have clothing rites (for the baptized, the ordained, the married), the Evangelical movement typically does not.

3.   Jack Tresidder, *Symbols and Their Meanings* (London: Duncan Baird Publishers, 2000), 134.

4.   Douglas R. Edwards, "Dress and Ornamentation," in *The Anchor Bible Dictionary*, 6 vols., ed. David Noel Freedman (New York: Doubleday, 1992), 2:232. As examples, Saul rips the hem of Samuel's cloak as a symbolic statement about Saul's kingdom being lost to David (1 Samuel 15:27), Elijah gives Elisha his mantle to indicate that the latter would be the former's successor (1 Kings 19:19), The removal of a shoe was used as the verification of a business transaction (Ruth 4:7–10), and so on.

5.   Leland Ryken, James C. Wilhoit, and Tremper Longman III, eds., *Dictionary of Biblical Imagery* (Downers Grove, Illinois: InterVarsity Press, 1998), 317. See also, Edwards, in *The Anchor Bible Dictionary*, 2:232.

6.   See John Tvedtnes, "Priestly Clothing in Bible Times" in *Temples of the Ancient World*, ed. Donald W. Parry (Provo, Utah: Foundation for Ancient Research and Mormon Studies, 1994), 665–66. Elsewhere we read, "The fact that God Himself revealed the pattern for these vestments should alert us to the possibility that they imitate the clothing that is worn by heavenly beings. And indeed, there is some evidence to support this view. A post-biblical Jewish commentary on the book of Exodus explains that the high priest's garments were like those worn by the Lord. And one extrabiblical source also describes an angel wearing eight garments, alluding to those worn by the earthly high priest. With this connection between the heavens and the earth, it is little wonder that they were called 'holy garments' (Exodus 28:2, 4; 31:10; Leviticus 16:4)." Matthew B. Brown, *The Gate of Heaven: Insights on the Doctrines and Symbols of the Temple* (American Fork, Utah: Covenant Communications, 1999), 81.

7.   See Ryken, Wilhoit, and Longman, eds., *Dictionary of Biblical Imagery*, 319.

8.   Cyril of Jerusalem, "Catechetical Lectures," Lecture 20:2, in *Nicene and Post-Nicene Fathers—Second Series*, 14 vols., ed. Philip Schaff and Henry Wace (Peabody, Massachusetts: Hendrickson Publishers, 2004), 7:147; emphasis in original.

9.   Ryken, Wilhoit, and Longman, eds., *Dictionary of Biblical Imagery*, 318. Even fabric, like wool and linen, had symbolic importance. Only priests, for example, were allowed to mix the two in ancient Jewish tradition (Leviticus 19:19; Deuteronomy 22:11).

10.   Hebrews 10:19–12 states, "Having therefore, brethren, boldness to enter into the holiest by the blood of Jesus, By a new and living way, which he hath consecrated for us, through the veil, that is to say, his flesh." In the spirit of these verses, the veil of

the temple was seen by many of the ancients as a symbol for the flesh of Christ—God incarnate. Margaret Barker, *The Gate of Heaven: The History and Symbolism of the Temple in Jerusalem* (Sheffield, England: Sheffield Phoenix Press, 2008), 104. Barker added: "Texts which describe [the high priest's] vestments show that these were made in exactly the same way as the temple curtain" or veil. Barker, *The Gate of Heaven*, 111. Blake Ostler wrote: "It should be noted that the ancient garment bore the same tokens as the veil of the temple at Jerusalem. . . . Many ancient texts confuse the garment with the veil of the temple, such as Ambrose of Milano's Tractate of the Mysteries or the Hebrew Book of Enoch where the 'garment' and 'veil' are used interchangeably." Blake Ostler, "Clothed Upon: A Unique Aspect of Christian Antiquity," in *BYU Studies* 22, no. 1 (Winter 1982): 35. Similarly, Hugh Nibley pointed out that the garment and the veil of the temple bear "the same markings" and have "the same cosmic significance." Hugh Nibley, *Mormonism and Early Christianity* (Provo, Utah: Foundation for Ancient Research and Mormon Studies, 1987), 75. Since the veil of the temple represents the flesh of Jesus, the garment (which was patterned after the veil) carries that same symbolic connotation.

11. See Edwards, in *The Anchor Bible Dictionary*, 2:234. See also, Philip J. Hyatt, "Dress," in *Dictionary of the Bible*, rev. ed., ed. James Hastings (New York: Charles Scribner's Sons, 1963), 223.

12. See Janet Mayo, *A History of Ecclesiastical Dress* (London: B. T. Batsford, 1984), 153. The 1609 Douday Bible's rendering of Leviticus 6:10 is as follows: "The priest shall be revested with the tunike and the linen femoralles."

13. The words "liturgy" and "liturgical" have to do with any fixed set of ceremonies— including words, actions, clothing, etc.—that are used during corporate (or group) worship.

14. See Ramban Nachmanides, *Commentary on the Torah*, 5 vols. (New York: Shilo Publishing, 1973), 2:484–85; Edwards, in *The Anchor Bible Dictionary*, 2:233; Walter C. Kaiser Jr., "Exodus," in *The Expositor's Bible Commentary*, 12 vols., ed. Frank E. Gaebelein (Grand Rapids, Michigan: Zondervan, 1976–92), 2:467.

15. While Christians typically describe the meaning of these articles of clothing in terms of Christocentric symbolism, that view is generally held by scholars to be eisegetical. Most academics assume the priests of the ancient temple cult did not have the messianic lenses we do when it comes to their rites, rituals, or ordinances. Of course, this is a point of debate.

16. Charles W. Slemming, *These Are the Garments: A Study of the Garments of the High Priest of Israel* (London: Marshall, Morgan Scott, Ltd., 1945), 127, 31.

17. See Arnold Van Gennep, *The Rites of Passage*, trans. Monika B. Vizedom and Gabrielle L. Caffee (Chicago: The University of Chicago Press, 1960), 29–30.

18. This garment is worn by Ultra-Orthodox and Modern Orthodox Jews, but not typically by Conservative, Reformed, or secular Jews. Orthodox women do not wear the fringed undergarment (*tallit katan*). Although in recent years, some females in Conservative, Reform, or Reconstructionist groups have begun to wear it.

19. Similarly, in AV Numbers 15:37–41, we find, "And the Lord spake unto Moses, saying, Speak unto the children of Israel, and bid them that they make them fringes in the borders of their garments throughout their generations, and that they put upon the

fringe of the borders a ribband of blue: And it shall be unto you for a fringe, that ye may look upon it, and remember all the commandments of the Lord, and do them; and that ye seek not after your own heart and your own eyes, after which ye use to go a whoring: That ye may remember, and do all my commandments, and be holy unto your God. I am the Lord your God, which brought you out of the land of Egypt, to be your God: I am the Lord your God."

20. In the opinion of many, this sacred undershirt is related to, though not identical with, the aforementioned "fine linen" shirt (Exodus 28:39) of the temple priests.

21. Rarely, a special belt, known as a "gartel," may be worn in connection with the *tallit katan*. This likely stems from the "curious girdle" worn by the ancient priest (Exodus 28:8).

22. Louis Ginzberg, *The Legends of the Jews*, 7 vols. (Philadelphia: The Jewish Publication Society of America, 1967–69), 3:241.

23. Cecil Roth, Geoffrey Wigoder, and Fred Skolnik, eds., *Encyclopaedia Judaica*, rev. ed., 17 vols. (Jerusalem: Keter Publishing, 1996), 15:745, s.v. "tallit katan."

24. Rabbi Nahman of Bratzlav maintains the garments "are a safeguard against immorality," pointing to examples in drunken Noah and in the Genesis creation myth. Thus by wearing the pure white *tallit katan*, we mitigate darkness and destruction. See Tzvi M. Rabinowicz, *The Encyclopedia of Hasidism* (Maryland: Jason Aronson Publishers, 1977), 512–13.

25. See *The Babylonian Talmud*, Tractate Menachot 44a.

26. Roth, Wigoder, Skolnik, eds., *Encyclopaedia Judaica*, 15:744, s.v. "tallit."

27. Ibid., 16:1187, s.v. "ẓiẓit."

28. See ibid.

29. As noted earlier, some liberal Jewish women have begun to wear the *tallit katan*, but it is only commanded of men—and has traditionally only been worn by men.

30. Among the faithful, this rite of passage always takes place by the end of the fifteenth year—as the age fifteen is seen by Zoroastrians as the age of adulthood. Those who do not become initiated into the faith by that age are seen as "ill-behaved" and as placing themselves "in the power of the evil druj" (in the way of error and deceit). See Jivanji Jamshedji Modi, *The Religious Ceremonies and Customs of the Parsees* (New York: Garland Publishing, 1979), 144.

31. The term *Navjote* (or *Naojot*) means "new birth," as the initiate is seen as a "new person," one just now "born into" the faith of Zoroastrianism. See Gherardo Gnoli, "Zoroastrianism," in *The Encyclopedia of Religion*, 16 vols., ed. Mircea Eliade (New York: Macmillan, 1987), 15:587. The ceremonial investiture is preceded by a sacred washing rite, called *Nahn*.

32. See Modi, *The Religious Ceremonies and Customs of the Parsees*, 145–46.

33. Ibid., 149.

34. Behman Sorabji Banaji, "The Warfare of Zoroaster," in *Advocate of Peace through Justice*, vol. 86, no. 1 (January 1924): 35.

35. See Modi, *The Religious Ceremonies and Customs of the Parsees*, 150–52. See also Michael Strausberg, "The Significance of the 'kusti': A History of Its Zoroastrian Interpretation," in *East and West*, vol. 54, no. 1 (December 2004), 15.

36. See Sad Dar, *Pahvlavi Texts,* 10:1, 4, trans. E. A. West (New York: Charles Scribner's Sons, 1901), 268.

37. See Firoze M. Kotwal, "Ritual Aspects of the Gathas and Their Continuity in Later Tradition," in *Iran & the Caucasus,* vol. 3 (1999–2000), 8.

38. See Strausberg, "The Significance of the 'kusti,'" 10.

39. Some Sikhs seem uncomfortable with connecting the *Amrit Sanskar* to baptism, as its meaning and purpose are not the same as Christian baptism—though the forms are akin to each other. See W. Owen Cole, "Review of W. H. McLeod's, *The Chaupa Sing Rahit-Nama,*" in *Journal of the Royal Asiatic Society of Great Britain and Ireland,* no. 1 (1989): 184.

40. Sikh Missionary Center, *Sikh Religion* (Detroit, Michigan: Sikh Missionary Center, 1990), 200. One scholar of Sikhism has pointed out that while most Sikhs accept that Guru Gobind Singh was the source for these special items of clothing, some historians believed that they were not part of the faith until the end of the nineteenth century. See, for example, Hew McLeod, "The Five Ks of the Khalsa Sikhs," in *Journal of the American Oriental Society,* vol. 128, no. 2 (April–June, 2008): 328–31.

41. This is sometimes also spelled *Kes.*

42. The *Kangha* is openly worn in the hair of female Sikh. On male Sikhs, however, it is often obscured by their turban. This is not an attempt to hide the comb, as they hide the undergarment. It is a practical matter (the turban helps to control their hair).

43. Early in their history, Sikhs were heavily persecuted by Muslims.

44. "These are a reminder of the duty of purity and also a reminder to Sikhs to act for the faith." Though a less common interpretation, one source suggested that the Sikh underpants were "to indicate alertness and readiness to fight." Michael Molloy, *Experiencing the World's Religions: Tradition, Challenge, and Change,* 5th ed. (New York: McGraw-Hill, 2010), 206.

45. Willard G. Oxtoby and Alan F. Segal, eds., *A Concise Introduction to World Religions* (New York: Oxford University Press, 2007), 334. Men and women can participate in the amrit initiation and wear the 5 Ks, which were originally associated with the Khālsā, but today are generally embraced by all Sikhs. There is no specified age of initiation. One must simply be old enough to read scripture and to comprehend the articles of the Sikh faith. See Nikky-Guninder Kaur Singh, "Sikhism," in *Encyclopedia of Religion,* 2nd ed., 16 vols., ed. Lindsay Jones (New York: Macmillan Reference USA, 2005), 12:8395, 8397.

46. McLeod, "The Five Ks of the Khalsa Sikhs," 327.

47. John Bowker, *World Religions—The Great Faiths Explored and Explained* (New York: DK Publishing, 2006), 84.

48. Ibid., 95. See also *Sikh Religion,* 200.

49. See Taxiarchae-Archangels Greek Orthodox Church, *The Consecration of Our Beloved Church* (Watertown, Massachusetts: Taxiarchae-Archangels Greek Orthodox Church, 2000), xvi.

50. See Isabel F. Hapgood, *Service Book of the Holy Orthodox-Catholic Apostolic Church* (New York: Association Press, 1922), 493–511, 613; Taxiarchae-Archangels, *The Consecration of Our Beloved Church,* xv–xvi. Hapgood notes that this white garment carries several symbols: that it encircles the neck symbolizes the wisdom and obedience

of the wearer; that it covers the body, particularly the breast, symbolizes the Word; that it shrouds the loins symbolizes the wearer's purity and strength. See Hapgood, *Service Book of the Holy Orthodox-Catholic Apostolic Church*, 613, n. 2.

51. One text on the rite states, "Functionally, the *savanon* is a large bright white garment in the shape of an alb that protects the bishop's vestments during the washing of the table. Symbolically, it represents the mortification of his body to all sin and the vesting of purity and blamelessness which he must possess in order to complete the consecration rite. The envelopment of his body with the brilliance of the cloak shows him to be mystically, on the one hand, Christ, and, on the other, a living altar." Gus George Christo, *The Consecration of a Greek Orthodox Church According to Eastern Orthodox Tradition: A Detailed Account and Explanation of the Ritual* (Lewiston, New York: The Edwin Mellen Press, 2005), 28, fn. 25.

52. Hapgood, *Service Book of the Holy Orthodox-Catholic Apostolic Church*, 501; Taxiarchae-Archangels, *The Consecration of Our Beloved Church*, xviii.

53. Greek Orthodox Church of the Annunciation, "Savanon" (Kansas City, Missouri: Greek Orthodox Church of the Annunciation, 1987), back cover. See also Christo, *The Consecration of a Greek Orthodox Church According to Eastern Orthodox Tradition*, 28, fn. 25, where we read, "Once the entire consecration procedure is over, the bishop divests of the *savanon*. It will be cut into tiny pieces and distributed to all the members of the congregation at the end of the Hierarchical Divine Liturgy of St. John Chrysostom. The tiny pieces are a phylacton or a phylactery (a blessed object worn as a protection against evil)." In addition, see Nicon D. Patrinacos, *A Dictionary of Greek Orthodoxy* (New York: Greek Orthodox Archdiocese of North and South America, Dept. of Education, 1984), 17–18.

54. For dissenters, the use of blessed objects, like the sacred garment (or vestment) of the Archbishop (the *savanon*), is superstitious nonsense. The notion of wearing a white piece of blessed or holy cloth somewhere on one's underclothing for protection against evil or temptation is, to some, superstitious at least, and potentially blasphemous at most. For those who are non-practicers (or non-wearers), this tradition sounds like an extension of the iconoclast controversy of the eighth and ninth centuries. See Timothy Ware, *The Orthodox Church*, new ed. (New York: Penguin Books, 1997), 30–35.

55. Greek Orthodox Church of the Annunciation, explanation of the power of phylakton (Kansas City, Missouri: October 4, 1987), back cover.

56. Helen Papanikolas, *An Amulet of Greek Earth* (Athens: Swallow Press/Ohio University Press, 2002), 4.

57. Ibid., 53.

58. Ibid., 29, 53.

59. Biblical Judaism is traditionally dated to the life of Abraham, placing its origins in the second millennium BCE. (Though some would place the wearing of sacred undergarments to the era of Adam and Eve—Genesis 3:21). Zoroastrianism dates somewhere between 1500 and 1000 BCE. Eastern Orthodoxy traces its origins to the founding of Christianity in the first century of the Common Era. Setting aside Mormonism, Sikhism is the most modern of the faith's we've discussed; originating in the fifteenth century. Though technically neither Sikhism nor Mormonism qualify

as "ancient," the culture from which Sikhism stems is, indeed, ancient, and Latter-day Saints see themselves as a "restoration" of primitive or ancient Christianity.

60. A lack of reverence for that which is sacred to one tradition ultimately shows disrespect to all, because those who are deeply religious are actually interconnected in ways that easily go unnoticed. The sacred undergarments of these various traditions, and the commonality of their purpose and meaning, are an invitation to ecumenism and appreciation for each other's tradition, and the deeply spiritual things that we share. Thus, we must never ridicule that which we do not understand. We are always better served by attempts at building bridges and understanding—and by seeking to highlight the ties that bind us one to another.

Chapter 4

DOCTRINE AND COVENANTS 129:8 AND THE REALITY OF SATAN'S PHYSICALITY[1]

Alonzo L. Gaskill

In section 129 of the Doctrine and Covenants, the Lord provides "three grand keys" by which the Saints may know whether any angelic ministration is from God or from the devil. Verse 8 informs us that should the devil (or one of his hosts) appear, attempting to deceive you into thinking he is a divine messenger sent from God, "when you ask him to shake hands he will offer you his hand, and you will not feel anything; you may therefore detect him."[2] For many, this verse gives the  impression that because Satan and his hosts lack mortal bodies, they are incapable of having physical contact with humans. In other words, the passage appears to focus on the nature of the bodies of Lucifer and his spirit followers, suggesting that their physical makeup is the reason their hands cannot be felt. However, a series of events that took place early in the Restoration suggest that this interpretation may not be completely accurate. In an effort to test the common interpretation of Doctrine and Covenants 129:8, this chapter will recount a handful of early encounters with the devil, and the implications for those encounters on our understanding of the temple endowment, the nature of Lucifer's person, and the doctrine conveyed in section 129.

THE PROPHET JOSEPH SMITH

Of course, the reader will be familiar with the first and most sacred of events tied to the Restoration—namely the appearance of the Father and Son to the Prophet Joseph Smith. That spring morning of 1820, Joseph had a very physical encounter with the adversary—an experience that left Joseph with no doubts about Satan's power in the physical realm:

> I kneeled down and began to offer up the desires of my heart to God. I had scarcely done so, when immediately I was seized upon by some power which entirely overcame me, and had such an astonishing influence over me as to bind my tongue so that I could not speak. Thick darkness gathered around me, and it seemed to me for a time as if I were doomed to sudden destruction, . . . and at the very moment when I was ready to sink into despair and abandon myself to destruction— not to an imaginary ruin, but to the power of some actual being from the unseen world, who had such marvelous power as I had never before felt in any being—just at this moment of great alarm, I saw a pillar of light. (Joseph Smith—History 1:15–16)[3]

Joseph describes here what must have been a terrifying and unimaginable encounter. Among other things, he notes that he was "seized upon" and was "entirely" overcome by Satan. He states that Lucifer bound his tongue so that he could not speak or cry out.[4] Elsewhere, Joseph noted that during this experience, the devil caused his tongue to physically swell up and cleave to the roof of his mouth.[5] He also spoke of hearing distinct footsteps walking toward him as he began his prayer, but he could not see Satan's person.[6] In one account of the experience, the Prophet noted that throughout the ordeal, he was "severely tempted" with "improper pictures," and his mind was "benighted . . . with doubts"—all via the devil's influence.[7]

This was certainly not the Prophet's only encounter with the adversary. Although we do not know all the details surrounding each of these experiences, we *do* know that Joseph confided to at least one of his brethren that Satan had made repeated attempts to physically destroy him. President Heber C. Kimball stated, "Brother Joseph . . . told me that he had contests with the devil, face-to-face. He also told me how he was handled and afflicted by the devil."[8] Heber shares the details of one of the many demonic encounters the Prophet had suffered:

I will relate one circumstance that took place at Far West, in a house that Joseph had purchased, which had been formerly occupied as a public house by some wicked people. A short time after he got into it, one of his children was taken very sick; he laid his hands upon the child, when it got better; as soon as he went out of doors, the child was taken sick again; he again laid his hands upon it, so that it again recovered. This occurred several times, when Joseph inquired of the Lord what it all meant; then he had an open vision, and saw the devil in person, who contended with Joseph face-to-face, for some time. He said it was his house, it belonged to him, and Joseph had no right there. Then Joseph rebuked Satan in the name of the Lord, and he departed and touched the child no more.[9]

Thus, the record shows that Joseph experienced Satan in a very real and tangible way. This was not isolated to the very strange encounter in the Sacred Grove; on the contrary, the devil—apparently on multiple occasions—physically and violently accosted the Prophet "face-to-face."

HEBER C. KIMBALL

We should not be surprised to learn that the Prophet Joseph was not the only member of the early Church to be attacked by Lucifer. Indeed, Elder Kimball's aforementioned conversation with Joseph regarding physical satanic attacks did not come up at random. Rather, the conversation was provoked by an encounter Heber had while serving a mission to the British Isles. Brother Kimball spoke of this experience on numerous occasions, each time sharing additional and different details. Because space will not allow us to provide each of Brother Kimball's many descriptions, what follows is an amalgamation of the salient points of the experience.

In 1837, Elders Heber C. Kimball, Willard Richards, Orson Hyde, and Isaac Russell were laboring as missionaries in Preston, England.[10] They were sharing a three-story flat on Wilford Street when the unthinkable happened. On Sunday, July 30, sometime around daybreak, Elder Russell rushed into the room of Elders Kimball and Hyde, waking them, and claiming that he was so afflicted with evil spirits that he would not live long if someone did not cast them out. The two brethren administered to him, rebuking

the devil and petitioning the Lord for relief from the enemy that held Isaac bound. Elder Kimball was voice during the blessing. Near the end of the administration, his voice began to falter, and then his tongue was bound so that he could no longer speak. Suddenly, he began to tremble and reel back and forth. At that moment, some invisible force threw him forward onto the floor. As he hit the floor, he let out a deep groan and then lay prostrate as though he were a dead man. Elder Hyde, with the assistance of Elder Russell, immediately laid hands on Elder Kimball, blessing him and rebuking Satan—at which point Heber regained consciousness, but had only partial strength. He noted that as he regained his senses, sweat began to roll from him so profusely that it was as though he had just stepped out of a river. Elders Hyde and Russell lifted Elder Kimball and placed him on his bed. However, his physical agony was so intense that he pulled himself back onto the floor. Reaching his knees, he began to plead with the Lord for intervention.

At some point during these bizarre happenings, Elder Willard Richards awoke and made his way up to the third floor where the events were unfolding. Elder Kimball noted that, having finished his prayer, he sat on his bed, and, to the surprise of all present, they were wrapped in a vision of the "infernal world." The four brethren said that they saw "legions" of evil spirits, company after company of them. According to Heber, these demonic hosts "struggled" to attack the elders and "exerted all their power and influence" to destroy them. These spirits were in the shape of men, with fully formed bodies, hands, eyes, hair, ears, and every other human feature—though some had hideous distortions in their face and body. With knives, they "rushed" upon the brethren "as an army going to battle." Elders Kimball and Hyde testified that they saw them as plainly as one would see a person standing in front of them. These demonic assailants came toward them, foaming at the mouth and "gnashing their teeth upon" the elders. Orson Hyde noted that there were also numerous snakes accompanying the satanic hosts, hissing, writhing, and crawling over each other. Willard Richards, who had his watch on his person, noted that these "foul spirits" remained in the room threatening the brethren for an hour and a half.[11] Elder Kimball indicated that the following day he was so weak from the physical attack that he could scarcely stand.

Years later, he spoke in detail of the encounter and then added, "I cannot even now look back on the scene without feelings of horror; yet, by it I learned the power of the adversary, his enmity against the servants of God, and got some understanding of the invisible world."[12]

Similarly, nearly two decades after the experience, Elder Hyde wrote, "Every circumstance that occurred at that scene of devils is just as fresh in my recollection at this moment as it was at the moment of its occurrence, and will ever remain so."[13] Although much of the foregoing account was visionary, rather than tangible, Heber was quite clear that he was physically assaulted with a force that felt like being punched in the face by the fist of a strong man—to say nothing of the faltering voice, bound tongue, and physical weakness he encountered.

WILFORD WOODRUFF

Not unlike the experiences of Joseph, Heber, Orson, Willard, and Isaac, Elders Wilford Woodruff and George A. Smith were physically attacked by the devil during the winter of 1840 as they labored in London. Elder Woodruff spoke of this assault on numerous occasions. On October 18, 1840, he wrote the following in his journal:

> We [Wilford Woodruff and George A. Smith] retired to rest in good season and I felt well in my mind and slept until 12 at night. I awoke and meditated upon the things of God until near 3 o'clock and while forming a determination to warn the people in London and overcome the powers of Darkness by the assistance of God; A person appeared unto me which I considered was the Prince of Darkness or the Devil. He made war with me and attempted to take my life. He caught me by the throat and choked me nearly to death. He wounded me in my forehead. I also wounded him in a number of places in the head.[14] As he was about to overcome me I prayed to the father in the name of Jesus for help. I then had power over him and he left me though much wounded.
>
> Three personages dressed in white came to me and prayed with me and I was immediately healed and [they] delivered me from all my troubles.[15]

Although he doesn't mention it in the foregoing account, on later occasions, Wilford indicated that Satan did physical harm to *both* him and George A. Smith—and had it not been for "three holy messengers . . . dressed in temple clothing" who gave them each a priesthood blessing, both of them would have been killed by Satan on that occasion.[16]

NEWEL KNIGHT

The Prophet and the early missionaries were not the only individuals to suffer physical attacks at the hands of the adversary. In what has come

to be known as the "first miracle of the Church," Newel Knight had a rather strange physical encounter with Lucifer. In the *History of the Church*,[17] we find the following reference to the event:

Amongst those who attended our meetings regularly, was Newel Knight son to Joseph Knight. . . . Newel had said that he would try and take up his cross, and pray vocally during meeting; but when we again met together, he rather excused himself. . . . Accordingly he deferred praying untill [*sic*] next morning, when he retired into the woods, where (according to his own accoount [*sic*] afterwards) he made several attempts to pray, but could scarcely do so. . . . He began to feel uneasy, and continued to feel worse both in mind and body, untill [*sic*], upon reaching his own house, his appearance was such as to alarm his wife very much. He requested her to go and bring me to him. I went and found him suffering very much in his mind, and his body acted upon in a very strange manner. His visage and limbs distorted and twisted in every shape and appearance possible to imagine; and finally he was caught up off the floor of the apartment and tossed about most fearfully. His situation was soon made known to his neighbours [*sic*] and relatives, and in a short time as many as eight or nine grown persons had got together to witness the scene. After he had thus suffered for a time, I succeeded in getting hold of him by the hand, when almost immediately he spoke to me, and with great earnestness requested of me, that I should cast the Devil out of him, saying that he knew he was in him, and that he also knew that I could cast him out. I replied "If you know that I can, it shall be done" and then almost unconsciously I rebuked the devil, and commanded him in the name of Jesus Christ to depart from him; when immediately Newel spoke out and said that he saw the devil leave him and vanish from his sight. . . .

The scene was now entirely changed for as soon as the devil had departed from our friend, his countenance became natural, his distortions of body ceased, and almost immediately the Spirit of the Lord descended upon him, and the visions of eternity were opened to his view. . . .

All this was witnessed by many, to their great astonishment and satisfaction.[18]

Knight confirms the *History of the Church* account in his autobiography, where he not only acknowledges that the event took place but also speaks in detail of the subsequent June 29, 1830, trial in which he was called as a witness and interrogated regarding the aforementioned Luciferian encounter.[19] Although Newel's experience may seem more like demonic possession than satanic attack, clearly he was being physically accosted. Not only was his body actually distorted and disabled by the experience, but he also notes that Satan physically lifted him off the floor and "tossed" him about the room as if he were a rag doll.

SIDNEY RIGDON

Lesser known is an event that took place in September of 1831. The Prophet Joseph decided to take his family, then dwelling in Kirtland, and move to Hiram, Ohio, where he could continue the work of translating the Bible. Sidney Rigdon was left to preside over the Saints in Kirtland. On one occasion during Joseph's absence, Sidney informed a body of Saints that the "keys of the kingdom" had been taken from the Church.[20] Those present were confused and dismayed by the announcement. Joseph was immediately sent for and, upon his return, declared that the  things Sidney had taught were false. The Prophet added that, because of the things Elder Rigdon had said and done, "the devil [would] handle him as one man handles another."[21] In fulfillment of Joseph's words, "a few weeks after this, Sidney was lying in bed alone, and suddenly 'an unseen power lifted him from his bed . . . and tossed him from one side of the room to the other.' His family heard the noises coming from the room and rushed in 'and found him going from one side of the room to the other.'"[22] This happened some three times over the course of the night.[23] Sidney was physically "laid up" for five or six weeks because of the effects of the experience. Thus, having spoken under the influence of the devil, Sidney was then turned over to the physical buffetings of Lucifer.

BENJAMIN BROWN

Although each of the aforementioned stories involved high-profile members of the Church, a number of lesser-known believers in the restored gospel had similar encounters. For example, one early Saint by the name of Benjamin Brown spent the years prior to his discovery of the Church looking for "the ancient gospel" of New Testament Christianity. In the process, he is said to have had a number of visions. However, when Brown shared these experiences with a local minister, he was told that both his visions and his desires to find "the ancient" Church of the Bible were "of the Devil."[24]

On one occasion after his conversion, Brother Brown and two friends were called upon to cast an evil spirit out of a possessed sister. While attempting to exercise the priesthood, Brown and one of his companions learned (via direct experience) of Satan's ability to physically interact with mortals. He notes:

> The evil spirit . . . came out full of fury, and, as he passed by one of the brethren, seized him by both arms and gripped them violently. Passing towards me, something, which by the feel appeared like a man's hand, grasped me by both sides of the face, and attempted to pull me sideways to the ground, but the hold appearing to slip, I recovered my balance immediately.
>
> My face was sore for some days after this. The other brother that was seized was lame for a week afterwards.[25]

Like so many others, Brother Brown and his companion learned first-hand that Satan's hands *can* be felt!

HARVEY WHITLOCK

One final experience is worth sharing here. It involves the ordination of Harvey Whitlock to the office of high priest. Brother Whitlock was an "on again, off again" Latter-day Saint who was baptized into the Church three times before finally becoming a member of the RLDS Church.[26] Brother Whitlock's experience with Satan was recorded by a number of individuals, some of whom were firsthand witnesses. For example, Levi Hancock wrote,

> The Fourth of June [1831] came and we all met . . . near Isaac Morleys in Kirtland, [Geauga] County, Ohio. . . . Joseph put his hands on Harvey Whitlock and ordained him to the high priesthood. He [Harvey Whitlock] turned as black as Lyman was white. His fingers were set like claws. He went around the room and showed his hands and tried to speak, his eyes were in the shape of oval O's. Hyrum Smith said, "Joseph, that is not of God." . . . Joseph bowed his head, and in a short time got up and commanded Satan to leave Harvey, laying his hands upon his head at the same time. At that very instant an old man said to weigh two hundred and fourteen pounds sitting in the window turned a complete summersault [*sic*] in the house and [landed on] his back across a bench and lay helpless. Joseph told Lyman to cast Satan out. He did. The man's name was Leamon Coply [Leman Copley], formally a Quaker [Shaker]. The evil spirit left him and as quick as lightening [*sic*] Harvey Green fell bound and screamed like a panther. Satan was cast out of him. But immediately entered someone else. This continued all day and the greater part of the night. . . . After this we . . . heard Harvey Whitlock say when Hyrum Smith said it was not [of] God, he disdained him in his heart and when the Devil was cast out he was convinced it was Satan that was in him and he knew . . . it. I also heard Harvey Green say that he could not describe the awful feeling he experienced while in the hands of Satan.[27]

Lucy Mack Smith also referred to the Harvey Whitlock experience in her 1844–45 preliminary manuscript that would become her *History of Joseph Smith by His Mother*. While she confirms Levi Hancock's account of the events, she adds a couple of additional insights that Hancock did not include. Mother Smith states that Whitlock convulsed when under

Philo Dibble

the physical influence of Satan and was left physically weak after the devil was cast out of him. She also notes that Copley had his tongue bound during the episode, preventing him from speaking.[28] Both of these "symptoms," if we can call them such, are comparable to the experiences of Joseph Smith, Heber C. Kimball, and Newel Knight. Philo Dibble, who was a firsthand witness to this experience, confirms Lucy Mack Smith's additions to the story. Dibble writes:

Harvey Whitlock stepped into the middle of the room with his arms crossed, bound by the power of Satan, and his mouth twisted unshapely.

Hyrum Smith arose and declared that there was an evil spirit in the room. . . .

Shortly Hyrum rose the second time, saying, "I know my duty and will do it," and stepping to Harvey, commanded the evil spirits to leave him, but the spirits did not obey.

Joseph then approached Harvey and asked him if he believed in God. Then we saw a change in Harvey. He also bore record of the opening of the heavens and of the coming of the Son of Man, precisely as Lyman Wight had done.

Next a man by the name of Harvey Green was thrown upon his back on the floor by an unseen power. Some of the brethren wanted to administer to him by laying on of hands, but Joseph forbade it. Harvey looked to me like a man in a fit. He groaned and frothed at the mouth. Finally he got upon his knees and came out of it.

Next thing I saw a man came flying through the window from outside. He was straight as a man's arm as he sailed into the room over two rows of seats filled with men, and fell on the floor between the seats and was pulled out by the brethren. He trembled all over like a leaf in the wind. He was soon . . . calm and natural. His name was Lemon [*sic*] Copley. He weighed over two hundred pounds. This I saw with my own eyes and know it is all true, and bear testimony to it.[29]

What seems significant here—at least as it relates to our discussion—is not so much the fact that Harvey Whitlock was possessed by the devil, as others apparently were. Rather, what seems noteworthy are the physical attacks upon Leman Copley and Harvey Green. Whereas Whitlock was clearly possessed, these brethren exhibited behavior that implied they were also being physically (not just spiritually) harassed by the adversary.

THE NATURE OF SATAN'S PERSON

What has been shared is only a sampling of the numerous examples of demonic attacks recorded in the diaries and journals of the early Saints and in the historical records of the Church. Were space not an issue, many more could be offered as evidence that Lucifer is capable of physical contact with mortals. As Elder Joseph Fielding Smith wrote, "We must not discount the power of the adversary of all righteousness. There are scores of cases, fully attested in our own day of demon influence."[30] Hauntingly, President George Q. Cannon spoke to this subject on more than one occasion, cautioning the Saints:

> I have come to the conclusion that if our eyes were open to see the spirit world around us, . . . we would not be so unguarded and careless, and so indifferent whether we had the spirit and power of God with us or not; but we would be continually watchful and prayerful to our heavenly Father for His Holy Spirit and His holy angels to be around about us to strengthen us to overcome every evil influence. . . .[31]

> If he could [Satan] would shed the blood of every man and woman on the face of the earth, rather than it should go into the hands of God. All those who are connected with him would, if they could, slay every man that stands in their pathway. The more faithful a man is in the cause of God, the more the hatred of the wicked is manifested against him.[32]

Of course, all these accounts raise a question: How is it possible that the devil and his minions—beings without physical bodies—are able to attack human beings in such a physical manner? Are we to be dismissive of these historical narratives as simple misunderstandings on the part of those who experienced the events described? This solution does not appear to be a viable one. Not only are a number of these brethren known to be men of character, righteousness, and trustworthiness,[33] but also each seems quite certain about what he saw, experienced, and described. Beyond this, there is a consistency in their experiences that suggests they are describing events that actually happened (such as being left weak, having one's tongue bound, being pinned or thrown to the floor, being tossed about the room, and so forth). Reason suggests that these events happened as described.

Perhaps one explanation of these happenings is to be found in the nature of Satan's body. We commonly cite the Prophet Joseph's comment, "We came to this earth that we might have a body and present it pure before God in the Celestial Kingdom. The great principle of happiness consists in having a body. The devil has no body, and herein is his punishment. He is pleased when he can obtain the tabernacle of man and when cast out by the Savior he asked to go into the herd of swine showing that he would prefer a swine's body to having none."[34]

Accurately, this statement points out that Satan's premortal rebellion and fall stripped him of the right to have a mortal body. However, the tendency is to assume that Joseph is here saying that Lucifer's "spirit body" is therefore void of any physical properties. Yet this is clearly not what the Prophet is claiming. Regarding the physical nature of the "spirit body," the Prophet notes "that the body is supposed to be organized matter, and the spirit, by many, is thought to be immaterial, without substance. With this latter statement we should beg leave to differ, and state that spirit is a substance; that it is material, but that it is more pure, elastic and refined matter than the body."[35] Similarly, approximately a year later, Joseph stated, "There is no such thing as immaterial matter. All spirit is matter, but it is more fine or pure, and can only be discerned by purer eyes; we cannot see it; but when our bodies are purified we shall see that it is all matter" (D&C 131:7–8). Latter-day Saint scholars Stephen E. Robinson and H. Dean Garrett write, "Spirits are made of matter. Just as matter can change form from matter to energy, so, apparently, matter can be refined and purified to the point where it is normally discernible only to bodies that have been similarly refined and purified. The universe is not composed of two mutually exclusive entities, matter and spirit, but of only one—matter in one or another stage of refinement."[36] The notion that Satan's spirit body—or the spirit body of any being—is immaterial, and thus intangible, appears to be incorrect. The devil's spirit body is made of matter, just as our physical bodies are made of matter. And the aforementioned encounters strongly suggest that spirit matter and mortal matter *can* interact.

As a parenthetical note, the material nature of spirits is not isolated to Luciferian angels. The physical makeup of righteous spirits is also material. For example, we understand that the priesthood continues to function in the spirit world, as it does here on earth.[37] Indeed, we have every reason to believe that part of the communication that takes place in the postmortal spirit world is physical—spirit to spirit.[38] They touch, interact, and so forth. We know that in the premortal world, where we were also spirits, men were ordained to the Melchizedek Priesthood in anticipation of their reordination here in mortality, and this was almost certainly done by the laying on of hands.[39] In addition, those who would serve in callings within the Church during their mortal experience were foreordained to those callings while they were still spirits.[40] Elders Orson Hyde and Neal A. Maxwell of the Quorum of the Twelve Apostles both taught that in our premortal state as spirits, we each entered into all the gospel covenants that would later be reintroduced to us in mortality.[41] These two Brethren suggest that we actually signed a document that would be retained in the heavens to be presented to us at the Judgment Day, attesting to the premortal covenants we had made.[42]

David Patten Kimball, son of President Heber C. Kimball, had an experience in which he had physical contact with the spirits of his deceased parents, who visited him from the spirit world. He had gotten lost in the desert of Arizona and was near death for want of water. His father and mother appeared to him and gave him a drink of water, which sustained his life until he could be found.[43]

Elder Parley P. Pratt had a similar experience. He was unjustly incarcerated in Richmond, Missouri, and had been fasting and pleading with the Lord to know if he would ever be freed from that "gloomy, dark, cold and filthy dungeon." In response to his prayer, his wife—who had been deceased for nearly two years—appeared to him. She held his hand and laid her cheek against his. Parley noted the warmth of her face as she pressed it against him. She had come in answer to his pleadings and informed him that he would again see the light of day.[44]

In the Gospel of Matthew, we are informed that it was an angel that rolled back the stone covering the opening of the sepulchre in which Jesus had been placed (see Matthew 28:2).[45] All of these accounts simply show that righteous spirits also have a material nature that is capable of touch, interaction, ordination, and so forth. Nothing is immaterial!

DOCTRINE AND COVENANTS 129:8

As we turn our attention back to Doctrine and Covenants 129:8, we are left with the impression that the passage is not primarily about the nature of Satan's body. As has been shown, the issue is not whether the devil can have physical contact with humankind. Indeed, the history of the Church is filled with examples that show he can. Rather, Doctrine and Covenants 129:8 appears to be highlighting some conditional restriction that has been placed upon Lucifer.[46]

As scripture attests (see D&C 121:4; Revelation 1:18; 9:1; Job), Satan does not have free reign to do as he wishes. Certainly, as President Joseph Fielding Smith noted, he "has some control over the elements. This he does by powers which he knows but which are hidden from weak mortal men."[47] However, he is bound by divine law, by which God keeps the adversary of all humankind "in check," as it were. Thus, as the Prophet Joseph states, we know that "wicked spirits have their bounds, limits, and laws by which they are governed or controlled."[48] We take it for granted that the devil simply is not allowed to do certain things. For example, he cannot tempt little children until they begin to become accountable (see D&C 29:47), he cannot tempt translated beings (see 3 Nephi 28:39), and he cannot come in the sign of the dove.[49] Some have even conjectured that he cannot imitate the witness of the Holy Ghost.[50] We can safely add to our list that Lucifer and his minions cannot shake hands with us if we request that they do so.[51]

As with any passage of scripture, the background of the passage examined is necessary if we are to understand the context of the words given. Section 129 is no different. When the context is understood, the meaning is much clearer.

First, this section offers "keys" that were intended for the Saints to protect them against the adversary. Bruce A. Van Orden writes, "These instructions and keys concerning angels became very useful for the Twelve in Britain, for in addition to being ministered to by righteous angels in the course of their missionary work, they were likewise plagued by evil spirits."[52] Professor Van Orden's point is that, as we have seen, the brethren who were sent on missions *greatly* needed the knowledge that Joseph received by revelation at least as early as 1839—knowledge that would eventually become section 129 of the Doctrine and Covenants.[53] This information would prove valuable, not so they would understand that Satan is void of a body, but rather so encounters with him might be discerned from encounters with divine beings. Certainly Joseph and Oliver learned the value of such knowledge. In one of his many efforts to deceive, at some point (likely in 1829) Satan appeared in the form of an "angel of light" to these two brethren. Of this experience the Prophet writes, "And again, what do we hear? . . . The voice of Michael on the banks of the Susquehanna, detecting the devil when he appeared as an angel of light!" (D&C 128:20). One contemporary of Joseph and Oliver said that he heard the Prophet say that this satanic appearance happened as these two brethren were running from a mob. It is conjectured by this same source that in their frightened and exhausted state, Lucifer tried to deceive them by giving them a false revelation.[54] The placement of this event in section 128 of the Doctrine and Covenants, immediately preceding section 129 on the discernment of spirits, is not coincidental. Section 129 appears to explain how to deal with situations like that described in Doctrine and Covenants 128:20.

As alluded to above, Joseph spoke on the subject of discerning angels on numerous occasions. Indeed, although section 129 is dated February 9, 1843, we know that the substance of this revelation was revealed to Joseph at least as early as June 27, 1839. On that date, Wilford Woodruff recorded in his journal the content of section 129, as delivered by Joseph to members of the First Presidency and Quorum of the Twelve before they left for their missions to England.[55] Indeed, Joseph conveyed the principles taught in section 129 on numerous occasions prior to February 1843.[56] As an example, on Sunday, May 1, 1842, Joseph preached in the grove, delivering a sermon on the keys of the kingdom. He stated,

> The keys are certain signs & words by which false spirits & personages may be detected from true.—which cannot be revealed to the Elders till the Temple is completed. . . . There are signs in heaven[,] earth & hell. the elders must know them all to be endued with power. to finish their work & prevent imposition. The devil knows many signs. but does not know the sign of the son of man. or Jesus. No one can truly say he knows God until he has handled something. & these this can only be [had] in the holiest of Holies.[57]

Clearly, Joseph saw the "signs" and "keys" of the holy temple as endowments of "power" to keep one from being "imposed" upon or deceived.[58] Nine of the Brethren learned of this connection when, on May 4, 1842, Joseph revealed to them the holy endowment.[59] Andrew F. Ehat and Lyndon W. Cook have noted that what was received that day was

> so sacred that when Heber C. Kimball wrote to fellow apostle Parley P. Pratt just a few weeks later, he said that Joseph had taught

them some precious things on the priesthood that would cause his soul to rejoice if he knew them, but that Joseph had given instructions that these keys not be written about. Heber concluded his description of the newly revealed endowment by saying that Parley would have to come to Nauvoo to receive the instructions for himself. . . . Parley arrived in Nauvoo on 7 February 1843, and . . . after only two days . . . [Joseph gave] him the instructions contained in D&C 129—the same instructions as given in [Joseph's] discourse, 27 June 1839.[60]

From the foregoing quote, there appears to be no question but that the "keys" delivered in section 129 were given to Heber, Parley, and others as part of the temple endowment. Hence, Stephen E. Robinson and H. Dean Garrett have noted that Joseph's public remarks on this section indicate that he "connected the substance of Doctrine and Covenants 129 with the ordinances of the temple and believed that the information in this revelation held increased significance for those who had been endowed."[61]

CONCLUSION

I conclude this chapter as I began it—with a recitation from D&C 129:4, 8: "When a messenger comes saying he has a message from God, offer him your hand and request him to shake hands with you. . . . If it be the devil as an angel of light, when you ask him to shake hands he will offer you his hand, and you will not feel anything; you may therefore detect him." By way of exegetical summary, several significant ideas are contained in these two verses—ideas that were discussed during the course of this article, but that warrant summary here:

- **When a messenger comes:** Angels are, at times, sent from the presence of God with communications from Him.
- **Offer him your hand:** According to the Prophet Joseph, in any such encounter, the temple-initiated Saints should request a "token" as a "key," or sign of the angel's divine commission.
- **If it be the devil as an angel of light:** Satan seeks to deceive us. He seeks to appear as an "angel of light"—or, in other words, as an angel sent from the light (from God and His celestial realms)—to deceive and draw away disciples after him.[62]
- **He will offer you his hand:** As shown above, the devil will either offer you his hand *or* he will shrink back, but he will not stand

still. He is obligated by some divine law to act in such a way that you will be able to clearly detect him and see through his efforts at deception.

- **You will not feel anything:** In any circumstance wherein Satan attempts to convey the "tokens" or "keys" offered patrons in the holy temple, Doctrine and Covenants 129:8 promises us that he will be bound and prevented from conveying that which he knows. Even though his spirit body is unquestionably made of refined matter that can be felt, under any circumstance in which he seeks to utilize the "keys" of the temple as a means of deception, God forbids and prevents him from acting.[63]
- **You may therefore detect him:** As the Prophet Joseph Smith notes, "The keys are certain signs and words by which false spirits and personages may be detected from true," and these "signs" are to be had only in the holy temple.[64]

Apparently, we can draw but one conclusion from the historical record—namely that, in Joseph's eyes, one of the purposes for which the endowed are given these "keys" is to enable them to have the power of discerning spirits. In other words, that which is learned in the Lord's holy house will enable those in possession of this knowledge not to be deceived by the "father of all lies" (2 Nephi 2:18). Additionally, we apparently can say with certainty that Doctrine and Covenants 129:8 is not a declaration about the non-corporeal nature of Satan's body. Nor is it a promise that the faithful will be physically protected from attacks by the devil and his angels. Rather, the crux of the message being conveyed in Doctrine and Covenants 129:8 is the doctrinal assurance that Satan may be able to appear to, deceive, and even accost God's children on the earth, but when it comes to the things conveyed to those endowed in the Lord's holy house, limitations have been placed upon the devil and his angels.[65] By divine decree, the fallen third-part of the hosts of heaven have been forbidden to "shake hands" with the temple-going Saints. They are bound by law! They have been strictly prohibited from utilizing that which is taught in the holy temple in order to gain the trust of mortals on the earth. This is the primary message of Doctrine and Covenants 129:8, and it is, indeed, a "grand key!"

NOTES

1. A version of this article was originally published under the title "Doctrine and Covenants 129:8 and the Reality of Satan's Physicality." See *The Religious Educator: Perspectives on the Restored Gospel*, vol. 8, no. 1 (2007): 31–54. Republished here by permission.

2. William Clayton's account of what the Prophet Joseph taught is slightly different from what is currently recorded in Doctrine and Covenants 129. In December of 1840, Clayton recorded, "If an Angel or spirit appears offer him your hand; if he is a spirit from God he will stand still and not offer you his hand. If from the Devil he will either shrink back from you or offer his hand, which if he does you will feel nothing, but be deceived." Extract from "William Clayton's Private Book, December 1840," in *The Words of Joseph Smith: The Contemporary Accounts of the Nauvoo Discourses of the Prophet Joseph*, ed. Andrew F. Ehat and Lyndon W. Cook (Provo, Utah: Religious Studies Center, BYU, 1980), 44. Of this, Ehat and Cook write, "Unlike other versions of these instructions given by Joseph Smith from 1839 to 1843, this account indicates that the Devil is not compelled to 'offer his hand.' Apparently Joseph Smith believed that the Devil had sense enough to avoid obvious detection but that unlike 'a spirit from God,' he would not remain motionless" (56n3; see also 20n21).

3. See also Karen Lynn Davidson, David J. Whittaker, Mark Ashurst-McGee, and Richard L. Jensen, eds., *The Joseph Smith Papers: Histories—Volume 1* (Salt Lake City: The Church Historian's Press, 2012), 212, 214; Joseph Smith, *Personal Writings of Joseph Smith*, ed. Dean C. Jessee (Salt Lake City: Deseret Book, 2002), 230; Milton V. Backman Jr., *Joseph Smith's First Vision: Confirming Evidences and Contemporary Accounts* (Salt Lake City: Bookcraft, 1971), 162–63.

4. See Davidson, Whittaker, Ashurst-McGee, and Jensen, eds., *Histories—Volume 1*, 212–13.

5. Joseph Smith, "Monday, November 9, 1835," in Dean C. Jessee, Ronald K. Esplin, and Richard Lyman Bushman, eds., *The Joseph Smith Papers: Journals—Volume 1, 1832–1839* (Salt Lake City: The Church Historian's Press, 2008), 88; Smith, *Personal Writings*, 104–5; Backman, *First Vision*, 159; Alexander Neibaur, *Personal Journal*, cited in Backman, *First Vision*, 177.

6. Smith, "Monday, November 9, 1835"; Smith, *Personal Writings*, 104–5; Backman, *First Vision*, 159.

7. Orson Pratt, "An Interesting Account of Several Remarkable Visions, 1840," cited in Davidson, Whittaker, Ashurst-McGee, and Jensen, eds., *Histories—Volume 1*, 523; Backman, *First Vision*, 171; Orson Hyde, *A Cry from the Wilderness, A Voice from the Dust of the Earth*, 1842, cited in Backman, *First Vision*, 174–75.

8. Heber C. Kimball, "March 2, 1856," in *Journal of Discourses* (London: Latter-day Saints' Book Depot, 1854–86), 3:229–30; see also Heber C. Kimball, "June 29, 1856," in *Journal of Discourses*, 4:2.

9. See Orson F. Whitney, *Life of Heber C. Kimball*, 4th ed. (Salt Lake City: Bookcraft, 1973), 258–59; see also *Discourses of the Prophet Joseph Smith* (Salt Lake City: Deseret Book, 1974), 177. I express appreciation to Dr. Scott Esplin of Brigham Young University for bringing this experience to my attention.

10. Laboring with these four brethren in Preston were John Snider, Joseph Fielding, and John Goodson. However, these three brethren were not present during the satanic encounter.

11. For accounts of this experience in the words of those present, see Heber C. Kimball, in *Journal of Discourses*, 3:229–30, 4:2, 11:84; Heber C. Kimball, "December 1860," *Journal History of the Church of Jesus Christ of Latter-day Saints*, 16:4 (Salt Lake City: The Church of Jesus Christ of Latter-day Saints, Church Archives); Heber C. Kimball, *Journal of Heber C. Kimball* (Nauvoo, Illinois: Robinson and Smith, 1840), 18–19. See also Whitney, *Life of Heber C. Kimball*, 129–32; Stanley B. Kimball, ed., *On the Potter's Wheel: The Diaries of Heber C. Kimball* (Salt Lake City: Signature Books, 1987), 9–10; Wilford Woodruff, "March 3, 1889," discourse, in *Collected Discourses*, ed. Brian H. Stuy (B. H. S. Publishing, 1999), 1:217–18; Myrtle Stevens Hyde, *Orson Hyde: The Olive Branch of Israel* (Salt Lake City: Agreka Books, 2000), 86–87; Joseph Fielding, *Diary of Joseph Fielding*, typeset (Provo, Utah: L. Tom Perry Special Collections, Harold B. Lee Library, BYU), 21–24; Heber C. Kimball, "A Letter From Heber C. Kimball to His Wife, Vilate Kimball," in *Elders' Journal*, October 1837, 4–5.

12. Kimball, *Journal*, 19.

13. Ibid., 101–2; see also Whitney, *Life of Heber C. Kimball*, 131.

14. The sentences "He wounded me in my forehead. I also wounded him in a number of places in the head" are written in the original but have been struck through with pencil by someone at a later date.

15. Wilford Woodruff, "October 18, 1840," *Wilford Woodruff's Journal*, 9 vols., ed. Scott G. Kenney (Midvale, Utah: Signature Books, 1983), 1:532; spelling and capitalization standardized.

16. Wilford Woodruff, "March 3, 1889," discourse, in *Collected Discourses*, 1:218; Wilford Woodruff, *Leaves from My Journal* (Salt Lake City: Juvenile Instructor Office, 1881), 109–10; Wilford Woodruff, "October 19, 1896," discourse, in *Collected Discourses*, 5:236–37. For some reason, no reference to this event by George A. Smith has survived. However, Elder Woodruff states that he and Elder Smith were sleeping on cots some three feet apart when Satan appeared to them that night. Thus, George A. was probably aware of what happened.

17. See Davidson, Whittaker, Ashurst-McGee, and Jensen, eds., *Histories—Volume 1*, 384.

18. Ibid., 380, 382, 384, 386. See also Joseph Smith, *History of the Church of Jesus Christ of Latter-day Saints*, ed. B. H. Roberts (Salt Lake City: The Church of Jesus Christ of Latter-day Saints, 1978), 1:82–83; see also B. H. Roberts, *A Comprehensive History of the Church of Jesus Christ of Latter-day Saints* (Orem, Utah: Sonos Publishing, 1991), 1:199–202.

19. See Newel Knight, *Newel Knight Autobiography* (Provo,Utah: L. Tom Perry Special Collections, Harold B. Lee Library, BYU), 3–4, 8–9, 13; see also Davidson, Whittaker, Ashurst-McGee, and Jensen, eds., *Histories—Volume 1*, 384; Smith, *History of the Church*, 1:91–93; Roberts, *Comprehensive History*, 1:207.

20. See Lavina Fielding Anderson, ed., *Lucy's Book: A Critical Edition of Lucy Mack Smith's Family Memoir* (Salt Lake City: Signature Books, 2001), 561; Lucy Mack Smith,

History of Joseph Smith by His Mother (Salt Lake City: Bookcraft, n.d.), 221. Richard Bushman conjectures that the reason for Rigdon's claim that the "keys of the kingdom [had been] rent from the Church" was a concern he had about property. See Richard L. Bushman, *Joseph Smith: Rough Stone Rolling* (New York: Alfred A. Knopf, 2005), 186.

21. Philo Dibble, "Philo Dibble's Narrative," in *Early Scenes in Church History* (Salt Lake City: Juvenile Instructor Office, 1882), 80; Anderson, ed., *Lucy's Book*, 563.

22. LeMar E. Garrard, *A Study of the Problem of a Personal Devil and Its Relationship to Latter-day Saint Beliefs* (master's thesis, Brigham Young University, 1955), 121; quoted material in Garrard is from Dibble, "Philo Dibble's Narrative," 80.

23. See Heber C. Kimball, in *Journal of Discourses*, 3:229–30, 4:2; Anderson, ed., *Lucy's Book*, 563–64.

24. Mark R. Grandstaff and Milton V. Backman Jr., "The Social Origins of the Kirtland Mormons," in *BYU Studies* 30, no. 2 (Spring 1990): 61.

25. Benjamin Brown, "Benjamin Brown Autobiography," in *Testimonies for the Truth* (Liverpool: S. W. Richards, 1853), ch. 2; Benjamin Brown, "Testimonies for the Truth," in *Gems for the Young Folks* (Salt Lake City: Juvenile Instructor Office, 1881), 72.

26. Today the RLDS, or Reorganized Church of Jesus Christ of Latter Day Saints, is known as Community of Christ. For information on Whitlock, see Susan Easton Black, *Who's Who in the Doctrine and Covenants* (Salt Lake City: Deseret Book, 1997), 326–27.

27. Levi Hancock, *Autobiography* (Provo, Utah: L. Tom Perry Special Collections Library, Harold B. Lee Library, BYU), 33–34.

28. She wrote, "When [Joseph] came to Kirtland he found . . . the Devil had been deceiving them with a specious appearance of power manifested by strange contortions of the visage and unnatural Motions which they supposed as being occasioned by an opperation [*sic*] of the power of God. . . . He . . . called upon one of the brethren who had been deceived by an evil spirit to speak[.] [W]hen he arose he was immediately convulsed in the most singular manner[,] his face[,] his arms[,] and his fingers being drawn like a person in [a] spasm[.] Joseph turned to Hyrum and said will you go and lay hands on that brother[?] [W]hen Hyrum did so the man fell back into his chair as weak as though he had exhausted himself by excessive hard labor[.] [H]e then called upon another who was standing . . . on the outside of the house leaning in the window[.] [T]his man . . . pitched forward into the house and[,] after trying sometime to speak without being able to do so[,] was administered to by the laing [*sic*] on of hands which affected him . . . the same as the one who had preceeded [*sic*] him." Lucy Mack Smith, "Unpublished Preliminary Manuscript" (Church Archives, 1844–45), 193; a transcript of this manuscript is available in Anderson, ed., *Lucy's Book*, 506–8.

29. Philo Dibble, "Recollections of the Prophet Joseph Smith," in *Juvenile Instructor* (May 15, 1892), 303.

30. Joseph Fielding Smith, *Man: His Origin and Destiny* (Salt Lake City: Deseret Book, 1954), 487.

31. George Q. Cannon, in *Journal of Discourses*, 11:30.

32. Ibid., 24:375–76.

33. The reader may be aware of comments suggesting that demonic attacks are allowed, if not caused, by disobedience to God's commands. For example, Joseph Smith reportedly

said, "The devil has no power over us only as we permit him; the moment we revolt at anything which comes from God the Devil takes power." Ehat and Cook, eds., *Words of Joseph Smith*, 60. Likewise, Charles W. Penrose teaches, "Satan cannot obtain the mastery over any human being, except by yielding to him" in *Conference Report* (October 1906), 57. Orson Pratt says, "The devil has not the power to take full possession of the tabernacles of human creatures, unless they give way to him and his influence to that degree that he gets power over them." "December 19, 1869," in *Journal of Discourses*, 13:64. In general terms, it seems correct to say that those who disobey God's commands place themselves outside the protection of the Holy Spirit and are thus in potential subjection to the devil and his influence. Nevertheless, the righteousness of men like Joseph Smith, Heber C. Kimball, Wilford Woodruff, or George A. Smith seems to be a given. In their specific encounters with Satan, a lack of personal righteousness does not appear to be the cause. Rather, as Joseph Smith taught, such attacks are evidence that the adversary feels his kingdom and power are being threatened by the work, faith, and righteousness of those whom he therefore chooses to attack. See Whitney, *Life of Heber C. Kimball*, 131–32.

34. Ehat and Cook, eds., *Words of Joseph Smith*, 60.

35. Smith, *History of the Church*, 4:575.

36. Stephen E. Robinson and H. Dean Garrett, *A Commentary on the Doctrine and Covenants* (Salt Lake City: Deseret Book, 2000–2005), 4:239. Elder John A. Widtsoe writes, "God, angels, spirits, men, and all the things in the universe belong to the same world, are organized from existing materials. They differ only in their various forms of organization." *Joseph Smith—Seeker after Truth, Prophet of God* (Salt Lake City: Bookcraft, 1951), 147.

37. Robert L. Millet and Joseph Fielding McConkie, *The Life Beyond* (Salt Lake City: Deseret Book, 1986), 51–53; Ezra Taft Benson, *Teachings of Ezra Taft Benson* (Salt Lake City: Bookcraft, 1998), 252–53.

38. See, for example, Brigham Young, "September 1, 1859," in *Journal of Discourses*, 7:239.

39. Joseph Fielding Smith, *Doctrines of Salvation* (Salt Lake City: Bookcraft, 1998), 3:81; Smith, *Teachings*, 157, 167, 365; see also Alma 13:7; Jeremiah 1:4–5. Perhaps we might argue that we do not know for certain that such "ordinations" were by the laying on of hands. True, this author knows of no official statement indicating that such is necessarily the case. However, as the earthly Church is patterned after the heavenly, we can logically assume that the premortal Church follows suit. Indeed, the notion that there was no physical contact between spirits in the premortal world—or between God and His spirit offspring—goes entirely against reason.

40. Joseph Smith taught that "every man who has a calling to minister to the inhabitants of the world was ordained to that very purpose in the Grand Council of heaven before this world was." Smith, *Teachings of the Prophet Joseph Smith*, 365.

41. This is not to suggest that we picked our spouses in the premortal world. Certainly the Brethren have discredited such a suggestion. See, for example, Boyd K. Packer, *Eternal Love* (Salt Lake City: Deseret Book, 1973), 11; *C.E.S. Seminary Old Testament Teacher's Outline* (Salt Lake City: The Church of Jesus Christ of Latter-day Saints, 1990),

57–59; Spencer W. Kimball, *Teachings of Spencer W. Kimball*, ed. Edward L. Kimball (Salt Lake City: Bookcraft, 1998), 305; Joseph Fielding Smith, *The Way to Perfection* (Salt Lake City: Genealogical Society of Utah, 1949), 44–45. However, because all covenants—including the new and everlasting covenant of marriage—are made between individuals and God (not between people), it is entirely possible for a man or woman to enter into such a covenant in the premortal world without having a specific spouse in mind. Indeed, when we are sealed in the Lord's holy temple, we make covenants regarding our spouse, but not to our spouse. All temple covenants are made between a singular person and God.

42. See Orson Hyde, in *Journal of Discourses*, 7:314–15; Neal A. Maxwell, *But for a Small Moment* (Salt Lake City: Bookcraft, 1986), 99–100.

43. See David P. Kimball to Helen Mar Whitney, "January 8, 1882," cited in Orson F. Whitney, "A Terrible Ordeal," in *Helpful Visions* (Salt Lake City: Juvenile Instructor Office, 1887), 9. In a somewhat related vein, according to our history, when Joseph and Oliver went to Cumorah to return the plates to Moroni, the hill opened up and inside was a room some sixteen feet square. (Some accounts only mention Joseph and Oliver, but when the various accounts of the experience are combined, the list of those present includes Joseph, Oliver, Hyrum Smith, David Whitmer, and Joseph Smith Sr.) The room was said to be filled with plates—"wagon loads" of them—lining the walls. There was light in the cave, a table in the center of the room, and the sword of Laban hanging upon the wall. See Brigham Young, in *Journal of Discourses*, 6:508, 19:38; Edward L. Stevens, *Reminiscences of Joseph, the Prophet, and the Coming Forth of the Book of Mormon* (Salt Lake City: Edward Stephens, 1893), 14–15; H. Donl Peterson, *Moroni: Ancient Prophet—Modern Messenger* (Salt Lake City: Deseret Book, 2000), 135–37. Joseph and Oliver handled items in the room, yet Joseph reportedly believed that these "wagon loads" of plates were not actually deposited in the hill in New York from which he acquired the Book of Mormon. Rather, sources suggest that Joseph believed that the room he and Oliver entered—the room in which they touched items pertaining to the Nephite nation—was somewhere in Central America. See H. Donl Peterson, "Moroni, the Last of the Nephite Prophets," in *The Book of Mormon: Fourth Nephi Through Moroni—From Zion to Destruction*, ed. Monte S. Nyman and Charles D. Tate Jr. (Provo, Utah: Religious Studies Center, BYU, 1995), 243–47. Thus, Joseph and Oliver had a physical encounter with items they were seeing with their "spiritual eyes."

44. See Parley P. Pratt, *The Autobiography of Parley Parker Pratt*, 5th ed., ed. Parley P. Pratt Jr. (Salt Lake City: Deseret Book, 1961), 238. I express appreciation to Paul E. Damron, who directed me to this source.

45. Although it is possible that this angel was a resurrected being—having been one of those who obtained his resurrection with Christ (see Matthew 27:52–53)—Greek scholar Joseph Thayer suggests that the "angel" in Matthew 28:2 is a spirit rather than a resurrected personage. See Joseph H. Thayer, *Thayer's Greek-English Lexicon of the New Testament* (Peabody, Massachusetts: Hendrickson Publishers, 1999), 5. Of course, we cannot rule out the possibility that this was a translated being either.

46. It is also possible—although unlikely—that some "restriction" has been placed on mortals too, as D&C 129:8 states that we will not be able to feel his hand. This

may imply that, although Lucifer and his angels have a material nature, you and I are prohibited by some divine law from making any conscious physical connection with that which is purely spiritual.

47.   Joseph Fielding Smith, *Church History and Modern Revelation* (Salt Lake City: The Church of Jesus Christ of Latter-day Saints, 1946–49), 1:207.

48.   Smith, *History of the Church*, 4:576.

49.   Ibid., 5:261.

50.   See, for example, Truman G. Madsen, *Joseph Smith the Prophet* (Salt Lake City: Bookcraft, 1989), 17. In light of Satan's appearance as an "angel of light" to the Prophet Joseph (D&C 128:20), not everyone agrees with this assumption.

51.   "One might suppose that these devils would refrain from shaking hands to make us believe they come from God. But there is something, perhaps a divine law, that compels them to respond as verse 8 specifies." Richard O. Cowan, *Answers to Your Questions about the Doctrine and Covenants* (Salt Lake City: Deseret Book, 1996), 144; see also Joseph Fielding McConkie and Craig J. Ostler, *Revelations of the Restoration* (Salt Lake City: Deseret Book, 2000), 1042; L. G. Otten and C. M. Caldwell, *Sacred Truths of the Doctrine and Covenants* (Springville, Utah: LEMB, 1983), 2:337.

52.   Bruce A. Van Orden, "Important Items of Instruction (D&C 129–31)," in *Scripture: Volume One—The Doctrine and Covenants Studies*, ed. Robert L. Millet and Kent P. Jackson (Salt Lake City: Deseret Book, 1989), 504.

53.   Doctrine and Covenants 129 is dated February 9, 1843, because that is the date on which the Prophet's secretary, William Clayton, recorded the information. Clayton penned this as he listened to Joseph explain the principles to Parley P. Pratt, who had just returned from a mission to England. However, we know that Joseph taught the content of this revelation to the Twelve as early as June 27, 1839. See *Joseph Smith Papers—Journals Volume 2: December 1841–April 1843*, ed. Andrew H. Hedges, Alex D. Smith, and Richard Lloyd Anderson (Salt Lake City: The Church Historian's Press, 2011), 257–58; McConkie and Ostler, *Revelations of the Restoration*, 1038.

54.   See letter from Addison Everett to Oliver B. Huntington, "February 17, 1881," recorded in Oliver B. Huntington's journal, journal 14, "January 31, 1881" (L. Tom Perry Special Collections). See also Alma 30:53, where Korihor indicates that Satan appeared to him in the "form of an angel."

55.   "June 27th I spent the day in Commerce in Council with the Presidency & Twelve. We had an interesting day. Joseph was president of the Council. Brother Orson Hide was restored to the Church and the quorum of the Twelve in full fellowship by a full vote of the Council, after making an humble Confession & acknowledgement of his sins &c. Among the vast number of the Keys of the Kingdom of God Joseph presented the following one to the Twelve for there benefit in there experience & travels in the flesh which is as follows: In order to detect the devel [*sic*] when he transforms himself nigh unto an angel of light. When an angel of God appears unto man face to face in personage & reaches out his hand unto the man & he takes hold of the angels hand & feels a substance the same as one man would in Shaking hands with another he may then know that it is an angel of God, & he should place all Confidence in him. Such personages or angels are Saints with there resurrected Bodies. But if a personage appears unto man

& offers him his hand & the man takes hold of it & he feels nothing or does not sens [*sic*] any substance he may know it is the devel [*sic*], for when a Saint whose body is not resurrected appears unto man in the flesh he will not offer him his hand for this is against the law given him & in keeping in mind these things we may detec [*sic*] the devil that he decieved [*sic*] us not." Journal of Wilford Woodruff, "June 27, 1839."

56. Numerous people record hearing Joseph teach the content of Doctrine and Covenants section 129. For example, sometime before August 8, 1839, Willard Richards recorded it. In December 1840, William Clayton recorded it. An anonymous pamphlet published in Nauvoo in 1841 recorded it. Joseph addressed the subject before the Relief Society on April 28, 1842. He also commented on it to the general membership of the Church on May 1, 1842. See Robinson and Garrett, *Commentary on the Doctrine and Covenants*, 4:215–16. See also Ehat and Cook, eds., *Words of Joseph Smith*, 56n3; Robert J. Woodford, *The Historical Development of the Doctrine and Covenants*, PhD diss. (Provo, Utah: Brigham Young University, 1974), 3:1701–4; McConkie and Ostler, *Revelations of the Restoration*, 1038–39; Van Orden, in Millet and Jackson, *Studies in Scripture*, 498, 502–4. Hyrum M. Smith and Janne M. Sjodahl write, "It should be noted that this Revelation came . . . before so-called spirit-rapping had been discovered, or invented, by the Fox family at Hydeville, N.Y., . . . giving birth to Spiritism with all its delusions. By this Revelation the Saints were forewarned and therefore saved from being deceived by false pretensions or by evil spirits." *Doctrine and Covenants Commentary*, rev. ed. (Salt Lake City: Deseret Book, 1978), 811.

57. Joseph Smith, "Sunday, May 1, 1842," in Dean C. Jessee, Ronald K. Esplin, and Richard Lyman Bushman, eds., *The Joseph Smith Papers: Journals—Volume 2, 1841–1843* (Salt Lake City: The Church Historian's Press, 2011), 53. See also Smith, *History of the Church* 4:608; Ehat and Cook, eds., *Words of Joseph Smith*, 119–20.

58. *Noah Webster's First Edition of an American Dictionary of the English Language, 1828 Facsimile Edition* (San Francisco: Foundation for American Christian Education, 1967), s.v. "imposition." In this discourse, Joseph also indicated that "to know God," a person "must handle 'something.'" Of course, Joseph knew what that "something" was. His vagueness here may be because it would not be for another three days before any of his hearers received their endowment. Thus, detailed reference to the activities of the endowment ceremony would have little meaning to them. It is also possible that the Prophet's comment regarding "handling something" in the "holiest of holies" has reference to the receipt of the Second Comforter—a subject Joseph also discoursed on almost three years earlier. See Smith, *Teachings of the Prophet Joseph Smith*, 149–50; Ehat and Cook, eds., *Words of Joseph Smith*, 5–6. Which of these two ideas Joseph intended is uncertain. Joseph indicated that the "devil knows many signs" but does not know—or at least cannot utilize—"the sign of the Son of Man." Traditionally, the phrase "sign of the Son of Man" was used by the Prophet in reference to the Second Coming of Christ. However, the context of the quotation under examination here does not lend itself to such an interpretation. As there is only one source for this comment, we cannot say with certainty what Joseph meant. However, the context is clearly the temple endowment, and those familiar with the ordinances of the temple will also find the language "sign of

the Son of Man" somewhat familiar. It seems fair to say that no one can truly know God until he or she has received the Second Comforter.

59. The nine brethren were Hyrum Smith (assistant president of the Church and Patriarch to the Church), William Law (a counselor in the First Presidency), Brigham Young, Heber C. Kimball, and Willard Richards (all three members of the Quorum of the Twelve Apostles), William Marks (president of the Nauvoo Stake), George Miller (president of the Nauvoo high priests quorum and Presiding Bishop), Newel K. Whitney (Presiding Bishop), and James Adams (patriarch and branch president). See *Joseph Smith Papers—Journals Volume 2: December 1841–April 1843*, 53; Andrew F. Ehat, "Joseph Smith's Introduction of Temple Ordinances and the 1844 Mormon Succession Question" (master's thesis, Brigham Young University, 1981), 27–28.

60. Ehat and Cook, eds., *Words of Joseph Smith*, 21n21; *Joseph Smith Papers—Journals Volume 2: December 1841–April 1843*, 54, n. 198.

61. Robinson and Garrett, *Commentary on the Doctrine and Covenants*, 4:216; see also McConkie and Ostler, *Revelations of the Restoration*, 1040–1041; *Joseph Smith Papers—Journals Volume 2: December 1841–April 1843*, 54, n. 198; M. Catherine Thomas, "Hebrews: To Ascend the Holy Mount," in *Temples of the Ancient World*, ed. Donald W. Parry (Salt Lake City: Deseret Book, 1994), 483.

62. Curiously, the Hebrew word translated as "serpent" in the Genesis account of the Fall (Genesis 3:1–5) is related to the Hebrew word for "luminous" or "shining." Thus, some have suggested that it was not a "serpent" that approached Adam and Eve in Eden but Lucifer appearing as an "angel of light." See, for example, Victor Hamilton, *Handbook on the Pentateuch* (Grand Rapids, Michigan: Baker Book House, 1982), 42; see also "Revelation of Moses," in Alexander Roberts and James Donaldson, eds., *Ante-Nicene Fathers: The Writings of the Fathers down to A.D. 325* (Peabody, Massachusetts: Hendrickson Publishers, 1994), 8:566. Louis Ginzberg records, "Satan assumed the appearance of an angel." *The Legends of the Jews* (Philadelphia: Jewish Publication Society of America, 1967–69), 1:95; "Life of Adam and Eve," Latin version 9:1 and Greek version 17:1–2, 29:15, in James H. Charlesworth, *The Old Testament Pseudepigrapha* (New York: Doubleday, 1983, 1985), 2:260–61, 277; Robert Jamieson, A. R. Fausset, and David Brown, Jamieson, *Fausset and Brown One Volume Commentary* (Grand Rapids, Michigan: Associated Publishers, n.d.), 19; Adam Clarke, *The Holy Bible Containing the Old and New Testaments . . . With a Commentary and Critical Notes* (New York: Methodist Book Concern, n.d.), 1:48. Of course, prior to the Fall, the serpent was a symbol or type for Christ, His atoning death, and His Resurrection—hence its use in Numbers 21:8; Alma 33:19–20; and Helaman 8:13–15. See Andrew C. Skinner, "Savior, Satan, and Serpent: The Duality of a Symbol in the Scriptures," *The Disciple as Scholar—Essays on Scripture and the Ancient World in Honor of Richard Lloyd Anderson*, ed. Stephen D. Ricks, Donald W. Parry, and Andrew H. Hedges (Provo, Utah: Foundation for Ancient Research and Mormon Studies, 2000), 359–84; Walter L. Wilson, *A Dictionary of Bible Types* (Peabody, Massachusetts: Hendrickson Publishers, 1999), 363; Bruce Vawter, *On Genesis: A New Reading* (Garden City, New York: Doubleday, 1977), 78. Thus, whether Satan talked to Adam and Eve through a snake or appeared to them as an "angel of light,"

his intent was the same: he was seeking to usurp the role of Christ by appearing to Adam and Eve in a form that would make then think he was the Christ (see 2 Nephi 9:9).

63.   By this we mean that, even though there are times when—the veil being lifted or thinned—we can see and feel spirits (good and evil), under any circumstance wherein Satan would seek to physically convey things associated with the temple, God will (in some way unknown to us) prevent us from having a sensory encounter with the devil. Satan's material spirit may make contact with our physical body (or our personal spirit), but the Father of us all will prevent us—in such a circumstance—from feeling anything, thereby preventing the attempted deception of the devil.

64.   Smith, *History of the Church*, 4:608; see also Ehat and Cook, eds., *Words of Joseph Smith*, 119–20.

65.   Ehat and Cook, eds., *Words of Joseph Smith*, 6; Smith, *History of the Church*, 208; Ezra Taft Benson, *The Teachings of Ezra Taft Benson* (Salt Lake City: Bookcraft, 1998), 402; George Q. Cannon, in *Journal of Discourses*, 24:145.

Chapter 5

THE "THREE PILLARS OF ETERNITY" AND THE HOLY ENDOWMENT

Alonzo L. Gaskill

There is a somewhat popular phrase in Mormonism, originally coined by Elder Bruce R. McConkie, who taught that "the Creation, the Fall, and the Atonement are the three pillars of eternity."[1] For years I cited that statement when teaching about one of these three—and I saw Elder McConkie's teaching largely as a testament to the importance of the doctrines of the Creation, the Fall, and the Atonement. There is no question—these three are foundational teachings of the Restoration. As Elder McConkie pointed out, "the Creation, the Fall, and the Atonement . . . are inseparably woven together to form one plan of salvation. No one of them stands alone; each of them ties into the other two; and without a knowledge of all of them, it is not possible to know the truth about any one of them. . . . The Creation is the father of the Fall, and . . . the Fall made possible the Atonement, and . . . salvation itself comes because of the Atonement."[2] And so it is!

While we may get distracted by the high liturgical forms of the endowment and, thereby, not realize that the holy temple is heavily doctrinal in its content; nevertheless, it certainly is. I am struck that Elder McConkie's declaration that the Creation, Fall, and Atonement are "the three pillars of eternity" may find its fullest realization in the endowment, rather than in Sunday School. Permit, if you will, this brief vignette as an illustration.

Every time the story of the Creation (pillar 1) is told in scripture or the temple, the story of the Fall (pillar 2) immediately follows. Why is that? What is the Lord seeking to teach us by tying those two narratives so closely together? In the story of the Creation the Lord does something instructive. At the end of the sixth "day" we are informed, "And God saw every thing that he had made, and, behold, it was very good. . . . Thus the heavens and the earth were finished, and all the host of them. And on the seventh day God ended his work . . . and he rested on the seventh day from all his work which he had made" (Genesis 1:31–2:2). Of this, President Joseph Fielding Smith pointed out, "When the Lord formed the earth and its heaven, he pronounced them very good. He sanctified them, and when man was placed on the earth, this condition of goodness and sanctification prevailed."[3] In other words, for all of the principles we can draw from the story of the Creation, perhaps one of the most important is simply this: God made *everything* "good"—in a state of goodness or perfection.[4] And immediately after informing us of this truth, He introduces us to the narrative of the Fall; a story about how *you and I* have messed everything up! (Remember what the endowment teaches us: we must think of ourselves as if we are Adam and Eve. This is *our* story, *our* fall. It is informing us of how *we* succumb to the enticements of the evil one.)[5] Thus, in the endowment we have presented to us (in a very intentional way) *paradise lost* (sorry Milton!).[6] God gives us perfection (in His creation), and we turn it into chaos (through our sins)! He offers us a state of paradise, but, through heeding Satan's enticements, we lose paradise and walk in a lone and dreary world.

Of course, the third "pillar of eternity" is the Atonement of the Lord Jesus Christ. Symbolically speaking, the endowment is entirely Christocentric. Every aspect of it—covenants, commands, clothing, signs, tokens, etc.—is about Christ. And appropriately so, since the Atonement is exactly what you and I need; not only in the narrative told in the temple, but also in our day-to-day lives. In other words, we lost the paradise God created for each of us through our personal falls—through listening to Satan. The endowment is how God will bring us full circle. It is how He will bring us back to paradise. And what is the message of the endowment? It is entirely about Christ and His ransom sacrifice on behalf of you and me. Once again, from Elder McConkie, we learn that "the revealed accounts of the Creation are designed to accomplish two great purposes. Their *general purpose* is to enable us to understand the nature of our mortal probation. . . . Their *specific purpose* is to enable us to understand the atoning sacrifice of the Lord Jesus Christ."[7] Indeed, this is exactly what the endowment does. It explains to us the nature of our mortal probation by reminding us that all that is of God is "good" and perfect. And it informs us that each time we listen to Satan, we lose those blessings God has foreordained each of us to have. But, as Elder McConkie's statement also suggests, the endowment then goes on to teach us about how the Atonement of the Lord Jesus Christ can fix all of the chaos we have created. It can get us back to paradise where we can eternally dwell with God in a state of absolute perfection.

Of course, the process of returning us to paradise is not simply depicted in the endowment, but is enacted every day in our lives, as God sends us experiences in which He seeks to perfect and develop us. He is constantly trying to recreate us—to improve us and remake us so that we reach our full potential, so that we become as He is. Thus, "God's act of creation is a great ordering process."[8] In the story of the Creation, God takes matter—which is in a chaotic, unproductive state (Genesis 1:2)— and He organizes it so that it is useful, fruitful, and productive. He seeks to do the same in our lives. Likewise, in the story of the Creation, God separates the light from the darkness (Genesis 1:4), just as He constantly prompts us to do the same in our own lives. Similarly, in the Creation accounts, God gives life to all that He creates (Genesis 2:7; Abraham 5:7), and He constantly seeks to give us life "more abundantly" (John 10:10) and eternal life in the world to come (Moses 6:59). He even places fruits, flowers, and vegetation upon the earth (during the Creation) to beautify that which He has made. He then commands humans to nurture that beauty, to take care of it and tend to it (Genesis 2:9–15). In like manner, God places so much beauty in our lives and in our paths, and He then commands us to nurture it, that it might be a gift to others (as well as a gift to ourselves).

God created us, but we have all fallen. Through the Atonement of His Son—our Savior—the Father offers to recreate us and, thereby return us to paradise, where we may dwell with Them forever! The "Three Pillars of Eternity" are at the heart of the message of the endowment. As we contemplate those sacred ordinances, the Spirit can reveal to us our place in the Plan, and the reasons why God allows us to have the tough experiences that constitute mortal life. Paradise was once ours. As we embrace the Plan and all it sends, we will—through Christ's ultimate act of love—dwell in paradise again. And we shall be like He who has created us (1 John 3:2; Moroni 7:48)!

NOTES

1.   Bruce R. McConkie, "Christ and the Creation," in *Doctrines of the Restoration: Sermons and Writings of Bruce R. McConkie*, ed. Mark L. McConkie (Salt Lake City: Bookcraft, 1989), 190.

2.   Ibid., 177, 179. Elder McConkie added, "God himself, the Father of us all, ordained and established a plan of salvation whereby his spirit children might advance and progress and become like him. It is the gospel of God, the plan of Eternal Elohim, the system that saves and exalts, and it consists of three things. These three are the very pillars of eternity itself. They are the most important events that ever have or will occur in all eternity. They are the Creation, the Fall, and the Atonement," 177.

3.   Joseph Fielding Smith, *Doctrines of Salvation*, 3 vols. (Salt Lake City: Bookcraft, 1998), 3:265. Elder McConkie similarly stated, "The first temporal creation of all things . . . was paradisiacal in nature. In the primeval and Edenic day all forms of life lived in a higher and different state than now prevails," McConkie, "Christ and the Creation," 178.

4.   Doctrinally speaking, the word was created in a terrestrial state. However—though not yet celestial—it was "perfect": perfect in its creation because it was perfect for God's purposes. There was no flaw in it.

5.   See Gordon B. Hinckley, *Teachings of Gordon B. Hinckley* (Salt Lake City: Deseret Book, 1997), 636; Rex E. Cooper, "Symbols, Cultural and Artistic," in *Encyclopedia of Mormonism*, 4 vols., ed. Daniel H. Ludlow (New York: Macmillan, 1992), 3:1430–1431; Elaine Pagels, *Adam, Eve, and the Serpent* (New York: Vintage Books, 1989), xx–xxi, xxiv; Bruce C. Hafen, *The Broken Heart* (Salt Lake City: Deseret Book, 1989), 33, 37, 50; Hugh Nibley, *The Message of the Joseph Smith Papyri: An Egyptian Endowment* (Salt Lake City: Deseret Book, 1975), xiii; Hugh Nibley, *Old Testament and Related Studies* (Provo, Utah: Foundation for Ancient Research and Mormon Studies, 1986), 87; Joseph Fielding McConkie and Donald W. Parry, *A Guide To Scriptural Symbols* (Salt Lake City: Bookcraft, 1990), 12; Joseph Fielding McConkie, "The Mystery of Eden," in *The Man Adam*, ed. Joseph Fielding McConkie and Robert L. Millet (Salt Lake City: Bookcraft, 1990), 29, 30, 23; Stephen E. Robinson, "The Book of Adam in Judaism and Early Christianity," in *The Man Adam*, 128; Jolene Edmunds Rockwood, "The Redemption of Eve," in *Sisters in Spirit*, ed. Maureen Usenbach Beecher and Lavina Fielding Anderson (Chicago: University of Illinois Press, 1992), 18; Steven C. Harper, "Endowed with Power," in *The Religious Educator: Perspectives on the Restored Gospel*, vol. 5, no. 2 (2004): 92; Donald G. Bloesch, *Essentials of Evangelical Theology*, 2 vols. (Peabody, Massachusetts: Price Press, 2001), 1:104–6. See also Pagels (1989), xxi, 74; Leland Ryken, James C. Wilhoit, and Tremper Longman III, eds., *Dictionary of Biblical Imagery* (Downers Grove, Illinois: InterVarsity Press, 1998), 9–10; Jacob Neusner, *The Enchantments of Judaism* (Atlanta: Scholars Press, 1991), 53–65; Jacob Neusner, *The Genesis Rabbah: The Judaic Commentary to the Book of Genesis* (Atlanta: Scholars Press, 1985), 174, 208–9, 211, 213, 224, 230; Bruce Vawter, *On Genesis: A New Reading* (New

York: Doubleday, 1977), 81, 90; Beverly Campbell, *Eve and the Choice Made in Eden* (Salt Lake City: Deseret Book, 2003), 52.

6.   In 1667, the seventeenth-century English poet, John Milton (1608–74) published his epic poem, *Paradise Lost.* Considered to be Milton's greatest work, *Paradise Lost* tells (in poetic form) the biblical story of the Fall of Adam and Eve, including their expulsion from Eden because they harkened to the enticements of Satan.

7.   *Doctrines of the Restoration*, 185.

8.   Ryken, Wilhoit, and Longman, eds., *Dictionary of Biblical Imagery*, 179.

Chapter 6

"THE SEAL OF MELCHIZEDEK"

The Invention of a Modern Mormon Symbol[1]

Alonzo L. Gaskill

Symbolism is the language of scripture and ritual. Thus, to be unversed in symbolism is to miss much of what God intends to convey through the scriptures and the ordinances of the gospel. As one text notes, "Symbols are the language in which all gospel covenants and all ordinances of salvation have been revealed. From the time we are immersed in the waters of baptism to the time we kneel at the altar of the temple . . . in the ordinance of eternal marriage, every covenant we make will be written in the language of symbolism."[2] While Latter-day Saints accept and utilize a number of symbols common to other religious traditions, we also have our own unique set of symbols foreign to most other faiths.[3]

In recent years, Mormonism appears to have adopted a new symbol, one quickly growing in popularity. It is commonly referred to as the seal of Melchizedek and consists of two interlocked (or overlapping) squares, making what appears to be an eight-pointed star. This design, according to a growing number of Latter-day Saints, is the ancient symbol of the Melchizedek Priesthood[4] and the act of making one's "calling and election sure."[5] Its increasing popularity among Church members is evidenced not only by

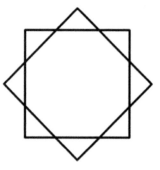

its placement in or on a number of LDS temples[6] but also by its presence in the Mormon market, where one can readily purchase necklaces, tie tacks, or cuff links sporting this newly adopted symbol.

THE DEVELOPMENT OF THE LORE

So how has this symbol made such inroads among Latter-day Saints? The story is a rather interesting one filled with both fact and fiction. The initial introduction of the seal of Melchizedek into LDS symbology came in 1992 with the release of Hugh Nibley's book *Temple and Cosmos*. In the chapter entitled "Sacred Vestments"[7] the following picture and caption (written by illustrator Michael Lyon) appear:

Figure 25. Another Ravenna mosaic, c. A.D. 520, shows the priest-king Melchizedek in a purple cloak, offering bread and wine at the altar (Gen. 14:18-20). The white altar cloth is decorated with two sets of gammadia, as well as the so-called "seal of Melchizedek," two interlocked squares in gold. Abel offers his lamb as Abraham gently pushes Isaac forward. The hand of God reaches down to this sacred meeting through the red veils adorned with golden gammadia on either side. The theme is the great sacrifice of Christ, which brings together the righteous prophets from the past as well as the four corners of the present world, thereby uniting all time and space.

While the caption under this picture says much about the primary theme of the mural being depicted, the sentence that has caught the attention of so many Saints—almost to the exclusion of everything else stated in the caption or the text—is this: "The white altar cloth is decorated with . . . the so-called 'seal of Melchizedek,' two interlocked squares." From this simple sentence has developed a symbol and a legend much bigger than anyone could have imagined when the line was initially penned by Michael Lyon, the illustrator of *Temple and Cosmos*.

According to the commonly repeated story, the architect of the San Diego California Temple, William S. Lewis Jr., was inspired to place the overlapping squares design throughout the temple without knowing what the symbol meant.[8] Sometime after the temple was constructed, it was brought to his attention that the design was actually the "seal of Melchizedek" and that it was an ancient symbol for the Melchizedek Priesthood, thus showing that he had unknowingly been inspired in his architectural design.[9] One website dedicated to the discussion of Latter-day Saint temples tells the story as follows:

> As we stood there looking at the temple, Brother Williams—or Williamson, the missionary, told us that he heard an interesting story about the symbol that appears all over the temple. He said the architect, who is a current temple sealer, gave a fireside not too long ago. He said that the symbol that appears all over the temple in the stone, the glass, even the fence surrounding the temple, was just an architectural design. He said he thought it would be nice to have a recurring design that ties the temple together. He worked on the simple design, for about six months, toying with different designs. He finally decided on the design, two interlocking squares turned 45 degrees from each other— sometimes containing a circle in the center, sometimes not. He put it in almost every stone wall, every glass window, and even the ornamental iron fence around the temple grounds. . . . I think the missionary said that someone (I don't know if it was a general authority or someone else from SLC) asked the architect at the temple open house where he got the design and what it means. The architect said that it was just an architectural design and didn't mean anything. The person said something like, "Oh I think there is more to it than that." The person came back to SLC, and some time later the word came back that the design was known as the seal of Melchizedek. I asked the missionary who it was in SLC that told them it was the seal of Melchizedek. He said it was Hugh Nibley. He said the architect said that if it is the seal of Melchizedek it would have saved him a lot of time if the Lord had just revealed it to him instead of the tinkering that he did to come up with it.[10]

According to some versions of this popular story, the architect "saw the symbol in a dream" and for that reason placed it throughout the temple.[11] Others have said that President Gordon B. Hinckley asked Hugh Nibley to confirm that this symbol was indeed the seal of Melchizedek, an ancient token of the Melchizedek Priesthood.[12] One member of the Church is reported as saying Hugh Nibley told him "something like, 'Oh sure, it is the seal of King Melchizedek. . . . It was a symbol of Melchizedek's power, kingdom, and . . . a type of name of Melchizedek, like a seal in wax.'"[13]

It is certainly not the purpose of this paper to call into question what various individuals say Dr. Nibley told them. There have been others who have reported conversations with Nibley on the subject wherein he said the opposite of what he apparently told the aforementioned individuals. For example, Robert J. Matthews, former dean of Religious Education at Brigham Young University and a colleague of Professor Nibley, asked him about this symbol and received a very different response than those represented above. Dr. Matthews indicated that Nibley "had little information about it as far as sources, other than the mural." Nibley thought the parallels between the San Diego Temple and the mural were "simply coincidental."[14] Another close associate of Nibley's, Michael Lyon (who has illustrated a number of Nibley's books), said, "Nibley was aware of [the eight-pointed star or interlocking square design], and his general sense of the design was this: 'It is a very interesting thing. But don't get too excited about it.'"[15] Thus, some who knew Nibley well relate a much different story about the symbol than others who inquired of him regarding it.

Of course, it is possible that Professor Nibley was not consistent in what he said or that he was misunderstood. Indeed, this—rather than dishonesty on the part of those who have reported conversations with Nibley—likely explains the strong contradiction between the various reports of his interpretation of the symbol. After all, Nibley himself stated, "As knowledge increases, the verdict of yesterday must be reversed today."[16] In other words, the more I know, the more I am compelled to change my mind. Hence his classic statement, "I refuse to be held responsible for anything I wrote more than three years ago."[17] Nibley was not ashamed of the fact that his views changed over time. He saw it as evidence that he was learning.[18] Of course, we cannot say dogmatically that Nibley changed his mind on this matter; though if we take the word of those who spoke with him about it, it seems the logical conclusion. What does seem evident is that, because of the inconsistency in his comments—and the lack of any written or public statement on this issue by Nibley—placing much credence in the varying and contradictory reports of his views on this matter is probably unwise. If we are to unravel the meaning of this symbol, we simply need to look beyond these reported comments for and against a connection to Melchizedek.

As to the design having been revealed in a dream, Lewis (the architect) has indicated that this did *not* happen. He noted that he and his architectural associates

> were working hard to find a common symbol, module, or pattern to give continuity to the design, or to give a certain character to the temple. They started with a square, but they thought that was too plain and boxy. Then they started chamfering the square's corners which brought it to an 8-sided figure. When they extended the lines it became two overlapping squares. They thought that worked well and so they started using it more and more in the design of the temple. He said the more they used it the better and better it worked. Some people asked about the symbolism of the design, and he told them he didn't know if it had any particular symbolism.[19]

On another occasion Lewis reported, "The Lord didn't show me anything. . . . In designing the temple the Lord expected us to do everything we could to get it right . . . I spent a lot of time in fasting and prayer . . . all through the project, simply to make sure I was getting it right. And then after you've done all you can do . . . I think the Lord begins to respond if you're getting in trouble."[20] Lewis also pointed out that "when the design was shown to the General Authorities in Salt Lake, . . . they didn't say anything about the interlocking squares symbol."[21] Thus there is no evidence that any of the presiding Brethren knew it to be a symbol of the Melchizedek Priesthood. Indeed, according to author Bryce Haymond, "Once the temple was finished, Elder David B. Haight of the Quorum of the Twelve Apostles escorted the media through the temple . . . Someone from the media asked him what the symbol was and what it represented, and Elder Haight . . . said that it was probably just an architectural detail."[22]

THE ORIGIN OF THE TERM

One fact consistently overlooked by those who circulate the story of the seal of Melchizedek is that Nibley was *not* the original source for that phrase. While the comment appears in his book *Temple and Cosmos*, the author of the caption (to which the legend can be traced) was Michael Lyon, the book's illustrator.[23] Lyon thought he had once seen the design in a book on Catholic symbolism, but he doubted the legitimacy of the name or title. In *Temple and Cosmos*, he used the term "so-called" to suggest caution about putting too much stock in the name or the seal's connection with Melchizedek.[24] I asked Lyon if Nibley approved his caption and the use of the phrase "seal of Melchizedek" under illustration 25 in *Temple and Cosmos*. Lyon told me:

> Over the years of submitting illustrations and captions for his approval, Bro. Nibley varied in his level of interest. Sometimes he read every caption, rarely making changes and at other times he said he didn't want to be bothered. . . . For *Temple and Cosmos* I remember him telling me to go ahead and write the captions and he would look through them. I left them with him and later picked them up hoping for some editorial changes but there weren't any. . . . I remember Sis. Nibley . . . thanking me for making the captions sound as much like his writing as we . . . could manage.[25]

Thus it seems likely that Nibley never actually examined or approved the caption, though he likely had been introduced to the mistaken connection between the symbol and Melchizedek through Lyon's innocent passing remark.

So what can we conclude thus far? There are a number of intriguing stories regarding why the architect of the San Diego temple placed the design (now commonly known as the "seal of Melchizedek") in and on the temple. Some of these stories misrepresent what Lewis himself has indicated actually happened. There are also conflicting stories as to what Dr. Nibley is said to have told various people when asked about this design. As previously noted, we know that Nibley never wrote the phrase "seal of Melchizedek" in any of his books or articles, including *Temple and Cosmos*. And we know that Michael Lyon was the source for the now-in-vogue phrase, though he personally doubts its legitimacy.[26] With that said, if we set aside the caption to figure 25 in Nibley's book and the accompanying stories that have become so popular, what, if anything, can we establish about the actual meaning of the symbol from historical and scholarly sources?

ASSOCIATIONS WITH MELCHIZEDEK

There is nothing in the mural that connects the symbol with the man Melchizedek. Indeed, if this figure was a standard ancient symbol for Melchizedek, or his priesthood, one would expect this emblem to appear with frequency—in association with Melchizedek—in the imagery and art of Judaism or Christianity or both. Yet the design is basically absent in traditional Jewish iconography, architecture, and symbology. While it appears occasionally in Christian art (mostly Byzantine), it would be unfair to say that it is a common Christian symbol. And where it does appear in Christianity, definitions of its symbolic meaning are inconsistent, though we can state dogmatically that they *never* have anything to do with Melchizedek or the Melchizedek Priesthood.[27]

One source—which has done much to add to the popularity of the "seal of Melchizedek" among Latter-day Saints—noted that "so far we have been unable to find any non-LDS scholars who have referred to this symbol as the 'seal of Melchizedek.'"[28] Nor do I expect that they will, as there is nothing ancient or scholarly to support such a connection. The only academic source that ever associates this design with Melchizedek is Lyon's passing comment, and even he in no way suggests that the design represents the priesthood or the temple, as a sizable number of Latter-day Saints claim. One might argue that Nibley is a second academic witness to this interpretation. However, as we have noted, his inconsistent and apparently contradictory private comments on the matter require us to place limited emphasis on these claims.

What is more significant is that, if one examines the San Vitale version of this mural[29] and the other murals found in that same church in Ravenna, this symbol is found nowhere on the clothing of Melchizedek. The so-called seal appears elsewhere, on the clothes of at least one other person—namely, a woman (who has the symbol on her cloak) standing immediately to the right of Theodora in her entourage.[30] If this symbol represented the man Melchizedek, it would not make sense to place it on the clothing of another individual depicted in the church's murals but not on Melchizedek himself. And if the design represents the Melchizedek Priesthood, it makes no sense that it does *not* appear on Melchizedek's clothes but *does* appear on the clothing of a woman.

Having established that there is nothing in scholarly or ancient sources to support the interpretation that this symbol represents Melchizedek or his priesthood, we must look at what else it might possibly represent.

There are five potential symbols in this design: (1) the gamma or right angle, (2) the square, (3) the number eight, (4) stars, and (5) the eight-pointed star. We will look at each of these respectively.

THE GAMMA

There is reason to question the claim that the design found on the altar cloth in the Ravenna mural is indeed an eight-pointed star in the form of two interlocked squares. Note that the focus of the portion of the chapter (of Nibley's book) in which the design appears is the ancient use (on liturgical clothing and items) of the square or right angle (also occasionally referred to as an upside-down gamma). Lyon's illustration,[31] copied from one of the original Ravenna murals, has some fourteen squares, right angles, or gammas clearly depicted in it. The illustration was included in the book specifically to highlight the use of that symbol (the right angle), as do illustrations 23, 24, 26b, 27a, b, and e, and 28 of that same chapter. There is no discussion in that chapter, or anywhere else in Nibley's book, regarding the design, nor is it the subject of illustration 25. Knowing that the symbol being illustrated is the right angle (L or Γ), it is possible that the pattern commonly interpreted as two interlocked squares or an eight-pointed star may actually instead be eight right angles arranged in a circular pattern.[32] It is thus possible that the design on the altar cloth may only be an attempt by the mural's artist to increase the number of gammas, or right angles, in the scene.

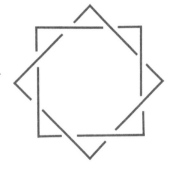

On a related note, Michael Lyon has suggested that the design, rather than being a star, may actually be nothing more than a rosette that "enhances [the] architectural design." He noted that the "geometric shape . . . is easier to put . . . onto a wall or stone frieze" than is a flower.[33] If that is the case, then another fascinating connection can be made. It has been suggested that rosette designs may carry the same symbolic meaning as a series of gammas in a circle, as lexicographers note "the great variety of forms in which the mark [of the square] could appear."[34] Curiously, a recently discovered Egyptian undergarment dating from the Greco-Roman period has "small rosettes . . . woven into the material in particular locations. There is one rosette over each breast and one on the right leg near the knee, but there is no corresponding rosette on the left leg. Across the lower abdomen, the material also has a hemmed slit about six inches long."[35] Thus the design in the middle in the San Vitale mural, which has come to be known as the "seal of Melchizedek," may instead be a rosette design made of gammas or right angles, specifically tying the design into the fourteen other gammas prominently displayed on the altar cloth. Hence, while we have no historic connection of the gamma with Melchizedek, its symbolic meaning has numerous connections with Christ.[36]

THE SQUARE

Because a variety of meanings can be found associated with the square (or box shape) as a symbol, it is rather difficult to speak emphatically about. In some cases it is juxtaposed with the circle (a symbol for the heavenly or the eternal), and therefore the square sometimes represents the mortal, the fallen, the earthly, or that which is limited.[37] None of these connotations seem applicable to the message of the Ravenna mural. On the other hand, one commentator noted that squares "in Christian tradition . . . symbolize a firm foundation."[38] They can also symbolize honesty, perfection, dependability, integrity, morality, protection, and unchangeability,[39] all attributes of Christ. One Latter-day Saint text notes that "interlaced squares signify man's regeneration,"[40] suggesting Christ's gift of resurrection. Elsewhere it is stated that the square can symbolize "the fixation of death as opposed to the dynamic circle of life and movement."[41] In this regard it also has connections with Christ, who died that we might live. Thus the square can quite logically be seen as a Christocentric symbol.

THE NUMBER EIGHT

The number eight is a very developed symbol in ancient and modern Christianity. It is traditionally associated with the concepts of resurrection, new beginnings, rebirth, renewal, and baptism.[42] Because of its association with these aforementioned ideas, it is sometimes also seen as the number of Christ. Indeed, one text notes, "Eight is the dominical number, for everywhere it has to do with the Lord. It is the number of His name, ΙΗΣΟΥΣ, Jesus," which totals 888 in Greek gematria.[43] This same source indicates that "other Dominical Names of Jesus are also marked by gematria and stamped with the number eight as a factor"—titles such as Christ, Lord, Savior, Emmanuel, or Messiah.[44] In reference to the symbolism of eight in the Resurrection, one author wrote, "Christ rose from the dead on 'the first day of the week,' that was of necessity the eighth day."[45] Additionally, for all of those born in the covenant, baptism is to be performed at the age of eight (D&C 68:27). The intricately connected symbols of baptism, new beginnings, resurrection, Christ, and the number eight are natural and appropriate. In each case, Christ is the source.

In antiquity, baptismal fonts were commonly eight sided to represent new beginnings, rebirth, renewal, resurrection, and Christ. Of this fact, one source notes, "The octagon draws on the symbolism of the number eight, emblematic of renewal. Eight-sided forms were felt to mediate between the symbolism of the square, representing earthly existence, and the circle (standing for heaven or eternity)."[46] Of course, Christ is the great mediator between heaven and earth—between man and God. Thus the number eight is best seen as a symbol of Jesus and that which he has done for those who seek to follow him.[47]

THE STAR

Anciently, stars were common symbols for angels.[48] Indeed, this is exactly how John the Revelator, Abraham, and Isaiah use the word *star* (see Revelation 1:20, 9:1, 22:16; Abraham 3:17–18; Isaiah 14:12–13; see also Numbers 24:17)—and quite possibly how Matthew intended the word to be understood in his gospel (see Matthew 2:2–10).[49] In the book of Revelation and in the Pearl of Great Price, Jesus is symbolized by a star. Harold Bayley, the noted early-twentieth-century Scottish scholar of language and symbolism, indicated that stars were common symbols for deity in many ancient cultures and religions and that the eight-pointed star is one of many star-symbols that represent the unity of the members of the Godhead.[50] Drawing on the book of Revelation, Bayley adds that "Christ . . . is described as the Bright and Morning Star."[51] Of the use of stars in art and architecture, the *Dictionary of Subjects and Symbols in Art* states, "To the Greeks and Romans the stars were divinities, a belief derived from the ancient religions of Persia and Babylon. . . . In a symbolic form the idea was absorbed by Christianity: Christ described as the 'bright star of dawn' (Revelations 22:16)."[52] Thus, more often than not, in religious symbolism, stars are associated with the divine—sometimes angels, but often Christ.[53]

THE EIGHT-POINTED STAR

As noted, the eight-pointed star in Christianity is sometimes symbolic of the Godhead and the unity of the Father, Son, and Holy Ghost.[54] For the Egyptians it was also a symbol of divinity or of God's influence.[55] One Catholic text noted, "The eight-pointed star symbolizes regeneration. The number eight is traditionally associated with the idea of regeneration or baptism."[56] Paul declares in the book of Romans that baptism is a type for the death, burial, and Resurrection of Christ—and the promise of resurrection or renewal for all who faithfully engage in that rite (see Romans 6:3–5). Thus one Latter-day Saint author wrote, "The eight-pointed star *signifies* man's regeneration."[57] The combination of the number eight (a symbol we have shown to be closely linked to Christ) and the symbolism of a star (also strongly tied in scripture to Jesus) suggest that the eight-pointed star is most likely a representation of the Savior.[58]

THE SACRIFICE OF CHRIST

When one takes all that is known from ancient and scholarly sources about the various symbolic elements of the so-called seal of Melchizedek, it appears in *all* cases to be Christocentric rather than Melchizedek-centric. At Ravenna it is *not* found on Melchizedek but rather on the altar, which is a symbol for Christ's sacrifice. It can represent honesty, perfection, dependability, integrity, morality, protection, and unchangeability—all attributes of Christ, but not explicitly stated to be attributes of Melchizedek. It has strong ties to the number eight, which foreshadows resurrection, new beginnings, rebirth, renewal, and baptism. These are all symbols of Jesus but *not* of Melchizedek (or *any* mortal man). The "seal" appears to many to be a star (and an eight-pointed star, at that)— a common scriptural symbol for the divine or for Christ but *never* for Melchizedek. Thus symbolically everything points to Jesus, but nothing really points to Melchizedek. Indeed, even the life of Melchizedek typologically points us to Christ.[59]

As we examine the murals from the churches at San Vitale and Sant'Apollinare,[60] it becomes evident that the focus is not Melchizedek but rather Christ. In the murals at both churches, the symbol is found on the altar cloth, not on the individuals surrounding the altar. In Christianity, altars suggest the presence of God, sacrifice, and union with God. They imply the passage from death to life and from time to eternity, which God offers to the faithful who approach the altar to sincerely worship him.[61]

As one expert in symbolism noted, "The altar represents both the tomb and the resurrection, death transformed into life, the sacrifice of Christ in the Eucharist [or sacrament] and Christ as the Son of Righteousness. [When an altar is made of wood,] the wood is [a symbol of] the cross, [and when it is made of stone,] the stone [is] the rock of Calvary and the raised altar is [a symbol of] both [Christ's] ascension and Christ's suffering on [Calvary's] hill."[62] Thus the placement of the symbol on an altar is a definite sign to the viewer that the symbol is about Christ's sacrifice on our behalf and *not* about the man Melchizedek.

In the San Vitale mural, Abel stands at the left side of the altar offering a lamb to God (see Genesis 4:4). God's hand is seen extended from the sky above the altar, implying both the focus of the offering and also God's acceptance of the same. To the right of the altar, rather than behind it, Melchizedek also makes a sacrificial offering, which is directed toward the extended hand of God. His sacrifice in the mural is a clear reference to Genesis 14:18, where Melchizedek is depicted as offering up the sacrament of the Lord's Supper. Though the so-called seal is present in the mural, it is associated with neither Abel nor Melchizedek, but instead with Christ and sacrifice.

In the Sant'Apollinare mural (illustrated in Nibley's book), the symbol of sacrifice is extended. Abel still offers up his lamb and Melchizedek is found offering up the sacrament, but Abraham is added to the mural, offering Isaac as an additional type of Christ's sacrifice on our behalf (see Genesis 22).[63] Once again the hand of God is depicted as evidence of his divine acceptance of the sacrifices offered.

While the San Vitale mural has the names of both sacrificers prominently displayed above their heads, the Sant'Apollinare mural, because of the veil to the left and right of the altar, is much more crowded. The prominent display of Melchizedek's name across the top gives the impression that the scene is specifically about Melchizedek. However, the symbolism makes it clear that, though Melchizedek is in the center of the picture, he is intended to be seen as one of several types for Christ. Indeed, though the *Temple and Cosmos* illustration shows Melchizedek's name across the top of the drawing, it deletes an important feature of the mural found underneath the altar. Written across the bottom of the mural in rather corrupt Latin is a descriptive caption that, though damaged, clearly sports the names of both Abel and Melchizedek.

From what can be read of the damaged caption, we learn that the picture is intended as a typological scene, illustrating the reality that several biblical figures typify Christ, including Abel and Melchizedek, and, in light of the mural above the caption, Isaac also.[64] Indeed, those who know the stories of the lives of Abel, Isaac, and Melchizedek know that each stand as an intricate typological foreshadowing of the offering or sacrifice of the Lord Jesus Christ.[65] The parallels between these three types are significant and sundry, and it is for this reason that the artist of the mural has depicted them together at the altar offering their respective typological sacrifices. The entire mural is a scene of sacrifice in honor of, and typification of, Christ's ultimate sacrifice. One expert on the Sant'Apollinare mural wrote,

> Noteworthy is the fact that Abel, Abraham, and Melchizedek are specifically mentioned in one of the solemn prayers of the Roman canon of the Mass: "Upon which (viz., the eucharistic offerings) do thou vouchsafe to look with a propitious and serene countenance, and to accept them, as thou wert graciously pleased to accept the gifts of thy just servant Abel, and the sacrifice of our Patriarch Abraham, and that which thy high priest Melchizedek offered to thee, a holy sacrifice, a spotless victim." . . . The representation of the three mystical antitypes

of Christ's priesthood in San Vitale is striking evidence of the importance of the liturgical theme in this church. . . . It must not be forgotten . . . that since apostolic times, the events narrated in the Book of
Exodus were looked upon as allusions to the events of redemption. . . .
The events narrated in the Book of Exodus are to be understood as
"shadows and types" of the salvation of mankind.[66]

This same source notes that the architectural shape of the church at
San Vitale was designed to suggest to the mind of the observer that the
church is a tomb—it is Christ's sepulchre, per se.[67] Sacrifice is the ultimate symbol of the building and the mural in question, as is suggested by
the lamb, the bread, and the boy Isaac, as well as by the sacrificial lives of
the three men offering their gifts to God.[68]

THE EVOLUTION OF SYMBOLS

Not surprisingly, symbols sometimes evolve in their meaning and
use. For example, in the two millennia since the founding of Christianity,
the cross has become the universally recognized symbol of the worldwide
body of believers in the divine mission of the Lord Jesus Christ. But the
fact is, the cross as a symbol predates Christianity. One noted expert in
symbolism referred to it as the "universal symbol from the most remote
times" and as "a cosmic symbol par excellence."[69] The Babylonians saw it
as a symbol of the four phases of the moon. To the Syrians it represented
the four great gods of the elements. In pre-Columbian America it was
a fertility symbol. In Egypt it was associated with Maat and in India
with Agni, but in Scandinavia it was a symbol for the fertilizing power
of Thor's hammer.[70] In addition to the cross's nearly universal acceptance
as a symbol, crucifixion was practiced for many centuries before the
Common Era by many peoples. The Phoenicians, Greeks, Babylonians,
Persians, and Romans all used it, and there is evidence that others such
as the Celts, Germans, Carthaginians, and Britons also employed it as a
form of capital punishment.[71] Thus, as a symbol and as an instrument of
death, the cross is pre-Christian in origin. Today, however, for Christians
it has a rather distinct and well-established meaning, though such meanings would have stood as contradictions to the actual ancient meanings of
the symbol in the Christian era.

The Star of David is another example of a symbol that has evolved in
its meaning over the centuries. One text suggests that the modern Jewish
Star of David is most likely a descendant of the ancient rosette, which

was connected to royalty.[72] Before the medieval period, it was not used within Judaism, and when it finally did find its first use in Jewry, it was the mystics or Kabbalists who utilized it. For them, it was not a symbol of Judaism or even of King David. Rather, it was a sign of protection placed on their amulets or good-luck charms.[73] Only in recent times has the Star of David become a distinctive Jewish symbol. For millennia it not only had no particular significance to Jews, but was completely absent in all things Jewish. The seven-branched menorah was the traditional symbol of Judaism and even appears on the official seal of the State of Israel.[74] The popular use of the Star of David in mainstream Judaism only started in the nineteenth century, when Jews of that period were looking for a symbol they could use "in contradistinction to the Christian use of the cross."[75] While adopted only recently by Jews, the Star of David was used by various societies as early as the Bronze Age. It was present in Mesopotamia, India, the Iberian Peninsula, and Britain. Its initial use in Judaism was entirely decorative or ornamental, and it is absent in Jewry during Hellenistic times.[76] During the Middle Ages, Muslims and Christians used the Star of David. It is seen in a number of medieval European churches and in some early Byzantine structures. Thus, like the cross of Christianity, the Star of David of Judaism is a symbol that was borrowed from ancient societies and reinterpreted to suit the needs of a more modern people who were looking for a symbol to represent an idea important to them. Hence a "new" symbol was born.

So what of the so-called seal of Melchizedek? There is no question that the two overlapping squares (or eight-pointed star) is an ancient design.[77] However, it has no strong connection to Judaism, and its connections to Christianity are mostly in the octagonal layout of various buildings, not in symbology. The design does appear sporadically from antiquity through modernity in various religions and cultures, but with no consistency in meaning and often as a purely aesthetic device.[78] For example, the pattern erroneously called the seal of Melchizedek appears frequently in the art of Islam, with no defined meaning. It was commonly used as a marker for the end of a chapter in Arabic calligraphy and is known as the *rub al-hizb*. It is customary in a number of Arabic texts, including older versions of the Qur'an.

The symbol is often simply an architectural design, as the architect reported it was intended to be on the San Diego Temple.[79] In predominantly Muslim cities, it is commonly found on mosques, votive objects, fobs, and even key chains.[80] Similarly, in the Khirbet Kanef synagogue of Palestine, there are two overlapping squares carved into one of its walls which, according to one expert, likely symbolize a rosette, thus again an aesthetic design with no specific meaning.[81] The overlapping squares appear as a pattern on the floor of the lobby of the House of Lords in the British House of Parliament, simply utilized for aesthetic appeal.[82] A number of flags and coats of arms employ the symbol of the eight-pointed star. For example, the Turkmenistan and Uzbekistan coats of arms employ it, as do the flags of Azerbaijan and the Azat (or "freedom") party of Kazakhstan. Until recently, the Iraqi Boy Scouts and Girl Guides employed the eight-pointed star as part of their official logo. Each of these utilizes the symbol for its own reasons and without any cross-cultural meaning.

The glory of Christ is often represented in Eastern Orthodox iconography as "eight rays of light emanating from the body of Christ."[83] A common way for that glory to be depicted in Orthodox art is through "two superimposed concave squares" forming an octagon.[84] In Hinduism the symbol sometimes known as the "star of Lakshmi" is an eight-pointed star, made of two superimposed squares. It symbolizes the many kinds of wealth offered to us by God, specifically the goddess Lakshmi.[85] While we could continue to list examples, it is evident that the pattern of two overlapping squares (or an eight-pointed star) is common in a variety of cultures. But there is no consistency in use or symbolic meaning, and certainly none of these faiths or cultures sees the symbol as a representation of the man Melchizedek or of priestly authority.

CONCLUSION

Weighing all of the evidence presented above, it seems clear to this author that the Ravenna murals made so popular by Nibley's *Temple and Cosmos* have utilized the design in question either as an aesthetic pattern, a means of multiplying right angles, or as a symbol for the atoning sacrifice of the Lord Jesus Christ. Of course, we will never be able to identify the true intention for sure, as the unknown artist of the murals left no known explanation of his objective.

What we can say for sure is that the design is not an ancient symbol of Melchizedek or priesthood authority (at Ravenna or in any ancient source). We know that it is primarily an aesthetic rather than religious design and that when it was used anciently, it never had a consistent defined meaning.

By popularizing this image, a handful of Latter-day Saints have created a new symbol—a modern Star of David or cross. The pattern of interlocked squares or an eight-pointed star has been endowed with religious meaning, and an entire folklore has developed around it to show that divine origins have been behind the symbol and its employment on certain temples.[86] Through a simple misunderstanding of a caption under a picture in a book, Mormons have unintentionally created a symbol that has erroneously been connected with Melchizedek and his priesthood.[87]

Given that the interlocked squares (or eight-pointed star) is *not* an ancient symbol for the Melchizedek Priesthood, and given that the proper ancient name for this design is *not* the seal of Melchizedek, we are left with the question, is it appropriate for modern Latter-day Saints to take an unaffiliated design, such as dual overlapping squares, and turn such a design into an official symbol for the Melchizedek Priesthood or for the act of making one's calling and election sure? As symbols can have many meanings—and a variety of applications, based on the needs of the person viewing them—I think the ultimate answer is "Yes!" I see no reason why this symbol can't be appropriately employed for Melchizedek and his priesthood. I suppose my one caveat would be this: as we do so, we should do what we can to be historically accurate. Thus, Latter-day Saints should not claim that it was used *in ancient times* as a symbol for Melchizedek, his priesthood, or making one's calling and election sure. But to say that the symbol reminds them of these aforementioned principles does not, to my mind, do violence to the symbol or damage to our doctrine. In the end, I realize that this chapter is unlikely to end the popular LDS practice of claiming the aforementioned design was Melchizedek-focused in antiquity. And I am entirely comfortable leaving it to readers to decide whether to embrace or reject the modern Mormon interpretation of this symbol.[88] For this author it matters little—though frankly, if we as a people are to adopt this symbol, it seems to me that it would be more appropriate to interpret it as a representation of Christ rather than as a symbol of one whose life typified him.[89]

NOTES

1. A version of this article was originally published under the title "The Seal of Melchizedek?" See *The Religious Educator: Perspectives on the Restored Gospel*, vol. 11, no. 3 (2010): 94–121. Republished here by permission.

2. Joseph Fielding McConkie and Donald W. Parry, *A Guide to Scriptural Symbols* (Salt Lake City: Bookcraft, 1990), 1; see also Bruce R. McConkie, *Mormon Doctrine*, 2nd ed. (Salt Lake City: Bookcraft, 1979), 773; Joseph Fielding McConkie, *Gospel Symbolism* (Salt Lake City: Bookcraft, 1985), 249.

3. Examples of symbols found in non-LDS traditions but also utilized by Latter-day Saints include white as a symbol of purity, victory, and happiness; the elements of the sacrament as representations of Christ's slain body and shed blood; the use of olive oil as a token of the Holy Ghost; the laying on of hands as a sign of conferral; and so forth. Examples of symbols unique to Latter-day Saints include statues of the angel Moroni, the CTR crest, sacred clothing associated with the temple and its rites, presidencies as symbolic mirrors of the Godhead, and so on.

4. See Val Brinkerhoff, *The Day Star: Reading Sacred Architecture* (New York: Digital Legend Press, 2009), 1:50, 52–53; 2:63, 131. "An eight-sided figure is . . . the seal of Melchizedek. The . . . mosaic in St. Apollinare in Classe . . . shows the seal of Melchizedek. . . . The seal of Melchizedek should remind us that it is the Melchizedek Priesthood that administers the ordinances of exaltation." Gerald E. Hansen Jr., *Sacred Walls: Learning from Temple Symbols* (American Fork, Utah: Covenant Communications, 2009), 47.

5. While most Latter-day Saints who utilize this symbol associate it with the Melchizedek Priesthood, some refer to it as the symbol of having made one's calling and election sure, and also of the principle of eternal progression. See Brinkerhoff, *Day Star*, 2:132, 142, 145; Bryce Haymond, "The Seal of Melchizedek—Part 3," *Temple Study: Defending and Sustaining the LDS Temple*, http://www.templestudy.com/2008/09/10/the-seal-of-melchizedek-part-3.

6. This design has been reported to appear in various places in the San Diego, Newport Beach, Redlands, Bountiful, Nauvoo, Salt Lake, Draper, and Albuquerque Temples. See Bryce Haymond, "The Seal of Melchizedek—Part 3."

7. See Hugh Nibley, *Temple and Cosmos: Beyond This Ignorant Present* (Salt Lake City: Deseret Book; Provo, Utah: Foundation for Ancient Research and Mormon Studies, 1992), 91–138.

8. See Brinkerhoff, *Day Star*, 2:155–56.

9. Ibid., 2:156.

10. See Haymond, "The Seal of Melchizedek—Part 1," *Temple Study: Defending and Sustaining the LDS Temple*, http://www.templestudy.com/2008/09/08/the-seal-of-melchizedek-part-1.

11. See Haymond, "The Seal of Melchizedek—Part 3."

12. See Haymond, "The Seal of Melchizedek—Part 4," *Temple Study: Defending and Sustaining the LDS Temple*, http://www.templestudy.com/2008/09/11/the-seal-of-melchizedek-part-4. See also Brinkerhoff, *Day Star*, 1:61. Val Brinkerhoff recounts a conversation he had with Bill Lewis on this matter. See *Day Star*, 2:61. Elsewhere he quotes Lewis as saying, "And so I wrote President Hinckley . . . and said now you're

too busy to respond, but just for your interest, for your information. And sure enough, a week later he responded very nicely. And [I] found out later, he called Brother Nibley and *checked* on it, talked with him about it." Val Brinkerhoff, "LDS Symbology Series: Interview of Bill Lewis, Private Architect of the San Diego, California LDS Temple" (unpublished manuscript in author's possession, 2006), 28; emphasis in original; transcribed by Jennifer Olson. Lewis indicated that President Hinckley did not tell him personally that he had spoken to Nibley about this, but Lewis heard through the grapevine that President Hinckley talked with Nibley at some point about the symbol. From his oral interview it is unclear what exactly President Hinckley explicitly conveyed to Lewis and how much Lewis learned through some secondary source or drew as a conclusion from inexplicit statements. Lewis never states in his interview that President Hinckley personally told him he had called Nibley or that President Hinckley informed him of what Nibley said about the symbol.

13. See Haymond, "The Seal of Melchizedek—Part 4." Another source reports that a member of the Temple Construction Department "became curious about the motif and asked Hugh Nibley (a professor at BYU at the time) if any ancient meaning was attached to the symbol. Nibley is said to have explained that in antiquity the 2 interlaced squares . . . is typically referred to as the Seal of King Melchizedek." Bill Lewis, in Brinkerhoff, *Day Star*, 2:156; see also 2:160 n.1; 1:60–61. While Nibley may have said this, there is no support for such a claim in antiquity.

14. Conversation with Robert J. Matthews, March 18, 2009; see also Paul E. Damron, "Melchizedek: A Personal Study" (unpublished paper presented to the Church Educational System Graduate Scripture Study of the New Testament class, Sacramento, 2000), 3–4. I express appreciation to Paul Damron for freely sharing with me his detailed research notes on this subject.

15. Michael Lyon, telephone conversation with the author, January 16, 2009.

16. Hugh W. Nibley, "A New Look at the Pearl of Great Price—Part 3: Empanelling the Panel," *Improvement Era*, July 1968, 54.

17. Hugh W. Nibley, "The Facsimiles of the Book of Abraham: A Response by H. W. Nibley to E. H. Ashment," *Sunstone*, December 1979, 49.

18. Brinkerhoff reported that Bill Lewis, the architect of the San Diego temple, told him, "Some in the academic world refute the meaning and its title. What is clear is that Hugh Nibley believed that it had connection to the ancient high priest and apparently Pres. Hinckley believed him." Brinkerhoff, *Day Star*, 1:61. As we have shown, it isn't clear at all what Nibley believed on this matter. It appears that he contradicted himself when he spoke to various people who inquired of him regarding the symbol. Unfortunately, because he is no longer living and thus cannot explain what he really said or believed, it seems wise to (1) trust the witness of those who knew Nibley and (2) more importantly, look at what scholarly sources tell us. In the end, Nibley may or may not have believed that this symbol was associated with Melchizedek. If he did, he may have been wrong. When one surveys ancient and scholarly sources on the matter, all evidence points to the fact that this design has absolutely nothing to do with Melchizedek or his priesthood. Every claim of its ancient connections to Melchizedek can be traced back to a one-on-one conversation with Nibley or to Michael Lyon's caption in Nibley's book. There is nothing

else to support the bold declaration that this is some ancient symbol of King Melchizedek and his priesthood. Thus, even if Nibley did believe the design was associated with Melchizedek, there is not a scrap of evidence to support such a belief. By this I mean no offense. I am simply trying to let the sources, ancient and modern, speak for themselves.

19. See Haymond, "The Seal of Melchizedek—Part 4."

20. Bill Lewis, oral interview with Val Brinkerhoff, August 2006. Brinkerhoff confirmed the accuracy of Lewis's words to me in personal correspondence on November 2, 2009.

21. See Haymond, "The Seal of Melchizedek—Part 4."

22. See ibid. Bill Lewis reported this same experience as follows: "Elder Haight was down, to usher the media through and answer questions, and so when they came back and they were asking questions, that was the first question that one of the reporters asked, 'What's that symbol mean? What part of the Church?' And it caught Brother Haight off guard I think. And he said the right answer in my opinion, he just said, 'Well, that's *the architectural* symbols they use.'" Bill Lewis, in "LDS Symbology Series," 27; emphasis in original.

23. Brinkerhoff has pointed out to me that some who have reported Nibley's comments about the symbol being somehow associated with Melchizedek say they spoke with Nibley prior to the actual publication of his book *Temple and Cosmos*. However, it should be noted that Nibley's book was being written, illustrated, and edited for a significant time prior to its publication in 1992. Consequently, Nibley had already likely been introduced to the so-called seal of Melchizedek by Michael Lyon well before his book reached the bookstore shelf and long before the April 1993 dedication of the San Diego Temple. Brinkerhoff's oral interview with Bill Lewis actually implies that the conversations with Nibley about this symbol came shortly after the temple open house and therefore well after Nibley's book was in print. See "LDS Symbology Series," 27–28. Time and again, those who suggest a Melchizedek connection to the symbol attribute it to Nibley and cite his book as evidence of the interpretation. While I am willing to concede that Lewis and a handful of others may trace their understanding to Nibley, since he never used that phrase in any of his writings, it is likely that he was influenced by Lyon's comment. And certainly the vast majority of those I have encountered who believe the symbol is associated with Melchizedek cite Lyon's caption as their source (though they attribute the caption to Nibley).

24. Conversation with Michael Lyon, January 16, 2009; see also Haymond, "The Seal of Melchizedek—Part 2," *Temple Study: Defending and Sustaining the LDS Temple*, http://www.templestudy.com/2008/09/09/the-seal-of-melchizedek-part-2. Lyon told me that though he has tried on numerous occasions to find the book in which he thought he had seen the symbol, he has been unsuccessful in locating it or any other text that connects the eight-pointed star with Melchizedek or that calls that design the seal of Melchizedek. In a conversation with Lyon in the year 2000, he indicated that he did not know whether the interlocking squares on the altar cloth were a deliberate construction of the artist of the mural or just an interesting shape that enhances the design. Lyon suggested that often the symbol of two interlocked squares was utilized as a representation of a flower because it would have been "easier to put onto a wall or stone frieze" than to carve a flower. Damron, "Melchizedek: A Personal Study," 8. More recently, Lyon told me

that "the eight-pointed star in the Ravenna mural may be nothing more than a pleasing design [with no particular meaning], developed by the mural's creator." Michael Lyon, conversation with the author, January 16, 2009; see also Allen H. Barber, *Celestial Symbols: Symbolism in Doctrine, Religious Traditions and Temple Architecture* (Bountiful, Utah: Horizon, 1989), 154, 168–69.

25. Michael Lyon, correspondence with the author, March 4, 2009.

26. Again, Nibley may well have shared Lyon's idea with a select few—perhaps even President Hinckley. But the general popularity of the symbol has come (in the opinion of this author) not from comments by Nibley to a couple of individuals, but rather from the widely seen and cited caption written by Lyon in *Temple and Cosmos*.

27. Michael Lyon stated, "The design is found in many Byzantine contexts where it does not seem to have any special meaning." Personal correspondence with author, November 19, 2009.

28. See Haymond, "The Seal of Melchizedek—Part 2."

29. There are two historic basilicas in the northeastern portion of Italy: San Vitale (in Ravenna) and Sant'Apollinare (in Classe). Construction on the San Vitale edifice began in AD 526. Upon completion, the building was dedicated to the martyrs of the city of Ravenna. Construction on San Vitale's sister basilica, Sant'Apollinare, began in AD 532. This second basilica was dedicated to Classe's first bishop. Sant'Apollinare is a more modest undertaking than its counterpart and predecessor. And the second of these two basilicas borrowed heavily from the motifs of its forerunner in San Vitale, including imitating and adapting its artwork. Indeed, one scholar noted that the mural in Sant'Apollinare, which is so heavily connected with the "seal of Melchizedek" myth, is "unquestionably an adaptation of the two mosaics in San Vitale. . . . The three antitypes of Christian priesthood [Abel, Isaac, and Melchizedek] have been brought together in one scene." Otto G. Von Simson, *Sacred Fortress: Byzantine Art and Statecraft in Ravenna* (New Jersey: Princeton University Press, 1987), 59. Upon their completion, both basilicas were dedicated by Bishop Maximian of Ravenna—San Vitale in AD 548 and Sant'Apollinare in AD 549.

30. Note that this woman is a political rather than a religious figure.

31. See Nibley, *Temple and Cosmos*, 109, fig. 25.

32. As to the meaning of the gamma, square, or right angle, one authoritative text on Jewish symbols notes that in antiquity, the square symbolized the hope "for immortality" by the wearer. Erwin R. Goodenough, *Jewish Symbols in the Greco-Roman Period* (New York: Bollingren Foundation, 1964), 9:163. In LDS writings we find interpretations such as the following: "An angle of a square . . . forms the sign of the square 'L' . . . which signifies moral rectitude." M. Garfield Cook, *Restoration In Geometric Symbolism*, rev. ed. (Salt Lake City: M. Garfield Cook, 2004), 38. A square or right angle "is a symbol of justice and uprightness, to act uprightly, justly and truthful; . . . and [it is] an emblem of morality, which taught the initiated to square their lives and actions according to the laws of God." Barber, *Celestial Symbols*, 36. One non-LDS text suggests that the square symbolizes staying "within . . . proper limits." Robert Macoy, *A Dictionary of Freemasonry* (New York: Gramercy Books, 2000), 674. Elsewhere we read, "The square was an emblem of morality, which taught them to square their lives and actions by the

unerring laws of God's word, and to regulate their conduct according to the doctrine laid down by their divine Creator, to preserve a lively faith in his holy gospel, and taught them to live in charity with all mankind." George Oliver, *The Ancient Landmarks of Freemasonry* (Silver Springs, Maryland: The Masonic Service Association, 1932), 249, cited in E. Cecil McGavin, *Mormonism and Masonry* (Salt Lake City: Bookcraft, 1956), 60. The square is "the implement of proof. 'Prove all things, hold fast that which is good' [1 Thessalonians 5:21]." Robert Morris, *The Poetry of Freemasonry* (n.c.: The Wrener Company, 1895), 119.

33.   Michael Lyon, conversation with the author, January 16, 2009; see also Damron, "Melchizedek: A Personal Study," 8; Barber, *Celestial Symbols*, 9:164.

34.   Goodenough, *Jewish Symbols*, 9:164.

35.   C. Wilfred Griggs et al., "Evidences of a Christian Population in the Egyptian Fayum and Genetic and Textile Studies of the Akhmim Noble Mummies," *BYU Studies* 33, no. 2 (1993): 226; see also 227; John W. Welch and Claire Foley, "Gammadia on Early Jewish and Christian Garments," in *Masada and the World of the New Testament* (Provo, Utah: BYU Studies, 1997), 254–55.

36.   One source notes that "in mediaeval times it was the gammadion [that was] used to symbolize Christ." J. C. Cooper, *An Illustrated Encyclopaedia of Traditional Symbols* (London: Thames and Hudson, 1995), 166. One expert on the evolution of symbols likewise suggested that "the gammadion . . . sometimes [takes] the place of the Cross of Christ" and that in certain cultures "the gammadion . . . [is a] representation of . . . god." Count Goblet d'Alviella, *The Migration of Symbols* (New York: University Books, 1956), 45, 50; see also 50–51, 71. He also says that for the Aryans, for example, the gammadion was a symbol of "the omnipotent God of the universe" or the "Heavenly Father" of subsequent mythologies (74, 75). One LDS source suggests that gammadia may be a "figure of victory" or "hoped for immortality." Welch and Foley, "Gammadia on Early Jewish and Christian Garments," 255. Indeed, "victory . . . commonly appears as a symbol of immortality." Goodenough, *Jewish Symbols*, 9:163, as cited in Welch and Foley, "Gammadia on Early Jewish and Christian Garments," 255. There is evidence that gammadia were "used . . . to ornament the garments of certain priestly personages" in the fourth century and that, in fact, they are constantly found on altars and priestly vestments in various cultures and religions. D'Alviella, *Migration of Symbols*, 35, 44.

37.   See Cooper, *Illustrated Encyclopaedia*, 157; Jack Tresidder, *Symbols and Their Meanings* (London: Duncan Baird, 2000), 154.

38.   Nadia Julien, *The Mammoth Dictionary of Symbols*, trans. Elfreda Powell (New York: Carroll and Graf Publishers, 1996), 398; see also J. E. Cirlot, *A Dictionary of Symbols*, 2nd ed., trans. Jack Sage (New York: Philosophical Library, 1971), 307; Cook, *Restoration in Geometric Symbolism*, 26; David Fontana, *The Secret Language of Symbolism* (San Francisco: Chronicle Books, 1993), 54.

39.   See Cooper, *Illustrated Encyclopaedia*, 157; Fontana, *Secret Language of Symbolism*, 54.

40.   Barber, *Celestial Symbols*, 165.

41.   Cooper, *Illustrated Encyclopaedia*, 157.

42. For examples of the number eight as a symbol of resurrection, see James F. White, "The Spatial Setting," in *The Oxford History of Christian Worship*, ed. Geoffrey Wainwright and Karen B. Westerfield Tucker (New York: Oxford University Press, 2006), 79–99; Cooper, *Illustrated Encyclopaedia*, 118; Robert D. Johnston, *Numbers in the Bible: God's Design in Biblical Numerology* (Grand Rapids, Michigan: Kregel Publications, 1990), 75; Julien, *Mammoth Dictionary of Symbols*, 135; E. W. Bullinger, *Number in Scripture: Its Supernatural Design and Spiritual Significance* (Grand Rapids, Michigan: Kregel Publications, 1967), 200; John J. Davis, *Biblical Numerology* (Grand Rapids, Michigan: Baker Book House, 2000), 122. For examples of eight as a symbol of new beginnings, see Johnston, *Numbers in the Bible*, 75; J. E. Cirlot, *A Dictionary of Symbols*, 2nd ed. (New York: Philosophical Library, 1971), 233; Julien, *Mammoth Dictionary of Symbols*, 135; Bullinger, *Number in Scripture*, 196, 200; Tresidder, *Symbols and Their Meanings*, 168. For examples of eight as a symbol of rebirth, see Julien, *Mammoth Dictionary of Symbols*, 135; Cook, *Restoration in Geometric Symbolism*, 40; Hansen and Brinkerhoff, *Sacred Walls*, 47. For an example of eight as a symbol of renewal, see Tresidder, *Symbols and Their Meanings*, 154, 168. For examples of eight as a symbol of baptism, see Cirlot, *Dictionary of Symbols*, 233; McConkie and Parry, *Guide to Scriptural Symbols*, 46; White, "The Spatial Setting," 798–99; Cook, *Restoration in Geometric Symbolism*, 41. "According to Clement of Alexandria, Christ placed those whom he gave a second life under the sign of eight." Julien, *Mammoth Dictionary of Symbols*, 135.

43. Cook, *Restoration in Geometric Symbolism*, 40; Hansen and Brinkerhoff, *Sacred Walls*, 47. "The Sibline Oracles 1:342–44 give the number of the name of the Savior in Greek as 888 (I=10, A=8, S=200, O=70, Y=400, S=200)." Richard D. Draper, *Opening the Seven Seals* (Salt Lake City: Deseret Book, 1991), 273, n. 29. "In the Hebrew alphabet this is the sacred number of Jesus." Cooper, *Illustrated Encyclopaedia*, 120.

44. Bullinger points out that, if spelled out in Greek gematria, "Christ" totals 1,480 (8 × 185); "Lord" totals 800 (8 × 100); "Our Lord" totals 1,768 (8 × 82); "Son" totals 880 (8 × 110). Additionally, in gematria "the names of the Lord's people are multiples of eight" in most cases. *Number in Scripture*, 203–7.

45. Bullinger, *Number in Scripture*, 200; see also Cook, *Restoration in Geometric Symbolism*, 41.

46. Tresidder, *Symbols and Their Meanings*, 154.

47. One expert on the church at San Vitale noted that the building's eight-sided design is Christocentric in its meaning. He wrote, "In Christian architecture the octagonal plan is an image of the Easter sepulcher. Liturgically and mystically, a martyr's sanctuary is both his tomb and Christ's sepulcher; and early Christian theology conceived the dignity of martyrdom as the martyr's mystical transfiguration into Christ. The architecture of San Vitale, evoking this relation of the death and resurrection of the titular saint to the death and resurrection of Christ, is a significant tribute to the Christlike dignity of St. Vitalis." Von Simson, *Sacred Fortress*, 4; see also Cooper, *Illustrated Encyclopaedia*, 111. Thus the structure of the very building in which the mural is found is Christocentric, sending a message to the mural's viewers as to what the architect and artists involved in constructing the building had in mind as the ultimate symbolism of the building and its art, including the so-called seal of Melchizedek.

48. Some might question our drawing a connection between eight-pointed stars and dual overlapping squares. Encyclopedias of symbolism do not always distinguish between these two symbols and their potential symbolic meanings. We have no way to tell what was intended at Ravenna, so we will treat here the eight-pointed star in case the artist intended his design to be perceived as such.

49. My interpretation of a star as a symbol for an angel is based on several early Christian infancy narratives that suggest that the "star" that the "wise men" followed was actually an angel. "There appeared to them an angel in the form of that star which had before been their guide in their journey; the light of which they followed till they returned into their own country." "The First Gospel of the Infancy of Jesus Christ," 3:3, in William Hone, comp., *The Lost Books of the Bible*, trans. Jeremiah Jones and William Wake (New York: Bell Publishing, 2004), 40; see also "The Arabic Gospel of the Infancy of the Saviour," 8:406, verse 7, in Alexander Roberts and James Donaldson, eds., *Ante-Nicene Fathers: The Writings of the Fathers down to A.D. 325* (Peabody, Massachusetts: Hendrickson Publishers, 1994), which reads basically the same: "There appeared to them an angel in the form of that star which had before guided them on their journey; and they went away, following the guidance of its light, until they arrived in their own country."

50. See Harold Bayley, *The Lost Language of Symbolism: An Inquiry into the Origin of Certain Letters, Words, Names, Fairy-Tales, Folklore, and Mythologies* (New York: Carol Publishing Group, 1993), 1:109–11 and fig. 299. Like Bayley, Nadia Julien suggests that stars "express the words 'god' and 'heaven.'" Julien, *Mammoth Dictionary of Symbols*, 401.

51. Bayley, *Lost Language of Symbolism*, 2:96.

52. James Hall, *Dictionary of Subjects and Symbols in Art*, rev. ed. (New York: Harper and Row, 1974), "star," 289.

53. See Brinkerhoff, *The Day Star*, 2:132, 138, 145, 160.

54. One text states that "the ancient seal of King Melchizedek [is] found in antiquity in many Christian contexts." Brinkerhoff, *Day Star*, 1:52. The reader should be aware that, while Christian churches occasionally display eight-pointed stars (✳) in their art and architecture, the overlain or interlocked squares (✦) that appear to form a type of eight-pointed star (being called by some Latter-day Saints the "seal of Melchizedek") are quite rare in Christianity—and are never referred to as the "seal of King Melchizedek," nor are they ever associated with Melchizedek. Thus, connections often made between stars in various churches and the design this article is examining are forced, as they are very different in appearance and meaning. See Brinkerhoff, *Day Star*, 2:131–81, particularly 157–58.

55. Julien, *Mammoth Dictionary of Symbols*, 404.

56. Friedrich Rest, *Our Christian Symbols* (New York: Pilgrim Press, 1987), 60.

57. Barber, *Celestial Symbols*, 30. Another penned this: "An eight-pointed star is symbolic of the way to heaven"—Jesus Christ being "the Way." Cook, *Restoration in Geometric Symbolism*, 40.

58. See Brinkerhoff, *Day Star*, 2:132, 138, 145, 160.

59. Little is known about Melchizedek's early life, just as little is known about Jesus's early life. Melchizedek manifested gifts of the Spirit in his youth (see JST, Genesis 14:26), as did Jesus (see JST, Luke 2:41–52). Melchizedek bore the title "King of Righteousness,"

which Jews associate with their Messiah, and Jesus was the "King of Righteousness" and the Jewish Messiah. Melchizedek is one of very few figures depicted in scripture as having offered the Lord's Supper (see Genesis 14:18–20; JST, Genesis 14:17–20). Jesus offered the Lord's Supper as the fulfillment of the Pascal feast (see Matthew 26:26–28). Scripture draws parallels between Christ and Melchizedek (see Hebrews 7:14–16; Psalm 110:4). Both were famous for preaching repentance to their hearers (see Alma 13:18; Matthew 4:17; D&C 18:22; 19:15–20), and for administering salvific ordinances for the remission of sins (see Alma 13:16; JST, Genesis 14:17; JST, John 4:1–3). The priesthood is called after Melchizedek's name (see D&C 107:3–4), whereas it used to be called after Christ's name, even the "Priesthood after the order of the Son of God" (D&C 107:3–4). Melchizedek is said to have reigned "under his father" (Alma 13:18), just as Christ reigns "under His Father" (see John 5:19). Melchizedek was king of Jerusalem (see Genesis 14:18; Psalm 76:2), and Jesus, by right, should have been king of the Jews and Jerusalem (see Matthew 1; 2; 5:35). Both were known for their miraculous powers (see JST, Genesis 14:26). Just as Melchizedek was called the "king of heaven" by his people (JST, Genesis 14:34–36), Jesus is the King of Heaven and is acknowledged as such by those who are his true followers (see 2 Nephi 10:14; Alma 5:50). Both were known as the "Prince of Peace" (JST, Genesis 14:33; Hebrews 7:1–2; Alma 13:18; Isaiah 9:6; 2 Nephi 19:6; see also John 14:27). Of Melchizedek it was said that no high priest was greater (see Alma 13:19), and Christ is the Great High Priest (see Hebrews 3:1; 9:11). Melchizedek is said to have overcome the world (see JST, Genesis 14:33–34), typifying that Jesus would overcome the world (see John 16:33).

60. Of the San Vitale mural, one expert wrote, "The scene on the right depicts Abel, Melchizedek, and Abraham on the three sides of an altar upon which they are offering their sacrificial gifts: Abel the lamb, Melchizedek the bread, and Abraham his son Isaac. The composition is unquestionably an adaptation of the two mosaics in San Vitale. . . . The three antitypes of Christian priesthood have been brought together in one scene." Von Simson, *Sacred Fortress*, 59.

61. See Cooper, *Illustrated Encyclopaedia*, 11.

62. Ibid., 111.

63. In San Vitale, next to the mural of Abel and Melchizedek is a mural of Abraham and Isaac. Thus, it appears that the artist of the Sant'Apollinare mural simply combined the two separate murals of San Vitale into one singular motif.

64. Because the Latin caption is incorrectly written, the best we can offer is a rough translation. But it appears to say, "Melchizedek illustrates, as Scripture demonstrates, of Christ, [unintelligible], similar to/more so than Abel." In other words, "As Scripture attests, Melchizedek is a type or symbol of Christ, as was Abel" or "even more so than was Abel." I express appreciation to Drs. Eric D. Huntsman and Jeffrey R. Chadwick for looking at this inscription and offering their interpretation of its meaning.

65. For example, Abel was a shepherd (see Moses 5:17) like Christ, the "Good Shepherd" (John 10:11). Abel offered an acceptable offering, which consisted of a male lamb, without blemish, of the first year (see Moses 5:20), just as Christ's offering was accepted by God and was typified by the slaying of a male lamb, without blemish, of the first year. Abel's offering involved the shedding of blood (see Moses 5:20), and Christ's

offering involved the shedding of his own blood (see Moroni 5:2). In making his offering, Abel was opposed by his brother (see Moses 5:21). So also, in making his offering and Atonement Jesus was opposed by his brother Lucifer (see Abraham 3:27–28). Scripture informs us that Abel walked in holiness before God (see Moses 5:26), as did Jesus (see 2 Nephi 31:7; 3 Nephi 11:7). As an example of how Isaac was a type for Christ, note that Isaac was the birthright son of a righteous father (see Genesis 21), as was Jesus (see D&C 93:21). Isaac's birth required a miracle (see Genesis 11:30; 17:15–22), as did Jesus' (see Luke 1:26–38). In his mid-thirties, Isaac was offered as a sacrifice by his father. Jesus was offered up by the Father apparently sometime during his thirty-fourth year of life. Genesis Rabbah 56:8 suggests that Isaac was somewhere between thirty-five and thirty-seven years of age; see also Victor P. Hamilton, *Handbook on the Pentateuch* (Grand Rapids, Michigan: Baker Book House, 1982), 108; Bruce R. McConkie, *The Mortal Messiah* (Salt Lake City: Deseret Book, 1979–81), 1:364. The attempted sacrifice of Isaac took place on Mount Moriah (see Genesis 22:2), the same location at which Jesus was crucified (see Mark 15:22). Isaac carried the wood to which he would be bound up to the top of Mount Moriah (see Genesis 22:6) just as Jesus carried the wooden cross on which he would be bound to the top of Golgotha's hill (see John 19:17). An angel ministered to both Isaac and Jesus during their hour of sacrifice (see Genesis 22:11; Luke 22:43). It is traditionally understood that Isaac willingly went to his place of sacrifice trusting his father's judgment and decision, just as Jesus willingly went to his place of sacrifice trusting in his Father's judgment and decision (see Abraham 3:27; Moses 4:2). A goat was provided for Isaac so that he wouldn't have to die (see Genesis 22:13), and Christ is the scapegoat for Isaac, and all mankind, having died in our stead (see Romans 5:8; Revelation 5:6). The ram, which died in Isaac's place, had the top of his head caught in some thorn bushes (see Genesis 22:13), and as part of his sacrifice, a crown of thorns had been placed on Christ's head (see Matthew 27:29). Regarding how Melchizedek is a type for Christ, see note 58 above.

66. Von Simson, *Sacred Fortress*, 25, 26; see also William J. Hamblin and David Rolph Seely, *Solomon's Temple: Myth and History* (London: Thames and Hudson, 2007), 53, 111.

67. See Von Simson, *Sacred Fortress*, 4, 15.

68. See ibid., 25. Because the emperor who commissioned the building of the church was trying to associate himself with Christ (and thus, by default, with Abel, Melchizedek, Isaac, and Abraham), these standard symbols of Christ are used in the Church's murals as symbols of the Emperor too; see Von Simson, *Sacred Fortress*, 31.

69. Cooper, *Illustrated Encyclopaedia*, 45.

70. See Tresidder, *Symbols and Their Meanings*, 146–47; see also Cooper, *Illustrated Encyclopaedia*, 45–46.

71. See Raymond E. Brown, *The Death of the Messiah* (New York: Doubleday, 1994), 2:945; Gerald G. O'Collins, "Crucifixion," in *The Anchor Bible Dictionary*, ed. David Noel Freedman (New York: Doubleday, 1992), 1:1206–8.

72. See Goodenough, *Jewish Symbols*, 2:198.

73. See ibid., 2:199; Nathan Ausubel, *The Jewish Book of Knowledge* (New York: Crown Publishers, 1964), "Magen David," 263; Morris N. Kertzer, *What Is a Jew?* rev. Lawrence A. Hoffman (New York: Macmillan, 1993), 174–75.

74. Ausubel, *Jewish Book of Knowledge*, "Magen David," 263.

75. Geoffrey Wigoder, ed., "Magen David," *Encyclopedia of Judaism* (Jerusalem: Jerusalem Publishing, 1989), 44; see also Cecil Roth, Geoffrey Wigoder, and Fred Skolnik, eds., "Magen David," *Encyclopaedia Judaica* (Jerusalem: Keter Publishing, 2007), 11:688, 697.

76. Roth, Wigoder, and Skolnik, eds., *Encyclopaedia Judaica*, "Magen David," 11:687.

77. As we noted above, the so-called seal may not actually be two overlapping squares or an eight-sided star. It may only be eight gammas arranged in a circular pattern.

78. Indeed, after looking at literally dozens of books on symbolism, including some of encyclopedic length, I could find only one text that presented this exact design and then offered a specific definition of its meaning. Though the text did not give a name to the design, nor did it indicate whether it was intended to be viewed as an eight-pointed star, two interlocked squares, a rosette, or a series of gammas arranged in a circle, it did offer the following definition: "Material generation through the interaction of two opposing principles." Cirlot, *Dictionary of Symbols*, 122. What does this definition mean? In less than clear language, it appears to be suggesting that the symbol represents reproduction or the generating of some temporal thing through the interaction of two opposites. But the symbol in the singular definition available to researchers is not connected to Melchizedek, to priesthood authority or power, or to anything innately religious.

79. Keith Critchlow, *Islamic Patterns: An Analytical and Cosmological Approach* (London: Thames and Hudson, 1976), 29, diagrams C and F; see also 55, 151, 192; Andreas Andreopoulos, *Metamorphosis: The Transfiguration in Byzantine Theology and Iconography* (New York: St. Vladimir's Seminary Press, 2005), 239.

80. One of my colleagues pointed out that "the symbol is so frequent in Islam that it is even represented in Microsoft Word's symbol cache for Arabic!" Jeffrey R. Chadwick, personal correspondence with author, October 21, 2009.

81. See Goodenough, *Jewish Symbols*, 2:198; see also vol. 3, fig. 547.

82. M. H. Port, ed., *The Houses of Parliament* (London: Yale University Press, 1976), 126, fig. 79.

83. Andreopoulos, *Metamorphosis*, 85.

84. Ibid., 228, 230. Other divine or angelic beings also have their glory depicted through the use of the two interlocked squares. See, for example, Yaroslav School, *John the Theologian, ca. 1820*, in S. Kent Brown, Richard Neitzel Holzapfel, and Dawn C. Pheysey, *Beholding Salvation: The Life of Christ in Word and Image* (Salt Lake City: Deseret Book, 2006), 44, fig. 43.

85. These kinds of wealth are gifts such as prosperity, good health, knowledge, strength, posterity, and power.

86. I wish the reader to be aware that I do not accuse the temple's architect (Bill Lewis), Professor Val Brinkerhoff, or illustrator Michael Lyon of creating the folklore of the "seal of Melchizedek" that I hear from various members of the Church at least once a month. Rather, lay (and I believe, well-intending) members have glommed onto bits of truth and

popularly told sensationalized stories and combined these into a tale beyond anything Nibley could have imagined—a tale which circulates as well as any faith-promoting rumor since the dawning of the Restoration.

87.   While I once again acknowledge that Nibley's inconsistent comments on this issue have added to this, I remind the reader that the vast majority of Latter-day Saints remain unaware of his handful of personal comments to various people. Lyon's caption in Nibley's book has been a major catalyst in the advancement of this tradition. On a related note, President Boyd K. Packer said, "Instruction vital to our salvation is not hidden in an obscure verse or phrase in the scriptures. To the contrary, essential truths are repeated over and over again." *Let Not Your Heart Be Troubled* (Salt Lake City: Bookcraft, 1991), 286. Obviously, the seal of Melchizedek is not essential to our salvation. Nor is it a symbol discussed or taught publicly by the presiding Brethren, employed in the salvific ordinances of the temple, or found in the holy scriptures.

88.   As one who feels it is appropriate to create our own modern symbols, Val Brinkerhoff wrote, "We as Latter-day Saints *can* take a motif and apply our own meaning to it. . . . If we want this historic motif to represent the Melchizedek Priesthood in the late 1980s or now (no matter what it may have represented for others), then so be it." Personal correspondence, July 13, 2010; emphasis in original.

89.   It is worth noting that while Brinkerhoff is an advocate of calling the design in question the "seal of Melchizedek," he does rightfully see this symbol as strongly connected to, and representative of, Christ and his saving acts and ordinances. He is less dogmatic than some and offers several interpretations of the design, though the most common interpretation found in his writings being the "seal" explanation. Consequently, while he and I disagree on the symbol's connection to Melchizedek, we are in agreement on the Christocentric nature of the symbol. See Brinkerhoff, *Day Star*, 2:131–81, specifically 2:132, 138, 145, 160.

Chapter 7

CLOTHED IN HOLY GARMENTS

A STUDY OF THE APPAREL OF THE TEMPLE OFFICIANTS OF ANCIENT ISRAEL[1]

Alonzo L. Gaskill

There are a variety of approaches to holy writ.[2] Some feel the most valid methodological approach is exegetical—seeking to discover what the authors meant when they originally penned the words many centuries ago.[3] Some, on the other hand, feel that an apologetic approach is most correct—reading scripture in an effort to find "evidences" for one's personal denominational persuasion. Certain students of scripture approach God's word as literature—looking not for its doctrinal or theological teachings, but for its beauty in structure or language. And there are, of course, a number of individuals who read scripture for its moral teachings—seeking to draw an application-oriented homily from what they read.

Perhaps it is no surprise that subscribers to these various schools of thought do not always agree with each other on which approaches are valid and which are not. Those in the exegetical camp, for example, sometimes feel that the homiletic approach "does violence to scripture," as they say, by offering applications that were never intended by the original author. Those in the homily camp, on the other hand, sometimes argue that to not apply scripture to one's personal situation is to miss the entire point of God's word. The dispute, which is more heated than many lay Christians realize, brings to mind the words of the Prophet Joseph: "Who of all these parties are right; or, are they all wrong together? If any one of them be right, which is it, and how shall I know

it?" (Joseph Smith—History 1:10). Regardless of which camp the reader falls into, what *is* certain is that many Christians throughout the centuries have felt comfortable with a homiletic approach to scripture. Such an approach was very common in the early post-New Testament church, and it has been a popular approach for many modern commentators—including a fair number of Latter-day Saint authors.[4]

Among those who read scripture for its homiletic value, it has long been noted that the garments of the Aaronic high priest[5] were, through their symbolic design, a teaching device given by divine revelation to the prophet Moses. Many Christian commentators suggest that the articles of apparel associated with this priestly office were designed as a type or foreshadowing of Jesus Christ.[6] The author of the book of Hebrews goes so far as to call Christ the "great high priest" (Hebrews 4:14). Thus one commentator noted that "Aaron, as a High Priest, was a breathing statue—a type—of Christ."[7] Another suggested, "The ways in which Aaron typified Christ are numerous and varied. In many respects he is to be considered the most illustrative type of the spiritual work of Christ to be found in the entire Old Testament."[8] If this is the case, the symbolism associated with the priestly officiant's dress should have significance for followers of Jesus Christ who, in baptism, "put on Christ" (Galatians 3:27), thereby becoming "the body of Christ, and members individually" (1 Corinthians 12:27, New King James Version). "When we *put on* Jesus Christ we accept him and his Atonement, and we become like him."[9] Consequently, the robes of the Aaronic high priest have the potential to teach us much about Christ and his attributes. They can also teach us about the people who make up Christ's Church, and the ideal attributes of faithful followers of the Savior. One expert on the garments of the ancient temple has noted, "As the High Priest was a type of the Great High Priest, Jesus, so the garments of the High Priest were typical of the character of Jesus Christ. Likewise, as the sons of the High Priest were priests and as we who are the sons of God are called to be priests, even so the dress of the priests typifies the character of the believers."[10] Elsewhere we read that the officiant "represented all Israel when he ministered in the tabernacle."[11] Accordingly, in the symbolic clothing of the temple high priest, we may draw a message about the nature and attributes of the Messiah and also of the characteristics each sincere follower of Christ should seek to develop if he or she seeks for an eternal inheritance in God's kingdom.[12]

Naturally, this understanding of the priestly garments implies a reading of scripture done through the lens of a "believer"—one who acknowledges Jesus Christ as the promised Messiah, of whom *all things*, including the Old Testament, testify (see Moses 6:63). This being the case, it is expected that those who do not share this belief are prone to arrive at different conclusions. Reading the scriptures through a Latter-day Saint lens, or even through a general Christian lens, will lead one to interpret symbols differently than would be the case otherwise. For this reason, a strictly exegetical analysis is unlikely to produce the same Christocentric results. Instead, we may hope to find Christ in the garments of the ancient high priests through a more homiletic approach.[13] From a traditional Latter-day Saint perspective, however, we can assume that those ancient Israelites who were enlightened by the Holy Ghost understood the ultimate messianic types embedded in the garments worn by the High Priest.[14] After all, the didactic symbols of which God makes abundant use are meant to open our eyes to greater truths—often, in fact, to the *greatest* truths. Thus, as we examine the clothing of the ancient temple's high priest, Latter-day Saints (who engage in the rites of modern-day temples) should deeply contemplate the meaning of their *own* priestly clothing—and what attributes those sacred symbols invite *them* to develop in their personal lives.

THE LINEN COAT
(LEVITICUS 8:7; EXODUS 28:4, 39; 39:27)

The first item that was placed upon the high priest, immediately after washing (see Leviticus 8:6–7), was the linen coat. In Exodus 28:39 we read, "And thou shalt embroider the coat of fine linen." The Hebrew of this verse may also be rendered, "And thou shalt weave a shirt-like undergarment of fine white cloth."[15] Josephus suggested that (according to the understanding of those in the first century) the coat or undershirt was "made of fine flax doubled" and that the "vestment reaches down to the feet, and sits close to the body."[16] Another source submits that this undershirt's sleeves reached "to the wrists."[17] Thus, this linen coat appears to have covered the entirety of the high priest's body.

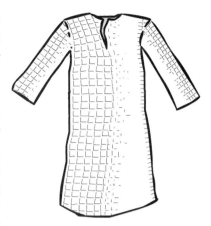

Not only was this undergarment made of the finest of materials, but the making of it apparently required significant effort. Indeed, the Hebrew root word used for "embroidered" implies something akin to our modern damask[18] (a lustrous fabric made with flat patterns in a satin weave). Thus, the garment is believed to have been skillfully woven so as to have a pattern within the fabric.[19] The embroidery may have been a "checkered" pattern[20] or one that utilized a design that looked like the Greek letter gamma (Γ) or a square (L).[21]

The symbols contained in this single article of clothing are manifold. For example, the material of its construction, being pure white, is often seen as "an emblem of moral purity."[22] The ultimate referent of this symbol is Jesus Christ, who is our exemplar in moral purity and perfection.[23] Thus on Yom Kippur (the Day of Atonement), the priest wore the linen coat, which (in the minds of many Christians) indicated that he was officiating as a type of Christ (see Leviticus 16). It is important that the linen coat was placed upon the high priest as the very first article of clothing, since this demonstrates that moral purity is foundational. Likewise, this sacred undergarment "was a full-length garment covering the entire body," which suggests to Christian commentators that Christ's salvation is "for the whole man; body, soul and spirit."[24] True moral purity requires totality, nothing lacking.

The embroidery pattern also contains important symbolic implications for the wearer and the viewer. One commentator notes that from a distance the linen coat may have appeared plain. However, "upon a closer examination there was skill and beauty attached to the make up [*sic*] of the fabric."[25] If this is the case, the implications this has for Jesus Christ are significant.

> To the many who take a casual glance at the "Jesus of Nazareth"
> and the "Man of Galilee" they see an ordinary yet good man, but study

that character, look into that life, note those works, and meditate upon His words. Here is no ordinary person, even though he is found in fashion as a man. There is a Divine pattern most intrinsically worked into the human frame which reveals Him to be the Son of God.[26]

Thus, the garment can remind us that something more than a casual look at the sacred is required if we wish to see and recognize the divine imprint.[27] This is as applicable to the doctrines of Christ as it is to Christ the man.

Beyond its reference to the Messiah, this linen coat may also allegorically suggest that the Church,[28] as a community of Christ's followers, must be completely morally pure.[29] That moral purity can only be obtained *through* Christ, whom the garment is said to represent. The undershirt, therefore, can be seen as an invitation to the Church to "awake" and "put on thy strength, O Zion; put on thy beautiful garments, O Jerusalem" (Isaiah 52:1). Additionally, the symbolism suggests that the Church of Christ is, like the linen coat, a work of fine craftsmanship, designed by heavenly hands and often referred to as a "marvelous work."[30] The Church, like its namesake (Christ), often looks plain upon a cursory glance. However, when sincerely and closely examined, the divine miracles and handiwork of God manifested in bringing it forth are apparent.

THE BREECHES
(LEVITICUS 6:8–10; EXODUS 28:42–43)

While the Leviticus passage doesn't specifically mention it, Baruch Levine points out that "it is to be assumed that at the beginning of the robing the priests were wearing their linen breeches,"[31] which reached to the knees. These breeches, or underpants, were made of linen, which is *not* a product of animals (which are subject to death and corruption). Thus, they become a fitting symbol of both incorruptibility and immortality.[32] From the perspective of a Christocentric reading of the passage, the implication is that Christ is both incorruptible and also

immortal. By extension, the breeches can suggest to the observer that (in this increasingly immoral world) Christ's followers should not allow their lives to become corrupted. Significantly, the fact that these breeches cover the loins—in other words, the reproductive area—is itself a potential symbol that the wearer needs to control his appetites and passions, lest defilement and corruption ensue. As the faithful followers of Christ reject all that corrupts, they have reason to hope that through Christ they shall also obtain immortality and "eternal lives" (D&C 132:24, 55).

THE GIRDLE
(LEVITICUS 8:7)

The Aaronic high priest donned two separate girdles as part of his holy clothing: "one of which was fastened over the coat [or undershirt] and was assumed [or donned] by the priests generally; the other was emphatically *the* curious, or embroidered, 'girdle of the ephod,' and belonged to the robes of the High Priest alone."[33] Our focus here will be on the former of these—that which was common to high priest and priest alike.

According to Josephus, this inner girdle (over which other vestments were worn) was rather long: it was wrapped twice around the high priest and yet still reached to the ankles.[34] It was apparently worn on top of the coat (undershirt) and breeches (underpants), but beneath the other garb of the priest. The symbols associated with the girdle buttress the symbols of the linen coat beautifully.

During certain periods in the ancient Near East, a girdle represented chastity and fidelity, including fidelity to covenants.[35] The fact that this girdle was used to bind up the loins suggests a likely origin of its symbolism. It potentially reminded the wearer of those virtues which must

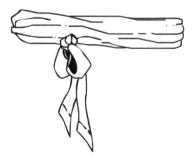

be tightly bound to the righteous individual—virtues present in the character of Israel's God and future Messiah. The fact that the girdle bound the coat and breeches close to the wearer's body was important, for, as one commentator suggested, "This is nearly always a symbol of service, the girded loins denoting readiness for action. This must always be the attitude of the priest and it is certainly true of Christ."[36] By implication, this hidden girdle can remind the Church of its need to be closely tied to the virtues of Christ and to ever be willing and ready to serve. This manifests the reality of the Christian virtues that the girdle symbolizes. The Lord's words to the Saints in section 4 of the Doctrine and Covenants exemplify the implied meaning of the under-girdle. Saints must develop qualities such as "faith, virtue, knowledge, temperance, patience, brotherly kindness, godliness, charity, humility, diligence" (D&C 4:6). And in the spirit of those virtues, they must diligently attend to the needs of God's children: "O ye that embark in the service of God, see that ye serve him with all your heart, might, mind and strength, that ye may stand blameless before God at the last day" (D&C 4:2).

THE ROBE OF THE EPHOD
(LEVITICUS 8:7; EXODUS 28:4)

The Lord informed Moses that this distinctive robe was to be made "all of blue" (Exodus 28:31)[37] and that it would reach past the ephod to the knee.[38] Remarkably, the robe of the ephod was constructed out of a

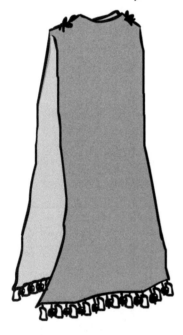 single sheet of material; having no seams, only a hole for the head and arms. The neck hole was reinforced to insure "that it be not rent" (Exodus 28:32). Indeed, the garment was "made in such a way that it was not possible for man to rend it."[39] At the bottom of the robe, stitched onto the fringe, were a series of alternating gold bells and cloth pomegranates.[40] According to Josephus, the practical function associated with these bells was to inform the priests and those within the temple precinct as to when the high priest was approaching the veil. It was hoped that upon hearing this sound "the people might have notice of it, and might fall to their own prayers at the time of incense [at the veil]."[41] Concerning the pomegranates, it is quite probable that their pattern was chosen due to their association with the Promised Land (see Deuteronomy 8:7–8; Numbers 13:23), which is a symbol of the celestial city. However, as will be demonstrated, their symbolic depth goes beyond that.

As a teaching device, a number of components of the robe of the ephod seem significant. First of all, the blue color of the garment is often seen as representative of the heavens—the abode of God. This color can symbolize the spiritual or celestial nature of a thing.[42] Thus Joseph Fielding McConkie associates the robe with Christ: "This [robe of the ephod] appears to have been a reference to the heavenly origin, character, and ministry of Christ, the great high priest."[43] Another author suggests that if a person in the Bible was adorned in blue, it indicated that he or she was divinely sanctioned.[44] For members of the Lord's Church, then, the robe can symbolize the divine origin of the Church and the requirement that they maintain the Lord's sanction through striving to be a Zion people.

The fact that the garment was donned by the high priest *after* the linen coat has been seen as an indication that divine sanction comes only to those who have purified their lives and taken virtue to the entirety of their beings, confirming such virtue through their actions.

Additionally, the seamless design of the robe serves as a reminder that Christ's divinity has no beginning and no end. The inability to tear the robe, its having the strength of armor, can signify his divine call as God's Only Begotten.

> How many would strip Jesus our Great High Priest, of His Divinity? But they could not and cannot. Every time man inflicted a doubt, saying: "*If* Thou be the Son of God" God was there to prove that He was. The Devil said: "*If* Thou be the Son of God" in Judea's wilderness, but he was vanquished with the "It is written." While Christ was on the Cross the people said, "Let Him save Himself *if* He be Christ the chosen of God" (Luke xxiii. 35). The soldiers said: "*If* Thou be the king of the Jews save Thyself" (Luke xxiii. 37). One of the malefactors joined the cry of doubt, saying: "*If* Thou be Christ, save Thyself and us" (Luke xxiii. 39) But to all these "ifs" came the challenge of the resurrection on the third day. Man said "Is not this the carpenter's son?" (Matt. xiii. 55). God said: "This is My Beloved Son in Whom I am well pleased" (Matt. iii. 17).[45]

Men were free to reject Jesus's chosen and divine status, but their rejection could not change the fact that he was heavenly in his origin, authorization, and nature. For the Church, the fact that the robe was seamless suggests that they too must be seamless (one), for "if ye are not one ye are not mine" (D&C 38:27). If they who make up his Church seek that unity, they will be covered (protected) by Christ, just as the high priest was covered by the garment. The indestructibility of the robe can symbolize the fact that the Church in its righteousness shall not be broken up by the cunning or strength of the natural man. The Lord brought to pass "the establishment of the kingdom of God in the latter days, never again to be destroyed nor given to other people" (D&C 138:44). The seamless garment reminds us of the necessity of seeking full obedience to God's commands, so that apostasy—individual or collective—may never breach the protective parameters that we call "the Church."

The pomegranates and golden bells along the bottom of the robe are equally rich in symbolism. Among other things, the pomegranate is known for its multiplicity of seeds. This seems to represent well both Christ's role as father of all who are reborn through him and also the laws and ordinances of his gospel—each of which typify the Master. The golden bells, on the other hand, have been seen as a symbol of divine protection.[46] Thus, one commentator states, "This robe is a type of that which preserves from death."[47] Owing to the fact that the sounding of these bells likely represented the "sounding forth" of the word of God, it is no wonder that they symbolize divine protection.[48] Christ, who sounded forth the word of God boldly and upon whose heart God's word was inscribed perfectly, was granted protection until his mission was complete. He offers that same protection to those who are faithful to their covenants and callings—to those who heed his warning and the warning of his prophets.

THE EPHOD
(LEVITICUS 8:7; EXODUS 28:4, 6–7)

To date, there continues to be some debate within the scholarly community as to what exactly the ephod was. Thus the term remains untranslated in the King James Version. Most scholars maintain that it was an apron of unsurpassable beauty, having gold woven into it (see Exodus 39:3)[49] and being very colorful in its appearance. Matthew B. Brown speculates that the ephod may have been decorated with "figures" or symbols.[50] Regardless, we know that it

was the outermost garment upon which the onyx shoulder stones and the breast piece of judgment were fastened. It was the vestment upon which some of the most emblematic and important features of the high priest's dress were to be secured. And it was the location in which the Urim and Thummim was stored.

The symbolism in this particular garment is rich and extensive. First, upon the shoulder-straps of the ephod were found two stones—one on each shoulder. Inscribed on these were the names of the twelve tribes of Israel (six on either stone). By implication, the Messiah bears the burdens of covenant Israel, as do His authorized servants. For the Church, on the other hand, this symbol can be seen as an invitation to keep the baptismal covenant to "bear one another's burdens, that they may be light" (Mosiah 18:8). Christ, the high priest, and every member of the Church must each shoulder the burdens (spiritual and otherwise) of God's children. That is what followers of the Messiah are called to do.

Beyond the aforementioned symbolism, aprons also served anciently as symbols for "priesthood"[51] and "work."[52] For Christians, the ephod signified Jesus's diligence in moving forward the will and work of the Father, and it likely reminded the high priest of the ancient temple that he too was called to do the work of the Lord in—a work that required priesthood power. For the Latter-day Saints, the ephod may suggest one of the major differences between them and other Christian denominations: restored priesthood keys and a divine call to build up the latter-day kingdom before the return of the Son of God.

Lastly, the coloration on the ephod would have been deeply important. Exodus 28:6 commands, "Make the ephod of gold, of blue, and of purple, of scarlet." As previously pointed out, blue (being the color of the sky) typically represents the heavens. Scarlet (or red) would have commonly represented the earth. As one text on the clothing of the high priest states, red "is the colour of the earth. Blue and red are therefore opposites. The name Adam comes from a root word 'Adham' which means 'red earth', and from this he was made." This same source notes that purple is "an intermediary colour to blend them [blue and red]."[53] Thus, the ephod can imply that Christ was made in the likeness of man (red) that he might bring us back to the likeness of God (blue). By taking upon himself flesh and blood, Jesus was equipped to meet our every need and also to set the perfect example for us to follow. He was a combination (purple) of the divine (blue) and the human (red)—as are each of us, being the literal "offspring of God" (Acts 17:29). Finally, that thread of gold, woven into the ephod, can remind us of his eternal and celestial nature: "[Gold] is not affected by exposure to the air and it will not deteriorate if buried for thousands of years. Acid will not destroy it, and fire will not burn it; from these it only comes out purified."[54] How perfectly this typifies Christ. And how significant is the invitation it offers to each of us to strive for life eternal though Christ's blood and through the faithful observance of his words.

THE CURIOUS GIRDLE OF THE EPHOD (LEVITICUS 8:7; EXODUS 28:5–8)

As with the ephod, information concerning the pattern and appearance of the "curious girdle" is limited. Since this vestment was directly associated with the ephod, it was only worn by the high priest. Unlike the inner girdle spoken of previously, the curious girdle would have resembled the pattern of the ephod in fabric and embroidery. One source notes, "The skillfully woven band [known as the curious girdle] seems to have been a girdle with which to fasten the ephod close about the waist (Lev. 8:7). It was permanently attached to the ephod and made of the same material."[55] As discussed above, a girdle represents fidelity or faithfulness to covenants as well as preparation for action.

Regarding the symbolism, the fact that the curious girdle (and the ephod which it bound) was worn *only* by the high priest indicates that certain functions and responsibilities were his alone to perform.[56] In obvious ways, this seems to typify both Christ and the presiding high priest of the Church today (the latter-day Prophet). For members of Christ's Church, this symbol stands as a reminder that, while other Christians may serve in significant ways to spread the message of "Jesus Christ, and him crucified" (1 Corinthians 2:2), Latter-day Saints have a mission and ministry that is unique to them. Theirs is a call that cannot be performed by any other.

THE BREASTPLATE OF JUDGMENT AND THE URIM AND THUMMIM (LEVITICUS 8:8; EXODUS 28:4, 15–30)

The breastplate (or "breastpiece") of judgment was made from the same materials and in the same manner as the ephod. It was made, like the ephod, out of one continuous piece of fabric.[57] The fabric was folded in half "upward to form a sort of pouch."[58] It was a span in length and width (about 9 x 9 inches), thus forming a perfect square.[59] Upon the front of the breastplate were twelve stones, arranged in four rows of three, each stone being different from the others. Every stone was engraved with the name of one of the tribes of Israel. The breastplate was secured over the chest of the high priest by gold chains. The function of the breastplate of judgment was to serve as a pouch that held the Urim and Thummim—a device through which seers and prophets received revelation on behalf of covenant Israel. The book of Exodus records, "And thou shalt put in the breastplate of judgment the Urim and Thummim; and they shall be upon Aaron's heart, when he goeth before the Lord" (Exodus 28:30). According to the Jewish sage, Nachmanides, Moses didn't make the Urim and Thummim—nor did anyone in Israel. It was given to Moses by God as a divine instrument of knowing and receiving.[60]

The Christocentric symbolism associated with the breastplate of judgment and with the Urim and the Thummim is rich and diverse. To begin, the shape and the size of the breastplate are of significance. We are informed that the shape was a perfect square, 9 x 9 inches. In the description of the tabernacle, the square is repeatedly present: we see it in the brazen altar (Exodus 38:1), the golden altar (Exodus 37:25), and the breastplate (Exodus 39:9). Each was required by God to be geometrically square—a symbol of balance, solidity, and equality. The number four typically symbolizes geographic completeness or totality.[61] In other words, if the number four is associated with an event or thing, the indication is that it will affect the entire earth and all its inhabitants. The breastplate over the heart of the high priest seems, therefore, to suggest Christ's love and awareness for *each* of God's children. The foursquare breastplate suggests that, through the Atonement of Christ, the entirety of the house of Israel shall be bound to Christ's heart just as the breastplate is bound to the heart of the priest. Significantly, unlike the twelve names written upon two stones on the shoulders of the High Priest, on the breastplate "each name is now on a separate stone so every individual believer in Him who has made the all-covering atonement has a special place in that all-prevailing intercession which is continually going on at the throne of grace."[62]

Since the Urim and Thummim within the pouch was a revelatory device, its placement in the squared pouch can suggest Christ's desire to reveal himself to all of God's children. It potentially implies that Christ's word will eventually fill the earth.

Interestingly, the various types of stones fastened into the breastplate itself may also be significant.[63] The stones in the breastplate are identical with the precious or semi-precious stones that, according to Ezekiel 28:13, were to be found in Eden, "the garden of God."[64] This reference to the original garden of God could have served as a reminder to the high priest that his work as mediator was to seek to return man to his spiritual station "in the Garden of Eden, when man was free from all sin."[65] Accordingly, when Christ performs his intercessory work, it is to bring us back into the state that we were in at Eden—a state of innocence wherein we were permitted to dwell in the presence of the Lord.

Finally, two facts about the Urim and Thummim—that it was likely not of earthly make and that it was also concealed—can teach us two significant truths about Christ. First, his origins are not of this earth. Matthew records the query of the Jews:

> And when he was come into his own country, he taught them in their synagogue, insomuch that they were astonished, and said, Whence hath this man this wisdom, and these mighty works?
>
> Is not this the carpenter's son? is not his mother called Mary? and his brethren, James, and Joses, and Simon, and Judas?
>
> And his sisters, are they not all with us? Whence then hath this man all these things? (Matthew 13:54–56)

Jesus was the Son of God—not the son of a lowly carpenter. Yet, as Isaiah reminds us, "He hath no form nor comeliness; and . . . there is no beauty that we should desire him" (Isaiah 53:2). His divinity truly is hidden from most.

In regards to the Church of Christ and how each of these symbols applies, note the following. Just as Christ's message and mission is to all the world, Latter-day Saints have a vocation to bless, serve, and convert the world to Christ and His ways. A requisite part of fulfilling that mission is having a love for our fellow men and a spirit of revelation that will guide us in teaching and ministering to individuals. Both of those necessary qualities are gifts of the Spirit.[66] Like the Urim and Thummim (with its individual names) over the heart of the high priest, we too must seek revelation and a spirit of love and compassion if we, as the bride of Christ, will be of use to our Groom in this most sacred work. And like the stones with individual names, we are reminded through the symbolism that Christ knows us intimately; he knows our needs and our gifts. He can aid us in all that we seek to do in his name, and on his behalf. Finally, like the Urim and Thummim, this work is of God, not of man. Yet, it is as a bed of gold concealed. It is our responsibility to uncover it and bring it to the entire world.

THE MITER AND THE HOLY CROWN
(LEVITICUS 8:9; EXODUS 28:4, 39–40; 39:30–31)

The miter (or headdress) of the high priest was made of linen. It was "of the distinctive design worn by royalty."[67] Upon the front of the miter was fastened the "Holy Crown" which consisted of a golden plate that bore the inscription "HOLINESS TO THE LORD" (Exodus 28:36). Additionally, the holy crown was secured to the miter with "a blue lace" ribbon (Exodus 28:37).

Christ-centered symbolism can be found in the miter. For example, one commentator notes, "The head is that which denotes authority. It is the head that controls the whole of the body. Christ as the Head of the Church controls that Church."[68] Since linen is a "symbol of holiness and righteousness,"[69] it seems clear that "the linen of the miter speaks

of the righteousness of the Lord."[70] The fact that it was the attire of royalty suggests he is the King of Kings (Revelation 17:14). Additionally, the blue ribbon attaching the holy crown to the miter can point to the reality that Christ's mind is that of the Father. He knows the Father's will, and all that he says and does is an attempt to bring that will to pass.

For the priest and the parishioner, the miter is a potential reminder of what God has promised each of us: that we might become "kings and priests unto God" (Revelation 1:6).[71] It also informs us as to how this is to be done: we must develop the mind of God. As Elder Bruce R. McConkie noted, "[when we] walk in the light as he is in the light . . . [we] thereby have his mind. [We then] think what he thinks, know what he knows, say what he would say, and do what he would do . . . all by revelation from the Spirit."[72] Though only the high priest was commanded to wear such an inscription, certainly what it represented is expected of all of God's servants. Without personal worthiness, all we do in the temple or in the Church is but a mere form and a mockery of holiness! The high priest represented the people before God. Thus, God's call to him to be holy before the Lord was, by application, a call to all in Israel to be holy before the Lord and to consecrate their hearts and minds to Jehovah. That declaration of "holiness to the Lord" was to influence their labors, their utterances, their thoughts and desires, and the paths they pursued—not just in the temple but also in their daily walk.[73] Thus, symbolically speaking, all who donned the cap of the priest were really donning a commitment to live in holiness *before* the Lord because they had dedicated their lives *to* the Lord.[74] The placement of the plate on the forehead can remind us of the fact that "it is the head that controls the whole of the body."[75] "For as he thinketh . . . so is he" (Proverbs 23:7).

CONCLUSION

What I have offered above is but a homily—an application of ancient Jewish symbols seen through Christian lenses. But, lest it be assumed that I have looked "beyond the mark" (Jacob 4:14), I remind the reader of the words of Nephi, who wrote, "Behold . . . *all things* which have been given of God from the beginning of the world, unto man, are the typifying of [Christ]" (2 Nephi 11:4, emphasis added). "The literary evidence of that," Elder Jeffrey R. Holland pointed out, "is seen throughout the holy scriptures."[76] Jacob recorded that the scriptures "truly testify of Christ" (Jacob 7:11). In the book of Moses, the Lord stated, "And behold, all things have their likeness, and all things are created and made to bear record of me, both things which are temporal, and things which are spiritual; things which are in the heavens above, and things which are on the earth, and things which are in the earth, and things which are under the earth, both above and beneath: all things bear record of me" (Moses 6:63). Clearly, the scriptures are replete with testaments of Jesus's Messianic call and divine nature. As I have pointed out above, much of Christianity acknowledges that the sacred clothing of the high priest can serve as a symbol of the consecrated attributes of the Holy Messiah.

As the priest of the temple served to mediate Israel's relationship with God, he too functioned as a type for the Redeemer. In donning the sacred garments, he served well as a representation of Jesus's role on behalf of the covenant people.

Finally, the attire of the high priest has much it can teach those who trust in Christ for their salvation. Peter reminded us that, in all things, Jesus is our exemplar (1 Peter 2:21). As the clothing of the high priest has the ability to teach us what the Savior is like, it also has the potential to teach us what we must become if we wish to inherit eternal life in God's presence. One commentator suggested that the function of the priestly garments "was to remind the Israelites that a powerful, holy and just God was indeed present with them in so far as the wearer of the garments was held to be linked to Him."[77] As covenant Israel continues seeking to develop the attributes of the Great High Priest, they have reason to trust in his promises. The Apostle Paul reminded us, "Wherefore the law was our schoolmaster to bring us unto Christ, that we might be justified by faith. But after that faith is come, we are no longer under a schoolmaster. . . . For as many of you as have been baptized into Christ have put on Christ" (Galatians 3:24–25, 27). For Christians, this is the invitation of the garments of the high priest: to "put on Christ"!

NOTES

1.   A version of this article was originally published under the title "Clothed in Holy Garments: The Apparel of the Temple Officiants of Ancient Israel," in David R. Seely, Jeffrey R. Chadwick, and Matthew J. Grey, eds., *Ascending the Mountain of the Lord: Temple, Praise, and Worship in the Old Testament* (Provo, Utah: Religious Studies Center, BYU, 2013), 85–104. Republished here by permission.

2.   See William W. Klein, Craig L. Blomberg, and Robert L. Hubbard Jr., *Introduction to Biblical Interpretation* (Dallas: Word Publishing, 1993).

3.   An exegetical approach typically includes word-studies—trying to find the various shades of meaning behind the original Greek or Hebrew words.

4.   Though this chapter is a homily, I am not arguing generally for or against a homiletic approach either to scripture or to the clothing of the high priest. What this Chapter seeks to do is to report the Christocentric reading of these things by various interpreters and to suggest the implications of those readings for practicing Christians today.

5.   The term Aaronic high priest in this chapter will refer to the high priests of the Mosaic dispensation, primarily the direct firstborn male descendants of Aaron. See Richard Neitzel Holzapfel and David Rolph Seely, *My Father's House: Temple Worship and Symbolism in the New Testament* (Salt Lake City: Bookcraft, 1994), 59. However, the term should not imply that each held only the Aaronic Priesthood. We know, for

example, that Aaron and his sons held the Melchizedek Priesthood. See John A. Widtsoe, *Priesthood and Church Government in the Church of Jesus Christ of Latter-day Saints* (Salt Lake City: Deseret Book, 1961), 14; Bruce R. McConkie, *The Promised Messiah: The First Coming of Christ* (Salt Lake City: Deseret Book, 1981), 411.

6.   Along with the examples quoted directly within this chapter, see also B. Maureen Gaglardi, *The Path of the Just: The Garments of the High Priest* (Dubuque, Iowa: Kendall/Hunt, 1971), 5: "There are, I suppose, numerous and undoubtedly profound volumes obtainable on the ministry and vestments of the High Priest. The great High Priestly office of Christ is the supreme lesson taught us by this type." Likewise, see Paul F. Kiene, *The Tabernacle of God in the Wilderness of Sinai*, trans. John S. Crandall (Grand Rapids, Michigan: Zondervan, 1977), 164: "The details of the high priest's garments speak of the Lord Jesus in His glory. They help us the better to recognize His incomparable qualities and the worth of His person, in order that we will love and honor our Lord more." Also, Stephen F. Olford, *The Tabernacle: Camping with God*, 2nd ed. (Grand Rapids, Michigan: Kregel, 2004), 123: "Each part of [Aaron's] attire speaks eloquently of the glories, virtues, and excellencies of our Great High Priest, the Lord Jesus Christ."

7.   David Fenton Jarman, *The High Priest's Dress; Or, Christ Arrayed in Aaron's Robes* (London: W. F. Crofts, 1850), ix.

8.   Kenneth E. Trent, *Types of Christ in the Old Testament: A Conservative Approach to Old Testament Typology* (New York: Exposition Press, 1960), 52. See also Ada R. Habershon, *Study of the Types* (Grand Rapids, Michigan: Kregel, 1974), 183.

9.   Donald W. Parry and Jay A. Parry, *Symbols and Shadows: Unlocking a Deeper Understanding of the Atonement* (Salt Lake City: Deseret Book, 2009), 27; emphasis in original.

10.   C. W. Slemming, *These Are the Garments: A Study of the Garments of the High Priest of Israel* (London: Marshall, Morgan & Scott, 1945), 22.

11.   Walter C. Kaiser Jr., "Exodus," in *The Expositor's Bible Commentary*, ed. Frank E. Gaebelein (Grand Rapids, Michigan: Zondervan, 1976–92), 2:466.

12.   In this chapter, we will be examining the garments in the order in which they are described in Leviticus 8:7–9, while also drawing upon descriptions of these same articles in the book of Exodus. I freely acknowledge that the garments of the high priest likely underwent modification in Israel's later periods; see Margaret Barker, *The Great High Priest: The Temple Roots of Christian Liturgy* (New York: T&T Clark, 2007), 210. This chapter will be concerned primarily with the information Moses preserved for us in the Pentateuch, though (due to lack of detail in certain areas) we may occasionally look at other descriptions of the garments to arrive at a more complete picture. The reader will be benefited by briefly reviewing Exodus 25–30 (the revelation), Exodus 36–39 (the making), and Leviticus 8–9 (the investiture and inauguration of temple service). The scope of this article will not allow for a discussion of those details here. Suffice it to say, these three units are intimately related but describe different stages of implementation of God's revelation to Moses.

13.   Moreover, this homily will occasionally analyze symbols from a Latter-day Saint perspective, showing possible meanings hidden in the garments that provide one with a greater understanding of the specific work of this last dispensation.

14. Just like the New Testament writers who were quick to identify Christ in Old Testament symbolism, all men and women can benefit from understanding the symbolism which God has embedded in all things. This symbolism is designed to bear testimony of his Son. While we must "be watchful that we do not force the text and make it say things it does not say." Sidney Greidanus, *Preaching Christ from the Old Testament* (Grand Rapids, Michigan: William B. Eerdmans, 1999), 37. Our homiletic approach will imitate the allegorical methodology found in the New Testament and in the early church fathers; see, for example, Luke 24:27 or Augustine, "The Epistle of John," Homily 2.1, in Nicene and Post-Nicene Fathers: First Series, ed. Philip Schaff (Peabody, Massachusetts: Hendrickson, 2004), 7:469. Augustine states that everything in the Old Testament speaks of Christ, but only to those who have the ears to hear it.

15. This optional rendering is based on the following: "And thou shalt embroider [Hebrew: *shabats*, meaning to 'weave' or 'plait'] the coat [Hebrew: *kthoneth* or *kuttoneth*, meaning an 'under-garment' or 'shirt-like garment,' sometimes rendered 'tunic'] of fine linen [Hebrew: *shesh* or *shshiy*, meaning something 'bleached white' or of white 'linen']." Admittedly, scholars have translated the passage variously. I have offered only one rendering, but it does appear to be a valid rendering of the Hebrew. See Kenneth Barker ed., *The NIV Study Bible* (Grand Rapids, Michigan: Zondervan, 1995), 128, s.v. Exodus 28:39 and footnote 28:39; *Good News Bible* (New York: American Bible Society, 1978), 96, s.v. Exodus 28:39.

16. Flavius Josephus, "Antiquities of the Jews 3.7.2," in *The Complete Works of Josephus*, trans. William Whiston (Grand Rapids, Michigan: Kregel, 1981), 73. See also Kaiser, "Exodus," 2:467 and J. H. Hertz, *The Pentateuch and Haftorahs*, 2nd ed. (London: Soncino Press, 1962), 343. Josephus may or may not be right about the design of the clothing of the Aaronic high priest. Nevertheless, his explanation represents the views of his day—both Jewish and Christian. It is quite possible that the Christocentric reading of these items by Christians of the post-New Testament era was colored by explanations of the design given by first century witnesses like Josephus. In that regard, his views are germane to our study—particularly since our examination is homiletic rather than exegetical.

17. Leslie F. Church, ed., *The NIV Matthew Henry Commentary in One Volume* (Grand Rapids, Michigan: Zondervan, 1992), 107. See also Patrick Fairbairn, *Typology of Scripture* (Grand Rapids, Michigan: Kregel, 1989), 242, n.1.

18. See Slemming, *These Are the Garments*, 25.

19. See Parry and Parry, *Symbols and Shadows*, 130–31; Slemming, *These Are the Garments*, 25.

20. See Jacob Milgrom, *The Anchor Bible: Leviticus 1–16* (New York: Doubleday, 1991), 502 and fig. 11, 506; James G. Murphy, *A Critical and Exegetical Commentary on the Book of Exodus, with a New Translation* (Boston: Estes and Lauriat, 1874), 320; Willem A. VanGemeren, ed., *New International Dictionary of Old Testament Theology and Exegesis* (Grand Rapids, Michigan: Zondervan, 1997), 4:340–41.

21. See Matthew B. Brown, *The Gate of Heaven: Insights on the Doctrines and Symbols of the Temple* (American Fork, Utah: Covenant Communications, 1999), 104, n. 139. See also Hugh Nibley, *Temple and Cosmos* (Provo, Utah: Foundation for Ancient research

ALONZO L. GASKILL

and Mormon Studies, 1992), 91–138; John W. Welch and Claire Foley, "Gammadia on Early Jewish and Christian Garments," *BYU Studies* 36, no. 3 (1996–97): 253–58. Brown states, "In the paintings of the Dura Europos synagogue (ca. AD 245), Moses is depicted standing before the tabernacle dressed in a white robe that is decorated at chest and knee level with two different checkered marks. . . . Examples of Jewish clothing with marks shaped like the Greek letter gamma (Γ) have been recovered in archeological sites at Masada, Bar-Kokhba, and Dura-Europos."

22. Murphy, *Critical and Exegetical Commentary on the Book of Exodus*, 320.

23. Parry and Parry have suggested, "Various parts of the ancient priestly sacred vestments symbolize aspects of the atonement." *Symbols and Shadows*, 138. The whiteness of the linen coat has obvious connections to Christ's ability to cleanse.

24. Gaglardi, *Path of the Just*, 28.

25. Slemming, *These Are the Garments*, 25.

26. Ibid.

27. See Augustine, "The Epistle of John," Homily 2.1, in *Nicene and Post-Nicene Fathers: First Series*, ed. Philip Schaff, 7:469, who states that everything in the Old Testament "tells of Christ," but only if you and I have the ears to hear what is being symbolically taught.

28. The "Church" of the Old Testament was quite different from the "Church" of the New Testament, just as the Church of today is quite different from the "Church" of antiquity; see John A. Tvedtnes, *The Church of the Old Testament* (Salt Lake City: Deseret Book, 1967). The use of the term "Church" here is intended generically, referring only to followers of YHWY (God) or Christ in any gospel dispensation.

29. Of course, commentators are extrapolating a meaning which was quite possibly foreign to Jews of the Mosaic dispensation, but which would have meaning to Christian readers of the Hebrew Bible. Holzapfel and Seely have written, "There is no scriptural evidence for the clothing of the Levites, but Josephus records that at the time of Jesus the Levites had gained the privilege of wearing priestly linen robes." *My Father's House*, 60. Though we cannot be certain of how far back this practice goes, it is clear that it would have allowed all Levites to gain a greater appreciation for and understanding of the symbolism behind the linen robe—not just the high priest and Aaronic priests.

30. For examples, see Doctrine and Covenants 4:1; 6:1; 11:1; 12:1; and 14:1.

31. Baruch A. Levine, *The JPS Torah Commentary: Leviticus* (Philadelphia: The Jewish Publications Society, 1989), 50. Eight articles of sacred clothing are mentioned in association with the high priest. The four undergarments—the linen coat, the breeches, the girdle or sash, and the headband—were worn by all Aaronic priests who worked in the tabernacle or the temple. The four outer garments—the breastplate with the Urim and Thummim, the ephod, the robe, and the miter—were worn only by the high priest. See Kaiser, "Exodus," 2:465.

32. See Brown, *The Gate of Heaven*, 81–82; Stephen D. Ricks, "The Garment of Adam," *Temples of the Ancient World*, ed. Donald W. Parry (Salt Lake: Deseret Book, 1994), 709, 727, n. 23. While plants were technically also subject to corruption and death, they were not seen as symbols of such because their level of life was not equivalent to the level of life of an animal. Thus, animal products carried negative symbolic connotations, whereas

132

linen carried positive ones. See also Trent, *Types of Christ in the Old Testament*, 56, who associates the "linen breeches" with "the righteousness of Christ."

33. Jarman, *High Priest's Dress*, 19; emphasis in original.

34. See Josephus, "Antiquities of the Jews 3.7.2." See also Brown, *The Gate of Heaven*, 84.

35. See Douglas R. Edwards, "Dress and Ornamentation," in The Anchor Bible Dictionary, ed. David Noel Freedman (New York: Doubleday, 1992), 2:237; James Hall, *Dictionary of Subjects and Symbols in Art* (New York: Harper and Row, 1974), 138; Jack Tresidder, *Symbols and Their Meanings* (London: Duncan Baird Publishers, 2000), 134. See also J. C. Cooper, *An Illustrated Encyclopaedia of Traditional Symbols* (London: Thames and Hudson, 1995), 73–74; Hugh T. Henry, *Catholic Customs and Symbols* (New York: Benziger Brothers, 1925), 69–70.

36. Slemming, *These Are the Garments*, 28. See also Gaglardi, *The Path of the Just*, 45: "Biblical girdles had various uses, the most common of which was to tighten the coat or clothes, bringing the folds together to enable the party wearing it to be prepared for work, or action such as running." See also 1 Peter 1:13; Walter L. Wilson, *A Dictionary of Bible Types* (Peabody, Massachusetts: Hendrickson Publishers, 1999), 196; Ralph Gower, *The New Manners and Customs of Bible Times* (Chicago: Moody Press, 1987), 14.

37. The Hebrew word translated as "blue" here is also sometimes translated as "violet." Though we are not explicitly told within the text whether the robe was made from linen, wool, or some other comparable fabric, commentators suggest it was most likely made of wool. See Levine, *The JPS Torah Commentary: Leviticus*, 50; Sol Scharfstein, *Torah and Commentary: The Five Books of Moses* (Jersey City, New Jersey: KTAV Publishing, 2008), 259.

38. See Brown, *The Gate of Heaven*, 82; Milgrom, *The Anchor Bible: Leviticus*, 1–16, 506, fig. 11; Hertz, *The Pentateuch and Haftorahs*, 342; Eerdmans' *Handbook to the Bible* (Grand Rapids, Michigan: Eerdmans, 1973), 169.

39. Slemming, *These Are the Garments*, 34.

40. See Levine, *JPS Torah Commentary: Leviticus*, 50.

41. See Whiston, *Complete Works of Josephus*, 74.

42. See Ada R. Habershon, *Study of the Types* (Grand Rapids, Michigan: Kregel Publications, 1974), 95; Cooper, *An Illustrated Encyclopaedia of Traditional Symbols*, 40.

43. Joseph Fielding McConkie, *Gospel Symbolism* (Salt Lake City: Bookcraft, 1985), 111.

44. See Kevin J. Conner, *Interpreting the Symbols and Types* (Portland, Oregon: City Bible Publishing, 1992), 61.

45. Slemming, *These Are the Garments*, 34; emphasis in original.

46. They represent "divine protection" because they are said to scare away demons. See Milgrom, *The Anchor Bible: Leviticus 1–16*, 504.

47. Murphy, *Critical and Exegetical Commentary on the Book of Exodus*, 319.

48. Charles F. Pfeiffer and Everett F. Harrison, eds., *The Wycliffe Bible Commentary* (Chicago: Moody Press, 1975), 79.

49. See, for example, Carol Meyers, "Ephod," in *The Anchor Bible Dictionary*, ed. David Noel Freedman, 2:550; John L. McKenzie, *Dictionary of the Bible* (Milwaukee,

Wisconsin: The Bruce Publishing Company, 1965), 241; Allen C. Myers, ed., *The Eerdmans Bible Dictionary* (Grand Rapids, Michigan: Eerdmans, 1987), 342; Kaiser, "Exodus," 2:468; George Arthur Buttrick, ed., *The Interpreter's Bible* (New York: Abingdon Press, 1951–57), 1:1039; Michael D. Coogan, ed., *The New Oxford Annotated Bible*, 3rd ed. (New York: Oxford University Press, 2001), 122 (Hebrew Bible section). Some English translations render the Hebrew word "ephod" as "apron." See, for example, James Moffatt, trans., *A New Translation of The Bible: Containing the Old and New Testaments* (New York: Harper & Brothers, 1950), 92 (Hebrew Bible section); J. M. Powis Smith and Edgar J. Goodspeed, eds., *The Complete Bible: An American Translation* (Chicago: University of Chicago Press, 1949), 76 (Hebrew Bible section).

50. Brown, *The Gate of Heaven*, 86.

51. Conner, *Interpreting the Symbols and Types*, 141; Merrill F. Unger, *Unger's Bible Dictionary* (Chicago: Moody Press, 1975), 317.

52. Nadia Julien, *The Mammoth Dictionary of Symbols* (New York: Carroll and Graf Publishers, 1996), 24. Cooper writes "fertility." *Illustrated Encyclopaedia of Traditional Symbols*, 14.

53. Slemming, *These Are the Garments*, 41. Purple is traditionally the color of royalty—and, in this sense, certainly applies to Jesus. However, Slemming is using the symbol in a slightly different way.

54. Ibid., 39–40.

55. Buttrick, *Interpreter's Bible*, 1:1039.

56. See Jarman, *High Priest's Dress*, 3.

57. While Latter-day Saints traditionally associate the word "breastplate" with the metal garment the Prophet Joseph found (in the hill Cumorah) with the plates of the Book of Mormon, the "breastplate" of the Old Testament High Priest was quite different in its makeup. The Hebrew, translated "breastplate" (in the King James Version), can also be rendered "breastpiece." The latter of these two translations is less likely to be misunderstood.

58. Kaiser, "Exodus," 2:467. Murphy, *Critical and Exegetical Commentary on the Book of Exodus*, 315.

59. See Ramban Nachmanides, *Commentary on the Torah*, trans. Charles B. Chavel (New York: Shilo Publishing House, 1973), 2:481. Whether Nachmanides is right on this point is anyone's guess. However, there seems to be scriptural support for his claim. For example, the Urim and Thummim mentioned time and again in the Hebrew Bible (Exodus 28:30; Leviticus 8:8; Numbers 27:21; Deuteronomy 33:8; 1 Samuel 28:6; Ezra 2:63; Nehemiah 7:65) never has an origin attached to it, and the one given to Joseph Smith by Moroni (see Joseph Smith—History 1:35) had belonged to Mahonri Moriancumer, and it was "given to the brother of Jared upon the Mount, when he talked with the Lord face to face" (D&C 17:1). Additionally, Doctrine and Covenants 130 and Revelation 2 speak of a Urim and Thummim which will be given to "each individual" who proves worthy of an inheritance in the celestial kingdom—again implying divine origin. Abraham spoke of "the Urim and Thummim, which the Lord my God had given unto me" (Abraham 3:1). Thus, Nachmanides's claim that this was not a man-made device finds support.

60. See Richard D. Draper, *Opening the Seven Seals: The Vision of John the Revelator* (Salt Lake City: Deseret Book, 1991), 24, 77, 94; Mick Smith, *The Book of Revelation: Plain, Pure, and Simple* (Salt Lake City: Bookcraft, 1998), 288; Robert D. Johnston, *Numbers in the Bible: God's Design in Biblical Numerology* (Grand Rapids, Michigan: Kregel Publications, 1990), 61; Carol L. Meyers and Eric M. Meyers, *The Anchor Bible: Haggai, Zechariah 1–8* (New York: Doubleday, 1987), 317.

61. Murphy, *Critical and Exegetical Commentary on the Book of Exodus*, 316.

62. The stones of the breastplate were sardius, topaz, carbuncle, emerald, sapphire, diamond, ligure, agate, amethyst, beryl, onyx, and jasper (Exodus 28:17–20).

63. The stones mentioned in Ezekiel 28:13 are sardius, topaz, diamond, beryl, onyx, jasper, sapphire, emerald, and carbuncle.

64. Umberto Cassuto, *A Commentary on the Book of Exodus*, trans. Israel Abrahams (Jerusalem: Magnes Press of the Hebrew University, 1983), 375–76.

65. See Marvin J. Ashton, "There Are Many Gifts," *Ensign*, November 1987, 23; Bruce R. McConkie, *Mormon Doctrine*, 2nd ed. (Salt Lake City: Bookcraft, 1966), s.v. "gifts of the Spirit."

66. Brown, *The Gate of Heaven*, 84.

67. Slemming, *These Are the Garments*, 118.

68. Ibid.

69. Gaglardi, *Path of the Just*, 216.

70. "Dressing in special clothing in the temple denotes a change in role, from that of mortal to immortal, from ordinary human to priest or priestess, king or queen." John A. Tvedtnes, "Priestly Clothing in Bible Times," in *Temples of the Ancient World*, ed. Donald W. Parry (Salt Lake City: Deseret Book, 1994), 666.

71. Bruce R. McConkie, *Doctrinal New Testament Commentary* (Salt Lake City: Bookcraft, 1987–88), 2:322.

72. Slemming wrote: "The mitre that adorned [the temple priest's] head would speak of holiness of thought and control." *These Are the Garments*, 127.

73. See Slemming, *These Are the Garments*, 124–25.

74. Ibid., 118. See also Gaglardi, *Path of the Just*, 216: "'HOLINESS TO THE LORD' is the ultimate complete holiness of the body, soul and spirit, essential in order for this old mortal to put on immortality when Jesus returns. All who have this hope certainly are purifying themselves today."

75. Jeffrey R. Holland, *Christ and the New Covenant: The Messianic Message of the Book of Mormon* (Salt Lake City: Deseret Book, 1997), 159.

76. R. K. Harrison, *Leviticus: An Introduction and Commentary* (Downers Grove, Illinois: InterVarsity Press, 1980), 92.

Chapter 8

LOCATION VENERATION

MISSOURI, THE TEMPLE, AND THE CHURCH'S FUTURE[1]

Alonzo L. Gaskill and Richard G. Moore

Since at least as early as 1831, Independence, Missouri, has held a position of significance in the theology of the Restoration. To this day, many branches of the restored gospel see it as sacred, either for Joseph's declaration that it was once the Garden of Eden, or because he decreed it to be the site where a holy temple would be erected to our God, or in some cases because it was designated as a place of gathering for the Saints. Today The Church of Jesus Christ of Latter-day Saints, members of the Community of Christ (or RLDS),[2] the Church of Christ—Temple Lot (Hedrickites), the Church of Jesus Christ (Cutlerites), and a number of other Restoration branches, have a presence in Independence; venerating it as a place of significance for believers in the Restoration of the Gospel through the Prophet Joseph Smith.

The idea of venerating sacred ground or a sacred place is not unique to Latter-day Saints. Throughout history, kings, priests, and peasants have sought interaction with the divine. When the transcendental or miraculous occurred, they would often erect an altar or monument on the spot to commemorate the occasion, and also as a testament to their sense of the hallowed nature of the location in which God revealed Himself. Such locations typically became places of pilgrimage for the faithful. Sacred places serve as a "focusing lens" of sorts.[3] They are a constant reminder to pilgrims and patrons of a tradition's past, but also of the chosen status of a people and place.

In the Abrahamic traditions—Judaism, Christianity, and Islamism—the concepts of sacred space and sacred place are prevalent and enduring. The Western ("Wailing") Wall, Mecca and Medina, and the Holy Sepulchre are persistent places of pilgrimage. For practitioners, locations of veneration hold a place of profundity for their past significance but also because they offer hope for a bright future, a future which potentially brings again spiritual experiences akin to those which took place there in days past. Each of the Abrahamic faiths has expectations of what God will do with, through, and for them *if* they hold out faithful to their God.

As suggested, the various denominations associated with the Prophet Joseph hold Independence, Missouri, as a sacred location of significance and veneration for different reasons. Certainly each has its own history with that part of the Lord's vineyard (D&C 72:2), and each has its own theology about what *did* and *will* happen there. Our focus here will be on the LDS branch of the Restoration: their history and thought regarding the significance of Independence, Missouri, and its place in the "gathering of Israel" (Articles of Faith 1:10 and D&C 110:11).

While the Community of Christ (formerly known as the RLDS Church) has a much more visible presence in Independence, Missouri, than does the Utah-based faith, nevertheless, many members of The Church of Jesus Christ of Latter-day Saints have a fixation with Independence, not only as a place of pilgrimage but also as a location they venerate because of a long-held belief that at one point, the Mormons would return to Missouri, transferring their headquarters from Utah to Jackson County. From whence do such beliefs arise? Are they accurate perceptions of the doctrine or position of the LDS Church? Has there been an evolution in the official position on this matter? These, and other questions like them, will be the focus of this chapter.

JOSEPH SMITH AND THE MORMON MISSOURI DOCTRINE

One of the greatest single contributions Joseph Smith made to the religious traditions of nineteenth-century Christianity was the assertion of a native sacred history for the Western Hemisphere; a history described in the Book of Mormon.[4] With the introduction of this "new scripture," Joseph offered the Americas as the "chosen land" which God had prepared for scattered Israel, and for the Restoration of the gospel of Jesus Christ. Indeed, the Book of Mormon indicates that God revealed the consecrated and sacred nature of the Americas to prophets millennia before the arrival of European explorers. Joseph's revelations expounded the virtues of the American Zion, indicating the principles of religious freedom that would largely define the land.

Of course, portions of Joseph's teachings on this subject were not unique to him or the Restoration.[5] One scholar noted, "The saints did not invent the concept of America as chosen; it surrounded America's Puritan beginnings"[6] Nevertheless, what Joseph restored, and what the Book of Mormon articulated, convinced many in the early days of the Restoration, that this common belief of America's "chosenness" was true.[7]

Additionally, while early followers of Joseph Smith held in common with other inhabitants of North America the view of that parcel as a promised land, there was much in what the Prophet revealed that went beyond the understandings or beliefs of those outside of the newly restored faith. For example, Joseph provided the context of communication with the divine in the American Zion by narrating its history. It became the place where God first spoke to man (the Garden of Eden[8]) and where Christ would return and speak during both the Restoration and the Millennium, for "out of Zion shall go forth the law" (Isaiah 2:3). The fact that the Mormon city of Zion was to be primarily a temple city[9] exemplifies its divine communicative symbolism: a place where the throne of God can be approached. (This idea was paramount in Joseph's mind, but not necessarily clear in the minds of all of his followers, as we shall shortly discover.) For Joseph, the temple and Zion went hand-in-glove. As he stated in 1843,

> The object of Gathering the . . . people of God in any age of the world . . . was to build unto the Lord an house whereby he could reveal unto his people the ordinances of his house and glories of his kingdom & teach the peopl [sic] the ways of salvation for their [sic] are certain ordinances & principles that when they are taught and practiced [sic], must be done in a place or house built for that purpose[.] This was purposed in the mind of God before the world was & it was for this purpose that God . . . gathers togethe [sic] the people in the last days to build unto the Lord an house to prepare them for the ordinances & endowment washings & anointings &c.[10]

Before Joseph sent men on missions to "gather Israel" and thereby build Zion, he revealed to them what members of the LDS Church have come to call "the Holy Endowment."[11] For Joseph, Zion could not exist aside from the temple. Hence, when he gathered the Saints to Ohio, he had them construct a temple. When he gathered them in Independence, Missouri, they dedicated a spot for a temple (which, had they not been expelled, would have been built there prior to the Prophet's death). When Joseph gathered his followers in Far West, Missouri, again, they laid cornerstones for a temple (which, to this day, remains unrealized because of their exodus). Around the same time that members were gathering in Far West, some of the Saints settled at Adam-ondi-Ahman where, in the fall of 1838, they set stakes for a temple, and dedicated the plot.[12] Finally, the Prophet gathered the Saints in Nauvoo, Illinois, and, once again, they built a temple. For the early Latter-day Saints, the temple and Zion were inseparable.

"We ought to have the building up of Zion as our greatest object," the Prophet declared in 1839.[13] One year earlier the Lord informed Joseph, "Arise and shine forth, that thy light may be a standard for the nations; And that the gathering together upon the land of Zion, and upon her stakes, may be for a defense, and for a refuge from the storm, and from wrath when it shall be poured out without mixture upon the whole earth" (D&C 115:5–6). Thus, one of the chief components of the gathering to this "promised land" of North America was protection. Zion was to provide "defense" and "refuge" for the members of the fledgling Church—protection from their enemies, but also from the sin and evils of a fallen world (John 17:15).[14] Through gathering to Zion the Saints would quickly come to realize an additional influence of being part of that holy society—namely, its influence on the lives, faith, and purity of the inhabitants. In August of 1833, the Spirit of revelation uttered these pertinent words, "Therefore, verily, thus saith the Lord, let Zion rejoice, for this is Zion—the pure in heart; therefore, let Zion rejoice, while all the wicked shall mourn" (D&C 97:21).

While the Prophet's early conversations about Zion highlighted the Book of Mormon teaching that God had established the Americas as a "choice land" (See 2 Nephi 10:19), over time, Joseph introduced into his discourse details regarding a small portion of the central United States. This new level of detail in the Zion doctrine may have come, in part, from Joseph's early 1830s work on the Inspired Version (or Joseph Smith Translation) of the Bible. Through that, he learned new things regarding the origins of man, the first Gospel dispensation, and the prototypical city of Zion built by the prophet Enoch.[15] It was revealed that, while Zion encompassed (at the very least) North America, a location within the boundaries of the state of Missouri held special significance. Joseph wrote:

> I received, by a heavenly vision, a commandment in June [1831], to take my journey to the western boundaries of the State of Missouri, and there designate the very spot which was to be the central place for the commencement of the gathering together of those who embrace the fullness of the everlasting Gospel. Accordingly I undertook the journey, with certain ones of my brethren, and after a long and tedious journey, suffering many privations and hardships, arrived in Jackson County, Missouri, and after viewing the country, seeking diligently at the hand of God, He manifested Himself unto us, and designated, to me and others, the very spot upon which he designed to commence the work of the gathering, and the upbuilding of an "holy city," which should be called Zion—Zion, because it is a place of righteousness, and all who build thereon are to worship the true and living God, and all believe in one doctrine, even the doctrine of our Lord and Savior Jesus Christ.[16]

In revealing this new and unequivocally exciting news, Joseph not only gave the Saints a location to which they should gather, but he also restored the concepts of "sacred place" and "location veneration" which had been so prevalent in antiquity.

EMOTIONAL IMPLICATIONS OF ZION'S FAILURE

The idea of a city implies planning, forethought, and order—which are distinctive traits of God, who harnesses the chaos to create an ordered universe. Thus, the "City" of Zion was really symbolic of the divine ordering of human disorder. It seems evident from the history that this is what Joseph sought to accomplish. Unfortunately, history also preserves the fact that the Saints did not realize the Zion they sought to establish. Many factors played a role: personal selfishness, a lack of prompt and faithful attention to God's commands, the prejudice of non-believers, economic impoverishment, block-voting, the exclusivity in the Saints' economic model, mobocracy, and so on. The Independence, Missouri, Zion that Joseph sought to establish (at the command of his God) did not come to fruition. The temple was not built. Lives were lost. Possessions were confiscated. And, ultimately, the Saints were incrementally driven from the state.

Oh, how this must have affected the psyche of the people! Had they been rejected by God? Was this expulsion a result of *their* sins? Or had the government's wicked behavior brought trouble to the Saints and, more particularly, God's wrath upon the state? No doubt being persecuted gave them a kinship with the ancient Israelites and the first-century Christians. But the devastating blow of Governor Boggs's "extermination order"[17] took them from their anticipation of a "utopia"[17] to utter destitution and homelessness. It seemed that all had been stripped away. And while the Prophet's words offered some measure of comfort, they also strongly implied that some of the fault for the Saints' failure to establish their Missouri Zion was their own sinfulness. Joseph wrote:

> We have the satisfaction of knowing that the Lord approves of us, and has accepted us, and established His name in Kirtland for the salvation of the nations: for the Lord will have a place whence His word will go forth, in these last days, in purity; for if Zion will not purify herself, so as to be approved of in all things, in His sight, He will seek another people; for His work will go on until Israel is gathered, and they who will not hear His voice, must expect to feel His wrath. Let me say unto you, seek to purify yourselves, and also the inhabitants of Zion, lest the Lord's anger be kindled to fierceness. Repent, repent, is the voice of God to Zion; . . . Hear the warning voice of God, lest Zion fall, and the Lord swear in his wrath the inhabitants of Zion shall not enter into His rest. . . . Our hearts are greatly grieved at the spirit which is . . . wasting the strength of Zion like a pestilence; and if it is not detected and driven from you, it will ripen Zion for the threatened judgments of God.[18]

Being driven from Jackson County, and then from Caldwell and Davies Counties, and finally from the state of Missouri, left the members of the restored Church reeling. On top of that, to then lose their presence in Kirtland, Ohio—including having to walk away from their beloved temple—certainly caused some to question the revelations of the Lord. No doubt this newfound destitution surely opened the door for later reinterpretations of what Zion *really* meant for the Latter-day Saints.

MISSOURI THROUGH THE LENSES OF NAUVOO AND BEYOND

As the Saints began to build up their settlement in Nauvoo, including the erection of a temple, certainly some emotionally "moved on" from Missouri and set their sights on Nauvoo as the "new Zion." However, this emotional divesting of the Independence "New Jerusalem" was not universal. Wilford Woodruff, who was called as an Apostle in 1839, wrote in his journal that some determined they would not go west in the mass migration from Illinois but would, instead, stay in the area "so when the church got ready to go back to Jackson County [they] would have but a short way to go."[19] Similarly,

Oliver Olney, a convert to the Church during the Kirtland era, penned this in his journal: "They speak of Missouri from whence we was drove. . . . They prophesy [sic] in the name of the Lord that they will be six hundred thousand strong in ten years. Thus a spirit of encouragement is held out by those that lead that they will gain in numbers and become a terror to the nations of the earth. They have now sent to England and to all parts for the saints to come in and that without delay."[20] Olney perceived the Church as biding its time in Nauvoo while their numbers increased, with the intention of returning to Missouri to reclaim their land once they were numerically large or strong enough to do so. This anticipation of return lasted for some time—and among many of the Saints. Indeed, as late as 1870, leaders of the Church offered the perspective that a return to Missouri was inevitable. For example, John Young (a prominent LDS Patriarch) taught, "If the people will keep humble and do as they are told, they will . . . go back and build the Temple in the centre [sic] stake of Zion."[21] Similarly, Elder Orson Pratt declared:

> There is one thing sure—as sure as the sun shines forth in yonder heavens, so sure will the Lord fulfil [sic] one thing with regard to this people. What is that? He will return them to Jackson county, and in the western part of the State of Missouri they will build up a city which shall be called Zion, which will be the head-quarters of this Latter-day Saint Church; and that will be the place where the prophets, apostles and inspired men of God will have their head-quarters. It will be the

place where the Lord God will manifest Himself to His people, as He has promised in the Scriptures, as well as in modern revelation.[22]

Thus, the view of a return to Missouri—and the eventual transference of the LDS Church's headquarters there—continued for some time. The Saints could not readily divest themselves of the notion, and the visions of vindication that accompanied a doctrine of return.

Curiously, following the death of Brigham Young (in August 1877) the leaders of the Church ceased to publicly discuss a return to Missouri. Certainly some still expected it, but formally, it disappeared from the public discourse of the presiding Brethren.[23]

In June of 1894, the First Presidency and Quorum of the Twelve Apostles began to counsel members of the Church to *not* immigrate to Utah—at least, not "until they are firmly founded in the religion" they had embraced. The leadership of the Church said members "should not be encouraged to immigrate to this place."[24] Rather, they were encouraged to stay in their homelands and build the Church there. Similarly, in 1898, George Q. Cannon (a member of the First Presidency) counseled "the Saints in the various lands where they embrace the Gospel to . . . not be anxious to . . . gather to Zion."[25] Significantly, "Zion" at the turn of the nineteenth century was being used in reference to Utah, not Missouri.

In 1903, President Joseph F. Smith suggested that the Church now begin to construct meetinghouses in Great Britain—something they had neglected to do in the first sixty years of the Church's presence in that country.[26] This new building phase implied permanence to the Church's presence in Great Britain, and it also discouraged immigration to the United States. Less than ten years later, the Utah-based church built its first temple outside of that state.[27] Again, the message was immigration is unnecessary and, perhaps, unwanted. That was the beginning of what would become an aggressive temple building program for the Saints. David O. McKay (who served as President of the Church from 1951 to 1970) initiated the construction of temples outside of North America. Only eight months after becoming president he purchased property for a temple near London. A month later he proposed another European temple—this one in Switzerland. As he described it, his rationale was to "contribute to the stability and growth of the Church in Europe"[28]—a goal that was significantly different from the earlier position of seeking to get *all* of the Saints to "gather in unto one place upon the face of *this* land": America (see D&C 29:8).

In the years that followed, a number of prophets and apostles spoke of the place of gathering as the homeland of the convert, rather than Utah or Missouri. President Spencer W. Kimball encapsulated the Church's position this way:

> Many people have been holding their breath waiting to see the gathering of Israel. We are in Israel and are being gathered. Now, in the early days of the Church we used to preach for the people to come to Utah as the gathering process, *largely because that was the only place in the whole world where there was a temple.* Now we have sixteen temples, and two more that have been approved, scattered throughout the world. So it is no longer necessary that we bring the people all to Salt Lake City. Our missionaries preach baptism and confirmation. And then we come to you with conferences and to organize stakes. So we say again, stay in Korea. This is a beautiful land. In this land you can teach your children just as well as you could in Salt Lake City. Stay in Korea where you can teach the gospel to millions of people.
>
> And so the gathering is taking place. Korea is the gathering place for Koreans, Australia for Australians, Brazil for Brazilians, England for the English. And so we move forward toward the confirmation of this great program the Lord has established for us.
>
> The First Presidency and the Twelve see great wisdom in the multiple Zions, many gathering places where the Saints within their own culture and nation can act as a leaven in the building of the kingdom— a kingdom which seeks no earthly rewards or treasures.
>
> Sometimes, inadvertently, we have given artificial encouragement to individuals to leave their native land and culture and, too often, this has meant the loss of the leaven that is so badly needed, and the individuals involved have sometimes regretted their migrations.
>
> I am hopeful that each of you will ponder carefully what it is the Lord would have you do with your lives, with the special skills, training, and testimonies you have.[29]

Elder Bruce R. McConkie, a rather influential doctrinal voice among the twentieth-century leadership of the Church, taught:

> The place of gathering for the Mexican Saints is in Mexico; the place of gathering for the Guatemalan Saints is in Guatemala; the place of gathering for the Brazilian Saints is in Brazil; and so it goes

throughout the length and breadth of the whole earth. Japan is for the Japanese; Korea is for the Koreans; Australia is for the Australians; every nation is the gathering place for its own people.[30]

Today members of The Church of Jesus Christ of Latter-day Saints are consistently taught to stay where they are—build Zion in their homeland; whether that's Pittsburgh or Paris, London or Los Angeles.

While records of the LDS Church's landholdings in Jackson County, Missouri, are not public, one can quite readily view their activities in Utah. The rate of Church building on the Wasatch Front is mind-boggling. Church properties are everywhere—with new chapels and church facilities being dedicated weekly. A few rather significant projects have been undertaken in the last decade and a half. For example, in 1996,

Church President, Gordon B. Hinckley, announced plans to build a facility to be known as the "Conference Center."[31] This massive building, which would largely replace the old Tabernacle (on Temple Square), seats over twenty-one thousand people, and has an auditorium "large enough to hold two Boeing 747s side by side."[32] A building of this size and cost suggests a Church that is putting down roots, rather than preparing to uproot itself.

In October 2006, the LDS Church announced plans to renovate downtown Salt Lake City through its commercial real estate arm, "Property Reserve, Incorporated" (PRI).[33] President Hinckley emphasized, "The Church is undertaking a huge development project in the interest of protecting the environment of Temple Square. While the costs will be great, it will not involve the expenditure of tithing funds."[34] According to KSL, a Church-owned media outlet, the renovation cost 5 billion dollars.[35] Again, this is evidence of a faith that is settling in, not heading out.

Perhaps one of the developments most germane to this discussion was the October 2008 announcement by current Church President Thomas S. Monson that an LDS temple would be built in "the greater Kansas City area."[36] This Kansas City Missouri Temple (dedicated May 6, 2012) is less than fourteen miles from the Independence Missouri Temple Lot, dedicated August 3, 1831, under the direction of the Prophet Joseph. To justify building another LDS temple some fourteen miles away would require a membership so dense in population as to rival that of any city in the state of Utah.[37] The Church's choice to build a temple that close to Independence, but not *in* Independence, seems to send a rather clear message as to how imminent an LDS "return" to Jackson County is.[38]

This handful of examples of public statements by LDS General Authorities and publicly performed actions by the Church certainly gives the impression that the Church does not wish the bulk of its membership to gather to any one place—be it Utah, Missouri, or anywhere else.

HAS THE DOCTRINE CHANGED?

This very brief survey might cause one to ask, has the doctrine or position of the LDS Church with regards to Independence, Missouri, changed? Is Independence a "sacred place," or is it not? Was the Church, in the days of Joseph Smith, planning on building a permanent headquarters in Jackson County, Missouri—to which they would gather *all* members of the Church? If so, have they abandoned that plan? A survey of members of the LDS Church tends to produce very different answers to these questions.[39] Certainly some observers have taken the stance that the Church *has* changed its position on the location of Zion—the place of gathering.[40] But does the evidence support such a conclusion? While some members of The Church of Jesus Christ of Latter-day Saints—in the nineteenth century as well as today—have held that the Church will *eventually* return to Jackson County *en masse*, this may stem from a combined hopeful nostalgia and a misunderstanding of the teachings of the Prophet Joseph.

It will be remembered that in 1833 Joseph prophetically stated, "Brethren, . . . I want to say to you before the Lord, that you know no more concerning the destinies of this church and kingdom than a babe upon its mother's lap. You don't comprehend it. . . . It is only a handful of priesthood you see here tonight, but this church will fill North and South America *it will fill the world.*"[41] Two things seem significant about this statement. First of all, Joseph seems to foretell the confusion that would exist within the Church regarding the gathering of Israel and the building up of Zion. Second, as early as 1833, Joseph is already talking in terms of Zion not being in one city, county, or state, but throughout the entire world.

In September of 1835, Joseph informed the Saints that God had "manifested Himself unto us, and designated, to [him] and others, the very spot upon which he designed to *commence* the work of the gathering."[42] Note that last clause: God revealed to Joseph and others that Independence, Missouri, (in Jackson County) was the place where "the work of gathering" the Saints was to "commence." Independence was *not* the end of the Saints' geographic "promised land"—it was the beginning (or center) of it.

In 1838 the Lord informed Joseph, "Arise and shine forth, that thy light may be a standard for the nations; And that the gathering together upon the land of Zion, *and upon her stakes*, may be for a defense, and for a refuge from the storm, and from wrath when it shall be poured out without mixture upon the whole earth" (D&C 115:5–6). In that same year Joseph announced, "The time is soon coming, when no man will have any peace but in Zion *and her stakes*."[43] Notice that the prophet is consistently speaking of Zion *and* her stakes. And he notes that both—Jackson County (Zion) and stakes outside of that region—would function as a "defense" and "refuge" from the "storms" and "wrath" that would be coming upon the "whole earth." In the midst of the coming "scourge" and "desolation," the Lord declared that safety could be found *if* the Saints would "stand in holy places, and . . . not be moved" (D&C 45:32; emphasis added).[44] As early as 1831, the prophet is suggesting that there is not a single geographic location that will provide protection from the world. The key is holiness, not geography. Thus, it is clear, even before the 1838 extermination order of Governor Boggs, that Joseph saw a broader picture than many have given him credit for. LDS Church President, Ezra Taft Benson, taught: "Holy men and holy women stand in holy places, and these holy places include our temples, our chapels, our homes, and the stakes of Zion, which are, as the Lord declares, 'for a defense, and for a refuge from the storm, and from wrath when it shall be poured out without mixture upon the whole earth' (D&C 115:6)."[45]

On August 6, 1842, Joseph prophesied: "The Saints would continue to suffer much affliction and would be driven to the Rocky Mountains."[46] According to Elder Woodruff, Joseph taught that the Church would

> fill the Rocky Mountains. There will be tens of thousands of
> Latter-day Saints who will be gathered to the Rocky Mountains, and

there they will open the door for the establishing of the gospel among the Lamanites, who will receive the gospel and their endowments and the blessings of God. This people will go into the Rocky Mountains; *they will there build temples* to the Most High. They will raise up a posterity there, and *the Latter-day Saints who dwell in these mountains will stand in the flesh until the coming of the Son of Man.* The Son of Man will come to them *while in the Rocky Mountains.*[47]

Here, Joseph not only predicts an exodus from Nauvoo, but he indicates that in the new land to which the Saints would go (the Rocky Mountains), they would build many temples,[48] and they would remain there until the return of Christ. Joseph declared the land of the Rocky Mountains was the new place of gathering. This prophetic declaration by the Prophet seems to indicate that, in Joseph's mind, Missouri had largely served its purpose and that the main body of the Church would not be returning. This hardly excludes some from going back at some future date. But Joseph speaks of the Rockies—not Jackson County, Missouri—as the location of the Church (or its headquarters) at the time of the Second Coming.

Perhaps others of Joseph's contemporaries didn't fully grasp his vision of Zion and the gathering, but Brigham Young seemed to. In 1864 he taught, "Remarks have been made as to our staying here [in Utah]. I will tell you how long we shall stay here. If we live our religion, we shall stay here in these mountains forever and forever, worlds without end, and a portion of the Priesthood will go and redeem and build up the centre [*sic*] Stake of Zion."[49] In response to another's query as to our return to Missouri, in 1853 Brigham said, "When our Elders go out to preach the Gospel, they tell the people to gather to Zion. Where is it? It is at the City of the Great Salt Lake, in the Valleys of the Mountains; in the settlements of Utah Territory—there is Zion *now.*"[50] He then added this:

> And what is Zion? In one sense Zion is the pure in heart. But is there a land that ever will be called Zion? Yes, brethren. What land is it? It is the land that the Lord gave to Jacob, who bequeathed it to his son Joseph, and his posterity, and they inhabit it, and that land is North and South America. That is Zion as to land, as to Territory, and location. The children of Zion have not yet much in their possession, but their territory is North and South America *to begin with.* As to the spirit of Zion, it is in the hearts of the Saints, of those who love and serve the Lord with all their might, mind, and strength.[51]

In July of 1861 Brigham Young stated, "Zion will extend, *eventually*, all over this earth. There will be no nook or corner upon the earth but what will be in Zion. It will all be Zion."[52] From Brigham's perspective, North and South America were the place where the gathering would "begin." But he clearly saw Zion in broader terms. Spiritual Zion was, for him, the purity of heart found in a faithful Saint. Geographic Zion, he suggested, had become Utah, but would include North and South America and, "eventually," the entire earth. Brigham understood Joseph's construct of Zion and the gathering of Israel. And he certainly recognized that Jackson County, Missouri, was *not* the totality of the Mormon utopia. It was but a stopping place on a lengthy journey.

As suggested earlier in this chapter, Joseph saw the idea of Zion (and the gathering) as inextricably connected to the building of temples—particularly after God revealed to him the endowment (in early 1842). Thus, in the Church's infancy—when temples were scarce—the Saints *needed* to gather to a singular location. In September of 1830 the Lord revealed, "Wherefore the decree hath gone forth from the Father that they shall be gathered in unto *one place* upon the face of this land, *to prepare their hearts and be prepared in all things against the day when tribulation and desolation are sent forth upon the wicked*" (D&C 29:8; emphasis added). Was that "one place" to which they were to gather the state of Missouri? Would being in Independence, Missouri, somehow "prepare their hearts and . . . all things against the day when tribulation and desolation are sent forth upon the wicked"? Or was the "one place" to gather—the "place of preparation"—actually the temple of the Lord, wherever it was found? From what Joseph taught, it appears that there was to be a physical gathering to one singular location. But that was not necessarily Missouri; nor, for that matter, was it Ohio, Illinois, or Utah. Shortly after the official organization of the Church, Joseph began to speak of the gathering as being to Zion's "stakes" rather than to one place. And Joseph sensed that Zion could be built up wherever a temple had been reared unto the Most High God. He had hoped to accomplish this in Missouri—first in Independence, but then later at Far West. Ultimately, it wasn't until Nauvoo that he was able to accomplish his design. But the place of gathering, for Joseph, was *not* as much a *geographic* location as it was a *spiritual* location—the holy temple. President Spencer W. Kimball well encapsulated Joseph's doctrine of gathering, and the Doctrine and Covenants idea of "one place" to gather. As we noted previously, he taught that the reason members of the Church were asked (after the Nauvoo era) to gather in one place was because there was only one location upon the face of the earth where liturgically functioning temples existed—Utah. Once the LDS Church was large enough to have temples in various parts of the world, the council was for members to stay put, rather than to gather to the Wasatch Front.[53] "So it is no longer necessary that we bring all of our people to Salt Lake City."[54] While Joseph understood this, and Brigham appears to have understood this too, many Mormons have not—hence the persistent view that the Church *en masse* would be returning to Independence to reclaim its inheritance and there reestablish its headquarters.

RETORT

Some argue that the Doctrine and Covenants insists upon a return to Independence, and the ultimate establishment of Zion—for *every member* of the Church—in Jackson County, Missouri. In addition, there are those who see in the scriptures evidence that The Church of Jesus Christ of Latter-day Saints will move its headquarters to Independence, Missouri some time prior to Christ's Second Advent. A number of passages are cited to support this position. As an example, section 57 states:

> Hearken, O ye elders of my church, saith the Lord your God, who have assembled yourselves together, according to my commandments, in this land, which is the land of Missouri, which is the land which I have appointed and consecrated for the gathering of the saints.
>
> Wherefore, this is the land of promise, and the place for the city of Zion.
>
> And thus saith the Lord your God, if you will receive wisdom here is wisdom. Behold, the place which is now called Independence is the center place; and a spot for the temple is lying westward, upon a lot which is not far from the courthouse. (D&C 57:1–3)

This July 1831 revelation, received in Jackson County, speaks of the Lord's command that the Saints gather in the land of Missouri. It even goes so far as to call it the land "consecrated for the gathering" and a "land of promise." However, the fact that the Lord also declares in these verses that Independence is to be "the center place" of gathering implies that it is "*a* location" but not "the *only* location" of gathering. As the Lord clarifies in Doctrine and Covenants 84:4, "Verily this is the word of the Lord, that the city New Jerusalem shall be built by the gathering of the saints, *beginning* at this place, even the place of the temple" (emphasis added). One commentator pointedly noted:

> As for the New Jerusalem gathering, Independence was to be the center place, not the center stake as some are inclined to say. The symbolism of the gathering of Israel had also been used by the Prophet Isaiah: "Enlarge thy place of thy tent, and let them stretch forth the curtains of thy habitations; spare not, lengthen thy cords and strengthen thy stakes" (Isaiah 22:2; 3 Nephi 22:2). In the center of the tent was normally a large pole, and cords were fastened to it, and each cord was extended to a perimeter surrounding the tent. A large tent pin or stake was driven into the ground, and the cord extended from the center pole was fastened to the stake and pulled tight to raise the tent. Thus, stakes were to be established all around Independence so that the tent of Israel, the New Jerusalem, could be equally supported on all sides.[55]

The Prophet Joseph also indicated that Independence "was to be the central place for the *commencement* of the gathering."[56] Said Brigham Young, "A woman in Canada asked if we thought that Jackson County would be large enough to gather all the people that would want to go to Zion. I will answer the question really as it is. Zion will extend, eventually, all over this earth. There will be no nook or corner upon the earth but what will be in Zion."[57] Regarding the language of section 57, Robinson and Garrett pointed out, "Since Zion will eventually grow to encompass all the Saints of God in all their many stakes, *Zion* is not always a very specific term geographically."[58] Clearly Independence is where the gathering was to *begin*—not where it was to end.

Parenthetically, Otten and Caldwell point out what we have already suggested: "The Lord asserts us to a vital aspect of the Zion concept. We learn [in D&C 57:3] that a temple is to be an essential part of such an endeavor. . . . It is in this section . . . that we first learn that Zion cannot be established without a temple. The two are inseparably connected."[59]

Section 57 is demonstrative of the exegetical problem associated with this subject. So often, when verses are cited to prove that Independence, Missouri, is the permanent destination of the Saints and the Church's headquarters, the verses don't actually claim that. There can be no question but that at one point in the history of the Church that revered spot was where the Saint's sought to settle. There can also be no doubt but that the Lord appointed that venerated location as a place of gathering. But, in case after case, where Independence is highlighted, holy writ typically speaks of it as "a" place of gathering, the "central" place of the gathering, or the "beginning" place for the gathering.[60]

> The 'regions westward' were only the beginning. 'Every region,' until the city of the New Jerusalem was prepared (D&C 42:8–9), would include all around the city since it was [only] the center place of Zion (D&C 57:3). . . . When the city of the New Jerusalem is built, the people in that city and in the supporting regions round about will be one. They will be the Lord's people, and He will be their God (D&C 42:9). This promise has been given to Israel whenever they are or will be gathered (see Exodus 6:7; Zacharias 8:8).[61]

The scriptures simply do *not* declare Independence or Jackson County to be the *sole* or *ultimate* place of gathering. To claim scriptural support for an *en masse* return, or for a premillennial transfer of the Church's headquarters, is to wrest the scriptures and to ignore the teachings of the latter-day prophets and apostles.

When verses speak of gathering to "one place"[62] those must necessarily be taken in the context of the time in which they were given, the Church's overarching soteriology, and the teachings of the oracles of the Church.[63] When read with such context, one cannot make an argument for Independence as *the* "one place" or the singular "final" place. Joseph was quite clear: the Holy Temple, at the center of Zion communities, is "the place" of gathering, the place of safety, the place of refuge.[64] Monte S. Nyman wrote, "The people are to gather to *their* 'one place' in preparation for the tribulation and desolation that will come upon the wicked."[65] Elder Bruce R. McConkie stated that the President of the Church has received the "keys" of gathering "to lead all Israel, the ten tribes included, from all the nations of the earth, coming as the prophetic word affirms, one by one and two by two, to the mountains of the Lord's houses, there to be endowed with power from on high."[66]

CONCLUSION

Like first-century Jews and Christians, the Prophet Joseph introduced or "restored" a belief in a Zion concept and a doctrine of "sacred place." And while not all branches of the Restoration movement continue to stress this concept, it was certainly prevalent among the early Saints, and remains strong in the psyche of many of the Saints of the Utah-based Church.[67]

Could Jackson County, Missouri, play a significant role in some future stage of the Church's development? Certainly! Will the Saints *en masse* return there prior to the Second Coming? From what Joseph Smith and Brigham Young taught, not likely. Is it *necessary* that Independence play a role in the future of the Church in order to fulfill scriptural or prophetic pronouncements? Such does not appear to be the case. That which prophets and apostles have stated about the gathering of Israel and the establishment of Zion seems generally applicable to any location upon the face of this earth—though certainly Independence was the "beginning" place for this work. Nevertheless, the gathering seems less about a physical city and primarily about temples and personal righteousness.[68] Elder Orson F. Whitney taught that "the redemption of Zion is more than the purchase or recovery of lands, the building of cities, or even the founding of nations. It is the conquest of the heart, the subjugation of the soul, the sanctifying of the flesh, the purifying and ennobling of the passions."[69] The metaphor of a tent and its stakes was drawn by the prophet from the book of Isaiah: "Enlarge the place of thy *tent*, and let them stretch forth the curtains of thine habitations: spare not, lengthen thy cords, and strengthen thy *stakes*" (Isaiah 54:2). Tents were designed to be movable, and so was the gathering place of the faithful, fondly referred to as "Zion."[70] After the organization of the Church, several cities seemed to qualify for the central post that supported the rest of the Church: Kirtland, Independence, and Nauvoo, among others. Where persecution required it, the Saints frequently picked up and moved the tent. For members of The Church of Jesus Christ of Latter-day Saints today, Utah has become the center stake—the headquarters of the Church, and the location from which the gathering is conducted.[71] As Elder Jeffrey R. Holland recently noted, "We no longer think of Zion as where we are going to live. We think of it as how we are going to live."[72] Similarly, Elder D. Todd Christopherson pointed out, "Zion is Zion because of the character, attributes, and faithfulness of her citizens."[73] Brigham reminded the Saints, "When we conclude to make a Zion we will make it, and this work commences in the heart of each person."[74]

The evolution of Zionist tradition in Mormonism has not *really* been in the teachings of the leaders of the Church. Rather, it has come as lay Latter-day Saints have struggled to keep in perspective and context comments made by the Prophet Joseph. Various ideas have been misunderstood, leaving the appearance that the doctrine has evolved. In reality, folklore has become fact in the minds of some, and the consequence has been the apparent laying down of true doctrine and the taking up of "Missouri myths."[75]

NOTES

1. A version of this article was originally published under the title "Location Veneration: Independence, Missouri, in Latter-day Saint Zionist Tradition and Thought." See *Mormon Historical Studies*, vol. 14, no. 1 (Spring 2013): 163–83. Republished here by permission.

2. Technically speaking, the proper name of the Church formally known as the RLDS Church is "Community of Christ," not "The Community of Christ." However, grammatically, the article "the" before the name helps with sentence structure and stylistic issues. Hence its employment here, and throughout this chapter.

3. Joel P. Brereton, "Sacred Space," in *The Encyclopedia of Religion*, 16 vols., ed. Mircea Eliade (New York: Macmillan, 1987), 12:526.

4. The early missionary efforts and subsequent revelations in the Doctrine and Covenants summarize the initial Latter-day Saint obsession with the American eschatology.

5. The concept of America as a "promised land" blessed and watched over by God quickly took root in the newly founded nation. During the first half of the nineteenth century, most Americans felt a strong sense of mission or "choseness." There was a common belief that their nation had been selected by God—"set apart," per se—for a special and divine mission. That belief certainly existed at least as early as the mid-eighteenth century. As Jonathan Edwards announced in 1742, "The latter-day glory, is probably to begin in America." See *The Works of Jonathan Edwards*, vol. 1, part 2, sec. 2 (http://www.ccel.org/ccel/edwards/works1.html). By the end of the Revolutionary War, America was being hailed as the sanctuary of Christianity, and the "leader in an attack on the Antichrist," which naturally was assumed (on the tail of the war) to be England. See Craig S. Campbell, Images of the New Jerusalem—Latter Day Saint Faction Interpretations of Independence, Missouri (Knoxville, Tennessee: The University of Tennessee Press, 2004), 4. One eighteenth century source echoed this view of America's chosen status and divine calling: "Pure religion will revive and flourish among us in a greater degree than ever it has done before: . . . this country will become the seat of civil and religious liberty; the place from which Christian light and knowledge shall be dispersed to the rest of the world; so that our Zion shall become the delight and praise of the whole earth, and foreign nations shall suck of the breasts of her consolations, and be satisfied with the abundant light and knowledge of Gospel truth which they shall derive from her." Samuel West, cited in James W. Davidson, *The Logic of Millennial Thought: Eighteenth-Century New England* (New Haven, Connecticut: Yale University Press, 1977), 250, cited in Campbell, *Images of the New Jerusalem*, 4. While most American Puritans spoke of the "New Jerusalem" in terms of a symbolic "heavenly condition" rather than an actual place, in the eighteenth and nineteenth centuries there were

numerous communities created around religious ideals; towns and villages plotted with the religious meetinghouse at the center, and emphasizing the covenant, "a two-way pact with God, kept by observing the proper Puritan life." In return, they believed, "God was 'under obligation to supply grace' to those who kept the contract." Campbell, *Images of the New Jerusalem*, 6.

6. Campbell, *Images of the New Jerusalem*, 2.

7. In some cases, early in the history of the United States, millennial accounts appeared, supposedly written by Native Americans themselves. One such document was titled *Apocalypse of Chiokoyhikoy, Chief of the Iroquois*. See Earnest Lee Tuveson, *Redeemer Nation: The Ideal of America's Millennial Role* (Chicago: The University of Chicago Press, 1968), 113–16. See also Robert Griffin and Donald A. Grinde Jr., *Apocalypse of Chiokoyhikoy, Chief of the Iroquois* (Québec City, Canada: University of Laval Press, 1997). In it, a vision describes a people who would rise up on American soil, be an agent for blessed revolution, after which the "supreme god" would return, bringing "good times" to the land and people of the Americas. Tuveson, *Redeemer Nation*, 3.

8. As is well known, Joseph and a number of his contemporaries and successors believed that the Garden of Eden was in Independence, Missouri. Joseph Smith is said to have taught this (see Wilford Woodruff, *Wilford Woodruff's Journal*, 9 vols., ed. Scott G. Kenney [Midvale, Utah: Signature Books, 1983], 7:129; see also Melvin R. Brooks, *LDS Reference Encyclopedia*, 2 vols. [Salt Lake City: Bookcraft, 1960], 1:114; Ben E. Rich, *Scrapbook of Mormon Literature*, 2 vols. [Chicago: Henry C. Etten & Co., 1913], 1:101–2), as did Brigham Young (discourse given October 7, 1860, in *Journal of Discourses*, 8:195), Wilford Woodruff (see Brooks, *LDS Reference Encyclopedia*, 1:114–15), Heber C. Kimball (*Journal of Discourses*, 10:235), George Q. Cannon (discourse given March 3, 1867, in *Journal of Discourses*, 11:337), Joseph Fielding Smith, *Doctrines of Salvation*, 3 vols. (Salt Lake City: Bookcraft, 1998), 3:74), Bruce R. McConkie (*Mormon Doctrine*, 2nd ed. [Salt Lake City: Bookcraft, 1979], 303), and others (Milton R. Hunter, *Pearl of Great Price Commentary* [Salt Lake City: Stevens & Wallis, Inc., 1951], 109; Hoyt W. Brewster Jr., *Doctrine and Covenants Encyclopedia* [Salt Lake City: Bookcraft, 1988], 201–2; Orson F. Whitney, *The Life of Heber C. Kimball* [Salt Lake City: Bookcraft, 1973], 207, n.2; John A. Widtsoe, *Evidences and Reconciliations* [Salt Lake City: Bookcraft, 1960], 127).

9. Joseph had planned to have a complex of twenty-four temples at the heart of the Independence, Missouri, Zion community. See B. H. Roberts, *A Comprehensive History of The Church of Jesus Christ of Latter-day Saints*, 6 vols. (Orem, Utah: Sonos Publishing, Inc., 1991), 1:311; Ronald E. Romig, "Temple Lot Discoveries and the RLDS Temple," in Arnold K. Garr and Clark V. Johnson, *Regional Studies in Latter-day Saint Church History—Missouri* (Provo, Utah: Department of Church History and Doctrine, Brigham Young University, 1994), 313–35. It seems evident, however, that these twenty-four "temples" were not all ordinance buildings. Many were effectively the same thing as you see around the Salt Lake Temple (the Church Administration building, the Church Office building, the Relief Society building, and so on).

10. Joseph Smith, "Wilford Woodruff Diary: 11 June 1843," in *The Words of Joseph Smith: The Contemporary Accounts of the Nauvoo Discourses of the Prophet Joseph*, ed.

Andrew F. Ehat and Lyndon W. Cook (Provo, Utah: Religious Studies Center, BYU, 1980), 212–13.

11. On May 4, 1842, Joseph revealed the holy endowment to nine prominent leaders in the Church. These men were Hyrum Smith (Assistant President of the Church and Patriarch to the Church), William Law (a counselor in the First Presidency), Brigham Young, Heber C. Kimball, and Willard Richards (all three, members of the Quorum of the Twelve Apostles), William Marks (president of the Nauvoo Stake), George Miller (president of the Nauvoo high priests quorum and Presiding Bishop), Newel K. Whitney (Presiding Bishop), and James Adams (patriarch and branch president). See Andrew F. Ehat, "Joseph Smith's Introduction of Temple Ordinances and the 1844 Mormon Succession Question" (master's thesis, Brigham Young University, 1981), 27–28.

12. Heber C. Kimball recorded, "While there we laid out a city on a high elevated piece of land, and set the stakes for the four corners of a temple block, which was dedicated, Brother Brigham Young being mouth; there were from three to five hundred men present on the occasion." See Orson F. Whitney, *Life of Heber C. Kimball,* 4th ed. (Salt Lake City: Bookcraft, 1973), 208–9. Robert J. Matthews noted, "Although the 'temple block' was dedicated, apparently no corner stones were laid." Robert J. Matthews, "Adam-ondi-Ahman," in *BYU Studies* 13, no. 1 (1972): 34.

13. Joseph Smith, *History of the Church,* 2nd rev. ed., 7 vols. (Salt Lake City: Deseret Book, 1978), 3:390. See also Joseph Smith, *Teachings of The Prophet Joseph Smith,* comp. Joseph Fielding Smith (Salt Lake City: Deseret Book, 1976), 160; Ehat and Cook, eds., *Words of Joseph Smith,* 11. Parallel with the Saints' efforts to establish Zion in North America, Joseph prayed that the Jews might "from this hour" begin to be redeemed and receive again their promised land. See Joseph Smith's dedicatory prayer of the Kirtland Temple, in D&C 109:62–63. One source notes, "Latter-day scripture declares that Jerusalem will become the spiritual-temporal capital of the whole Eastern Hemisphere, 'One Great Centre, and one mighty Sovereign' . . . , while Zion will be the place of refuge and divine direction in the Western Hemisphere." In 1840 to 1841, the Apostle Orson Hyde dedicated the land of Jerusalem under the direction of Joseph Smith. "His prayer petitioned for the gathering home of the exiles, the fruitfulness of the earth, the establishing of an independent government, the rebuilding of Jerusalem, and 'rearing a Temple in honor of thy name.'" See Truman G. Madsen, "Zionism," in *Encyclopedia of Mormonism,* 4 vols., ed. Daniel H. Ludlow (New York: Macmillan, 1992), 4:1626. The nineteenth century saw the fusing of traditional messianism with modern nationalism, creating a true Zionist movement among Jews for a variety of factors. This led to the conception and eventual establishment of a Jewish homeland.

14. See Robert L. Millet, "Zion," in *Encyclopedia of Latter-day Saint History,* ed. Arnold K. Garr, Donald Q. Cannon, and Richard O. Cowan (Salt Lake City: Deseret Book, 2000), 1397.

15. In later revelations, it was revealed to Joseph that the Saints should "establish a like community of faith in the last Days"—and that this community should be built upon the same "foundational principles of consecration and stewardship" that Enoch's city of Zion adhered to. Millet, in *Encyclopedia of Latter-day Saint History,* 1397.

16. Smith, *History of the Church*, 2:254. See also "Revelation, 6 June, 1831 [D&C 52]," in Michael Hubbard MacKay, Gerrit J. Dirkmaat, Grant Underwood, Robert J. Woodford, and William G. Hartley, eds., *The Joseph Smith Papers: Documents—Volume 1: July 1828–June 1831*, ed. Dean C. Jessee, Ronald K. Esplin, Richard Lyman Bushman, and Matthew J. Grow (Salt Lake City: The Church Historian's Press, 2013), 327–32.

17. In their Kirtland attempt at establishing a utopia (which, parenthetically, collapsed when the Kirtland Safety Society collapsed), they included economic communalism, a store, a bank, a newspaper, a clerical school for training missionaries, and even a temple. No doubt each of these components, and more, would have been part of the Missouri Experiment—though it was not to be.

18. Smith, *History of the Church*, 1:316–17. See also Matthew C. Godfrey, Mark Ashurst-McGee, Grant Underwood, Robert J. Woodford, and William G. Hartley, eds., *Documents, Volume 2: July 1831–January 1833, vol. 2 of the Documents series of The Joseph Smith Papers*, ed. Dean C. Jessee, Ronald K. Esplin, Richard Lyman Bushman, and Matthew J. Grow (Salt Lake City: The Church Historian's Press, 2013), 364–68. Joseph referred to this letter, written January 11, 1833 to W. W. Phelps, as the "Olive Leaf." Harmonious with Joseph's rebuke of the Saints, D&C 105:9 states, "Therefore, in consequence of the transgressions of my people, it is expedient in me that mine elders should wait for a little season for the redemption of Zion." Similarly, Community of Christ D&C 98:1a states, "Verily, I say unto you, concerning your brethren who have been afflicted, and persecuted, and cast out from the land of their inheritance, I, the Lord, have suffered the affliction to come upon them, wherewith they have been afflicted in consequence of their transgressions" (See also LDS D&C 101:1–2; CofC D&C 98:1a).

19. See Wilford Woodruff, *Wilford Woodruff's Journal*, 9 vols., ed. Scott G. Kenney (Midvale, Utah: Signature Books, 1983), 4:370, s.v. December 16, 1855.

20. Oliver Olney, *Oliver Olney Journal*, s.v. May 7, 1842. *The Oliver Olney Papers* are housed in the Beinecke Rare Book and Manuscript Library at Yale University. There are twelve folders consisting of over 450 pages of handwritten journal entries and letters. A copy of Oliver's unpublished journal is in the possession of this author.

21. John Young, discourse given October 25, 1857, in *Journal of Discourses*, 26 vols. (Liverpool: Latter-Day Saints' Book Depot, 1855–86), 5:371.

22. Orson Pratt, discourse given April 10, 1870, in *Journal of Discourses*, 13:138.

23. Some discussion of a return would resurface in the latter-half of the twentieth century. However, those who had known the Prophet Joseph and had sought the establishment of a Missouri Zion during his day rarely spoke of it from the pulpit after Brigham's passing.

24. See V. Ben Bloxham, ed. *Truth Will Prevail: The Rise of the Church of Jesus Christ of Latter-day Saints in the British Isles 1837–1987* (Solihul, England: The Church of Jesus Christ of Latter-day Saints, 1987), 189.

25. George Q. Cannon, discourse given October 6, 1898, in *Conference Report* (Salt Lake City: The Church of Jesus Christ of Latter-day Saints, 1898), 4.

26. See Joseph F. Smith, discourse given October 4, 1903, in *Conference Report* (Salt Lake City: The Church of Jesus Christ of Latter-day Saints, 1903), 4.

27. Of course, the Church had previously built temples in Kirtland, Ohio, and in Nauvoo, Illinois. However, by 1913, the Kirtland Temple no longer belonged to the Mormons, nor did it offer the types of salvific ordinances the Saints were then practicing. The Nauvoo Temple had long since been destroyed. Thus, in 1913 the Cardston Alberta Temple was the LDS Church's only non-Utah temple.

28. In a 1952 joint meeting of the First Presidency and Quorum of the Twelve it was noted that the reason for "carrying temples to the people in Europe" was so that "they will build up strong branches" of the Church there. Gregory A. Prince and Wm. Robert Wright, *David O. McKay and the Rise of Modern Mormonism* (Salt Lake City: The University of Utah Press, 2005), 262–63.

29. This is an amalgamation of President Kimball's teachings on this matter, found in Spencer W. Kimball, *The Teachings of Spencer W. Kimball*, ed. Edward L. Kimball (Salt Lake City: Bookcraft, 1998), 439–40; emphasis added.

30. Bruce R. McConkie, discourse given at a 1972 area conference in Mexico City, cited in Richard O. Cowan, "The Great Temple of the New Jerusalem," in *Regional Studies in Church History—Missouri* (Provo, Utah: Religious Studies Center, BYU, 1994), 151.

31. See Gordon B. Hinckley, "This Glorious Easter Morn," in *Ensign*, May 1996, 65. The Conference Center was dedicated on October 8, 2000.

32. See http://en.wikipedia.org/wiki/LDS_Conference_Center. In addition to the 21,000 seats, the Conference Center also has an overflow which seats some 900 people. See Don L. Searle, "The Conference Center: 'This New and Wonderful Hall'," in *Ensign*, October 2000, 33. While the LDS Church has never published, so far as I can find, the total cost to build the Conference Center, *The Salt Lake Tribune* reported its price tag at 240 million dollars. See "Questionable Spending" in *The Salt Lake Tribune*, April 22, 2000, A-10.

33. See http://www.mormonnewsroom.org/article/downtown-redevelopment-plans-announced.

34. Gordon B. Hinckley, "We Bear Testimony to the World," in *Ensign*, November 2006, 4–5.

35. See Carole Mikita, "A look inside as City Creek Center's Completion Nears," March 1, 2012, posted on the KSL website, http://www.ksl.com/?nid=148&sid=19428181.

36. See Thomas S. Monson, "Welcome to Conference," in *Ensign*, November 2012, 6.

37. The Kansas City Missouri Temple serves some 12 stakes, 102 wards, and 25 branches of the Church. Approximately 25,000 members of the LDS Church live in the "temple district" associated with the Kansas City Missouri Temple.

38. Parenthetically, the Kansas City Missouri LDS Temple isn't even in Jackson County. It is in Clay County. Thus it could not qualify as fulfilling Joseph's initial vision of a temple in Jackson County, let alone in Independence.

39. The current LDS Bible Dictionary gives this flowing definition of Zion: "The word Zion is used repeatedly in all the standard works of the Church and is defined in latter-day revelation as 'the pure in heart' (D&C 97:21). Other usages of Zion have to do with a geographical location. For example, Enoch built a city that was called Zion (Moses 7:18–19); Solomon built his temple on Mount Zion (1 Kgs. 8:1; see also 2 Sam. 5:6–7); and Jackson County, Missouri, is called Zion in many of the revelations in the D&C,

such as 58:49–50; 62:4; 63:48; 72:13; 84:76; 104:47. The city of New Jerusalem, to be built in Jackson County, Missouri, is to be called Zion (D&C 45:66–67). The revelations also speak of 'the cause of Zion' (D&C 6:6; 11:6). In a wider sense all of North and South America are Zion (HC 6:318–19). For further references see 1 Chr. 11:5; Ps. 2:6; 99:2; 102:16; Isa. 1:27; 2:3; 4:3–5; 33:20; 52:1–8; 59:20; Jer. 3:14; 31:6; Joel 2:1–32; Amos 6:1; Obad. 1:17, 21; Heb. 12:22–24; Rev. 14:1–5; and many others. (In the New Testament, Zion is spelled Sion.)" See LDS Bible Dictionary (Salt Lake City: Intellectual Reserve, Inc., 2013), 746.

40. See, for example, Jan Shipps, "The Scattering of the Gathered and the Gathering of the Scattered: The Mormon Diaspora in the Mid-Twentieth Century," in *The Juanita Brooks Lecture Series—Issue 3* (Saint George, Utah: Dixie College, 1991), 4–5.

41. Joseph Smith, in Wilford Woodruff, *The Discourses of Wilford Woodruff* (Salt Lake City: Bookcraft, 1964), 38–39; emphasis added.

42. Smith, *History of the Church*, 2:254; emphasis added. See also Smith, *Teachings of The Prophet Joseph Smith*, 79.

43. Smith, *History of the Church*, 3:391; emphasis added. See also Smith, *Teachings of The Prophet Joseph Smith*, 161.

44. See also D&C 87:8. McConkie and Ostler penned this: "The safety known to the General body of the church will center in its stakes. That these stakes will dot the whole earth suggests that the safety of the Saints will center not in a particular location but rather through the garment of protection that rests upon them in and through keeping their covenants with exactness and honor. As the stakes of Zion spread across the face of the earth, we expect temples to follow. The hope is that in some not too far distant day every faithful Latter-day Saint will find themselves within some reasonable proximity of a temple. 'Let us . . . recite the crowning reason for gathering to Zion or to her stakes,' taught Elder Bruce R. McConkie. 'It is to receive the blessings found in the temples of the Lord.'" McConkie and Ostler, *Revelations of the Restoration*, 918. Elsewhere we read, "Note that it is Zion, wherever she is established in all her stakes, and not exclusively in Far West [where this revelation was received] or even in Missouri, that the Saints will find refuge at the last day." Robinson and Garrett, *A Commentary on the Doctrine and Covenants*, 4:111. As we have noted, according to LDS doctrine, protection is not about geography; it is about faithfulness to covenants. And where the temple is, there is Zion. Hence D&C 124:36 informs us, "For it is ordained that in Zion, and in her stakes, and in Jerusalem, those places which I have appointed for refuge, shall be the places for your baptisms for your dead." D&C 45 says nothing about a return to Independence, but it says a great deal about the multiple locations of Zion at the time the Lord returns—and the protective power of the House of the Lord upon those who worship therein.

45. Ezra Taft Benson, "Prepare Yourselves for the Great Day of the Lord," *Brigham Young University Fireside and Devotional Speeches* (Provo, Utah: Brigham Young University, 1981), 68.

46. Joseph Smith, letter to Moses C. Nickerson, in "History of Joseph Smith," published in *Times and Seasons*, 6 vols. (Commerce and Nauvoo, Illinois: The Church of Jesus Christ of Latter-day Saints, 1839–46), 6:899.

47. Joseph Smith, in Woodruff, *The Discourses of Wilford Woodruff*, 39; emphasis added. It has been pointed out that Wilford Woodruff is the only source for this statement by Joseph. Wilford doesn't record this "testimony of the Prophet Joseph" in his personal journal until Sunday, October 5, 1884. He indicates that he heard Joseph teach this in Kirtland, Ohio, in April of 1834. It seems worth noting that the period in which this discourse by Joseph was said to have been given is one in which many things are without multiple attestations—largely because the members had yet realized the importance of keeping detailed records. Thus, the fact that Wilford Woodruff is the only one to make a note of this specific discourse—and a late note at that—may not be sufficient reason to discount this source. Indeed, under the date of Saturday, August 6, 1842, Joseph's History states, "I had a conversation with a number of brethren in the shade of the building on the subject of our persecutions in Missouri, and the constant annoyance which has followed us since we were driven from that State. I prophecied [*sic*] that the Saints would continue to suffer much affliction and would be driven to the Rocky Mountains, many would apostatize, others would be put to death by our Persecutors, or lose their lives in consequence of exposure or disease, and some of you will live to go, and assist in making settlements and build cities and see the Saints become a mighty people in the midst of the Rocky Mountains." See http://josephsmithpapers.org/paperSummary /history-1838-1856-volume-d-1-1-august-1842-1-july-1843?p=5&highlight=would%20 be%20driven%20to%20the%20Rocky%20Mountains. This would suggest that Wilford Woodruff's recollection of Joseph's teaching was accurate, even though others did not cite the teaching publicly as Wilford did.

48. Once again Joseph connects Zion and the gathering with the building of temples and the receiving of the sacred, saving ordinances the prophet labeled as the "endowment."

49. Brigham Young, discourse given December 11, 1864, in *Journal of Discourses (1855–86)*, 11:16.

50. Brigham Young, discourse given June 5, 1853, in *Journal of Discourses (1855–86)*, 2:253; emphasis added.

51. Brigham Young, discourse given June 5, 1853, in *Journal of Discourses (1855–86)*, 2:253; emphasis added.

52. Brigham Young, discourse given July 28, 1861, in *Journal of Discourses (1855–86)*, 9:138; emphasis added.

53. At the writing of this chapter, the LDS Church had 148 operating temples, 14 under construction, and 11 announced.

54. Kimball, in *The Teachings of Spencer W. Kimball*, 439; emphasis added. Elder Erastus Snow taught, "The work before us is a great one, and very much remaineth to be accomplished according to the prophecies—Israel is to be gathered, Jerusalem rebuilt, Zion established, the vineyard of the Lord pruned and the corrupt branches cut off and cast into the fire, while the good branches shall be grafted in and partake of the root and fatness of the tame olive tree. There is a great work to be accomplished in the earth. . . . As our minds grew, and our ideas enlarged, we began to perceive that we were only children in our views and feelings, our ideas and expectations. We have the views, ideas and expectations of children; and we see how the Lord has enlarged Israel and expanded His work. . . . The time was that we looked for one temple. The early revelations

given to the Latter-day Saints predicted a temple in Zion, and Zion in our minds at that time was a little place on the Missouri River in Jackson County, Western Missouri—a town and a few surrounding villages, or a country, peradventure it may be as large as a county. When we first heard the fullness of the Gospel preached by the first Elders, and read the revelations given through the Prophet Joseph Smith, our ideas of Zion were very limited. But as our minds began to grow and expand, why we began to look upon Zion as a great people, and the Stakes of Zion as numerous, and the area of the country to be inhabited by the people of Zion as this great American continent, or at least such portions of it as the Lord should consecrate for the gathering of His people. We ceased to set bounds to Zion and her Stakes. We began also to cease to think about a single temple in one certain place. Seeing the different Stakes of Zion that were being organized we perceived the idea, possibly, of as many temples. Having had one spot pointed out in the revelations for the temple in Jackson County, our minds expanded so that in a short time we were building another temple in a Stake of Zion in Kirtland, Ohio. A little while afterwards we were laying the foundation of a temple in Far West, Missouri, and driven before our enemies; from that place we next laid the foundation and built up a temple unto the Lord in Nauvoo. When we located in the mountains and laid the foundation of a temple in Salt Lake City, who of us had an idea that before it should be completed we would be administering in a temple in St. George, and another in Logan, and another in Manti, and who conceives the idea to-day, that by the time these are completed and the Saints have officiated in them, we will be scattered over the American continent, building temples in a hundred other places? All this comes within the range of possibility, nay, probability, almost amounting to certainty. One of my brethren behind me here, who understands these things, and who can speak knowingly in regard to them, says, that we may put it down as a certainty, that by and by, there will be hundreds of these temples throughout the land. Our minds are beginning to comprehend the object and purpose of the temples of our God." Erastus Snow, discourse given February 2, 1884, in *Journal of Discourses*, 25:30–31.

55. Monte S. Nyman, *Doctrine and Covenants Commentary*, 2 vols. (Orem, Utah: Granite Publishing, 2008–9), 1:474.

56. Smith, *History of the Church*, 2:254; emphasis added.

57. Brigham Young, discourse given July 28, 1861, in *Journal of Discourses* 9:139.

58. Stephen E. Robinson and H. Dean Garrett, *A Commentary on the Doctrine and Covenants*, 4 vols. (Salt Lake City: Deseret Book, 2000–5), 2:143.

59. Leaun G. Otten and C. Max Caldwell, *Sacred Truths of the Doctrine and Covenants*, 3rd ed., 2 vols. (Springville, Utah: LEMB, 1982–83), 1:275.

60. President Joseph F. Smith declared, "May Israel flourish upon the hills and rejoice upon the mountains, and assemble together unto the place which God has appointed, and there prosper, multiply and replenish the earth, and thence spread abroad throughout the land; for the time will come when we will find it necessary to fulfil the purposes of the Almighty by occupying the land of Zion in all parts of it. We are not destined to be confined to the valleys of the mountains. Zion is destined to grow, and the time will come when we will cry aloud, more than we do today, 'Give us room that we may dwell!'" Smith, *Doctrines of Salvation*, 75.

61. Nyman, *Doctrine and Covenants Commentary*, 1:353.

62. For example, D&C 29:7–8; 42:8–9, 34–36; 45:64–71; 49:24–25; 63:33–36; 101:43–62. See also Moses 7:63 and Ether 13:3–5.

63. Curiously, in several places, the Lord doesn't say "into one place" but, instead, "into one." Of course, He has reminded us, "I say unto you, be one; and if ye are not one ye are not mine" (D&C 38:27). McConkie and Ostler note, "We are not saved alone. Salvation is a community affair, as is the redemption of Zion or the building of a temple. The covenants we make with God on an individual bases require that we also be part of a covenant community. . . . Zion can be built up only by a community of Saints who are 'of one heart and one mind, and dwell in righteousness' (Moses 7:18)." McConkie and Ostler, *Revelations of the Restoration*, 309.

64. Section 45 (D&C 45:64–71) is quite clear that Zion will be a place of refuge from a wicked and fallen world. However, it does not say that Missouri is the only portion of Zion that has this protective power. Indeed, in April of 1838 the Lord informed the Prophet Joseph that this protective power was absolutely not reserved for only those gathered to Missouri. He promised that any who gathered to Zion, or "her stakes," would find "refuge from the storms" that were to come (D&C 115:6). Thus, while this verse supports the notion that some members of The Church of Jesus Christ of Latter-day Saints will undoubtedly gather to stakes in Jackson County, it argues against a universal gathering to that location. As one source notes, "Zion will be larger than just one city." Robinson and Garrett, *A Commentary on the Doctrine and Covenants*, 2:69. McConkie and Ostler penned this: "The safety known to the General body of the church will center in its stakes. That these stakes will dot the whole earth suggests that the safety of the Saints will center not in a particular location but rather through the garment of protection that rests upon them in and through keeping their covenants with exactness and honor. As the stakes of Zion spread across the face of the earth, we expect temples to follow. The hope is that in some not too far distant day every faithful Latter-day Saint will find themselves within some reasonable proximity of a temple. 'Let us . . . recite the crowning reason for gathering to Zion or to her stakes,' taught Elder Bruce R. McConkie. 'It is to receive the blessings found in the temples of the Lord.'" McConkie and Ostler, *Revelations of the Restoration*, 918. Elsewhere we read, "Note that it is Zion, wherever she is established in all her stakes, and not exclusively in Far West [where this revelation was received] or even in Missouri, that the Saints will find refuge at the last day." Robinson and Garrett, *A Commentary on the Doctrine and Covenants*, 4:111. As we have noted, according to LDS doctrine, protection is not about geography; it is about faithfulness to covenants. And where the temple is, there is Zion. Hence D&C 124:36 informs us, "For it is ordained that in Zion, and in her stakes, and in Jerusalem, those places which I have appointed for refuge, shall be the places for your baptisms for your dead." Thus D&C 45 is saying nothing about a return to Independence. But it says a great deal about the multiple locations of Zion at the time the Lord returns—and the protective power of the House of the Lord upon those who worship therein.

65. Nyman, *Doctrine and Covenants Commentary*, 281. George Horton wrote, "During the impending wars, as the wicked slay the wicked, the situation will be so severe that 'the saints also shall hardly escape' (D&C 63:34). They are admonished to 'gather

together, and stand in holy places,' e.g., stakes of Zion (D&C 101:22)." George A. Horton Jr., "Knowing the Calamity," in *Studies in Scripture—Volume One: The Doctrine and Covenants*, ed. Robert L. Millet and Kent P. Jackson (Salt Lake City: Deseret Book, 1989), 46. Smith, *Doctrines of Salvation*, 75.

66. Bruce R. McConkie, "The Keys of the Kingdom," in *Ensign*, May 1983, 22. Millet and Backman wrote, "Only through the establishment and strengthening of stakes throughout the world could the full concept of Zion be realized; only then could the Lord make it possible for the blessings of the temple to be had universally. Joseph Smith taught: 'The main object [of gathering] was to build unto the Lord a house whereby He could reveal unto His people the ordinances of His house and the glories of His Kingdom, and teach the people the way of salvation.'" Milton V. Backman and Robert L. Millet, "Heavenly Manifestations in the Kirtland Temple," in *Studies in Scripture—Volume One: The Doctrine and Covenants*, ed. Robert L. Millet and Kent P. Jackson (Salt Lake City: Deseret Book, 1989), 425. "Now I call your attention to the facts, set forth in these scriptures, that the gathering of Israel consists of joining the true church; of coming to a knowledge of the true God and of his saving truths; and of worshiping him in the congregations of the Saints in all nations and among all peoples. Please note that these revealed words speak of the folds of the Lord; of Israel being gathered to the lands of their inheritance; of Israel being established in all their lands of promise; and of there being congregations of the covenant people of the Lord in every nation, speaking every tongue, and among every people when the Lord comes again." Bruce R. McConkie, quoted by President Harold B. Lee, "Strengthen the Stakes of Zion," in *Ensign*, July 1973, 4. Similarly, 2 Nephi 9:1–2 states, "And now, my beloved brethren, I have read these things that ye might know concerning the covenants of the Lord that he has covenanted with all the house of Israel—That he has spoken unto the Jews, by the mouth of his holy prophets, even from the beginning down, from generation to generation, until the time comes that they shall be restored to the true church and fold of God; when they shall be gathered home to the *lands* of their inheritance, and shall be established in all their *lands* of promise"; emphasis added.

67. Mario S. De Pillis noted, "Western Missouri was holy millennial ground to the early Mormons—and remains fraught with millennial expectations for Mormons today." Mario S. De Pillis, "Christ Comes to Jackson County: The Mormon City of Zion and Its Consequences," in *John Whitmer Historical Association*, vol. 23 (2003): 26.

68. Significantly, Scott Esplin pointed out that from D&C 58 onward "focus shifted from Zion as a place to Zion as a process" by which "the Saints could become his promised people." Scott C. Esplin, "'Let Zion in Her Beauty Rise': Building Zion by Becoming Zion," in *You Shall Have my Word: Exploring the Text of the Doctrine and Covenants*, ed. Scott C. Esplin, Richard O. Cowan, and Rachel Cope (Provo, Utah: Religious Studies Center, BYU, 2012), 136.

69. Orson F. Whitney, *The Life of Heber C. Kimball*, 4th ed. (Salt Lake City: Bookcraft, 1973), 65.

70. The Hebrew root from which our English word Zion comes means literally "signpost" or "monument." This seems appropriate in light of the veneration of Zion

among Restorationists. It is a "signpost" or "monument" to God's work through His covenant people. It is a symbol of His efforts to gather them.

71.   We take no negative position on the potential that a percentage of Latter-day Saints may by assignment one day gather in Independence, Jackson County, Missouri. Such is certainly possible; though the activities of the Church in Utah and other parts of the world may suggest that a general return is not likely. Ultimately, it is not our place to speculate. What the reader should know is that Alonzo tends to see Independence as playing a smaller role in the future of the Church than does Rich, who suspects that its role might be a bit more significant. Neither author is certain, and neither feels dogmatic about that city's future role in Church history.

72.   Jeffrey R. Holland, "Israel, Israel, God is Calling," *CES Fireside for Young Adults*, September 9, 2012.

73.   D. Todd Christofferson, "Come to Zion," in *Ensign*, November 2008, 38.

74.   Brigham Young, *Discourses of Brigham Young*, comp. John A. Widtsoe (Salt Lake City: Bookcraft, 1998), 118.

75.   See Graham W. Doxy, "Missouri Myths," in *Ensign*, April 1979, 64–65. LDS.org has a section on "General Topics" of interest. In that section of the website, under "Zion," one finds two significant statements. First, "In the early days of this dispensation, Church leaders counseled members to build up Zion by emigrating to a central location. Today our leaders counsel us to build up Zion wherever we live. Members of the Church are asked to remain in their native lands and help establish the Church there. Many temples are being built so Latter-day Saints throughout the world can receive temple blessings." And second, "The New Jerusalem, which will be built in Jackson County, Missouri" is sometimes called "Zion." LDS.org is quoting from the official Church publication, *True to the Faith* (Salt Lake City: The Church of Jesus Christ of Latter-day Saints, 2004), 189–90. In that publication and on the website, "Zion" is defined in several different ways.

CHAPTER 9

THE "CEREMONY OF THE SHOE"

A RITUAL OF GOD'S ANCIENT & MODERN COVENANT[1]

Alonzo L. Gaskill

"Put off thy shoes from off thy feet, for the place whereon thou standest is holy ground" (Exodus 3:5). So spoke the premortal Jehovah to the prophet Moses—and so practiced ancient and modern Hindus, Muslims, Hare Krishnas, and various other faith traditions. Shoes have played an important role in establishing sacred space and sacred rites from the beginning of time. However, the removal of one's shoes as a ritual act or gesture is not always about sacred soil. As a singular example, the ancient practice of levirate marriage is often associated with the removal of the shoes—but entrance into sacred space is not at the heart of the act. Indeed, an entirely different connotation is implied. In this chapter, I will examine the "ceremony of the shoe" as it appears in Ruth 4, with its common interpretations, likely implications, and significant relations to Latter-day Saint temple practices.

Levirate marriage is the name given to the ancient law requiring the surviving brother of a deceased man to unite in an intimate relationship with the childless widow of his brother. This was done in order to raise up seed unto the name of his prematurely deceased sibling (see

165

Deuteronomy 25:5–6).[2] As with many Hebrew laws, levirate marriage had accompanying rituals requisite for its formal and legal enactment. Thus, near the end of the Deuteronomic passage dealing with this law comes an explanation of what a woman should do if her surviving brother-in-law (or *levir*) refuses to marry her. We read, "Then shall his brother's wife come unto him in the presence of the elders, and loose his shoe from off his foot, and spit in his face, and shall answer and say, So shall it be done unto that man that will not build up his brother's house. And his name shall be called in Israel, The house of him that hath his shoe loosed" (Deuteronomy 25:9–10).

We know that the practice of levirate marriage was known in biblical times at least as early as the writing of the Pentateuch and remained culturally acceptable perhaps as late as the penning of the gospel of Luke (see Luke 20:28). Unfortunately there is some confusion surrounding this rite; namely, it is common for scholars to make blanket assumptions about this law and its ritual enactment in scripture and history—perhaps in part because what does appear in scripture regarding levirate marriage is scant at best. Thus commentators will sometimes see in certain cultic practices or biblical passages what appear to be parallels between those rites or verses and the law of levirate marriage. However, many of these suppositions are not necessarily warranted.

For an example of one such unwarranted assumption, we turn to the book of Ruth and the story of Boaz's marriage to that icon of faithfulness and devotion, Ruth. In the fourth chapter of Ruth we read, "Now this was the manner in former time in Israel concerning redeeming and concerning changing, for to confirm all things; a man plucked off his shoe, and gave it to his neighbour: and this was a testimony in Israel. Therefore the kinsman said unto Boaz, Buy it for thee. So he drew off his shoe" (Ruth 4:7–8).

At least as early as the first century of the Common Era, commentators were reading the Ruth passage as an example of levirate marriage. Josephus clearly saw the ritual portrayed in the book of Ruth as a representation of this rite, as is evidenced by his comments in his work *Antiquities of the Jews*. He wrote that Boaz "bid the woman to loose his shoe and spit in his face, according to the law; and when this was done [Boaz] married Ruth, and they had a son within a year's time."[3] Likewise, Methodist commentator Adam Clarke (circa 1760–1832) wrote that the laws explaining what was happening in Ruth chapter 4 are "given at large in Deut.xxv.5–9."[4] Like Josephus and Clarke, most scholars, whether LDS[5] or non-LDS,[6] tend to see the rite described in Ruth chapter 4 as a biblical example of levirate marriage.

Admittedly, on a superficial level, there appear to be significant correlations between the passages in Ruth 4 and those in Deuteronomy 25. In the end, however, there are a number of reasons why Ruth chapter 4 is likely not intended to be a representation of a traditional levirate marriage ritual.[7]

First of all, unlike the widowed woman in Exodus chapter 25, Ruth does not spit in the face of the man who refuses to marry her, which many sources indicate is a requisite part of the ceremony of levirate marriage.[8] One commentator noted that the Boethusians, or Sanhedrin, "held that the *yevamah* is required actually to spit in the levir's face and this is also stated in two manuscripts of the Septuagint, in Josephus's *Antiquities*, and in some of the apocryphal books, but the talmudic scholars held it to be sufficient if the elders see her spitting."[9] Thus, since Ruth neither spits in the face of her intended, nor on the ground, hers cannot be a levirate marriage. It will also be noted that the unnamed male kinsman-redeemer (*gō'ēl*) in the story of Ruth incurs no disgrace when he declines to play his part.[10] If this is an example of levirate marriage, it runs contrary to scripturally dictated practice.

Second, in the story of Ruth and Boaz it is *not* the woman who removes the man's shoe. Rather, the unnamed male kinsman-redeemer (*gō'ēl*) is depicted as removing his own shoe. This too is contrary to the law surrounding levirate marriage and contrary to what happens in the Deuteronomic passage in question.[11] Thus, again, something other than the standard levirate marriage ceremony is being depicted here.

Third, in the book of Ruth the unnamed kinsman-redeemer (*gō'ēl*) is *not* Ruth's husband's brother—as is required by Jewish law. He appears to be, at best, a distant relative.[12] Thus, again, this cannot be an effort to fulfill the custom of levirate marriage. Something entirely different is being depicted here.

Fourth, the words for the levirate obligation (*yābām*) and for the kinsman-redeemer (*gā'ēl*) are totally unrelated. *Yābām* can mean either "husband's brother," or to perform the duty of such to "a brother's widow."[13] However, the book of Ruth does not use *yābām* but rather the term *gā'ēl*, which indicates a redeemer (particularly of consecrated things or people) or an avenger and signifies that these roles are performed based on the authority of kinship. A "kinsman-redeemer" purchases a relative from slavery (actual or potential); a "kinsman-avenger" provides justice on behalf of a relative.[14] Of course both concepts are in the image of God as Redeemer—but the implications and linguistic connotations are entirely different. Thus, again, the connection between levirate marriage and the rite depicted in Ruth chapter 4 seems stretched.

Fifth, Obed—the son born to Boaz and Ruth—is spoken of as the son of Boaz rather than as the son of Ruth's deceased husband, Mahlon (see Ruth 4:18–22; LXX Ruth 4:13). This would be contrary to levirate marriage, which is primarily for the purpose of raising seed up to a deceased brother.[15] In other words, when the *levir* fathers a child through his sister-in-law, it is not considered his offspring but, rather, the offspring of his deceased brother. Since Obed is described as being Boaz's son, the rite performed in Ruth chapter 4 cannot be an example of levirate marriage.[16]

Finally, one text notes, "In biblical law the levir [or brother-in-law] does not require a formal marriage (*kiddushin*) to the *yevamah* [or sister-in-law] since the personal status tie, the *zikkah* between them, arises automatically upon the death of the husband of the *yevamah*."[17] Elsewhere we read, "If a man died childless, his widow was not free to remarry but was considered to be already betrothed to his brother."[18] Thus, whereas levirate marriage did not require—nor allow—a marriage contract to be initiated (as the couple were considered already married), in the book of Ruth a formal marriage *is* expected and, in the end, *is* performed. Thus, the rites depicted in Deuteronomy 25 and Ruth 4 appear to be different—one having to do with the loss of a family member and the other to do with something that is potentially different altogether.

So if Ruth 4:7–8 is not an example of levirate marriage, what is it? While we cannot say for certain, and the chapter offers us little by way of clues,[19] there are a couple of elements which may at least help us to form a hypothesis about what the author intended his audience to understand. Our primary focus here will be the removal of the shoe. However, we must be cautious to approach the passage exegetically rather than eisegetically[20] if we wish to avoid the pitfalls encountered by previous exegetes.

In modern as well as ancient cultures, shoes have served not only a practical function but also an aesthetic one. However, when employed in biblical ritual, shoes have an almost exclusively symbolic purpose.[21] For example, they can represent one's preparation for a task (see Exodus 12:11; Ephesians 6:15; Matthew 10:10; Mark 6:9). Sometimes they imply the status of the wearer—freedom for the shod (see Luke 15:22) and enslavement or poverty for the barefoot individual (see 2 Chronicles 28:15; Isaiah 20:2). In contrast, going barefoot is occasionally utilized as a sign of mourning (see 2 Samuel 15:30; Ezekiel 24:17, 23).[22] Finally, perhaps the most commonly associated meanings have to do with the removal of shoes when one enters hallowed ground (see Exodus 3:5; Joshua 5:15; Acts 7:33).[23] Thus, we see footwear as more than a convenience and more than an accessory. Shoes, slippers, and sandals are important symbolic articles for ancient and modern Israel—God's covenant people. Aside from the aforementioned symbolic uses of the shoe or slipper, there is one additional use worthy of our examination—the ceremony of the shoe[24] alluded to in the Hebrew Bible, in the records of ancient Mesopotamia,[25] and in the sacred rites of modern covenant Israel.

It appears from a number of sources, scriptural and otherwise, that the transfer of property in ancient times was accompanied by a rite or ritual consisting primarily of the removal of shoes. The Hebrews referred to this ritual by the name of *halitzah* ("to draw off").[26] One text notes, "When someone sells his property . . . he loses permanently or temporarily his legal right to it . . . and he 'lifts up his hand or foot from it, and places that of the new owner in it.' Thus it is logical to conclude that this expression which had at first only a legal meaning developed into a symbolic meaning. Then the biblical tradition took a step further. The 'lifting up of the foot' became more concrete and real with the 'pulling off of the shoe.'"[27] This act before witnesses was a legal attestation[28] that the party divesting itself of a particular piece of property was doing so willingly—and had formally and officially relinquished all future claims to that particular piece of property.[29] The removal of the sandal, slipper, or shoe at the end of the rite signified that the transaction was completed and that the ritual was legally binding.[30] One commentary described the meaning of the rite as follows: "A person's garments are, so to speak, part of himself, and . . . if a person removes his garments in order to show his willingness to deprive himself of everything in life, he ought also to remove his shoes."[31] This same author continues:

> Amongst the Hebrews business transactions took place publically in the market-place so that the presence of the whole community, or at least ten of the elders, served to confirm them. (Gen. xxiii.) . . . As an aid to the memory, therefore, there arose the custom of drawing off

the shoes in transferring a possession or domain. (Ruth iv, 7.) The idea was that the person who gave up a possession should show by removing his shoe that he was thus divesting himself of something before the witnesses. This could then be regarded as a public declaration that he was withdrawing from the property and handing it over to another person.[32]

Because the shoe was a natural symbol of possession, the removal of the same implied divestment.[33] As noted, this act (although symbolic) had binding, legal implications clearly understood by all who were called upon to witness the rite,[34] and in a time when the ability to write was greatly limited, it allowed even the illiterate to participate in legal transactions. Because of biblical evidence and extracanonical support, scholars believe that this rite was at one time very widespread in the ancient Near East.[35]

Although the common assumption is that the rite depicted in Ruth 4 is an example of levirate marriage, it appears likely that it is instead a prime example of the ceremony of the shoe. The salient portion of Ruth reads, "(Now in earlier times in Israel, for the redemption and transfer of property to become final, one party took off his sandal and gave it to the other. This was the method of legalizing transactions in Israel.) So the kinsman-redeemer said to Boaz, 'Buy it yourself.' And he removed his sandal" (N, Ruth 4:7–8).[36] One commentary on this passage states:

> When the unnamed[37] kinsman-redeemer (*gō'ēl*) arrives the next morning at the city gate, Boaz is waiting for him. The dialogue is brief. Boaz brings together the kinsman-redeemer and 10 elders. In typical patriarchal fashion the subject matter is not the women—Naomi and Ruth—but rather the dead man Elimelech's land. Boaz tells the kinsman-redeemer that Naomi is selling it and he is the first in line to acquire it. . . . The kinsman-redeemer agrees to redeem Elimelech's land. Boaz, however, counters that the Moabite Ruth is part of Elimelech's property. Since Elimelech's daughter-in-law is still able to provide an heir for her dead husband's name and land, the kinsman-redeemer is, in effect, committing himself to providing that heir by buying the land. . . . This new information changes things. It is one thing to buy land—and convenient that being a close relative to the deceased gives one the first option to do so. It is quite another thing to realize that the land will ultimately belong to the son whom one will raise up for the deceased. The kinsman-redeemer understands the purchase of Elimelech's land to entail risk to his own inheritance and

so declines the opportunity to purchase it. He then passes on to Boaz the right to redeem the land. . . . A narrative parenthesis explains the significance of what happens next. . . . Transfer of right or ownership of property was solemnized not by a handshake nor by a written contract as it is today but by each party's removing his sandal and giving it to the other.[38]

So the subject is the transfer of property—specifically land (traditionally associated with this ritual), but also Ruth, who, in an ancient patriarchal milieu, would have had the status of property in such circumstances.[39] Here the removal of a shoe symbolizes the fact that rights to the land Elimelech once owned—and rights to his daughter-in-law (who might provide a legal heir)—are now being transferred.[40] Indeed, one commentator noted that Ruth 4:7 "is best understood as an overly terse way of describing shoe symbolism in two different kinds of transaction; in an exchange transaction, the parties exchanged shoes, while in the matter of giving up the right of redemption, the one ceding the right gave his shoe to the one taking over the right."[41] As noted above, the right to freely walk on or dwell upon an estate belonged only to the owner—and the shoe served as the perfect symbol of the right of possession.[42] Anciently, the foot symbolized power or possession (see Psalm 8:6; Psalm 36:11; Joshua 10:24) as well as territorial claims (see Deuteronomy 1:36; 11:24; Joshua 1:3; 14:9).[43] Here the kinsman-redeemer (*gōʾēl*) was acknowledging that he had willingly divested himself of his natural right to Elimelech's former property. Thus one commentator states that the book of "Ruth has preserved the older meaning of the shoe ceremony—a renunciation of a right."[44]

Of course, it is possible that at some point in history there was a connection between, or blending of, the ceremony of the shoe and levirate marriage[45]—after all, the latter of these was not solely concerned with producing a male heir for a deceased relative. It was just as concerned, if not more so, with the perpetuation of family property within the immediate family.[46] Regardless, clearly the meaning of the rite described in the book of Ruth is different from that of levirate marriage, and it appears that there are limited connections that can be made between these two rites. Despite involving the removal of a shoe, the context of the Deuteronomic rite shows that what is intended is significantly different from what is represented in the book of Ruth.

The connections sometimes made between the ceremony of the shoe and the removal of footwear when entering sacred space are not so tenuous, however. As noted above, a prime message in the removal of shoes as a ritual act is that one is divesting oneself of ownership or property. It is a legally binding acknowledgment that what was once yours is no longer such, of your own free will and choice. We see examples in scripture of individuals removing their shoes upon entering sacred space, Moses (see Exodus 3:5) and Joshua (see Joshua 5:15) being the chief among them. In what sense are they divesting themselves of something when they perform such an act? The answer to that question seems obvious. In his fourth-century *Instructions to Initiates into the Mysteries,* Cyril of Jerusalem stated, "As soon, then, as ye entered [the inner chamber], ye put off your tunic [or street clothes]; and this was an image of *putting off the old man with his deeds.*"[47] In the spirit of Cyril's comments, it seems fair to say that the removal of shoes upon entering sacred ground symbolizes the temporary divesting of oneself of the world and its ways—exchanging temporal property for a spiritual residence. It is a symbolic effort to set aside the natural man and the things of this fallen world in order to consecrate one's life and embrace the things of God, including his presence, glory, and Spirit. Thus, one typologist wrote, "putting off shoes on entering a holy place represents leaving earthly contact outside . . . and [divesting] oneself of vice."[48] Another source states, "Shoes are necessary only on the earth because of the filth of the ground. By removing them, we symbolically leave the world outside the Lord's sanctuary."[49]

Elsewhere we read of a connection between the ceremony of the shoe and the removal of one's footwear when entering sacred ground; anciently, "washing was a symbol of consecration, and it was necessary for the worshiper to wash his garments previous to his taking part in any special sacred function (Lev. xvi, etc.), but as shoes, on account of the material from which they were made, could not be washed, they were removed as an act of consecration."[50] Thus, when you and I participate in the ordinances of the temple, we technically divest ourselves of the world via approaching the temple physically clean and also via removal of not only our street clothing but also our shoes. Such actions do not constitute the ceremony of the shoe, but they do prepare us to divest ourselves of the world in the ordinances of the house of the Lord—and they do suggest a subtle connection between the ceremony and our actions of preparation.

We now turn our attention to the specifics of how this ancient rite of property transferal specifically relates to God's modern covenant people and their worship patterns today. The symbolic meanings underlying the ceremony of the shoe, as delineated in this chapter, seem germane to modern temple worship.

First of all, removing shoes—as part of the covenant-making process in ancient Semitic societies—signaled the participants' willingness to divest him or herself of some possession; often property which he or she formerly had a right to. Then is it not possible that the rite manifests their hope of gaining something better through the fulfillment of their part in the covenant?[51] For example, when Adam and Eve willingly partook of the fruit of the tree of knowledge of good and evil, they divested themselves of Eden (with its ease and luxury) in hopes of gaining the celestial kingdom.[52] They made a choice to renounce that property because they knew something better awaited them.

Similarly, in the holy temple, patrons symbolically divest themselves of their inheritance in the premortal existence (the "first estate") so that they can live in the "lone and dreary world" (the "second estate")—all in the hopes of gaining the celestial kingdom. Thus, like Adam and Eve— or Ruth's unnamed kinsman-redeemer—we once willingly covenanted to relinquish our right to remain in the premortal existence because we knew something better awaited us, namely, the celestial kingdom. We made a trade, as it were. We took a calculated risk. In the temple, when entering into that covenant with God, we physically remove our shoes as a symbolic statement that such was done of our own free will and choice, and with the knowledge and belief that God will fulfill his portion of that covenant by preparing for us a "promised land," even the celestial kingdom. John Tvedtnes has suggested "the Hebrew word for sandal (na'al) is probably a wordplay with (nahal), meaning 'inheritance.'"[53] So the removal of the footwear when participating in the ceremony of the shoe actually highlights what that rite is about. It suggests to the participant that inheritance (or land) is the focus—and in a temple context those lands are the premortal existence, Eden, and the yet-future celestial kingdom.[54]

On a related note, David R. Mace explained that in biblical times, "possession of the land and marriage with the widow went together."[55] As it relates to the story of Ruth, there appears to be symbolic implications in this concept. Just as the land and the bride are connected in the story, so also do the promised land (or celestial kingdom) and membership in the Church (which is the "bride of Christ"—Ephesians 5:22–33) go together. It is through the restored rites of the fullness of the gospel of Jesus Christ that those who believe become Christ's bride and lay hold upon an inheritance in the land that belongs to him.[56] We each seek a place in the celestial kingdom of our God. The ceremony of the shoe highlights that desire and our commitment to connect ourselves to the Bridegroom, that redemption might take place and an inheritance might be received. Of the symbolism inherent in the story of Ruth, one commentator wrote that Boaz "is a type for the Lord Jesus who owns the field and who marries those who were formerly foreigners and strangers, but who put their trust in Him and become His bride, the church."[57] Symbolically speaking, removal of the shoe is a ritualistic way of exhibiting faith in the Bridegroom and his ability to save or redeem. The early twentieth-century Scottish linguist and typologist Harold Bayley saw connections between the shoe, or slipper, and Christ. He noted that just as a shoe protects the wearer and shields him or her from dirt—"*by taking it upon itself*"—so also does Jesus shield those who seek to be his bride from the spiritual dirt we call sin.[58] This has relevance in the story of Ruth, both because Ruth and Boaz seem to typify the Church and her Bridegroom, and also because Boaz redeems Ruth via shouldering her burden and taking upon himself her trial—just as Christ willingly shoulders our burdens and takes upon Himself our trials. Significantly, as in the story of Ruth, we must seek out a covenant relationship with Christ (our Bridegroom) and, metaphorically speaking, offer him our shoe as a representation that we have given up all we have because we trust in him and in all that he has promised to do for us and to give to us.[59]

As the evidence shows, levirate marriage and the ceremony regarding the transferal of property are not equivalent, or even harmonious, rites. Indeed, as one commentator noted, "they are in open conflict" with each other.[60] Thus, rather than assuming that the book of Ruth preserves a traditional example of the former Deuteronomic rite, it seems more fitting to draw from Ruth's experience a message about property or inheritance rites and their application to our modern covenant relationship with Christ and the work which we do in His holy temples.

NOTES

1. A version of this article was originally published under the title "The 'Ceremony of the Shoe': A Ritual of God's Ancient Covenant People," in *By Our Rites of Worship: Latter-day Saint Views on Ritual in Scripture, History, and Practice*, ed. Daniel L. Belnap (Provo, Utah: Religious Studies Center, BYU, 2013), 133–50. Republished here by permission.

2. See David R. Mace, *Hebrew Marriage: A Sociological Study* (New York: Philosophical Library, 1953), 95, 113. See also Richard Kalmin, "Levirate Law," in *The Anchor Bible Dictionary*, ed. David Noel Freedman (New York: Doubleday, 1992), 4:296.

3. Flavius Josephus, "Antiquities of the Jews," in *The Complete Works of Josephus*, trans. William Whiston (Grand Rapids, Michigan: Kregel, 1981), 121.

4. Adam Clarke, *Clarke's Commentary on the Holy Bible* (New York: Methodist Book Concern, 1930), 2:201.

5. See, for example, James R. Baker, *Women's Rights in Old Testament Times* (Salt Lake City: Signature Books, 1992), 140–48; Victor L. Ludlow, *Unlocking the Old Testament* (Salt Lake City: Deseret Book, 1981), 74; Daniel H. Ludlow, *A Companion to Your Study of the Old Testament* (Salt Lake City: Deseret Book, 1981), 213; Ellis T. Rasmussen, *A Latter-day Saint Commentary on the Old Testament* (Salt Lake City: Deseret Book, 1993), 228.

6. See, for example, Arthur E. Cundall and Leon Morris, *Tyndale Old Testament Commentaries: Judges and Ruth* (Downers Grove, Illinois: InterVarsity Press, 1968), 306–7; Edward F. Campbell Jr., "Ruth: A New Translation with Introduction, Notes, and Commentary," *Anchor Bible*, vol. 7 (New York: Doubleday, 1975), 161; Clarke, *Clarke's Commentary*, 2:201; Kalmin, "Levirate Law," 4:296.

7. Mace notes that Ruth "is not a very good illustration" of levirate marriage "because there are several irregularities in the account—so much so that some scholars have doubted whether it is really an instance of the levirate at all." Mace, *Hebrew Marriage*, 98. See also Kalmin, "Levirate Law," 4:296.

8. See Cecil Roth, Geoffrey Wigoder, and Fred Skolnik, eds., *Encyclopaedia Judaica* (Jerusalem: Keter Publishing, 1971–72), 11:126. See also Louis Ginzberg, *The Legends of the Jews* (Philadelphia: The Jewish Publication Society of America, 1967–69), 6:193n65; Josephus, "Antiquities of the Jews," 121; Mace, *Hebrew Marriage*, 97, 110; Baker, *Women's Rights*, 147; E. John Hamlin, *Surely There Is a Future: An International Theological Commentary on the Book of Ruth* (Grand Rapids, Michigan: Eerdmans, 1996), 59.

9. Roth, *Encyclopaedia*, 126.

10. See Mace, *Hebrew Marriage*, 100; George Arthur Buttrick, ed., *The Interpreter's Bible* (New York: Abingdon, 1953), 2:848.

11. See Deuteronomy 25:7–10; Roth, *Encyclopaedia*, 122, 126, 130; David Bridger, ed., *The New Jewish Encyclopedia* (New York: Behrman House, 1962), s.v. "halitzah"; Ginzberg, *Legends*, 193–94; Mace, *Hebrew Marriage*, 99; Josephus, "Antiquities of the Jews," 121; Baker, *Women's Rights*, 147; Buttrick, *Interpreter's Bible*, 848.

12. See Roth, *Encyclopaedia*, 122; Bridger, *Jewish Encyclopedia*, s.v. "Halitzah"; Ginzberg, *Legends*, 193–94 n.65; Mace, *Hebrew Marriage*, 99; Buttrick, *Interpreter's Bible*, 848; Hamlin, *Surely There Is a Future*, 59.

13. See Francis Brown, S. R. Driver, and Charles A. Briggs, *The Brown-Driver-Briggs Hebrew and English Lexicon* (Peabody, Massachusetts: Hendrickson, 1999), 386; Claude F. Mariottini, "Onan," in *Anchor Bible Dictionary*, 5:21; Victor P. Hamilton, "Marriage (Old Testament and Ancient Near East)," in *Anchor Bible Dictionary*, 4:567.

14. Brown, Driver, and Briggs, *Lexicon*, 145; R. B. Taylor, "Avenger of Blood," in *Dictionary of the Bible*, rev. ed., ed. James Hastings (New York: Charles Scribner's Sons, 1963), 80; A. R. S. Kennedy and A. G. MacLeod, "Kin (Next of), Kinsman, Avenger of Blood, Go'el," in *Dictionary of the Bible*, 550–51.

15. See Mace, *Hebrew Marriage*, 101, 103.

16. See ibid., 99; Campbell, *Ruth*, 160–61. See also Baker, *Women's Rights*, 148, who sees this problem in the text but seems dismissive of it (as he is a proponent of the theory that the book of Ruth is a case of levirate marriage).

17. Roth, *Encyclopaedia*, 124.

18. Jacob Neusner, ed., *Dictionary of Judaism in the Biblical Period: 450 B.C.E. to 600 C.E.* (Peabody, Massachusetts: Hendrickson, 1999), 674. I express gratitude to Dr. RoseAnn Benson for bringing this source to my attention.

19. Buttrick, *Interpreter's Bible*, 847.

20. Whereas exegesis is the practice of drawing out of a text the original author's intended meaning, eisegesis is reading into a text with preconceived notions held by the reader. The former is appropriate methodology, whereas the latter does violence to the text and is often pejoratively referred to as "proof-texting."

21. E. A. Speiser, "Of Shoes and Shekels," in *Bulletin of the American Schools of Oriental Research*, vol. 77 (1940), 15; Frank E. Eakin Jr., *The Religion and Culture of Israel: An Introduction to Old Testament Thought* (Boston: Allyn and Bacon, 1971), 238.

22. Maurice H. Farbridge, *Studies in Biblical and Semitic Symbolism* (London: Kegan Paul, Trench, Trubner, 1923), 214, 224.

23. I say this is the most common connotation not because it appears the most frequently in scripture, as it certainly does not. Simply put, lay Latter-day Saints more often than not gravitate toward this meaning when they contemplate the removal of shoes. Of course, this is a generalization, but in my experience there is a statistically high number of Saints who make this connection, even when it is not intended by the passage.

24. Speiser, "Shoes," 18. See also Hamlin, *Surely There Is a Future*, 57; Buttrick, *Interpreter's Bible*, 849.

25. Records from Nuzi, an ancient Mesopotamian city, attest to a ceremony of property transfer or land ownership wherein the person selling (or transferring property) must remove his shoes as evidence that the transfer had indeed taken place. See Hamlin, *Surely There Is a Future*, 58.

26. Bridger, *Jewish Encyclopedia*, "Halitzah."

27. Ernest R. Lacheman, "Note on Ruth 4:7–8," in *Journal of Biblical Literature*, vol. 56 (1937), 53, 56. Thomas Thompson and Dorothy Thompson, "Some Legal Problems in the Book of Ruth," *Vetus Testamentum*, vol. 18 (1968): 92; Thompson and Thompson make a similar claim.

28. Farbridge, *Symbolism*, 274; Leland Ryken, James C. Wilhoit, and Tremper Longman III, eds., *Dictionary of Biblical Imagery* (Downers Grove, Illinois: InterVarsity Press, 1998),

s.v. "shoe, sandal"; Speiser, "Shoes," 15; Charles F. Pfeiffer and Everett F. Harrison, eds., *The Wycliffe Bible Commentary* (Chicago: Moody Press, 1975), 271; Eakin, *Religion and Culture*, 238; G. A. Cooke, *The Book of Ruth* (Cambridge: Cambridge University Press, 1913), cited in Cundall and Morris, *Tyndale Commentaries*, 306; Francis I. Andersen and David Noel Freedman, *Amos: A New Translation with Introduction and Commentary, Anchor Bible* 24A (New York: Doubleday, 1989), 312–13; G. M. Tucker, "Shorter Communications: Witnesses and 'Dates' in Israelite Contracts," *The Catholic Biblical Quarterly*, vol. 28 (1966): 42.

29. As one commentator put it, "The meaning of this custom was that the adopter would never go again and put his foot in his former property." Lacheman, *Biblical Literature*, 53. Elsewhere we read that by removing the shoe he was "intimating in this that, whatever right he had to walk or go on the land, he conveyed and transferred it. . . . This was the method of legalizing transactions in Israel." Leslie F. Church, ed., *The NIV Matthew Henry Commentary in One Volume* (Grand Rapids, Michigan: Zondervan, 1992), O.T. 293. See also Mace, *Hebrew Marriage*, 97–98; Tucker, "Shorter Communications," 44. Of course, from a gospel perspective, the forfeiture of the premortal world (or "first estate") is permanent only in that we will never again be in that same state (as spirits abiding in the presence of the Father). However, those who successfully traverse the mortal experience will certainly return to the Father, then inhabiting this earth as a celestialized orb. Hence, our forfeiture of the "first estate" is somewhat tentative.

30. Cundall and Morris, *Tyndale Commentaries*, 307.

31. Farbridge, *Symbolism*, 223–24.

32. Ibid., 9.

33. Mace, *Hebrew Marriage*, 98.

34. One commentator on the rite noted, "To confirm whatever was agreed upon, one man drew off . . . his sandal. . . . It is a curious custom, but at least its unusualness would mean that it attracted attention, and this probably was its object. . . . People would know of the agreement reached." Cundall and Morris, *Tyndale Commentaries*, 306. Elsewhere we read, "A man renouncing property rites removed a sandal . . . , a gesture that everyone understood and considered binding if witnessed by the elders." "Great People of the Bible and How they Lived," *Readers Digest* (Pleasantville, New York: Readers Digest, 1974), 133, cited in *Old Testament: Genesis–2 Samuel (Religion 301) Student Manual*, 2nd ed. rev. (Salt Lake City: The Church of Jesus Christ of Latter-day Saints, 1981), 263.

35. See, for example, Thompson and Thompson, *Vetus*, 90.

36. One commentator noted that, in the book of Ruth, "the delivering of a shoe signified that the next-of-kin transferred to another a sacred obligation." Farbridge, *Symbolism*, 9.

37. According to Jewish legend, the unnamed kinsman-redeemer was Boaz's older brother, Tob. See Ginzberg, *Legends*, 4:34 and 6:188n34.

38. Alice L. Laffey, "Ruth," in *The New Jerome Biblical Commentary*, ed. Raymond E. Brown, Joseph A. Fitzmyer, and Roland E. Murphy (Englewood Cliffs, New Jersey: Prentice Hall, 1990), 557. See also Church, *Matthew Henry Commentary*, 293.

39. See, for example, Speiser, "Shoes," 18; Laffey, "Ruth," 557.

40. Campbell, *Anchor Bible*, 150.

41. Ibid.

42. See James Strahan, "Ruth," in *A Commentary on the Bible*, ed. Arthur S. Peake (New York: Thomas Nelson and Sons, 1919), 272. "The Halakah explains Ruth 4:7 to refer to the form of acquisition known in rabbinic jurisprudence as Halifin, consisting in the handing over of an object by the purchaser to the seller, as a symbolical substitute for the object bought." Ginzberg, *Legends*, 6:194n65.

43. See Hamlin, *Surely There Is a Future*, 58.

44. Buttrick, *Interpreter's Bible*, 849. "The shoe ceremony at the Bethlehem gate was probably like signing a document of transfer. . . . The purpose of the ceremony was to give legal status to a transfer of responsibility involving 'redeeming and exchanging' (4:7)." Hamlin, *Surely There Is a Future*, 57–58.

45. One commentator suggests that perhaps "the Book of Ruth was written late, at a time when the old custom [of levirate marriage] had been modified." See Mace, *Hebrew Marriage*, 100.

46. See Hamilton, "Marriage," 567.

47. Cyril of Jerusalem, "Catechetical Lectures," in *Nicene and Post-Nicene Fathers—Second Series*, ed. Philip Schaff and Henry Wace (Peabody, Massachusetts: Hendrickson, 2004), 7:147; emphasis in original. Hugh Nibley offers the following rendering of the passage: "Immediately upon entering you removed your street clothes. And that was the image of putting off the old man and his works." Hugh Nibley, *The Message of the Joseph Smith Papyri: An Egyptian Endowment* (Salt Lake City: Deseret Book, 1976), 280; or Hugh Nibley, *The Message of the Joseph Smith Papyri: An Egyptian Endowment*, 2nd ed. (Provo, Utah: Foundation for Ancient Research and Mormon Studies; Salt Lake City: Deseret Book, 2005), 516.

48. J. C. Cooper, *An Illustrated Encyclopaedia of Traditional Symbols* (London: Thames and Hudson, 1995), 152.

49. John A. Tvedtnes, "Priestly Clothing in Bible Times," in *Temple of the Ancient World*, ed. Donald W. Parry (Provo, Utah: Foundation for Ancient Research and Mormon Studies, 1994), 671.

50. Farbridge, *Symbolism*, 273.

51. See ibid., 9, 224; Merrill F. Unger, *Unger's Bible Dictionary* (Chicago: Moody Press, 1966), 1021; Allen C. Myers, ed., *The Eerdmans Bible Dictionary* (Grand Rapids, Michigan: Eerdmans, 1987), 911–12; Douglas R. Edwards, "Dress and Ornamentation," in *Anchor Bible Dictionary*, 2:234. Typologist J. C. Cooper noted that shoes represent control. Thus, removal of the shoe symbolizes the relinquishing of control. See Cooper, *Illustrated Encyclopaedia*, 152. W. C. Hazlitt noted that the Semites were not the only ones to use the "ritual of the shoe" as a symbol for divestment rites. He wrote, "It appears to have been a custom among the Chinese for an official, on relinquishing his duties, to suspend his shoes in a conspicuous place." W. C. Hazlitt, *Dictionary of Faiths and Folklore: Beliefs, Superstitions and Popular Customs* (London: Bracken Books, 1995), s.v. "shoes."

52. See Jeffrey R. Holland, *Christ and the New Covenant* (Salt Lake City: Deseret Book, 1997), 203. This perspective is unique to Latter-day Saints.

53. The quote continues, "The medial consonants are both pharyngeal fricatives, one voiced and the other unvoiced." John Tvedtnes, cited in Baker, *Women's Rights*, 157n26.

54. One might argue that the temple rite during which one removes one's shoes is different from the rite of removal of shoes depicted in Ruth 4—particularly since during the endowment all ceremonial temple clothing is removed, not just the shoes. However, in Ruth 4 it is only the shoes that are taken off. Nevertheless, it should be remembered that in the temple the removal of the shoes is its own rite, even though it is performed alongside the ritual of clothing. This is evidenced by the fact that one puts on ceremonial clothes twice during the temple endowment, but one removes and replaces the shoes only once—specifically when Adam and Eve leave Eden and you and I metaphorically leave the premortal realm. Thus, the rite of clothing and that of the removal of shoes are separate, even though they are once placed side-by-side in the temple. Therefore, the distinctions between the ceremony of the shoe in Ruth 4 and that which takes place in the holy endowment are more perceived than real.

55. Mace, *Hebrew Marriage*, 106.

56. Matthew Henry drew a similar analogy. See Church, *Matthew Henry Commentary*, 293. Of course, Christ received his inheritance of the land just as each of us does—through obedience to the Father.

57. Walter L. Wilson, *A Dictionary of Bible Types* (Peabody, Massachusetts: Hendrickson Publishers, 1999), 48. Typologist Ada Habershon wrote, "Boaz was a type of Christ . . . as the lord of the harvest, the near kinsman, the supplier of wants, the redeemer of the inheritance, the man who gives rest, the wealthy kinsman, and the bridegroom." Ada R. Habershon, *Study of the Types* (Grand Rapids, Michigan: Dregel, 1974), 134. See also Joseph Fielding McConkie and Donald W. Parry, *A Guide to Scriptural Symbols* (Salt Lake City: Bookcraft, 1990), 22; Kevin J. Conner, *Interpreting the Symbols and Types* (Portland, Oregon: City Bible, 1992), 110–11.

58. Harold Bayley, *The Lost Language of Symbolism: An Inquiry into the Origin of Certain Letters, Words, Names, Fairy-Tales, Folklore, and Mythologies* (New York: Carol Publishing, 1990–93), 1:227.

59. Their covenant depicted by the removal of the shoe appears primarily focused on the surrender of temporal things, or property. However, the connotation or implications in temple worship is that we are surrendering more than just property (that is, the premortal abode), but also our personal wills. In return, Christ is said to offer us the celestial kingdom and to make us as He is. Thus today something highly spiritual is implied through a rite that initially had a rather temporal focus.

60. Mace, *Hebrew Marriage*, 104. See also Hamlin, *Surely There Is a Future*, 58–59. As another example of the misapplication of the "ceremony of the shoe," some see connections between this rite and the selling of slaves in Hebrew Bible times. For example, in Amos 8:6 we read, "That we may buy the poor for silver, and the needy for a pair of shoes." See also Amos 2:6. Of this verse David Noel Freedman and Francis I. Andersen wrote, "The circumstances of this nefarious and strictly illegal practice of buying and selling debtors into slavery is what the prophet [Amos] is talking about." Andersen and Freedman, *Amos*, 801. E. A. Speiser, however, noted, "The ordinary interpretation of this saying that the poor could be enslaved for so trifling a thing as a pair of shoes is unconvincing . . . and economically improbable." Speiser, "Shoes," 18. See also Andersen and Freedman, *Amos*, 312. Speiser rejects a literal reading of the verse, insisting instead that some connection

to the ceremony of the shoe is intended by the text. Speiser adds this: "Shoes . . . must be regarded in such instances as token payments to validate special transactions by lending them the appearance of normal business practice." Speiser, "Shoes," 17. True, slaves were seen as property and thus the owner had a right to them—and in this regard one might conjecture some connection between the passage and the "ceremony of the shoe." However, the context of the passage at hand suggests that these were not slaves in the proper sense of the word (those without legal rights). Rather, these were individuals who had incurred debt through the dishonesty and trickery of corrupt merchants. Thus, they were not slaves in the traditional sense of the word—and therefore the ceremony of the shoe would have had no place in this context. Indeed, the traditional interpretation of this passage (Amos 8:6) has to do with sandals as representations of the derisory amount of money a human's worth had been reduced to. See, for example, C. F. Keil and F. Delitzsch, "The Twelve Minor Prophets," in *Biblical Commentary on the Old Testament* (Grand Rapids, Michigan: Eerdmans, 1954), 1:315; Robert Martin-Achard and S. Paul Re'emi, *International Theological Commentary: Amos and Lamentations—God's People in Crisis* (Grand Rapids, Michigan: Eerdmans, 1984), 58–59; Andersen and Freedman, *Amos*, 801–2; Buttrick, *Interpreter's Bible*, 840; Clarke, *Clarke's Commentary*, 675. See also David Allan Hubbard, *Tyndale Old Testament Commentary: Joel and Amos* (Downers Grove, Illinois: InterVarsity Press, 1989), 220–21. Thus, contra Speiser's interpretation, most commentators see nothing ritualistic taking place in this passage.

"WHAT'S IN A NAME?"

"Appertaining" vs. "Pertaining" in Ritual

Alonzo L. Gaskill

I
t appears that I have stumbled upon the answer to Juliet's timeless
question, "What's in a name?" (Romeo and Juliet, Act 2, Scene 2).
While a 'rose, by any other name, may have smelled as sweet' to Juliet,
subtle differences in words and language *do* make a difference—particularly when those differences are found in rites, rituals, or covenants.

Case in point: A number of years ago I was participating in a sealing
session in the Provo Temple. Part way through the session the brother
performing the sealings took a break from the work at hand to share an
insight he had regarding a portion of the language of the sealing ceremony. He asked, "Do any of you know the difference between the words
'appertaining' and 'pertaining'?" I remember thinking to myself, "I seriously doubt that there *is* any difference." Indeed, I immediately thought
of a comment Elder Boyd K. Packer made in a leadership training meeting many years ago. He said to those in attendance: "What is the difference between a Special Witness and an Especial Witness?—*The letter E!*"
Translated: there isn't really a difference between these two words and
their meaning. Thus, when the sealer at the Provo Temple suggested to
those of us present that "appertaining" and "pertaining" actually meant
significantly different things, I remember feeling a measure of doubt
regarding his claim.

The word "appertaining" is used twice in the temple: once in the
initiatory ordinances and once in the sealing ordinance. The word

"pertaining," on the other hand, is used some three times in the ordinances of the house of the Lord: once in the endowment and twice in the sealing ordinance. Context does not make evident any meaningful difference in the meaning of these words.

Since an appeal to setting does not make obvious the difference, perhaps an appeal to dictionaries and lexicons might net us some measure of understanding.

Significantly, the exhaustive twenty-volume *Oxford English Dictionary* defines "appertaining"[1] as follows:

1. The fact of belonging to.
2. Pertaining, belonging, proper, appropriate (*to*).

This same text defines "appertain"[2] in the following ways:

1. To belong as parts to the whole, or as members of a family or class, and hence, to the head of the family; to be related, akin *to*.
2. To belong as a possession *to*.
3. To belong as a right or privilege *to*.
4. To belong naturally or by inherent fitness; to be suited, proper, appropriate *to*.
5. To belong as an attribute, function, or affecting circumstance; to pertain, relate.
6. Belonging to in an impersonal sense (see definitions 3 and 4).
7. To belong to, become, befit.

Similarly, Webster's 1828 dictionary—representative of the word's use in Joseph Smith's day—defines the word "appertaining" as "belonging."[3] It also defines "appertain"[4] as follows:

1. To pertain, to reach to, to extend to, hence to belong.
2. To belong, whether by right, nature, or appointment.

The Oxford English Dictionary also offers the following definition of the word "pertaining:[5]

1. To belong, to extend, stretch, tend (to), belong (to).
   a. To belong, be connected (in various ways); e.g. as a native or inhabitant, as part of a whole, as an appendage or accessory, as dependent.
   b. To belong as a possession, legal right, or privilege.

    c. To belong as one's care or concern. To pertain to: to matter to, to concern.

    d. To belong as an attribute, fitting adjunct, or duty; to be appropriate *to*.

2. To have reference or relation; to relate *to*.
3. Belong.
4. As regards, as concerns, in regard to, in relation to.

With a similar view, Webster's 1828 dictionary defines "pertain"[6] as:

1. To belong; to be the property, right, or duty of.
2. To have relation to.

As suspected, there appears to be no significant difference in the meaning of the words "pertain" and "appertain" as laymen in the English language use them. In traditional English usage, "appertaining" is simply the archaic version of the more modern word, "pertaining."[7] Legal dictionaries similarly suggest that "sometimes the word [*appertain*] appears to have been used merely as a fancy variant of the more usual *pertain*."[8]

Let's pause briefly so that I can gloat about this seeming confirmation of my initial suspicions regarding the supposed distinctions between these two temple terms. As the dictionary shows—and as I had suspected—these two words mean basically the same thing in modern layman's English.

Okay, prideful moment over: time for a reality check! While there may be no difference between these words in common English language usage, in legal documents "pertain" and "appertain" are actually sometimes used with distinction. One legal dictionary states, "Some differentiation is possible. Both take the preposition to, but *appertain* usually means 'to belong to rightfully' <the privileges *appertaining* to this degree>, whereas *pertain* usually means 'to relate to; concern' <the appeal *pertains* to defendant's Fifth Amendment rights>."[9] Elsewhere we read, "the word 'appertain' means to belong to" something.[10] Thus, from a legal standpoint, to "pertain" means to "relate to" something; whereas, "appertain" means to "belong rightfully to" something.

That being the case, in context of temple sealings, therefore, the implications of the legal meaning of the words are that you make a covenant and a promise that, from the day of your sealing forward, you will keep each of the laws, the rites, and the ordinances which are *related to* the sealing in which you have participated. But you also have sealed upon you all of the blessings which *belong rightfully to* the new and everlasting covenant of marriage. In other words, as used in the sealing, the word "pertain" suggests that there are rules or commandments associated with your covenants. But the word "appertain," suggests that there are blessings that are rightfully yours because of your covenants—assuming you manifest faithfulness to those covenants.

Owing to the fact that Joseph Smith and Brigham Young had no formal training in law—nor were they significantly schooled in letters generally—their use of these terms in the temple sealing ceremony seems inspired and significantly appropriate. Rather than using these words in the interchangeable manner in which they were used in their day (and ours), they instead incorporated them into the ordinances of the temple—particularly the sealing ceremony—to convey to participants a more specific and instructive meaning: namely, what we are obligated to do (once sealed), but also what powers and blessings we have a sacred right to (if we are faithful).

As always, "time vindicates the prophets"[11] and Joseph and Brigham's inspiration is once again on display! "Praise to" those men "who communed with Jehovah!"[12]

NOTES

1. "Appertaining," in J. A. Simpson and E. S. C. Weiner, eds., *The Oxford English Dictionary*, 20 vols. (New York: Oxford and Clarendon Press, 1991), 1:571.

2. "Appertain," in *The Oxford English Dictionary*, 1:571.

3. "Appertaining," in *Noah Webster's First Edition [1828] of an American Dictionary of the English Language*, 2 vols. (San Francisco: Foundation for American Christian Education, 1967), vol. 1, sec. 11.

4. "Appertain," in *Noah Webster's First Edition [1828] of an American Dictionary of the English Language*, vol. 1, sec. 11.

5. "Pertain," in *The Oxford English Dictionary*, 11:313.

6. "Pertain," in *Noah Webster's First Edition [1828] of an American Dictionary of the English Language*, vol. 2, sec. 34.

7. One LDS text, reaching a similar conclusion, stated, "'Appertain' means it belongs as part, right, possession, attribute, etc. and pertains or relates to the whole. The phrase 'hereunto appertaining' has similar meaning to 'contingent' or 'based upon.'" Richard H. Morley, *A Scriptural Glossary of Manti Temple Terms* (Price, Utah: Wix Plaza Book Sales, 2004), 40.

8. Bryan Garner, *Garner's Dictionary of Modern Legal Usage*, 3rd ed. (New York: Oxford University Press, 2011), 69, s.v. "appertain; pertain."

9. Garner, *Garner's Dictionary of Modern Legal Usage*, 69, s.v. "appertain; pertain."

10. See "What are 'appurtenant' private structures within provision," in 43 A.L.R. 3d 1362.

11. From March 7 through October 17, 1954, Hugh Nibley delivered a weekly radio lecture (on KSL) titled "Time Vindicates the Prophets." Much of Nibley's content from those lectures was reproduced in his book, *The World and the Prophets* (Provo, Utah: Foundation for Ancient Research and Mormon Studies, 1987).

12. "Praise to the Man," *Hymns*, no. 27.

Chapter 11

THE ANGEL MORONI

An Evolving Latter-day Symbol

Alonzo L. Gaskill and Seth G. Soha

One of the most recognizable symbols of The Church of Jesus Christ of Latter-day Saints is the image of the angel Moroni. Representations of this Book of Mormon prophet—and patron of the Americas[1]—top the majority of our temples, have been reproduced on the cover of the Book of Mormon, and have even been etched on the headstones of deceased Saints. While those outside our faith may not know who the angel represents, the youngest members of the Church are traditionally able to identify the cherub atop the temples. He is, for the Saints, a well-known and much loved icon.

What may be less known by the Latter-day Saint laity is the development of this standard symbol of the Restoration. The angelic figure has had many forms and even more than one name. And, while he generally has a sameness from temple to temple, our distant views have limited some of the unique distinctions between the various versions of the Moroni statue. What follows is a brief survey of the ways in which this Book of Mormon prophet—and ornament of the temples—has been depicted over the years.

Before we glance at the various physical depictions of Moroni, however, perhaps a word or two about his identity is worth mentioning. There is evidence that when the image we today call "Moroni" was first employed, it might have been intended as a generic symbol—not specifically of Moroni, but of the Restoration's angelic beginnings. For example, a statue of an angel was first utilized in an iconic manner on the spire of the original Nauvoo Temple. No source contemporary to the time referred to the angel as "Moroni." Thus, one text claims, "Although the original Nauvoo Temple did not feature an angel Moroni statue, it did feature an angel flying in the heavens."[2] In retrospect, many have called the Nauvoo angel "Moroni." Yet, while the original temple was still standing, the symbol seemed to have a more generic meaning.[3] Indeed, it seems that it was many years *after* the Nauvoo era that the Church settled on the identity of the statue atop the temples. Thus, in an April 1893 article in *The Contributor* magazine, the angel atop the Salt Lake Temple was depicted and discussed. However, rather than being called "Moroni," it was referred to time and again as "the angel" or "an angel." In the aforementioned article—published the same month the temple was dedicated—the figure atop the temple was never given a specific identity.[4] The article appears to intentionally avoid referring to the statue by Moroni's name, or by *any* personal name. If at that point in Church history the statue was perceived as a representation of Moroni, it makes no sense that the publishers of this Church periodical would consistently avoid calling it such but, instead, refer to the angel by generic titles, as they do repeatedly in this 1893 article. Similarly, in an 1875 *Deseret News* article, we read of a two-dimensional statue (or cut-out) that looked almost identical to the ones commonly employed on the tops of LDS temples

today. According to this article, this particular figure was placed atop the organ in the Tabernacle at the commemoration of "the 28th anniversary of the entrance of the Pioneers into Utah Territory."[5] Of it, the article states, "Surmounting the organ was a gilded and shaded figure of an angel sounding the gospel trumpet, to 'every kindred, tongue, and people.'"[6]

Once again, though seemingly indistinguishable from the traditional depictions of today—blowing a trump, holding a book in his left hand, and standing upon a ball—this angelic figure is simply referred to as "an angel" rather than as "the angel Moroni."

The reason for this vagueness in the early days may have been because it had not yet been decided whom the angel represented. However, it may also be that the early Church initially saw this angel as a representation of the numerous angels associated with the Restoration. In this spirit, and while commenting on Revelation 14:6 (so often associated with the angel Moroni), Elder Bruce R. McConkie explained:

> Now, as to the actual work of restoration—what angel performed this mighty deed, this work which involves the salvation of all men on earth in these latter-days? Who restored the everlasting gospel? Was it one angel or many?
>
> It is traditional (and true!) to reply: 'Moroni, son of Mormon, the now resurrected Nephite prophet, who holds the keys of "the stick of Ephraim" (D&C 27:5), the one through whose ministry the Book of Mormon was again brought to light.' . . .
>
> From [D&C 133:36–40] we learn two things relative to the identity of the angel John saw "fly in the midst of heaven":
>
> 1. The angel (Moroni) had by that date already come, and the gospel message in the Book of Mormon was then on earth and would without fail go forth to all of its inhabitants; and
>
> 2. The angel of the restoration was yet, in the future, to "appear unto many that dwell on the earth."
>
> Paul makes the apt statement that the gospel consists of two parts: the word and the power. (1 Thess. 1:5.) Thus Moroni brought the word, or at least that portion found in the Book of Mormon, for that record summarizes and teaches, in large part, what men must do to be saved. It records the terms and conditions of the plan of salvation. Also, before November 3, 1831, John the Baptist, and Peter, James, and John, as angelic ministrants, had brought keys and powers. But other angels were yet to come—Moses, Elias, Elijah, Gabriel, Raphael, and "divers angels,—all declaring their dispensation, their rights, their keys, their honors, their majesty and glory, and the power of their priesthood; giving line upon line, precept upon precept; here a little, and there a little." (D&C 128:21.)
>
> Thus the angel Moroni brought the message, that is, the word; but other angels brought the keys and priesthood, the power. And in the

final analysis the fulness [*sic*] of the everlasting gospel consists of all of the truths and powers needed to enable men to gain a fulness [*sic*] of salvation in the celestial heaven . . .

In a post-millennial setting; in a recitation of what is to be after the last man, including the sons of perdition, has been resurrected; in fact at the final great day when all things preceding the celestializing of the earth are past, then: "Another trump shall sound, which is the fifth trump, which is the fifth angel who committeth the everlasting gospel—flying through the midst of heaven, unto all nations, kindreds, tongues, and people; And this shall be the sound of his trump, saying to all people, both in heaven and in earth, and that are under the earth—for every ear shall hear it, and every knee shall bow, and every tongue shall confess, while they hear the sound of the trump, saying: Fear God, and give glory to him who sitteth upon the throne, forever and ever; for the hour of his judgment is come." (D&C 88:103–4.)

And so, as we ponder upon the identity, mission and ministry of the angel appointed to commit the everlasting gospel to men in latter-days, we are led to exclaim—'What wonders of eternal truth are found in one short sentence of the revealed word!"[7]

Elder McConkie's point was simply this: though we frequently identify that "angel fly[ing] in the midst of heaven, having the everlasting gospel to preach unto them that dwell on the earth" (Revelation 14:6) as Moroni, that scriptural symbol is really a composite representation of the many angels associated with the Restoration and the work of God in the latter-days. This reality may have caused early members of the Church—and even the Church's leadership—to look at the angel that would top the various temples of the Church as a broad symbol of God's outpouring of His spirit, and His choice to send *many* an angels to the earth to reveal truth and restore keys.[8]

While there was certainly a vagueness in those early days about the identity of the angel, at some point, members of the Church began to interpret that statue as a symbol for a specific angel, rather than as a broad icon. Surprisingly, however, it wasn't initially Moroni that they associated the angel with, but Gabriel[9]—the great annunciating cherub of Bible times.[10] As evidence of this understanding, in the personal papers of Joseph Don Carlos Young—the assistant architect of the exterior of the Salt Lake Temple, and chief architect of the temple's interior—there appears a picture of the statue atop the Salt Lake Temple. At the bottom of that picture appears the notation: "Statue of Angel Gabriel Made for Temple at Salt Lake City, Utah."[11] Joseph Don Carlos Young was in a position to know who the angel was intended to be, and yet this document does not refer to him as Moroni but, instead, as Gabriel. Similarly, in an October 4, 1891, article in *The Salt Lake Herald*, an artist's rendering of the statue appears—in traditional form, atop a ball, blowing a trumpet—but the article's description of the statue explains that "the sixth" spire of the temple "will be crowned by a bronze representation of the angel Gabriel."[12] Likewise, one 1891 publication says of the Salt Lake Temple, "when finished [it] will be surmounted with a mammoth statue of Gabriel blowing his trumpet."[13] Even the Temple Souvenir Album, published one year before the Salt Lake Temple was dedicated, depicts the trumpet-blowing angel with the caption: "Statue of the Angel Gabriel on East Center Tower."[14] Likewise, in the October 17, 1891, edition of *The Deseret Weekly*—an "Official Organ of The Church of Jesus Christ of Latter-day Saints"[15]—it states that sculptor "C. L. Dallin" had created "the statue of Angel Gabriel, designed for the [Salt Lake] temple."[16] A number of references, such as these, appear in early publications—each suggesting that, at some point, members of the Church saw the angel gracing the pillars of our temples as Gabriel, instead of Moroni. Frankly, such a designation would make sense, owing to the fact that Gabriel was—as we have noted—the angel of the Annunciation. Who better then to announce the Restoration of the fullness of the gospel of Jesus Christ? Additionally, "Gabriel's trump" is a famous euphemism in Christianity—often used as a symbol of proclamation.[17] There is no question that the early Brethren were aware of this symbol. Indeed, some even occasionally referred to it.[18] Thus, the inclination to connect the trumpet-blowing angel with Gabriel would have been a natural one.

All of this being said, it seems apparent that the identity of the angel which would grace the spires of Latter-day Saint temples was not well defined in the early days of the Church, and the leadership of the Church ostensibly did not decide with finality the identity of this iconic symbol until days before the capstone dedication, when Joseph F. Smith—second counselor in the First Presidency—explained to a reporter from *The Salt Lake Herald* that the

angel was to "represent, not the Angel Gabriel, sounding the trumpet on resurrection day, but the Angel Maroni [*sic*], proclaiming the gospel to all the world."[19] While President Smith—some forty-six years after the Church began using this image—finally defined its symbolic meaning to the world, this did not immediately squelch the misinformation. Even after the capstone dedication, prominent newspapers throughout the country continued to identify the angel as Gabriel. For example, on April 12, 1892, *The Boston Weekly Globe* printed this:

> The light on the central eastern tower is to be placed below the statue of the angel Gabriel, and it will be reflected upwards so that the figure will be illuminated by a bewitching halo. The statue of the angel Gabriel, which stands on the eastern tower, comes from the hands of a finished sculptor who has already attracted attention by his work and will yet achieve still greater fame, a goal towards which he has now made great advancement. He is C. E. Dallin, who was born in this city, and is yet not much more than 30.[20]

While we cannot say with certainty how long misunderstandings were common, it appears to have been quite some time after the dedication of the Salt Lake Temple before the angel was generally and permanently understood to be a symbol of the angel Moroni.[21]

We turn our attention now to the various ways in which Moroni has been artistically depicted in the years in which his image has been employed upon the towers of our most sacred edifices. From a distance, the subtle distinctions in design may escape the eye of the casual viewer. There have been, however, a number of notable differences in how various artists have rendered this icon of the Restoration. What follows is but a brief pictorial survey.[22]

THE ORIGINAL NAUVOO TEMPLE

While the temple that stands in Nauvoo, Illinois, today (dedicated June 27, 2002) has a vertical statue of the angel Moroni adorning its tower, the original Nauvoo Temple (dedicated May 1, 1846) sported instead a weather vane in the form of a horizontal angel blowing a trumpet and holding up an opened book. As noted above, contemporary accounts never call the original

angel "Moroni" but, instead, simply see the depiction as an angel representative of the divine source of the restored gospel.

In addition to being unique because of its horizontal stance, the original Nauvoo angel is also distinctive because of its dress. This angel was conspicuously clothed in a pleated robe with a round, flat cap. Perrigrine Sessions (1814–93)—an early Latter-day Saint who eventually settled the area today known as Bountiful, Utah—indicated in his journal that the unnamed angel atop the Nauvoo Temple was intended to be understood as wearing "priestly robes."[23] Sessions's interpretation seems confirmed by an 1861 painting of Joseph Smith, wherein the Prophet is depicted in the same semi-horizontal stance of the Nauvoo angel, and in the same clothing—however, the detail of the "priestly robes" is even more evident in the painting. This 1861 portrait was created for the 24th of July parade in Salt Lake City. Thomas Bullock designed the original image and Dan Weggeland, a prolific early Mormon artist, painted it.[24] Like the Nauvoo angel, here Joseph blows the trump while leaning forward, flying through "the midst of heaven" (Revelation 14:6). However,

in his hand he clutches, not the Book of Mormon but, instead, a scroll listing the names of the various pioneers who arrived in the valley in 1847. The parallels between these two depictions is unmistakable, and the temple theme evident.

In addition to the unique clothing of the angel, the weather vane of the original Nauvoo Temple also included a representation of a flame—which was a common symbol in antiquity for the Shekinah, or glory and presence of the divine.[25] Just beneath the Shekinah was a compass and square, holding covenantal significance. The horizontal angel was depicted as holding an open book in his right hand—which has been said to have been intended as the Book of Mormon.[26] In his left hand, and pressed against his lips, was a trumpet.

THE SALT LAKE TEMPLE

The statue atop the Salt Lake Temple is interesting both because it introduced a new representation of the angel—one which would hold a permanence in the iconography of the Church—but also because it too went through a measure of evolution. As we noted above, the earliest references to the Salt Lake Temple's angel were always Gabriel rather than Moroni. But, in addition to that shift, there was also a design shift during the process of creating this statue. Initially, it was intended to be a horizontal angel, following that atop the Nauvoo Temple. And, early artistic renderings indicate that it

was the intent to place an angel on the central tower of both the east and west ends of the temple. That plan was scrapped as the design of the angel evolved.

The sculptor of the Salt Lake Moroni was Cyrus Dallin, a member of the Unitarian faith, who initially rejected President Wilford Woodruff's invitation to sculpt the statue because he did not personally believe in angels and felt that someone of "greater spiritual capacity" should be asked to sculpt it.[27] Nevertheless, President Woodruff encouraged Dallin to talk to his LDS mother before formally turning down the commission. Dallin did so, and she is said to have reminded him that, while he claimed he did not believe in angels, "every time you return home and take me in your arms you call me your angel mother."[28] Apparently moved by this reminder, Dallin "accepted the commission."[29] He is said to have spent some time studying scripture and Latter-day Saint doctrine in an effort to grasp the "character" of angels;[30] and in the process of researching and sculpting the statue, Dallin had a conversion experience, of sorts. He didn't join the LDS Church, but he did feel something. Of the experience of making the statue, Dallin wrote, "my angel Moroni brought me nearer to God than anything I did" and in the process of making the statue "I came to know what it means to commune with angels from heaven."[31]

The current Moroni atop the Salt Lake Temple sports a crown instead of a temple cap—though the original blueprint drawings suggest that the initial intent was to depict him in temple regalia akin to that worn by the angel atop the Nauvoo Temple. Dallin's statue also originally had a light in its crown, which was illuminated at night. Of this, the *San Francisco Chronicle* recorded, Moroni "bears upon his crown an electric jet of 300-candle power."[32] This gave the statue a halo effect at night, though the lights were later removed.

The height of the statue—cast by W. H. Mullins Company of Salem, Ohio—is variously given in publications as 12 ½ feet, 14 feet, and 16 feet. Regardless of the inconsistent reporting, the actual height of the Salt Lake Temple's Moroni is 12 ½ feet.

THE WASHINGTON WARD CHAPEL

While not a temple, the Washington Ward chapel (located on Sixteenth Street, in Washington, DC) is the only Sunday meetinghouse of The Church of Jesus Christ of Latter-day Saints to have ever been adorned with an angel Moroni.[33] Designed by Joseph Don Carlos Young (assistant architect of the Salt Lake Temple) and Ramm Hansen (a Norwegian emigrant), this ward meetinghouse was dedicated November 5, 1933.

The artist of this statue was Torleif S. Knaphus—who modeled the Washington Ward Moroni after Dallin's Salt Lake Temple statue,[34] the latter of the two being 12 inches taller than the former.[35]

The last LDS Church meeting to be held in the Washington Ward building was on August 31, 1975. Because of its need of extensive and costly repairs, in September of 1977, the statue of Moroni was removed and the building was sold. Today the building is the property of the

Unification Church.[36] The statue that once graced the spire of this unique chapel is now in the LDS Museum of Church History and Art, in Salt Lake City.

According to some who attended church in that building, the statue drew many into the church to inquire about it and the faith that it represented. It was said to have been a great missionary tool—and possessed the ability to draw in non-Mormons in a way that many of our temples do.[37]

THE LOS ANGELES TEMPLE[38]

There are several things about the statue atop the Los Angeles Temple that make it unique among the various representations of the angel Moroni.[39] The first is that this is the only depiction of the angel with "Lamanite features" and "Mayan" garb.[40] If one looks closely at the detail, one is able to see that the headdress, the robe, and even the belt on this statue have a Lamanite, rather than angelic, appearance.

Another interesting symbol placed on this Moroni statue, but appearing on no other, are the initials of an Apostle, engraved on the back of the sculpture, at the approximate location of the right knee. As the story goes, Elder Matthew Cowley was enamored with the work of Millard F. Malin, the sculptor—and also with the uniqueness of this particular

statue. He visited the studio with some frequency during its creation, checking on the statue's progress. One source records, "The cornerstone of the Los Angeles Temple was laid in December 1953, while Malin's statue was still in its clay form, nearly ready for casting in aluminum. Elder Cowley visited Malin's studio again on the day before he left to attend the cornerstone ceremony. Elder Cowley examined the completed model from all sides. When Malin asked him what he thought, he said, 'It is superb! I like it— like everything about it.' Pleased, Malin handed Elder Cowley a modeling tool and invited him to 'sign' the clay figure. Elder Cowley did so, carving "MC" into the lower edge of the angel's robe, in back. He thanked Malin, wished him well, and left for his appointment in Los Angeles."[41] Sadly, Elder Cowley died of a heart attack only days later.[42]

It is said that Malin was heavily influenced by Arnold Friberg's paintings of scenes of the Book of Mormon. The evidence of that is apparent when one looks at this depiction of Moroni.[43]

To top off the distinctiveness of this particular representation of Moroni, we offer this last insight into the Los Angeles Temple's statue. The original Millard Malin sculpture, from which the cast was made, is currently in an abandoned warehouse in Bountiful, Utah.[44] There Moroni rests on top of an old abandoned Zion's Bank vault.

THE WASHINGTON DC TEMPLE

This sculpture of the angel was created by Avard Fairbanks.[45] It is the second of only six Moroni temple sculptures to hold a stack of plates—the others being the statues on the Los Angeles, Seattle, Jordan River, and Mexico City temples, and the Hill Cumorah statue.

Made of gilded bronze, this statue weighs over 4,000 pounds, whereas today the statues of Moroni are typically made out of fiberglass and weigh only approximately 350 pounds.[46]

Keith Wilcox, who served as the architect of the Washington DC Temple, tells one interesting note regarding the creation of this statue:

> A rather humorous incident occurred during the time Dr. Fairbanks worked on his enlarged 18 foot high sculpture in Pietrasanta, Italy. He invited the architects to [Italy to] see this enlarged sculpture first hand before casting it in bronze. . . . I told Dr. Fairbanks I didn't like the sculpture. He was shocked. After gasping for breath, he asked why. I told him that to me the Angel Moroni looked as if he were "drinking" from his horn rather than "blowing" it. [Dr. Fairbanks] asked what I meant. I responded by displaying how [I, as a] former trombone player "buzzed" with [my] lips to make the tone (amplified by the horn). . . . I demonstrated this. Immediately Dr. Fairbanks requested that I model this so that he could reform [the] muscles around the mouth of the

sculpture to give it the appearance of "blowing." This [modeling session] lasted for about 45 minutes.[47]

Fairbanks' son, Eugene, indicated that the orb on which the Moroni stands was "symbolic of the earth to which he has come. It represents his return to the world to reveal to humankind further scriptures which he had hidden in the Hill Cumorah."[48] While this was apparently Avard Fairbanks's interpretation of the DC angel, the symbolism seems generally applicable to any Moroni statue placed upon one of the Latter-day Saint temples today.

THE MONTICELLO UTAH TEMPLE

The Monticello Utah Temple sculpture, by artist LaVar Walgreen, is matchless in that it is the only of the temple statues to depict the prophet Moroni in his youth. Traditionally he is represented as being a middle-aged man.

Additionally, Walgreen's Moroni is unique in being the only of the  Moroni statues that was white, rather than gold-leafed. The original statue was six feet tall and made of white fiberglass. It was only on the temple for one year. President Hinckley made a visit to the Monticello Utah Temple on a cloudy day and noticed that the white statue was not visible. Feeling that such would not do, he had it removed and replaced by one with gold leafing. The original white statue was then gilded and placed atop the Columbus Ohio Temple.

The Monticello Utah Temple statue was also the first Moroni statue to hold a scroll in his hand—though today many of our temples depict Moroni in that way, the scroll being representative of the everlasting gospel spoken of by John in the Book of Revelation (Revelation 14:6).

THE HILL CUMORAH

While not formally a temple, no doubt in some ways the Hill Cumorah functioned as such for the Prophet Joseph. And, thus, perhaps it is appropriate that this is the one Church monument (outside of our temples) that *currently* sports a statue of the angel Moroni.

Cumorah's Moroni is the only one to be posed without a trumpet up to his lips. While he does hold a stack of golden plates, he holds his right arm to the square, while pointing upward. Of Moroni's posture, the sculpture (Torleif Knaphus) explained, "Moroni" is "in a position as though calling the inhabitants of the Earth to reverence of the Gospel message. His right hand is pointed towards heaven and in his left hand he holds the record."[49]

Moroni's body, on this monument, was modeled after a Salt Lake bricklayer named Elwin Clark. The angel's face was modeled after Elwin's rancher father, Hyrum Don Carlos Clark.[50] Ironically, when Knaphus individually approached these two men to pose for the statue, he did not know they were related. When they both arrived at his studio the same day and at the same hour, he was shocked to learn that he had selected a father and son to be his models.[51]

CONCLUSION

In its more than 150 years of use, our iconic statue has had several names and a variety of forms. Each has had unique meaning—to its sculptor and to those who viewed it. While this symbol has evolved in so many ways, there is a consistency about it too; and about the ultimate message it testifies to—namely, that the gospel has been restored, and that the fullness of the good news is again upon the earth.

In the introduction to his work on traditional symbols, Jack Tresidder pointed out, "Some of the most familiar things around us once had deeper and more fascinating meanings and associations that we now realize."[52] Such could certainly be said of the icon we today call "Moroni." The evolution of this symbol takes nothing away from its significance and impact. On the contrary, knowing its multiple depictions and manifold meanings throughout Church history may simply serve to deepen its significance, power, and connotations for those who, with faith-filled eyes, view it.[53]

NOTES

1. In a rather curious statement about Moroni, Elder Orson Hyde declared, "This . . . angel presides over the destinies of America, and feels a lively interest in all our doings. He was in the camp of Washington; and by an invisible hand, led on our fathers to conquest and victory; and all this to open and prepare the way for the Church and kingdom of God to be established on the western hemisphere, for the redemption of Israel and the salvation of the world. This same angel was with Columbus, and gave him deep impressions, by dreams and by visions, respecting this New World. Trammeled by poverty and by an unpopular cause, yet his persevering and unyielding heart would not allow an obstacle in his way too great for him to overcome; and the angel of God helped him—was with him on the stormy deep, calmed the troubled elements, and guided his frail vessel to the desired haven. Under the guardianship of this same angel, or Prince of America, have the United States grown, increased, and flourished, like the sturdy oak by the rivers of water." Orson Hyde, discourse given July 4, 1854, in *Journal of Discourses* 6:368.

2. R. Lane Wright, *Testament in Stone: Symbols of the Nauvoo Temple and Their Meanings* (Nauvoo, Illinois: The Nauvoo Press, 2014), 35.

3. See Matthew B. Brown and Paul Thomas Smith, *Symbols in Stone—Symbolism on the Early Temples of the Restoration* (American Fork, Utah: Covenant Communication, 1997), 105; Kelsey Berteaux and Jannalee Rosner, "10 Things You Didn't Know about the Angel Moroni Statue," in *LDS Living Magazine*, November 15, 2013. See http://ldsliving.com/story/74177-10-things-you-didnt-know-about-the-angel-moroni-statue.

4. See James H. Anderson, "The Salt Lake Temple," in *The Contributor: A Monthly Magazine*, vol. 14, no. 6 (April 1893): 274.

5. See "The Jubilee," in *Deseret News*, Wednesday, July 28, 1875.

6. Ibid.

7. Bruce R. McConkie, *Doctrine New Testament Commentary Volume III: Colossians-Revelation* (Salt Lake City: Bookcraft, 1988), 528–31.

8. A partial list of the keys believed to have been restored to the prophet Joseph include the keys of the Aaronic Priesthood—which included the keys of the "ministry of angels" (D&C 13) brought by John the Baptist; the apostolic keys (D&C 27:12; D&C 81:2; D&C 128:20) brought by Peter, James, and John; the keys of the "gathering of Israel" (D&C 110:11) brought by Moses; the sealing keys (D&C 110:13–16) brought by Elijah; the keys over "the dispensation of the gospel of Abraham" (D&C 110:12; 132:20) brought by Elias; and "the keys of the record of the stick of Ephraim" (D&C 27:5; JS—H 1:29–60) brought by Moroni.

9. See Wright, *Testament in Stone*, 35, who rightly points out that, during an earlier era, the angel atop the temple "was commonly referred to as the angel Gabriel."

10. Regarding his annunciating role, one text notes, "Gabriel foretold the birth of John the Baptist, and of the Virgin Mary. The angel who appeared to the mother of Sampson to announce his birth is, though unnamed, traditionally identified with Gabriel, as is the angel of the Nativity and the angel who announced Christ's resurrection. . . . Gabriel's predominant role in Christian art is that of the angel of the Annunciation." James Hall, *Dictionary of Subjects & Symbols in Art* (New York: Harper & Row, 1974), 134.

11. Annotated photo in the papers of Joseph Don Carlos Young, housed in the personal collection of Richard W. Young, Salt Lake City.

12. "The Temple," in *The Salt Lake Herald*, Sunday, October 4, 1891.

13. Charles A. Anderson and Henry B. Carrington, *A Trip From Ocean to Ocean—Or, Weekly Excursions to California and the West* (Boston, Massachusetts: C. A. Anderson, 1891), 65.

14. See "Temple Souvenir Album" (Salt Lake City: Magazine Printing Company, April 1892), 8.

15. This line appears on the masthead of the cover page of *The Deseret Weekly*.

16. See "The Territorial Fair," in *The Deseret Weekly*, vol. 43, no. 17, October 17, 1891.

17. See Jack Tresidder, *Symbols and Their Meanings* (London: Duncan Baird Publishers, 2000), 30; Leland Ryken, James C. Wilhoit, and Tremper Longman III, *Dictionary of Biblical Imagery* (Downers Grove, Illinois: InterVarsity Press, 1998), 32; Hall, *Dictionary of Subjects & Symbols in Art*, 134. The earliest known association of Gabriel with a trump comes in the year 1455, where he is depicted in Byzantine art as blowing a trump to call the dead from their graves. In the seventeenth century, Milton then appears to draw on this Byzantine image when, in Paradise Lost, he spoke of Gabriel's trump being blown at the Second Coming. Much later the image of Gabriel's trump frequently appears in the "negro spirituals" of the South. By the time of the Restoration this image would have been commonplace.

18. See, for example, Brigham Young, in *The Complete Discourse of Brigham Young*, 5 vols., comp. Richard S. Van Wagoner (Salt Lake City: The Smith-Pettit Foundation, 2009), 3:1737; Heber C. Kimball, in *Journal of Discourses*, 7:168.

19. See "The Temple," in *The Salt Lake Herald*, Sunday, April 3, 1892. President Smith acknowledges that the belief that the angel represented Gabriel had "gained considerable currency" in the Church because such had been stated in "previous publications." Ibid.

20. "The Great Temple" in *The Boston Weekly Globe*, Tuesday, April 12, 1892. From the content of the article, it appears that its author was present in Utah at the capstone dedication. The author seems intent on correcting misinformation about the temple—as he notes "erroneous statements" circulating regarding the cost of the temple. That being said, his attention to detail leaves one to assume that at the capstone dedication the identity of the angel was not mentioned, or the article's author most likely would have included that also. But, having been present at the services, he was still under the impression that the angel represented Gabriel rather than Moroni.

21. An entire year after President Joseph F. Smith clarified the angel to be a symbol of Moroni, a Church produced publication neglected to use that name when referring to the statue—simply referring to it as "the angel." See Anderson, "The Salt Lake Temple," 274, cited above.

22. In addition to the variation in the artistic depictions of Moroni (which will be our focus), there has also been significant variety in other aspects of the statue. For example, the earliest depictions were made of bronze, copper, or aluminum. Today, however, they are made of fiberglass, and then gold leafed. Some hold in their left hand the plates from which the Book of Mormon was translated. Others clutch a scroll instead. Some depict the angel with an empty left hand. Of course, not all temples are adorned with a statue

of Moroni; and some (like the Freiberg, Provo, and London Temples) had the statue added later. While most Moroni statues atop LDS temples are oriented toward the east, a handful have west-facing statues (largely due to the lot orientation). See Berteaux and Rosner, "10 Things You Didn't Know about the Angel Moroni Statue."

23. See Perrigrine Sessions, *The Diary of Perrigrine Sessions*, unpublished manuscript in the possession of the author, 41, s.v. "May 5, 1844."

24. See Robert C. Mitchell, "DUP Receives Historic Gift," in *Deseret News*, Thursday, October 7, 1965. The original banner was larger than the 45"×50" copy which was also made by Weggland (in 1897). While the original apparently still exists, according to Mitchell, it is housed in the First Presidency Vault, and only the smaller copy is on display.

25. See Leland Ryken, James C. Wilhoit, Tremper Longman III, eds., *Dictionary of Biblical Imagery* (Downers Grove, Illinois: InterVarsity Press, 1998), 287.

26. See Sessions, *The Diary of Perrigrine Sessions*, s.v. "May 5, 1844."

27. See Richard Neitzel Holzapfel, *Every Stone a Sermon* (Salt Lake City: Bookcraft, 1993), 48.

28. See Jane Dallin, cited in Holzapfel, *Every Stone a Sermon*, 48.

29. Ibid.

30. Ibid. It is commonly claimed that Dallin spent time reading the Book of Mormon before beginning his work on the statue—all in an attempt to get a sense of Moroni's character. While that is possible, there are no known primary sources to support this claim. Indeed, since all evidence suggests that the statue was not originally intended to be Moroni, it would make little sense for Dallin to take such an approach.

31. See Levi Edgar Young, "The Angel Moroni and Cyrus Dallin," in *The Improvement Era*, vol. 56, no. 4 (April 1953): 234. There is some question as to whether Dallin was actually told he was making a statue of Moroni, or just a statue of an angel. Some have suggested that it was only the latter, and that later Dallin himself landed on Moroni as the identity of the angel he created. While this has been theorized by various authors, and while it cannot be proven, the late date at which the Church began calling the angel Moroni might suggest that Dallin was not originally told the identity of the angel he was commissioned to sculpt.

32. *San Francisco Chronicle*, April 7, 1893. See also Holzapfel, *Every Stone a Sermon*, 98.

33. Reed Russell, "The Washington, D.C. Chapel," in *The Keepapitchinin*, September 26, 2012. See http://www.keepapitchinin.org/2012/09/26/guest-post-the-washington-d -c-chapel/.

34. See Allen P. Gerritsen, "The Hill Cumorah Monument: An Inspired Creation of Torleif S. Knaphus," in *Journal of Book of Mormon Studies*, vol. 13, nos. 1–2 (2004): 127.

35. See Gerritsen, "The Hill Cumorah Monument," 127.

36. See Russell, "The Washington, D.C. Chapel."

37. H. K. Abel, "Mormon Trivia: The Angel Moroni Statue," January 4, 2010. See http://mormonsoprano.com/2010/01/04/mormon-trivia-angel-moroni-statue/.

38. The Los Angeles Temple Moroni was placed atop the temple on October 19, 1954. See Jack Sears, "A Sacred Witness to All Men," in *The Instructor*, vol. 91, no. 3 (March

1956): 74; Richard O. Cowan, *Temples to Dot the Earth* (Springville, Utah: Cedar Fort, 1997), 154.

39. This statue of Moroni, made of cast aluminum, weighs some 2,100 pounds and is 15 feet, 5 ½ inches in height. The trumpet he blows is about 8 feet long. See Edward O. Anderson, "The Los Angeles Temple," in *The Improvement Era*, vol. 58, no. 11 (October 1958): 806; Sears, "A Sacred Witness to All Men," 73–74.

40. See Sears, "A Sacred Witness to All Men," 74.

41. Ardis E. Parshall, "The Angel Moroni's Secret," in *The Keepapitchinin*, April 30, 2009. See http://www.keepapitchinin.org/2009/04/30/the-angel-moronis-secret/. See also Sears, "A Sacred Witness to All Men," 74.

42. See Sears, "A Sacred Witness to All Men," 74; Elaine Cannon, *The Truth About Angels* (Salt Lake City: Bookcraft, 1996), 89–90. Cannon also records seeing the statue and the initials carved into it by Elder Cowley—though she writes her account more than forty years after she saw it and she misremembers exactly where on the statue the initials were carved.

43. See Sears, "A Sacred Witness to All Men," 73.

44. While this warehouse is on the property of the Wood Museum, it is not part of the museum proper.

45. Keith W. Wilcox, *A Personal Testimony Concerning the Washington Temple* (no publisher or city listed: 1974), 18.

46. See Berteaux and Rosner, "10 Things You Didn't Know about the Angel Moroni Statue." It takes about 2 ounces of gold leaf to completely cover the current Moroni statues.

47. Keith W. Wilcox, *The Washington, DC Temple—A Light to the World: A History of its Architectural Development* (Self-published by Keith W. Wilcox, 1995). The pages of this book are unnumbered. If one does not count the cover and front-matter/title page of the book, but begins one's count starting on the first page of traditional text, then this quote appears on page 27 of the book. If, instead, one counts starting with the cover of the book, then the quote is found on page 31.

48. Eugene F. Fairbanks, *A Sculptor's Testimony in Bronze and Stone: Sacred Sculpture of Avard T. Fairbanks*, rev. ed. (Salt Lake City: Publishers Press, 1994), 39.

49. Torleif S. Knaphus, "Description of the Hill Cumorah Monument," cited in Gerritsen, "The Hill Cumorah Monument," 129.

50. See Gerritsen, "The Hill Cumorah Monument," 131.

51. Ibid.

52. Jack Tresidder, *Symbols and Their Meanings: The Illustrated Guide to More Than 1000 Symbols—Their Traditional and Contemporary Significance* (London: Duncan Baird Publications, 2000), 6.

53. While some, no doubt, had already picked up on the variations from one statue to another—many may not have noticed these subtle, but real differences. Perhaps, even in this, there is a symbolic message. Sometimes we're guilty of missing the details—of something like these statues, but also in the rites and rituals of the temple. It takes attentiveness to notice, and spiritual consciousness to understand what it is that God is trying to convey through such symbols. At times we gloss over the symbols of the

endowment, or the details of the architecture, or the words of the scriptures, missing the hidden details that the Father pines for us to discover. However, if we are willing to make a concerted effort, we will be blessed with greater light and knowledge. We will notice details we did not see before, and our testimonies will be deepened and enhanced for the effort. In this spirit, Elder Neal A. Maxwell emphasized the importance of making an effort to find the truths our Father is waiting to grant us. He wrote, "The Book of Mormon will be with us 'as long as the earth shall stand.' We need all that time to explore it, for the book is like a vast mansion with gardens, towers, courtyards, and wings. There are rooms yet to be entered, with flaming fireplaces waiting to warm us. The rooms glimpsed so far contain further furnishings and rich detail yet to be savored, but décor dating from Eden is evident. There are panels inlaid with incredible insights, particularly insights about the great question. Yet, we as Church members sometimes behave like hurried tourists, scarcely venturing beyond the entry hall." Neal A. Maxwell, *Not My Will, But Thine* (Salt Lake City: Deseret Book, 1988), 36. Elder Maxwell's point seems germane to our study here. Having an eye attentive to the details will bring meaning otherwise missed, whereas a casual glance can bring nothing more than casual blessings. May we have the "eyes to see" (Matthew 13:15–17).

Chapter 12

THROUGH FEMALE EYES

AN INTERPRETIVE APPROACH TO THE
RITES OF THE TEMPLE[1]

Alonzo L. Gaskill

I have long had a love for the holy temple. When I received my endowment (a year after my conversion), the ordinances of the House of
the Lord simply confirmed for me the rightness of my decision to
become a Latter-day Saint. Of course, I realize that not everyone who
enters the temple has a powerful experience. As an example, I recently
read a temple-focused study that both intrigued and saddened me, as it
chronicled the experiences of a handful of Latter-day Saint women who
expressed frustration with the language, rites, and symbolic undertones of
the LDS temple.[2] The general concern expressed by several of the study's
female participants was that they felt the language of some of the temple
covenants represented women as second-class citizens and as subservient
silent partners. My sorrow came, not because these women see things differently than I but, because I am pained when I see *any* person hurting;
and the thought that one of the most powerful and uplifting influences in
my life is painful or distasteful to others fills me with a deep sadness, and
also significant concern.

As a male, it would be unfair of me to suggest that I completely
understand all of the pain my sisters in Christ have felt living in a world
that has, in so many ways, favored men over women. However, I *do* see
why, for some, elements of the initiatory, endowment, or sealing ceremony
cause some discomfort. Having read the comments of several females who
have expressed concern, I believe (at least in part) that I understand their

interpretation of the covenants and ordinances, and also why those readings of the rites have left them feeling as though their Church views them as "less than" men.

My intention here is not to call into question the interpretations of those who see things differently than me, nor to propose that they are somehow reading the rites of the temple in erroneous ways. Neither is it my intention to be understood as saying that I think the language and symbolism of the temple is flawed or sexist. Rather, my purpose here is to offer a model for viewing those sacred rites which might be helpful to members of the Church—both those who struggle with the manner in which the covenants are conveyed, and those who are quite comfortable with the content. I certainly am not challenging how some interpret the ordinances—nor even their justification for their views. Rather, what I am offering here is an alternate interpretation of that which, to some, feels offensive; an interpretation that *I feel* is both in harmony with the doctrine of the Church and the message of the temple ordinances—but which also potentially offers comfort to those who feel misrepresented by the rites and covenants of the temple.

As a preface to my approach, I remind the reader of something Elder Dallin H. Oaks wrote about the role of the Holy Ghost in helping us understand God's words. Elder Oaks explained:

> For us, the scriptures are not the ultimate source of knowledge, but [they are] what precedes the ultimate source. *The ultimate knowledge comes by revelation.* . . . Such revelations are necessary because, as Elder Bruce R. McConkie of the Quorum of the Twelve observed, "Each pronouncement in the holy scriptures . . . is so written as to reveal little or much, depending on the spiritual capacity of the student."[3] . . . *Many of the prophecies and doctrinal passages in the scriptures have multiple meanings.* The Savior affirmed that fact when he told his disciples that the reason he taught the multitude in parables was that this permitted him to teach them "the mysteries of the kingdom of heaven" (Matt. 13:11) while not revealing those mysteries to the multitude. His parables had multiple meanings or applications according to the spiritual maturity of the listener. They had a message for both children and gospel scholars. . . . "For in the wise words of St. Hilary, . . . '*Scripture consists not in what one reads, but in what one understands.*'"[4] . . . This is why the teaching of the Holy Ghost is a better guide to scriptural interpretation than even the best commentary.[5]

Elder Oaks added that "scripture is not limited to what it meant when it was written but may also include *what that scripture means to a reader today.*"[6] I could not agree more with Elder Oaks' point. While there is value in knowing the original intent of a passage, there is also great value in an openness to applications beyond "what was meant at the time the scriptural words were spoken or written." I think his point is as applicable to temple ritual as it is to the standard works of the Church. I do not speak for the Brethren, and I do not profess to know what exactly the Lord intended us to understand when He revealed the sacred temple ordinances to the Prophet Joseph and his successors.[7] But I *do* believe that the Spirit knows what you and I need; and, to some degree, the "right interpretation" of a ritual or ordinance *may* be the one that the Holy Ghost reveals to you at a given stage in your life. Certainly, what the ordinances mean to one person is not always what they mean to another. And that does not necessarily mean that one or both have an invalid interpretation or understanding. It may simply mean that the Spirit is revealing through those same rites the specific meaning that each needs at any given stage in his or her life. Consequently, following Elder Oaks' lead, I am proposing here a reading of the rites that I personally think might be helpful to some.

THE EMPLOYMENT OF A STANDARD MOTIF

The author of the study I cited in my introductory paragraph suggested that "ritual can be a vehicle of empowerment and oppression."[8] Truly, it can be. But perhaps it is the responsibility of the participant to determine whether empowerment or oppression is the chosen interpretation of a given rite or ritual. One can endow the forms with oppressive meanings or empowering meanings. The participant gets to choose what a rite or ritual means to him or her. The rites of the temple are clearly conveyed in symbolic fashion—as are *all* covenants in the Church.[9] The meanings we give to the words, actions, and clothing of the temple will determine the message we derive from those ritualistic articulations, acts, and

articles. Ultimately, ritual invites us to select our interpretive meanings.[10] That, in itself, is empowering.

Evidence that something symbolic is clearly intended in the telling of the story of Adam and Eve is to be found in the fact that, contrary to the majority of the world, the LDS doctrine regarding Eve is consistently positive—seeing her as a brave heroine who initiated mortality "that man may be."[11] Yet, contrary to that well-established latter-day doctrine, in the endowment Eve is portrayed in seemingly negative terms, as though she had succumb to the enticements of Satan; something we know she *did not* do.[12] Thus, clearly something symbolic is being conveyed via the endowment narrative. It is the patron's responsibility to uncover that symbolic message. What follows is my attempt at exactly that.[13]

While some of the symbols of the temple may have *many* potential applications—each very positive in its message and meaning; some very standard archetypes also appear in the temple rites. The story of the Fall appears to be one of those archetypes. One of the most important symbolic lessons of the endowment has to do with the symbolism of the Groom and His bride. Scripture frequently highlights Christ's covenant relationship with His Church by employing the symbols of bride and Bridegroom for the Church and Messiah respectively.[14] In context of that symbolic archetype, Adam well stands as a representation of Jesus and his prophets. Eve, on the other hand, can appropriately serve as a typological symbol of the Church, the bride of Christ, or Covenant Israel (female *and male*). Thus, when the story of the Fall is employed in liturgy, this metaphorical interpretation is traditionally understood to be at the heart of the message. As examples, note the following:

- Just as Adam was the first human to be created, Christ was the Firstborn of the Father (D&C 93:21). Adam was created in the image of God,[15] as was Jesus (who is said to be in the "express image" of the Father—Hebrews 1:3). Michael became the "first Adam" and Jesus is the "last Adam" (1 Corinthians 15:45).

- God gave Adam a "help meet" (Genesis 2:18; Moses 3:18), and He has given Jesus one also—the Church; this is Christ's work and it is His Church—but it was not in the design and will of the Father that Jesus do that work alone. As Eve was Adam's help and support, Christ's bride—the Church—serves as *His* help and support. After their Fall, Adam and Eve unitedly do the work

God sent them to earth to do. Similarly, the Church's members aided Jehovah in the Creation, in the writing of scripture, in the preaching of His message, in the administration of His ordinances, and so on. Their hands are His hands. Their work is His work. Adam and Eve were commanded to be one and, in like manner, Christ and His Church are to be one.

• One typologist wrote, "[Eve is] a type of the church as Adam is a type of Christ. As Eve was made out of a part of Adam, so the church is a part of the Lord Jesus. The church is called His bride as Eve was Adam's bride."[16] The covenant relationship between the bride and the Bridegroom is the most important of all eternal relationships. Adam and Eve were to become one; husbands and wives are all commanded to become one; and Christ and His Church are to be one. Eve is metaphorically said to have come out of Adam's side (Genesis 2:21–24; Moses 3:21–24), and the Church is called "Christian" because it comes out of the Man, Christ. Elsewhere we read:

> It is significant that the man [Adam] calls the woman [Eve] "bone of my bone and flesh of my flesh," a statement he could not have made about the animals. In Hebrew, these phrases indicate a closeness, a blood relationship between the two parties, and in this case a unified companionship between the man and the woman. But the phrases are also used in other places in the Old Testament to describe two parties who are not necessarily blood relatives but who have made a covenant with each other, such as when the northern tribes of Israel made a covenant with David, their new king, and confirmed: "Behold, we are thy bone and thy flesh." David makes a similar covenant with the elders of Judah: "Ye are my brethren, ye are my bones and my flesh." Some of the participants may have been related, but the phrase refers to a mutual covenant the two parties have made with each other.[17]
>
> There is a covenant relationship that exists between Christ and His Church. This is foreshadowed by Adam's relationship with Eve. The fact that in the story the man was made first, and then the woman was made from the man, has been seen as a statement about the covenant

people's dependence upon Christ—who was the Firstborn of Father's spirit offspring.[18] The rib metaphor suggests that the eternities are intended to be a partnership of man and woman[19]—or, as the endowment suggests, between Christ and His Bride.[20] Indeed, if any of us successfully lay hold upon exaltation, it will be *because* we had such a relationship with our Savior!

In the endowment, patrons are participants in a play. We are each actors who, by instruction, imagine ourselves as though we are playing the roles of the characters called "Adam" and "Eve."[21] Of course, the symbolism is important, and, visually speaking, the masculinity of men better suits them to symbolically represent Christ (and His prophets). Consequently, women can best represent the bride of Christ (His Church—female *and male*). As one participates in this holy play, keeping this archetype of the Groom and His bride in mind helps to avoid sexist interpretations of the rites, rituals, and covenants being conveyed. What follows is a reading of those sacred ordinances through lenses colored by this archetype.

THE ENDOWMENT[22]

In the view of some, there are several components of the temple endowment that seem to rub individuals—particularly females—wrong. Each is typically focused on the perception that Eve is represented in the temple endowment as subservient to, or less than, Adam. Chief among the concerns expressed are the following: how Eve is absent in the creation account, how she covenants to be obedient to her husband, how she is depicted as a silent partner, and how women (who portray Eve) veil their faces during certain rites. We will consider each of these respectively.

Eve and the Creation: One female Latter-day Saint lamented, "The endowment film depicts the six-day Creation as being carried out by the craftsmanship of men—Elohim, Jehovah, and Michael."[23] The same sister went on to suggest that not highlighting women in the creation narrative was "theologically inaccurate" and potentially offensive to women.[24]

Of course, we should be cautious when reading scripture or participating in ordinances to not draw our interpretations or applications from what is *not* said. In other words, if the scriptures or the temple endowment *do not* discuss a particular doctrine or historical event, we should *not* draw from that silence an assumption that something is not doctrinally true, or that it has no basis in history. The story of the Creation is a good example of this. In none of the authorized accounts—Genesis, Moses, Abraham, or the endowment—do we have a discussion of women participating in those sacred and foundational events. However, the *Encyclopedia of Mormonism* suggests that it is a teaching of the Church that women *did* participate in the Creation of this earth, as well as that of others earths.[25] The fact that females are not depicted as participating in the Creation, when we understand the teaching of the Church to be that they *did*, implies that something symbolic may be intended. In the Church's official teacher's manual for its temple preparation course, we are informed that "all the events covered in the temple are symbolic. When they are understood" to be such, "they will help each person recognize truth and grow spiritually."[26] So, with propriety we ask, what might we draw from the absence of women in the creation narrative?

One simple interpretation of a creation that is symbolically depicted as being solely accomplished by males (who figuratively represent God) is that we are reminded, in emblematic ways, of the Father's graciousness in creating for us this most remarkable gift we call earth. The creation of this earth, and its gifting to us by God, is an excellent symbol for the plan of salvation, which is unquestionably a gift to all of Father's children. Owing to the archetype of Christ and His bride/Church, including female figures in the account of the Creation would run the risk of distracting from the message of our dependence upon God for His Plan—typified by the creation of all things. Thus, the choice to not depict the woman (bride of Christ) as participating in the creation account helps us to place our focus, not on our own work during the Creation, but on God's—because He is ultimately the source of all things.[27]

That being said, I think it is worth pointing out that there are ways to find Eve (or the bride) in aspects of the Creation. Approaching the symbolism from an entirely different angle (than the bride/Bridegroom construct), one sister explained how she finds the feminine in the story of the Creation:

> The Semitic meaning of the term "Elohim" is plural and means Gods. . . . Elohim created us in his image, male and female, created he them. Elohim, *they.* So to me I see the Mother very involved in this whole creation and I don't think its [*sic*] really doctrinally erroneous for me to say that but we don't talk about it. And even in the temple,

curiously that's not there. Well, I should say, it's not there front and center but it is implicit when all is said and done. It . . . makes it quite clear that there is a Mother in Heaven and that she's very involved.[28]

In this same spirit, it is worth noting that, as soon as Eve arrives on the stage, we are told her name and its meaning, emphasizing the symbolic merit of the scene. As one sister explained, "Eve's name, 'the mother of all living,' powerfully evidenced Eve's role in the creation."[29] Elder Russell M. Nelson called women "a keystone in the priesthood arch of creation."[30] Thus, the creation account, as told in the endowment, may actually offer us some very positive images about women, in addition to offering an uplifting and focused message about how a great and loving God has given us (through the Creation) the ultimate opportunity—to come to an earth that we might become like Him.

Eve and obedience to the Bridegroom: As in scripture, so also during the ritual enactment of the story of the Fall, Eve and Adam walk hand in hand before God prior to being banished from Eden. During their stay in their garden paradise, each conversed with the Father. A pre-Fall equality is depicted. However, in the symbolic story, upon Eve's partaking of the "forbidden fruit" (at the enticement of Satan), things changed. After their transgression, Adam is depicted as having a continuing, unmediated and direct covenant relationship with the Father. However, post-Fall, Eve is symbolically depicted as having lost that. Thus, Eve is shown emblematically as accessing God through her groom, while Adam is portrayed as having direct access to the Father. For obvious reasons, this has been interpreted by some as offensive and sexist. As an example, one sister explained, "My main issue with the temple is having to covenant to my husband while he covenants to God. That's not how I've always thought it to be—I've always felt like I have direct access to God. At first with the temple that really bothered me and . . . the more I went it really bothered me that I was required to do that."[31] Similarly, another female explained her perception of what takes place in the temple: "The husband is covenanting with the Lord and the woman is covenanting with her husband and she's not covenanting directly with the Lord. I don't really know what sense to make of that."[32] Finally, one sister said, "It's hard for me to imagine how a single woman goes through and spends her whole life not even married and hears that over and over again."[33] While each of these interpretations are understandable, if one considers the archetype of bride and Bridegroom, as elucidated above, one can potentially see a different message in all of this.

When you and I experience our personal falls—through entrance into mortality and via our repeated choices to hearken unto the enticements of Satan—we are in need of an arbitrator to mediate our covenant relationship with the Father. When we lived with the Father in our premortal paradise, mediation was not needed because we had not yet fallen. But once our circumstances changed, we needed from that time forward one who could mediate our covenants and our return to God. Christ is that mediator! In this context, as the symbolic bride of Christ, Eve's post-Fall act of covenanting through Adam well represents the Church's act of making covenants with the Father through Christ. Donald W. Parry and Jay A. Parry wrote, "Because our sins separate us from God, we cannot act in our own names and have our acts be recognized by God. We must have a mediator, a savior, whose power of redemption will validate our righteous acts. We need One who is not separated from God to stand between us and God. Hence, all of our righteous acts, all of our testimonies and teachings—and all ordinances—must be done in the name of Jesus Christ, that perfect Redeemer."[34] Adam, as a representation of the Lord, has the ability (post-Fall) to directly access the Father because Christ (whom he typifies) was not disobedient to the Father. However, the bride of Christ (you and I) *are* at times disobedient and, thus, *do* need mediation. Consequently, if one understands Adam to symbolize Christ (the Bridegroom), the perceived offensiveness of the narrative seems mitigated. According to this perspective, Eve is not making a covenant to an earthly husband but, instead, to her Groom—the Mediator of all humankind. And, since Eve represents us, we can conclude that a similar symbolic message is being conveyed. We, the bride of Christ (female *and male*), are in a fallen state and thus need a mediator—which is Christ, the Lord. He is our Bridegroom; we are His bride. He has direct access to the Father, whereas we need Him to mediate our access. This seems a better reading of the narrative and covenant under examination.

In support of this interpretation, we should remember that we make no covenants *to* other people in the temple—even in the sealing ceremony. We only make covenants *about* other people.[35] Consequently, for one to read this portion of the temple endowment as being about making a covenant to one's spouse is to potentially miss what Eve is doing—and what we are called to do. Rather than seeing "this part of the ritual" as expressing "women's eternal subordination" to men,[36] we may be better suited by seeing in it evidence that we are eternally dependent upon Christ, our Mediator. The message is a positive one—for men *and for women*. It is a testament to the fact that, though we have estranged ourselves from God through our sins, Christ stands ready to mediate our salvation and return us to the Father if we will covenant *to* Him and live faithfully *for* Him. I like the language of Doctrine and Covenants 45, which reads:

> Listen to him who is the advocate with the Father, who is pleading *your* cause before him—Saying: Father, behold the sufferings and death of him who did no sin, in whom thou wast well pleased; behold the blood of thy Son which was shed, the blood of him whom thou gavest that thyself might be glorified; Wherefore, Father, spare these my brethren [and sisters] that believe on my name, that they may come unto me and have everlasting life. (D&C 45:3–5; emphasis added.)

This seems to me to be one of the primary messages that is being taught when Adam and Eve are symbolically represented as making their post-Fall covenants in divergent ways.

Eve as Silent Partner: It has been pointed out by some who are uncomfortable with the temple's narrative that Eve speaks during the endowment—but only *prior to* the Fall. Once she partakes of the "forbidden fruit"—and once the Fall is complete—she "never speaks again. She's there but she doesn't talk."[37] One sister, concerned about this, said, "I don't know what they're trying to say with that but it made me uncomfortable. It seemed like they'd taken something away from her because of what she'd done."[38] Another Latter-day Saint sister similarly said "after that covenant" that Eve makes when she falls, she "is gone. . . . They show her but she doesn't talk. [Peter, James, and John] don't address Eve, they always address Adam."[39]

While this may summarize how the symbolic narrative is portrayed, drawing from it a conclusion that women are being counseled to be "submissive" to men seems both emotionally harmful to sisters and potentially errant in interpretation.[40]

The archetype we have been working with says that Eve represents the entire Church—male and female. It also suggests that Adam represents the Lord. Thus, the symbolic message ought *not* be interpreted as a statement about women's subservience to men. On the contrary, it seems to me that there is a very specific message here about the consequence of sin in the lives of members of the Church—male and female. When we listen to the enticements of Satan, when we sin, we *do* lose our voice, *per se*. The symbolic representation of Eve as silent after she hearkened to the devil's bidding seems calculated to remind us that *our* access to God is curtailed through disobedience to covenants and commandments. After the Fall, Adam—who had obeyed the commands of the Father—still has voice because he is depicted as not having been deceived by the devil. Eve, on the other hand, falls silent—specifically because symbolically she is represented as ignoring the Father's commands while embracing the adversary's advice. Consequently, her access—meaning the Church's access—is now mediated through Christ.

Once again, it seems that a message can be found in this that does not tear down women but, instead, highlights the covenant relationship of the entire Church (male and female) to the Lord. In the context of the archetype, this portion of the narrative simply seems to testify of the dangers of sin. The *Dictionary of Biblical Imagery* points out that "Silence communicates. . . . It can express faithlessness . . . , rebellion . . . , defeat or destruction. . . . Significantly, there is one Hebrew verb that means both 'to destroy' and 'to keep silent.'"[41] The symbolic silence of Eve can remind us that when *we* act in faithless or rebellious ways, we allow Satan to defeat God's efforts to work in our lives. Such an act, if not repented of, can ultimately lead to our destruction. And, thus, Eve's silence after the Fall is only about subservience in the sense that each of us—male and female—must submit our lives and wills to God; otherwise we lose our voice and risk our destruction.

Eve and the Wearing of Veils: For a variety of reasons, veils have been used for centuries in multiple cultures and in many religious traditions. The symbolic meaning of veils is contingent upon the culture and context in which they are employed. Certainly for some patriarchal societies, veils imply modesty or chastity.[42] For others, they are a symbol of submission to authority.[43] Sometimes veils represent the need to conceal or hide something.[44] And, occasionally, they are even used as a symbol of separation from God.[45] None of these explanations seem to grasp the primary message of the act of veiling in Latter-day Saint temples.

Of course, not all Latter-day Saints interpret the veiled face in the same way. While some see veiling as a positive symbol, others draw from it oppressive connotations (such as that women are somehow being forced to submit themselves to the will and ways of mortal men). In the context of our archetype, the veiling of the face makes one a symbol for the bride of Christ and, consequently, should *not* be seen as a representation of the oppression of women by men who exercise "unrighteous dominion" (D&C 121:36–37, 39, 41–44). One scholar pointed out that anciently

> The relation between a god and his people was represented as one of marriage. . . . Thus, in the Old Testament Jahveh is frequently imagined as the husband of Israel. . . . Hosea, for example, thinks of Israel as an unfaithful wife who is still beloved by her husband and is forgiven and restored. Paul takes up the Old Testament idea and conceives of the relation between the Church and Christ as one of marriage. . . . The book of Revelation culminates in the glowing description of the Church as the Bride of Christ, and . . . the submission of a wife to her husband [as called for by Paul] is in some way to represent the obedience which the Church owes to Christ.[46]

Perhaps it might also be helpful to point out a related practice in ancient post–New Testament Christianity. One scholar spoke of a unique calling or designation, *per se*, of women in the ancient Christian Church: "The *virgins* . . . sat in special seats reserved for them. . . . Their number and their commitment to a life of chastity was one of the church's most esteemed emblems. These *virgins* signified their unmarried state by *not* wearing veils."[47] If the office of "virgin" was indeed a calling, so to speak, and if *not* wearing a veil symbolized being unmarried, then donning a veil appropriately represents getting married or entering into a covenant relationship with a bridegroom (namely Christ), as anciently it was a common cultural practice for married women to wear veils so as to show "propriety, specifically sexual modesty, since it preserved the sight of [their] hair for only [their] husband and family."[48] Thus, the veiling of the face— rather than being a negative symbol—has the potential to be an elevating symbol of covenant, commitment, and consecration, not to man, but to the Lord. And it is a symbol that is as applicable to temple-attending men as it is to endowed women.

Of course, wearing a physical veil over one's face or eyes obscures one's sight. It dims the vision, per se. Though only one interpretation of the meaning of this reality, note Paul's emphasis in Ephesians 5. He indicates that a wife's "cooperation with"[49] her husband is a symbol for the bride (or Church) subjecting herself (male and female) to the Bridegroom (Christ). The Church is to live in subjection to its Bridegroom and Savior. In this context, the donning of a veil can be seen as a symbol of the Church's willingness to do so. Anciently, the veil often carried very strong connotations of blindness, unbelief, a lack of faith, obscured vision or sight, the concealment of certain aspects of truth and/or deity, and so on. To be veiled implied that one stood in a "pre-enlightened state," and that one was in ignorance of certain bits of "hidden or esoteric knowledge."[50] The veiled face is best *not* interpreted as a statement about the spiritual ignorance of *women*. On the contrary, it is best to see this as a statement about the spiritual blindness of *all humankind*, including those in the Church—covenant Israel (male and female). Thus, one commentator wrote, "Paul reinterprets and spiritualizes this veil to represent the Jewish inability to understand the Scriptures correctly."[51] Similarly, Isaiah scholar Edward Young noted that God depicts the bride of Christ as veiled because she is spiritually blind and ignorant aside from her relationship with the Lord.[52] One dictionary of biblical imagery states, "As an image of concealment, the veil also has the negative meaning of a mind that is cut off from the truth. Paul pictured the unbelieving mind as having a veil over it (2 Corinthians 3:12–16) and the gospel as being veiled to people who disbelieve it (2 Corinthians 4:3)."[53] Thus, in antiquity, when the woman clothed herself in a veil, in part, that act symbolized her acknowledgment that the Church (or Covenant Israel) did not see clearly and, therefore, needed its God (and His earthly representatives) to guide the members of the Church safely home. Submission of the will to the Bridegroom was the only way that this safe return could be accomplished—and the veil was a frank acknowledgment of that fact. Thus, contrary to some interpretations, the veiled face can be a strongly positive image in scripture and particularly in the temple.[54] It does not speak of the submissive state of women, but of the spiritually ignorant state of humankind—male and female.

In summation: The bride of Christ does not see clearly because we—the Church—labor under a veil and are susceptible to the enticements of Satan. The Lord and His appointed prophets are not veiled as we are and, thus, can see what we cannot see. The veiling of the bride (male and female) is a symbolic reminder to us that she must attach herself to the Groom (Christ) so that she can safely be led home. It reminds us—via a play in which we all take part—that we need to cling to the Lord and His prophets because they have the power to lead us, in the words of President John Taylor, "in the ways of life and salvation."[55] *There is no other way!*

THE SEALING CEREMONY

In the sealing ceremony—wherein a husband and wife are united as a companionship for time and for all eternity—each partner is invited, by covenant, to do certain things. Elders Abraham H. Cannon and Orson Pratt, of the Quorum of the Twelve Apostles, and President Anthony W. Ivins of the First Presidency, each highlighted the difference in the language of the covenant made by men and women during the sealing ordinance.[56] The two genders do not make the exact same covenant about their spouses. Understandably, some have perceived this as suggesting that the two partners are on different planes; the one seemingly elevated above the other because the one does not "give" of their self, but only "receives"—whereas the other gives *and* receives.

In order to understand the potential symbolism in this ordinance, one should recognize (as we have pointed out above) that—contrary to popular opinion—in the sealing ceremony *no* covenant is made between the husband and the wife. Certainly covenants are made *about* how one will interact with the other person. But one does not make any specific covenant *to* any human during the sealing ceremony. Hugh Nibley indicated that the covenant made in the sealing ceremony "is between the individual and his [or her] Heavenly Father alone."[57] President Heber C. Kimball taught that "there are no covenants made between individuals in the church. All promises and agreements are between the individual and our Father in Heaven."[58] Latter-day Saint scholar, Lisle G. Brown, wrote, some "may feel that the couple" being sealed "actually enter into solemn covenants with each other. . . . However, in the actual wording of the marriage sealing ceremony there are no words that specifically mention any covenant made between the bride and groom. Indeed . . . , there are no covenants made between individuals in the priesthood ordinances."[59] The fact that the couple being sealed only makes a covenant with God, but not with each other, serves to heighten the potential positive symbolism in this rite.

If we again take our cues from the metaphor of bride and Bridegroom, what might otherwise be read as sexist, takes on a completely different meaning. In this model, the bride of Christ (the Church—male and female) covenants to "give" herself to her Lord (the Bridegroom, who is Christ), and to "receive" Him as her Lord.[60] In response, the Groom—Christ—promises that, if she does so, He will "receive" her (the

Church—male and female) unto Himself (into His Kingdom).[61] In this symbolic archetype:

- Giving one's self to the Groom represents laying one's will upon the altar. It symbolizes living for God, and not for one's self. In the words of Omni 1:26, "And now . . . , I would that ye should come unto Christ, who is the Holy One of Israel, and partake of his salvation, and the power of his redemption. Yea, come unto him, *and offer your whole souls as an offering unto him*, and continue in fasting and praying, and endure to the end; and as the Lord liveth ye will be saved" (emphasis added). To "give" ourselves to Christ requires more than simply having a testimony. It necessarily implies conversion, commitment, and consecration. As Elder Neal A. Maxwell taught, "The submission of one's will is really the only uniquely personal thing we have to place on God's altar. The many other things we 'give,' brothers and sisters, are actually the things He has already given or loaned to us. However, when you and I finally submit ourselves, by letting our individual wills be swallowed up in God's will, then we are really giving something to Him! It is the only possession which is truly ours to give!"[62]

- To "receive" the Bridegroom symbolically implies that we accept Him—as our Master and, thus, as our Savior. In so doing, we open ourselves up to the influence of God, and also to the salvation offered by Christ. As Doctrine and Covenants 11:30 states, "But verily, verily, I say unto you, that as many as *receive* me, to them will I give power to become the sons [and daughters] of God." President Joseph Fielding Smith reminded the members of the Church, "The privilege of exaltation is *not* held out to those who have had the opportunity to *receive* Christ and obey his truth and who have refused to do so."[63] Of course, to "receive" Christ necessarily implies that we "receive" His authorized messengers whom He has sent (D&C 84:36).

- Finally, for the Groom to "receive" you or me, symbolically implies that He has accepted us as His spiritual sons and daughters (Mosiah 5:7; 27:25). It implies that He has applied His atoning blood to our lives because we have placed our trust in Him, and because we have earnestly sought to live His commandments and be faithful to our covenants. As Alma 5:33 states, "Behold, he sendeth an invitation unto all men, for the arms of mercy are extended towards them, and he saith: Repent, and *I will receive you*" (emphasis added).

When we read the sealing ordinance through the lens of the standard archetype—that of the Groom and His bride—suddenly the message of this rite is more powerful and more personal.[64] We see that our covenants are individual; they are between ourselves and our God, rather than being between ourselves and another flawed human being.[65] We also understand better what  is required of us for salvation; namely, that we must let go of our rebellious hearts and turn our lives over to Him, accepting His acts of love and Atonement on our personal behalf. Then He can receive us unto Himself. Then, and only then, can we expect to dwell with Him for eternity.

THE INITIATORY ORDINANCES

Early in this chapter we referenced a study which chronicled how some Latter-day Saint women interpret the symbolism and covenants of the temple. Many of those interviewed in the study indicated that they took issue with what they perceived as the message conveyed through the covenants and narrative of the temple. That being said, one thing that there seemed to be universal agreement on was this: for the sisters, the initiatory ordinances of the temple did not cause the same visceral reaction that the other rites and rituals occasionally did. Indeed, each of those interviewed in the study quite literally raved about how meaningful and powerful the initiatory rites are to them. The *Encyclopedia of Mormonism* notes that, in the temple, "women are set apart to administer the ordinances to women."[66] Of that reality, one sister said, "I was really happy to see that women were performing ordinances in the temple. That made me happy. . . . I really love the blessings in the initiatory and I love that women are doing it."[67] Similarly, another woman explained, "I was really overwhelmed by my first initiatory experience. The biggest reason was that women were doing the temple work—no one told me—I could not believe it. I just loved it. It's my favorite part of temple work."[68] One female commentator on the ordinances wrote, "For contemporary LDS women,

ALONZO L. GASKILL

the physical experience of being administered to by another women is an often unexpected and entirely new religious experience culminating in what several women described as a transformative ritual experience."[69]

The importance of this cannot be underestimated. The depiction of women in the initiatory is as priestesses.[70] They are represented as empowered and authorized.[71] They act on behalf of God—and are in no way symbolically presented as functioning in submission to some lording male patriarch. The initiatory rites teach us of God's respect *for* and trust *in* faithful women. Because men are entirely removed from women during this rite—women now play a role acted out by men in the endowment. In the initiatory ordinances, the sisters engaging in the ritual drama are positioned to represent God, as He pours out His blessings upon His dearly loved daughters. All of this is important because it gives women reason to rejoice in knowing how God truly feels about them. But it is also important because it serves as a lens through which we might interpret every other temple rite, ritual, or ordinance that follows the initiatory. In other words, if the message of the washing and anointing rites is so very positive about women and their place in the kingdom, how can we then interpret all of the other rites as messages about male domination, patriarchy, and the oppression of women? Such a contradiction makes absolutely no sense. If the initiatory ordinances are so aggrandizing of women—and one cannot believe otherwise—then it seems evident that the other ordinances must have a similar message. And if we are seeing a contradiction between the obvious meaning of the initiatory rites and the more opaque meaning of the other rituals, surely we must be inadvertently misinterpreting the latter in erroneous ways.

CONCLUSION

While throughout this article I have focused on a singular symbol—namely men and women as representations of the bride of Christ—let us not forget Christ's love for His bride. Our fallen status is not the focus of the symbol of the bride but, rather, Christ's intent to love and redeem His bride: that is the focus. And that seems to be the emphasis of the endowment, which is—to me—a tremendously positive message about women generally, and about Christ's Church specifically. The Lord has described His Church—His bride (male and female)—in this way:

And when I passed by thee, and saw thee polluted in thine own blood, I said unto thee when thou wast in thy blood, Live; yea, . . . I have caused thee to multiply as the bud of the field, and thou hast increased and waxen great, and . . . thine hair is grown, whereas thou wast naked and bare. Now when I passed by thee . . . , I spread my skirt over thee, and covered thy nakedness: yea, I sware unto thee, and entered into a covenant with thee, saith the Lord God, and thou becamest mine. Then washed I thee with water; yea, I throughly washed away thy blood from thee, and I anointed thee with oil. I clothed thee also with broidered work, and shod thee with badgers' skin [slippers], and I girded thee about with fine linen, and I covered thee with silk. I decked thee also with ornaments, and I put bracelets upon thy hands, and a chain on thy neck. And I put a jewel on thy forehead, and earrings in thine ears, and a beautiful crown upon thine head. Thus wast thou decked with gold and silver; and thy raiment was of fine linen, and silk, and broidered work; thou didst eat fine flour, and honey, and oil: and thou wast exceeding beautiful, and thou didst prosper into a kingdom. And thy renown went forth among the heathen for thy beauty: for it was perfect through my comeliness, which I had put upon thee, saith the Lord GOD. (Ezekiel 16:6–14)

The language of the passage is beautiful because it is the language of redemption. The Lord speaks of His bride—male and female—as struggling to be faithful. And yet He loves her, blesses her, and redeems her, making a covenant of salvation *with* and *to* her. What a beautiful and positive message.

Aside from the archetype we've been discussing—and in addition to the positive feminine symbolism found in the initiatory—there are other potentially beautiful images of women in the temple. In my book, *The Lost Language of Symbolism*, I discuss the fact that the Apostle Paul saw the veiling of women's faces as evidence that angels acknowledged their "authority" before God.[72] Significantly, several sisters I spoke with each saw the veiling of their faces as "private time with God." Independently, they described it as their opportunity to commune with the Father unfettered by distractions—the veil shutting out all such things. One sister said to me, "I feel sad for men because they don't get to have that experience of veiling their faces, like we do. For me it is a profoundly spiritual time, where I feel closer to the Lord, and empowered by Him. It is a time to commune privately with the Most High God!" In my book, *Sacred Symbols:*

Finding Meaning in Rites, Rituals, and Ordinances, I discuss how women in the temple serve as perfect symbols of Christ in several ways, and on multiple levels.[73] In support of this, time and again, God uses feminine metaphors and symbols to represent some of His most holy and loving attributes (for example, Isaiah 49:15; Deuteronomy 32:11–12; Hosea 13:8; Matthew 23:37). I've ever found beautiful the fact that the Hebrew word for God's "compassion" means, quite literally, "womb love."[74] The implication is that God's love and compassion is of such a nature, that it can only be understood by comparing it to an exclusively feminine attribute. I suppose, on some level, this might explain the action of men when Eve is introduced in the endowment. The brethren all stand in her presence as a symbol of their respect for God's "crowning creation"—woman![75] This should be viewed as reverencing women; not as suppressing them. Men stand, not because they see women as "second class," but because they love, honor, and cherish them. Likewise, such empowering principles are taught by the declaration that women are "the mother of all living" (Genesis 3:20). There are so many symbols in the temple that speak to the power of women, and to God's love for them. Over and over we are presented with images and symbols that can be seen as exalting of women, and as evidence of their Christocentric nature. Certainly any symbol can be interpreted in negative terms—but why would we when such positive imagery is available to us? I reiterate here what I said above: with symbols of women—like those depicted in the initiatory rites—being so obviously positive, can we assume that the other feminine imagery of the temple is intended as sexist, condescending, or oppressive? To me, such makes absolutely no sense. And it seems to serve no helpful purpose—for men or women.

When contemplating symbols, it is my personal practice to avoid dogmatism regarding their likely meanings. As Elder Oaks noted regarding scripture, so also I suggest regarding symbolism: if we are Spirit-directed, the Holy Ghost will reveal to us the most helpful meaning of any given symbol, based on our current needs and our specific stage of life.[76] It is not my place to insist that one interpret the rites, covenants, and symbols of the temple in the same way that I do, nor do I claim to know all that God has intended by them. However, for me, I feel that there is a way to read such things that will foster inspiration rather than feelings of discontent. If my proposed model is in anyway offensive or insensitive, I not only apologize, but I also encourage the reader to reject it—as they might any offensive reading—and to seek from the Spirit an interpretation that brings hope and healing.

One might argue: If the models presented herein are true, the Church should teach and emphasize them; they should rework the temple rites so that such an interpretation is clear to all who participate—including to those whom might seek to misuse such rites to enforce patriarchy.[77] The problem with this suggestion is that it implies that all women find the messages of the temple offensive, oppressive, or harmful.[78] Since such is simply not the case, to forcefully interpret the narrative or covenants in a way that only meets the needs of one segment of the population would not be helpful. Rather, by depicting the rites in a symbolic way—and in a way, might I add, which is common to scripture—this leaves open to the patron the opportunity to interpret and apply the messages in ways best suited to the personal needs of the individual.

Might I also suggest, where one has questions, one ought not stew about them; do not let them fester. Study and seek understanding. Perhaps pay a visit to the temple president or the matron, and there discuss some of those concerns or questions. While I cannot promise that the president or matron will *always* have the answer to the questions being posed, the exchange may be helpful. Most importantly, remember that—as Elder Oaks has suggested—the Spirit is the ultimate counselor and teacher when one seeks to understand how to best interpret the symbols of the temple. In the words of the hymn: "Let the Holy Spirit guide."[79]

In the end, I realize this short chapter is not going to resolve all of the concerns that some have about the temple or the larger Church. However, it is my hope that the archetype presented herein might serve as a source of comfort to those who struggle, and also as a springboard for better and more meaningful interpretations of our most sacred rites—interpretations which are positive, empowering, and capable of providing the healing that the House of the Lord was intended to provide.

NOTES

1. Lest the reader misunderstand what I'm trying to do here, I would point out that I am offering in this chapter a singular interpretation and application of Eve and the story of the Fall. I, myself, have found many applications in this sacred narrative. The one presented here is offered, because it addresses a particular concern some have had. But it is hardly the only interpretation that I, or others, have proffered. Indeed, I would strongly encourage the reader to take a look at my book, *The Truth About Eden* (Springville, Utah: Cedar Fort, Inc., 2013), where I offer a much more in-depth look at Eve as a symbol,

and where I discuss in detail the doctrine surrounding her and the choice she and Adam made in Eden.

2. See Nazneen Kane, *"Priestess Unto the Most High God": LDS Women's Temple Rituals and the Politics of Religious Identity* (College Park, Maryland: doctrinal dissertation, University of Maryland, College Park, 2011). While I did not agree with many of the interpretations of LDS temple rites presented therein, I found Dr. Kane's study interesting because it brings to our attention a legitimate concern which needs to be addressed. Consequently, I am not writing by way of review, nor to criticize the study's author. Rather, I am attempting to be responsive to her research—as all research calls us to be. Additionally, while I have used her research as an example of an expression of a concern, I realize that there may be others who have the same concerns she does. Of course, I'm well aware that my response is limited by my own inadequacies as a scholar and human being, and may be less than perfect because of my own ignorance and because I am approaching the issue as a male. (By that I mean, as a male, I certainly cannot fully grasp what a woman encounters emotionally, or otherwise, when she participates in the rites of the temple. I acknowledge that and, thus, put forth that disclaimer at the onset of this study.) My purpose in writing is to offer my simple interpretation of certain rites and covenants in the hope that for those who have been hurt or feel disenchanted and, thus, disenfranchised, perhaps something shared herein will bring comfort and potentially even healing.

3. Elder Oaks is quoting from Bruce R. McConkie, *A New Witness for the Articles of Faith* (Salt Lake City: Deseret Book, 1985), 71.

4. Here, Elder Oaks is citing something he had heard Hugh Nibley quote.

5. Dallin H. Oaks, "Scripture Reading and Revelation," in *Ensign*, January 1995, 7–9; emphasis added.

6. Ibid.; emphasis added.

7. While Joseph is the one we hold to be the conduit through which the ordinances were restored and to whom they were revealed, a number of Joseph's successors have been instrumental in the packaging of and conveyance of those sacred ordinances—Brigham Young, chief among them. While several could be cited, as a singular example chronicling the unfolding of modern temple worship in the post-Joseph Smith era, see Devery S. Anderson, *The Development of LDS Temple Worship: 1846–2000, A Documentary History* (Salt Lake City: Signature Books, 2011).

8. Kane, "Priestess Unto the Most High God," 142.

9. Joseph Fielding McConkie and Donald W. Parry wrote, "Symbols are the language in which all gospel covenants and all ordinances of salvation have been revealed. From the time we are immersed in the waters of baptism to the time we kneel at the altar of the temple with the companion of our choice in the ordinance of eternal marriage, every covenant we make will be written in the language of symbolism." See Joseph Fielding McConkie and Donald W. Parry, *A Guide To Scriptural Symbols* (Salt Lake City: Bookcraft, 1990), 1; See also, Bruce R. McConkie, *Mormon Doctrine*, 2nd ed. (Salt Lake City: Bookcraft, 1979), 773.

10. While the symbolic meaning of some rites (such as baptism or the sacrament) are largely defined for us (by general authorities or by scripture), it seems fair to say that

many are not; and that leaves those rituals or ordinances open for us to find our own meaning and application.

11. Elder Dallin H. Oaks stated, "Some Christians condemn Eve for her act, concluding that she and her daughters are somehow flawed by it. Not the Latter-day Saints! Informed by revelation, we celebrate Eve's act and honor her wisdom and courage in the great episode called the Fall." Dallin H. Oaks, "The Great Plan of Happiness," in *Ensign*, November 1993, 73. Elder Bruce R. McConkie wrote, "As there are not words to extol the greatness of the Ancient of Days . . . so there is no language that could do credit to our glorious mother Eve." Bruce R. McConkie, "Eve and the Fall," in *Woman* (Salt Lake City: Deseret Book, 1979), 68. See also 57–68. Elder Marion G. Romney called Eve's decision to partake of the fruit "noble." See Marion G. Romney, "Mother Eve, A Worthy Exemplar," in *Relief Society Magazine*, 55 (February 1968): 84–89. In the LDS Bible Dictionary we are told that "the fall is a blessing, and . . . Eve should be honored." LDS Bible Dictionary (Salt Lake City: The Church of Jesus Christ of Latter-day Saints, 2013), 641, s.v. "Fall of Adam and Eve." See also, Megan Armknecht, "Mormon Women and Mother Eve: Perceptions, Parallels, and Pedestals," in *Student Symposium: 2015 BYU Religious Education* (Provo, Utah: Religious Studies Center, BYU, 2015), 123–34; Beverly Campbell, *Eve and the Choice Made in Eden* (Salt Lake City: Deseret Book, 2003).

12. See Alonzo L. Gaskill, *The Truth About Eden: Understanding the Fall and Our Temple Experience* (Springville, Utah: Cedar Fort, Inc., 2013), 5–42.

13. Again, the model I offer here is only one of many interpretations and applications.

14. See, for example, Isaiah 54:1–6; Jeremiah 31:32; Ezekiel 16:8; Hosea 2; Romans 7:1–6; 2 Corinthians 11:2; Ephesians 5:21–33; Revelation 19:7; 21:2, 9. See also Leland Ryken, James C. Wilhoit, and Tremper Longman III, eds., *Dictionary of Biblical Imagery* (Downers Grove, Illinois: InterVarsity Press, 1998), 120–22; Alonzo L. Gaskill, *The Lost Language of Symbolism: An Essential Guide for Recognizing and Interpreting Symbols of the Gospel* (Salt Lake City: Deseret Book, 2003), 79, 191–97, 321.

15. Elder McConkie spoke of Adam as being "a similitude of Christ." See Bruce R. McConkie, *The Promised Messiah* (Salt Lake City: Deseret Book, 1978), 449. Elder McConkie's comment comes in the context of the Apostle Paul's declaration that Christ is the "second Adam."

16. Walter L. Wilson, *A Dictionary of Bible Types* (Peabody, Massachusetts: Hendrickson Publishers, 1999), 139.

17. Jolene Edmunds Rockwood, "The Redemption of Eve," in Maureen Ursenbach Beecher and Lavina Fielding Anderson, eds., *Sisters in Spirit* (Chicago: University of Illinois Press, 1992), 17–18.

18. See, for example, Andrew Louth, ed., *Ancient Christian Commentary on Scripture: Genesis 1–11* (Downers Grove, Illinois: InterVarsity Press, 2001), 67, 71; Quodvultdeus, "Book of Promises and Predictions of God" 1:3, *Ancient Christian Commentary on Scripture*, 71; Augustine, "City of God" 22:17, in *Ancient Christian Commentary on Scripture*, 70; Jerome, "Homilies" 66, in *Ancient Christian Commentary on Scripture*, 70; Ambrose, "Letters to Laymen" 85, in *Ancient Christian Commentary on Scripture*, 71.

19. See John Sailhamer, "Genesis," in *The Expositor's Bible Commentary*, 12 vols., ed. Frank E. Gaebelein (Grand Rapids, Michigan: Zondervan, 1976–92), 2:47. This does not exclude those who, in mortality, have never had a chance to marry someone whom they truly loved—or those who in mortality have struggled with same-gender attraction—provided each remains faithful to his or her covenants.

20. "As Eve was bone of the bones of her husband and flesh of his flesh, we also are members of Christ's body, bones of his bones and flesh of his flesh." Ambrose, "Letters to Laymen" 85, in *Ancient Christian Commentary on Scripture*, 71. Late in the fourth century, St. Ambrose noted that Eve was not made in the same way Adam was. She was created from a rib, whereas Adam came from the dust. Ambrose, "Paradise" 10:48, in *Ancient Christian Commentary on Scripture*, 68. Similarly, Christ's mortal birth (represented by Adam's creation) was different than ours (typified by Eve's creation). Whereas we have come entirely from another mortal (symbolized by the rib), Christ's origin is clearly different (as highlighted by the elements utilized in the creation of Adam). It is this difference in His origin and makeup that enables Him to atone, and enables us to exercise faith in Him.

21. Stephen E. Robinson pointed out, "In the mind of first-century Jews and Christians, what Adam was, we are; what Adam could become, we can become." Stephen E. Robinson, "The Book of Adam in Judaism and Early Christianity," in McConkie and Millet, 128. Indeed, it is generally held within Mormonism that Adam and Eve "are symbolic representations of all men and women." See Jolene Edmunds Rockwood, "The Redemption of Eve," in *Sisters in Spirit*, ed. Maureen Usenbach Beecher and Lavina Fielding Anderson (Chicago: University of Illinois Press, 1992), 18.]

22. Technically speaking, each of the ordinances—from the initiatory, to the endowment, and including the sealing ceremony—can be considered part of the endowment since the word "endowment" means "gift," and each of those ordinances offers us gifts, including divine power. However, traditionally we use the term "endowment" to refer to a select portion of the temple's rites, regardless of the universally applicable nature of the term. Thus, in this chapter we will use the word "endowment" in the traditional, and more limited sense.

23. Kane, "Priestess Unto the Most High God," 120.

24. See Ibid., 121.

25. The *Encyclopedia of Mormonism* states, "Eve, Adam, Abraham, and others were among the noble and great ones involved with the creation of the earth." Beverly Campbell, "Eve," in *Encyclopedia of Mormonism*, 4 vols., ed. Daniel H. Ludlow (New York: Macmillan, 1992), 2:475. Elder Orson F. Whitney (of the Twelve) is said to have taught that there were as many females as there were males in that group we call the "noble and great"—that group which participated in the creation of the worlds (Moses 1:33–35). See Hugh Nibley, *Teachings of the Book of Mormon*, 4 vols. (Provo, Utah: Foundation for Ancient Research and Mormon Studies, 2004), 2:351.]

26. *Endowed From on High: Temple Preparation Seminary, Teacher's Manual* (Salt Lake City: The Church of Jesus Christ of Latter-day Saints, 1995), 23. That some of the symbols do not outright appear to include women is not intended to pit one gender

against another, or to place one above another. Rather, it reminds us that Christ is preeminent. For the Church (male and female) He must always be the supreme focus.

27.   One might argue that having Elohim, Jehovah, and Michael all involved in the Creation destroys the symbolism being proposed—namely that Adam is a symbol for Christ. I would simply suggest that that need not be the case. Jesus is a symbol of the Father, but when we see the Father and Son together in scripture we do not feel the symbolism is ruined. Thus, it need not be the case in the Creation. Having several divine and angelic male beings depicted as engaging in that historical event does not diminish their ability to each stand as a symbol of the divine. Indeed, when a group of Melchizedek priesthood holders—each acting as symbols of Christ—engage together in an ordinance (such as giving a priesthood blessing or performing a confirmation), this does not prevent each of them from symbolizing the Lord when they exercise their priesthood. Our lives are constantly filled with types and symbols of Christ—including competing symbols, such as the brazen serpent (Helaman 8:14) and the Lamb of God (John 1:29). One symbol with a different meaning need not negate another. Nor should two separate symbols of Christ concurrently present cause us to feel we must reject the one in order to embrace the other.

28.   "Molly," quoted in Kane, "Priestess Unto the Most High God," 121.

29.   "Hannah," quoted in Kane, "Priestess Unto the Most High God," 122. This sister is suggesting that "mother of all living" certainly includes giving birth to children, but also applies to other acts of creation—such as the Creation of this earth. Sheri Dew similarly suggested that "mother of all living" may have a broader application than giving birth to one's biological offspring in mortality. See Sheri L. Dew, "Are We Not All Mothers?," in *Ensign*, November 2001, 96–98.

30.   Russell M. Nelson, "Lessons From Eve," in *Ensign*, November 1987, 87.

31.   "Eliza," quoted in Kane, "Priestess Unto the Most High God," 124.

32.   "Kara," quoted in Kane, "Priestess Unto the Most High God," 127. Some women in Kane's study "rejected this covenant and challenged the verity of temple ritual" because of it. See Kane, "Priestess Unto the Most High God," 123. It should be noted that Kara inadvertently conflates the persons of the Father and the Son in her description. Thus, her perception of what happens in the temple is actually inaccurate. The "husband" does not make a covenant to the Lord. This may seem insignificant, but if one understands the archetype—and if Adam indeed symbolically represents the Lord—then the husband's covenant to the Father and the woman's covenant to the Groom each carry significant symbolic meaning. Consequently, we need to accurately represent who is covenanting with whom. Such subtleties do make a difference.

33.   "Lydia," quoted in Kane, "Priestess Unto the Most High God," 130.

34.   Donald W. Parry and Jay A. Parry, *Symbols and Shadows: Unlocking a Deeper Understanding of the Atonement* (Salt Lake City: Deseret Book, 2009), 9.

35.   See Hugh Nibley, *Approaching Zion* (Provo, Utah: Foundation for Ancient Research and Mormon Studies, 1989), 385; Heber C. Kimball, in *Journal of Discourses*, 6:127; Lisle G. Brown, "The First Seal of the Holy Priesthood: The Holy Order of Matrimony," (Huntington, West Virginia: unpublished paper in the possession of this author, 2012), 45. Of course, symbolism aside, the standard Latter-day Saint response is well represented

by a comment by Lydia, who said, "when men are unrighteous, women's obedience is no longer required." "Lydia," quoted in Kane, "Priestess Unto the Most High God," 131. Similarly, Molly explained that "there is absolutely no room for interpretation of second-class status submissiveness and subservience to one another—but only submissive[ness] to the will of the Father. . . . Nowhere is the man to be unrighteous over the woman or the woman to be erroneously subservient to the man. . . . All must submit to God and since contingencies are placed upon the women's obedience (a woman only submits to her husband if he submits to God), she is actually only submitting to God." "Molly," quoted in Kane, "Priestess Unto the Most High God," 134. This same idea was taught by President Spencer W. Kimball, who said that a woman should only follow a husband who was following Christ. "No woman has ever been asked by the Church authorities to follow her husband into an evil pit." Only a man who is following the "Savior of the world" is worthy of being followed by anyone, according to President Kimball. He added, "We have heard of men who have said to their wives, 'I hold the priesthood and you've got to do what I say.' Such a man should be tried for his membership." See Spencer W. Kimball, *The Teachings of Spencer W. Kimball*, ed. Edward L. Kimball (Salt Lake City: Bookcraft, 1998), 316.

36. Kane, "Priestess Unto the Most High God," 128.

37. "Ruth," quoted in Kane, "Priestess Unto the Most High God," 136. It should be noted, Eve has much more dialogue in the temple narrative of the Fall than she does in the scriptural account. Indeed, in the Genesis narrative, Eve's only lines are, "We may eat of the fruit of the trees of the garden: But of the fruit of the tree which is in the midst of the garden, God hath said, Ye shall not eat of it, neither shall ye touch it, lest ye die" (Genesis 3:2–3), and "The serpent beguiled me, and I did eat" (Genesis 3:13).

38. "Ruth," quoted in Kane, "Priestess Unto the Most High God," 136.

39. "Eliza," quoted in Kane, "Priestess Unto the Most High God," 137. See also 135–36.

40. See Kane, "Priestess Unto the Most High God," 137.

41. Leland Ryken, James C. Wilhoit, Tremper Longman III, eds., *Dictionary of Biblical Imagery* (Downers Grove, Illinois: InterVarsity Press, 1998), 790–91.

42. See, for example, James Hall, *Dictionary of Subjects & Symbols in Art*, rev. ed. (New York: Harper & Row, 1979), 318. This does not appear to be the message conveyed in the endowment.

43. See, for example, J. C. Cooper, *An Illustrated Encyclopaedia of Traditional Symbols* (London: Thames & Hudson, 1995), 184. Again, the veiled face in the endowment does not appear to be about submission to authority—except if God is the "authority" we are submitting ourselves to.

44. See, for example, J. E. Cirlot, *A Dictionary of Symbols*, 2nd ed. (New York: Philosophical Library, 1971), 359. In the case of the endowment, the veil of the temple accomplishes this, but not the veiling of the face.

45. See, for example, Kevin J. Conner, *Interpreting the Symbols and Types*, rev. ed. (Portland, Oregon: City Bible Publishing, 1992), 177. In a sense we can see this meaning implied in the endowment, in that we veil ourselves to symbolically say that we do not see what God sees and do not know what He knows. Thus, by inference, we are "separated" from Him—His presence, but also His knowledge and the fullness of His truth.

46. E. F. Scott, *The Moffatt New Testament Commentary: The Epistles of Paul to the Colossians, to Philemon, and to the Ephesians* (London: Hodder and Stoughton, 1952), 236–37. See also, W. Robertson Nicoll, *Expositor's Greek Testament*, 5 vols. (Grand Rapids, Michigan: Eerdmans, 1983), 3:366. While we acknowledge the power of Paul's analogy, some still find any literal interpretation of this as oppressive or offensive. We must certainly submit ourselves to God, but mortal married couples do best when they are an "equally yoked" companionship—which is another Pauline analogy (2 Corinthians 6:14).

47. Karen Jo Torjesen, *When Women Were Priests* (San Francisco, California: HarperCollins, 1993), 166; emphasis added.

48. See Torjesen, *When Women Were Priests*, 41.

49. The King James Version renders the verb "submit" rather than "cooperate." However, the Greek word translated "submit" does not mean to "give in" or "blindly obey." One scholar noted that the verb never implies "servile submissiveness" or the "elimination or breaking of the human will." Rather, it is a "voluntary" sustaining of the spouse. See Markus Barth, *The Anchor Bible: Ephesians 4–6* (New York: Doubleday, 1974), 609. Another scholar pointed out that "'cooperate' is a loose translation, but that is the working concept that Paul asks of all Saints—cooperation with Church and civil leaders, and cooperation of wives with the family leadership of their husbands." Richard Lloyd Anderson, Understanding Paul (Salt Lake City: Deseret Book, 1983), 353.

50. See Wilson, *A Dictionary of Bible Types*, 444; Conner, *Interpreting the Symbols and Types*, 177; Cirlot, *A Dictionary of Symbols*, 359; Kevin J. Todeschi, *The Encyclopedia of Symbolism* (New York: The Berkley Publishing Group, 1995), 274; Cooper, *An Illustrated Encyclopaedia of Traditional Symbols*, 184.

51. Allen C. Myers, ed., *The Eerdmans Bible Dictionary* (Grand Rapids, Michigan: Eerdmans, 1987), 1036.

52. See Edward J. Young, *The Book of Isaiah*, 3 vols. (Grand Rapids, Michigan: Eerdmans, 1997), 2:194–95.

53. Ryken, Wilhoit, and Longman, eds., *Dictionary of Biblical Imagery*, 911.

54. See Ibid.

55. John Taylor, discourse given October 8, 1871, in *Journal of Discourses*, 14:245.

56. See Orson Pratt, "Celestial Marriage (continued)," in *The Seer*, vol. 1, no. 2 (February 1853) (Roy, Utah: Eborn Books, 2000), 31; *Abraham H. Cannon Diary*, "Wednesday, September 28, 1892," BYU Special Collections; Anthony W. Ivins papers, "Sealing Ordinance," cited in Devery S. Anderson, *The Development of LDS Temple Worship, 1846–2000: A Documentary History* (Salt Lake City: Smith-Pettit Foundation, 2011), 102.

57. Hugh Nibley, *Approaching Zion* (Provo, Utah: Foundation for Ancient Research and Mormon Studies, 1989), 385.

58. Heber C. Kimball, cited in Nibley, *Approaching Zion*, 385. President Kimball also stated, "I want you to understand that [in the temple] you make covenants with God, and not with us." See Heber C. Kimball, discourse given December 13, 1857, in *Journal of Discourses*, 6:127. The *Encyclopedia of Mormonism* similarly states, "In the temple endowment all covenants are between the individual and God." Kenneth W. Godfrey,

"Freemasonry and the Temple," in *Encyclopedia of Mormonism*, 4 vols., ed. Daniel H. Ludlow, 2:529.

59. Lisle G. Brown, "The First Seal of the Holy Priesthood: The Holy Order of Matrimony" (Huntington, West Virginia, 2012), 45. A copy of this paper is in the possession of the author. All of this being said, the covenants made to God in the temple imply strong commitments to one's spouse—and duties to that spouse. In the opinion of this author, one cannot keep one's covenant with God about one's spouse, if a husband does not seek to love, honor, cherish, and even dote over his wife, and if a wife does not do the same for her husband. Additionally, I do not believe one can keep the covenants one has made in the temple if one resents one's spouse, or his/her gender and roles. Thus, while our covenants are always with God—not with other humans; we still have an obligation, by covenant, to our spouse once we are married and sealed. Even in the reading we have proposed herein, that must not be forgotten.

60. See Orson Pratt, "Celestial Marriage (continued)," 31; Cannon, "September 28, 1892"; Ivins in Anderson, *The Development of LDS Temple Worship*, 102.

61. What men and women do in the sealing ceremony seems merely a symbolic mirroring of what Christ does with His bride. Again, like the endowment, each partner in the sealing is an actor or actress, portraying an even greater truth than what seems evident. While they are being married and sealed to their earthly mate, in the same act they are foreshadowing their own marriage to the Bridegroom and, thus, their own exaltation through that covenant relationship.

62. Neal A. Maxwell, in *Conference Report*, October 1995, 30.

63. Joseph Fielding Smith, *Doctrines of Salvation*, 3 vols. (Salt Lake City: Bookcraft, 1998), 2:182; emphasis added.

64. Admittedly, it will be more difficult for some to see the bride/Bridegroom symbolism in the sealing ceremony than in the endowment, largely because we tend to put our focus on the actual bride (woman) and actual bridegroom (man) that are being sealed. Thus, to notice the larger symbolism at play (that of Christ and His bride) requires a major change in mind-set. Having said that, the sealing ceremony is the creation of an eternal family unit (which is the basic unit of the Church). In order to truly understand what is taking place when a couple is sealed—and in order to fulfill what God seeks to accomplish through the rite of sealing—one must understand one's personal relationship to Christ (the Groom). Minus this understanding, one cannot fulfill one's covenant with God.

65. Molly, a Relief Society president quoted in the Kane study, said, "I oft times have to tell some of the sisters, 'Listen carefully to the wording. Listen carefully to what is being said—what is said and what isn't said—how it's phrased.' . . . All of the covenants are made between the individual and the Father. . . . All covenants are with the Father and I think that's important to understand. . . . This is all about us individually, and our relationship to the Father." See Kane, "Priestess Unto the Most High God," 133.

66. Allen Claire Rozsa, "Temple Ordinances," in *Encyclopedia of Mormonism*, 4 vols., ed. Daniel H. Ludlow, 4:1444. Of course, "set apart" does not mean the same as "ordain." As early as the late second century that point was being emphasized. Hippolytus (circa AD 170–236), for example, was quite clear that women were not "ordained" to the priesthood but, rather, "appointed" or set apart to their calling to minister.

See Hippolytus, "Apostolic Tradition," Part 1, 11:1–5, in *The Apostolic Tradition of Hippolytus*, trans. Burton Scott Easton (Ann Arbor, Michigan: Archon Books, 1962), 40. See also Christine Chaillot, "The Ancient Oriental Churches," in *The Oxford History of Christian Worship*, ed. Geoffrey Wainwright and Karen B. Westerfield Tucker (New York: Oxford University Press, 2006), 135.

67. "Ruth," quoted in Kane, "Priestess Unto the Most High God," 93.

68. "Hannah," quoted in Kane, "Priestess Unto the Most High God," 93. Isabelle added, "I love that women are performing the ordinances." See Kane, "Priestess Unto the Most High God," 93. For Isabelle, it "was very powerful, a woman basically endowing another woman." See Kane, "Priestess Unto the Most High God," 94. Lydia also highlighted the role of women, saying, "It's women officiating for women and that is really significant to me." See Kane, "Priestess Unto the Most High God," 94.

69. Kane, "Priestess Unto the Most High God," 93. Dr. Kane adds, "The women in this study shared an affinity toward the ritual that unfold throughout this ceremony, finding them to be especially meaningful. Women's affinity for this ceremony is tied to the unique representation of women as ritual actors who performed the laying on of hands." Kane, "Priestess Unto the Most High God," 22.

70. See Joseph Fielding Smith, *Doctrines of Salvation*, 3 vols. in 1, comp. Bruce R. McConkie (Salt Lake City: Bookcraft, 1998), 3:178; Elder Parley P. Pratt spoke of the exalted woman in this way: "thou shalt sit down on [a] throne, as a queen and priestess unto thy lord, arrayed in white robes of dazzling splendor . . . and thy sons and daughters innumerable shall call thee blessed, and hold thy name in everlasting remembrance." See Parley P. Pratt, *Autobiography of Parley Parker Pratt*, 5th ed., ed. Parley P. Pratt Jr. (Salt Lake City: Deseret Book, 1961), 167. In spite of this, even in the initiatory ordinances—wherein sisters officiate for sisters—some see oppression and deference to one's "husband." However, if we see that "Husband" as the "Groom" or Christ, this seems a positive metaphor in all respects.

71. President Joseph Fielding Smith stated that "if [women] are faithful and true, they will become priestesses and queens in the kingdom of God, and that implies that they will be given authority." Smith, *Doctrines of Salvation*, 3:178. Such seems the symbolic depiction represented in the ordinances of the temple.

72. See Alonzo L. Gaskill, *The Lost Language of Symbolism* (Salt Lake City: Deseret Book, 2003), 80–82.

73. See Alonzo L. Gaskill, *Sacred Symbols: Finding Meaning in Rites, Rituals & Ordinances* (Springville, Utah: Cedar Fort, Inc., 2011), 78–86.

74. See Gaskill, *Sacred Symbols*, 82.

75. Gordon B. Hinckley, "The Women in Our Lives," in *Ensign*, November 2004, 83.

76. Oaks, "Scripture Reading and Revelation," 7–9.

77. While I'm certain there are times when this happens, I think such is less common today than at any time in the Church's history.

78. Kane, "Priestess Unto the Most High God," 57.

79. "Let the Holy Spirit Guide," *Hymns*, no. 143.

Chapter 13

"THE IDLE BRAIN IS THE DEVIL'S PLAYGROUND"

Labor, Loafing, and the Enticements of Satan

Alonzo L. Gaskill

A number of years ago, I was visiting England on an assignment for Brigham Young University. During my trip I, along with a number of my colleagues, took the opportunity to participate in an endowment session in the Preston England Temple. As we were exiting the temple, my friend Susan Easton Black said to me, "Alonzo, did you notice what Adam was doing when Satan tempted him?" I thought for a second, and then said, "No. What?" Susan replied: *"Absolutely nothing!"*[1]

Doctor Black's point, though seemingly simple, is really quite profound. In our personal lives, the adversary of all righteousness has increased access to us when we are idle; when we are not "anxiously engaged in a good cause" (D&C 58:27). This is not a condemnation of leisure. We all need time to rest from our day-to-day labors. What the endowment seems to be warning us about is not relaxation but, rather, the relaxing of our standards and the letting down of our guard. Never were truer words spoken than when Professor Harold Hill warned the residents of River City, Iowa, "the idle brain is the devil's playground."[2] The endowment depicts both Adam and Eve as idle when Satan makes his move—and in our own lives it is during those down times we are most prone to temptation. How many sins have started with an innocent, random surf of the internet?

Doctrine and Covenants 75:29 cautions us, "Let every man be diligent in all things. And the idler shall not have place in the church, except he repent and mend his ways." We typically interpret this passage as a statement about the need to work and contribute to the kingdom—to serve faithfully in our callings—and so it is. However, it is worth noting an additional application of the verse. Might it not also be said that "the idler shall not have place in the Church, except he repent" *because* idleness leads to temptation and sin? In other words, though it is sinful to be lazy, it is also spiritually dangerous to be idle because Satan is able to get his hand in our lives and, thereby, lead us away from Christ and salvation. Perhaps one reason "the idler shall not have place in the Church" is idleness leads us away from Christ and the keeping of covenants—as temptation always does.

This image from the endowment suggests that it isn't enough to simply avoid the bad. Adam wasn't being bad when Satan approached him; nor was Eve. Protection comes when we both avoid the bad, but also fill our lives with good. Again, the Lord has commanded that we be "anxiously engaged in a good cause, and do many things of [our] own free will, and bring to pass much righteousness" (D&C 58:27). The thirteenth Article of Faith states, "We believe in being honest, true, chaste, benevolent, virtuous, and in doing good to all men; indeed, we may say that we follow the admonition of Paul—We believe all things, we hope all things, we have endured many things, and hope to be able to endure all things. If there is anything virtuous, lovely, or of good report or praiseworthy, we seek after these things." It is one thing to not do evil. It is entirely another to fill our lives with good, to "seek after" the uplifting, the holy, inspiring. Thus, twice in holy writ the Lord counsels the Saints to take upon themselves the "whole armor" of God (Ephesians 6:11–18; D&C 27:15–18). This is an invitation to protect ourselves in all aspects of our lives: to watch ourselves morally ("loins girt about with truth"); to guard what we allow ourselves to desire or love ("breastplate of righteousness"); to be careful that we only allow ourselves to go where we can have peace—physically, mentally, and spiritually ("feet shod with the preparation of the gospel of peace"); to keep our faith strong ("taking the shield of faith"); to control our thoughts continuously ("the helmet of salvation"); and to use the Spirit to discern all things ("the sword of the Spirit"). The "whole armor of God" is a metaphor for those things we must do in our lives to keep Satan at bay. The idle man or woman is always guilty of setting aside at least some portion of that protective armor.

One Relief Society president noted, "I am so busy in my Church calling, my sins are dying of neglect." May this be the case in our own lives. And may we learn the lesson of spiritual idleness—and its dangers—as depicted in the temple. Such a subtle detail in the endowment, easily passed over, actually contains one of the greatest messages about how to secure one's salvation.

NOTES

1. The particular endowment film we were watching depicted Satan approaching Adam as he was casually sitting by a body of water, doing nothing.
2. See Meredith Wilson, *The Music Man* (1957).

BIBLIOGRAPHY

A

Abel, H. K. "Mormon Trivia: The Angel Moroni Statue." (January 2010). http://mor-monsoprano.com/2010/01/04/mormon-trivia-angel-moroni-statue/.

Alford, Kenneth L., and Richard E. Bennett. *An Eye of Faith*. Provo, Utah: Religious Studies Center, BYU, 2015.

Ambrose of Milan. "Letters to Laymen." In *Ancient Christian Commentary on Scripture: Genesis 1–11*, edited by Andrew Louth, 71. Downers Grove, Illinois: InterVarsity Press, 2001.

———. "Paradise." In *Ancient Christian Commentary on Scripture: Genesis 1–11*, edited by Andrew Louth, 68. Downers Grove, Illinois: InterVarsity Press, 2001.

Andersen, Francis I., and David Noel Freedman. *The Anchor Bible: Amos—A New Translation with Introduction and Commentary*. New York: Doubleday, 1989.

Anderson, Charles A., and Henry B. Carrington. *A Trip From Ocean to Ocean—Or, Weekly Excursions to California and the West*. Boston, Massachusetts: C. A. Anderson, 1891.

Anderson, Devery A. *The Development of LDS Temple Worship: 1846–2000, A Documentary History*. Salt Lake City: Signature Books, 2011.

Anderson, Edward O. "The Los Angeles Temple." *The Improvement Era* 58, no. 11 (1958): 803–7.

Anderson, James H. "The Salt Lake Temple." *The Contributor: A Monthly Magazine* 14, no. 6 (1893): 243–303.

Anderson, Lavina Fielding, ed. *A Critical Edition of Lucy Mack Smith's Family Memoir.* Salt Lake City: Signature Books, 2001.

Anderson, Richard Lloyd. *Understanding Paul.* Salt Lake City: Deseret Book, 1983.

Andreopoulos, Andreas. *Metamorphosis: The Transfiguration in Byzantine Theology and Iconography.* New York: St. Vladimir's Seminary Press, 2005.

"The Arabic Gospel of the Infancy of the Saviour." In *Ante-Nicene Father: The Writings of the Fathers down to A.D. 325*, edited by Alexander Roberts and James Donaldson, 8:405–15. Peabody, Massachusetts: Hendrickson Publishers, 1994.

Armknecht, Megan. "Mormon Women and Mother Eve: Perceptions, Parallels, and Pedestals." In *2015 BYU Religious Education Student Symposium*, 123–34. Provo, Utah: Religious Studies Center, BYU, 2015.

Ashton, Marvin J. "There Are Many Gifts." *Ensign*, November 1987, 20–23.

Augustine of Hippo. "City of God." In *Ancient Christian Commentary on Scripture: Genesis 1–11*, edited by Andrew Louth, 70. Downers Grove, Illinois: InterVarsity Press, 2001.

———. "Homilies on the First Epistle of John." In *Nicene and Post-Nicene Fathers: First Series*, edited by Philip Schaff, 7:459–529. Peabody, Massachusetts: Hendrickson Publishers, 2004.

Ausubel, Nathan. *The Jewish Book of Knowledge.* New York: Crown Publishers, 1964.

B

Backman Jr., Milton V. *Joseph Smith's First Vision: Confirming Evidences and Contemporary Accounts.* Salt Lake City: Bookcraft, 1971.

Backman Jr., Milton V., and Robert L. Millet. "Heavenly Manifestations in the Kirtland Temple." In *Studies in Scripture-Volume One: The Doctrine and Covenants.* Edited by Robert L. Millet and Kent P. Jackson, 417–31. Salt Lake City: Deseret Book, 1989.

Baker, James R. *Women's Rights in Old Testament Times.* Salt Lake City: Signature Books, 1992.

Banaji, Behman Sorabji. "The Warfare of Zoroaster." *Advocate of Peace Through Justice* 86, no. 1 (1924): 33–36.

Barber, Allen H. *Celestial Symbols: Symbolism in Doctrine Religious Traditions and Temple Architecture.* Bountiful, Utah: Horizon, 1989.

Barker, Kenneth, ed. *The NIV Study Bible.* Grand Rapids, Michigan: Zondervan, 1995.

Barker, Margaret. *The Gate of Heaven: The History and Symbolism of the Temple in Jerusalem.* Sheffield, England: Sheffield Phoenix Press, 2008.

———. *The Great High Priest: The Temple Roots of Christian Liturgy.* New York: T&T Clark, 2007.

Barth, Markus. *The Anchor Bible: Ephesians 4–6*. New York: Doubleday, 1974.

Bayley, Harold. *The Lost Language of Symbolism: An Inquiry into the Origin of Certain Letters, Words, Names, Fairy-Tales, Folklore, and Mythologies*. New York: Carol Publishing Group, 1990.

Belnap, Daniel L., ed. *By Our Rites of Worship: Latter-day Saint Views on Ritual in Scripture, History, and Practice*. Provo, Utah: Religious Studies Center, BYU, 2013.

Benson, Ezra Taft. "Prepare Yourself for the Great Day of the Lord," *New Era*, May 1982, 44–50.

———. *Teachings of Ezra Taft Benson*. Salt Lake City: Bookcraft, 1998.

Berteaux, Kelsey, and Jannalee Rosner. "10 Things You Didn't Know about the Angel Moroni Statue." *LDS Living Magazine*, November 2013. http://ldsliving.com /story/74177-10-things-you-didnt-know-about-the-angel-moroni-statue.

Black, Susan Easton. *Who's Who in the Doctrine and Covenants*. Salt Lake City: Desert Book, 1997.

Bloesch, Donald G. *Essentials of Evangelical Theology*. Peabody, Massachusetts: Price Press, 2001.

Bloxham, V. Ben, ed. *Truth Will Prevail: The Rise of the Church of Jesus Christ of Latter-day Saints in the British Isles 1837–1987*. Solihul, England: The Church of Jesus Christ of Latter-day Saints, 1987.

Bowker, John. *World Religions—The Great Faiths Explored and Explained*. New York: DK Publishing, 2006.

Brereton, Joel P. "Sacred Space." In *The Encyclopedia of Religion*, edited by Mircea Eliade, 12:526–35. New York: Macmillan, 1987.

Brewster Jr., Hoyt W. *Doctrine and Covenants Encyclopedia*. Salt Lake City: Bookcraft, 1988.

Bridger, David, ed. *The New Jewish Encyclopedia*. New York: Behrman House, 1962.

Brinkerhoff, Val. *The Day Star: Reading Sacred Architecture*. 3rd ed. New York: Digital Legend Press, 2012.

Brooks, Melvin R. *LDS Reference Encyclopedia*. Salt Lake City: Bookcraft, 1960.

Brown, Benjamin. *Testimonies for the Truth: A Record of Manifestations of the Power of God, Miraculous and Providential, Witnessed in the Travels and Experience of Benjamin Brown*. Liverpool: S. W. Richards, 1853.

———. "Testimonies for the Truth." In *Gems for the Young Folks*, edited by George Q. Cannon. Salt Lake City: Juvenile Instructor Office, 1881.

Brown, Francis, S. R. Driver, and Charles A. Briggs. *The Brown-Briggs Hebrew and English Lexicon*. Peabody, Massachusetts: Hendrickson, 1999.

Brown, Lisle G. "The First Seal of the Holy Priesthood: The Holy Order of Matrimony." Huntington, WV: unpublished manuscript in possession of author, 2012.

Brown, Matthew B. *The Gate of Heaven: Insights on the Doctrine and Symbols of the Temple.* American Fork, Utah: Covenant Communications, 1999.

Brown, Matthew B., and Paul Thomas Smith. *Symbols in Stone—Symbolism on the Early Temples of the Restoration.* American Fork, Utah: Covenant Communications, 1997.

Brown, Raymond E. *The Death of the Messiah.* New York: Doubleday, 1994.

Brown, S. Kent, Richard Neitzel Holzapfel, and Dawn C. Pheysey. *Beholding Salvation: The Life of Christ in Word and Image.* Salt Lake City: Deseret Book, 2006.

Bullinger, E. W. *Number in Scripture: Its Supernatural Design and Spiritual Significance.* Grand Rapids, Michigan: Kregel Publications, 1967.

Burton, Alma P., comp. *Discourses of the Prophet Joseph Smith.* Salt Lake City: Deseret Book, 1974.

Bushman, Richard L. *Joseph Smith: Rough Stone Rolling.* New York: Alfred A. Knopf, 2005.

Buttrick, George Arthur, ed. *The Interpreter's Bible.* New York: Abingdon Press, 1951–57.

C

Campbell, Beverly. "Eve." *Encyclopedia of Mormonism*, edited by Daniel H. Ludlow, 2:475–76. New York: Macmillan, 1992.

———. *Eve and the Choice Made in Eden.* Salt Lake City: Deseret Book, 2003.

Campbell, Craig S. *Images of the New Jerusalem: Latter-day Saint Faction Interpretations of Independence, Missouri.* Knoxville, Tennessee: The University of Tennessee Press, 2004.

Campbell Jr., Edward F. *The Anchor Bible: Ruth—A New Testament with Introduction, Notes, and Commentary.* New York: Doubleday, 1975.

Cannon, Abraham H. *Abraham H. Cannon Diary.* BYU Special Collections, 1892.

Cannon, Elaine. *The Truth About Angels.* Salt Lake City: Bookcraft, 1996.

Cannon, George Q. Discourse given October 6, 1898. In *Conference Report*, 3–6. Salt Lake City: The Church of Jesus Christ of Latter-day Saints, 1898.

Cassuto, Umberto. *A Commentary on the Book of Exodus.* Translated by Israel Abrahams. Jerusalem: Magnes Press of the Hebrew University, 1983.

C.E.S Seminary Old Testament Teacher's Outline. Salt Lake City: The Church of Jesus Christ of Latter-day Saints, 1990.

Chaillot, Christine. "The Ancient Oriental Churches." In *The Oxford History of Christian Worship*, edited by Geoffrey Wainwright and Karen B. Westerfield Tucker, 131–69. New York: Oxford University Press, 2006.

Christo, Gus George. *The Consecration of a Greek Orthodox Church According to Eastern Orthodox Tradition: A Detailed Account and Explanation of the Ritual.* Lewiston, New York: The Edwin Mellen Press, 2005.

Christofferson, D. Todd. "Come to Zion." *Ensign,* November 2008, 37–40.

Church, Leslie F., ed. *The NIV Matthew Henry Commentary in One Volume.* Grand Rapids, Michigan: Zondervan, 1992.

Cirlot, J. E. *A Dictionary of Symbols.* 2nd edition. Translated by Jack Sage. New York: Philosophical Library, 1971.

Clarke, Adam. "Clarke's Commentary." *The Holy Bible Containing the Old and New Testaments.* New York: Methodist Book Concern, 1930.

Coffin, William Sloane. *Credo.* Louisville, Kentucky: Westminster John Knox Press, 2004.

———. *The Riverside Preachers.* Edited by Paul Sherry. New York: The Pilgrims Press, 1978.

Cole, W. Owen. "Review of W. H. McLeod's, *The Chaupa Sing Rahit-Nama.*" *Journal of the Royal Asiatic Society of Great Britain and Ireland* 1 (1989): 183–84.

Compton, Todd. "Symbolism." In *Encyclopedia of Mormonism,* edited by Daniel H. Ludlow, 3:1428–30. New York: Macmillan, 1992.

Conner, Kevin J. *Interpreting the Symbols and Types.* Portland, Oregon: City Bible Publishing, 1992.

Coogan, Michael D., ed. *The New Oxford Annotated Bible.* 3rd ed. New York: Oxford University Press, 2001.

Cook, M. Garfield. *Restoration In Geometric Symbolism.* 2nd rev. ed. Salt Lake City: M. Garfield Cook, 2004.

Cooke, G. A. *The Book of Ruth.* Cambridge: Cambridge University Press, 1913.

Cooper, J. C. *An Illustrated Encyclopaedia of Traditional Symbols.* London: Thames and Hudson, 1995.

Cooper, Rex E. "Symbols, Cultural, and Artistic." In *Encyclopedia of Mormonism,* edited by Daniel H. Ludlow, 3:1430–31. New York: Macmillan, 1992.

Cowan, Richard O. *Answers to Your Questions about the Doctrine and Covenants.* Salt Lake City: Deseret Book, 1996.

———. "The Great Temple of the New Jerusalem." In *Regional Studies in Church History—Missouri,* 137–54. Provo, Utah: Religious Studies Center, BYU, 1994.

Critchlow, Keith. *Islamic Patterns: An Analytical and Cosmological Approach.* London: Thames and Hudson, 1976.

Cross, F. L., and E. A. Livingstone, eds. *The Oxford Dictionary of the Christian Church.* 2nd ed. New York: Oxford University Press, 1990.

Cundall, Arthur E., and Leon Morris. *Tyndale Old Testament Commentaries: Judges and Ruth*. Downers Grove, Illinois: InterVarsity Press, 1968.

Cyril of Jerusalem. "Catechetical Lectures." In *Nicene and Post-Nicene Fathers—Second Series*, edited by Philip Schaff and Henry Wace, 7:1–157. Peabody, Massachusetts: Hendrickson Publishers, 2004.

D

d'Alviella, Count Goblet. *The Migration of Symbols*. New York: University Books, 1956.

Dar, Sad. *Pahvlavi Texts*, 10:1, 4. Translated by E. A. West. (New York: Charles Scribner's Sons, 1901).

Davidson, James W. *The Logic of Millennial Thought: Eighteenth-Century New England*. New Haven, Connecticut: Yale University Press, 1977.

Davidson, Karen Lynn, Richard L. Jensen, and David J. Whittaker, eds. *Histories, Volume 2: Assigned Historical Writings, 1831–1847*. Edited by Dean C. Jessee, Ronald K. Esplin, and Richard Lyman Bushman. Salt Lake City: Church Historian's Press, 2012.

Davis, John J. *Biblical Numerology*. Grand Rapids Michigan: Baker Book House, 2000.

Dew, Sheri L. "Are We Not All Mothers?" *Ensign*, November 2001, 96–98.

De Pillis, Mario S. "Christ Comes to Jackson County: The Mormon City of Zion and Its Consequences." In *John Whitmer Historical Association* 23 (2003): 21–44.

Dibble, Philo. "Philo Dibble's Narrative." In *Early Scenes in Church History*, 74–96. Salt Lake City: Juvenile Instructor Office, 1882.

———. "Recollections of the Prophet Joseph Smith." *Juvenile Instructor* 27 (1892): 22–23.

Doxy, Graham W. "Missouri Myths." In *Ensign,* April 1979, 64–65.

Draper, Richard D. *Opening the Seven Seals: the Visions of John the Revelator*. Salt Lake City: Deseret Book, 1991.

Dunn, Paul H. "Put On Your Spiritual Clothes." BYU Devotional, Provo, Utah. December 7, 1976.

E

Eakin Jr., Frank E. *The Religion and Culture of Israel: An Introduction to Old Testament Thought*. Boston, Massachusetts: Allyn and Bacon, 1971.

Edwards, Douglas R. "Dress and Ornamentation." In *The Anchor Bible Dictionary*, edited by David Noel Freedman. New York: Doubleday, 1992.

Edwards, Jonathan. *The Works of Jonathan Edwards*. 1742. http://www.ccel.org/ccel/edwards/works1.html.

Ehat, Andrew F. "Joseph Smith's Introduction of Temple Ordinances and the 1844 Mormon Succession Question." Master's thesis, Brigham Young University, 1981.

Ehat, Andrew F., and Lyndon W. Cook, eds. *The Words of Joseph Smith: The Contemporary Accounts of the Nauvoo Discourses of the Prophet Joseph.* Provo, Utah: Religious Studies Center, BYU, 1980.

Elworthy, Frederick Thomas. *The Evil Eye: An Account of This Ancient & Widespread Superstition.* London: John Murray, 1895.

Endowed From on High: Temple Preparation Seminar Teacher's Manual. Salt Lake City: The Church of Jesus Christ of Latter-day Saints, 1995.

Esplin, Scott C. "'Let Zion in Her Beauty Rise': Building Zion by Becoming Zion." In *You Shall Have my Word: Exploring the Text of the Doctrine and Covenants,* edited by Scott C. Esplin, Richard O. Cowan, and Rachel Cope, 134–48. Provo, Utah: Religious Studies Center, BYU, 2012.

F

Fairbairn, Patrick. *Typology of Scripture.* Grand Rapids, Michigan: Kregel, 1989.

Fairbanks, Eugene F. *A Sculptor's Testimony in Bronze and Stone: Sacred Sculpture of Avard T. Fairbanks.* Rev. ed. Salt Lake City: Publishers Press, 1994.

Farbridge, Maurice H. *Studies in Biblical and Semitic Symbolism.* London: Kegan Paul, Trench, Trubner, 1923.

Fielding, Joseph. *Diary of Joseph Fielding.* Typescript. Provo, Utah: L. Tom Perry Special Collections, Harold B. Lee Library, BYU.

Fontana, David. *The Secret Language of Symbols: A Visual Key to Symbols and Their Meanings.* San Francisco, California: Chronicle Books, 1994.

Friedrich, Gerhard, ed. "The Games." In *Theological Dictionary of the New Testament,* 7:620. Grand Rapids, Michigan: Eerdmans, 1983.

Fronk, Camille. "Fruit." In *Book of Mormon Reference Companion,* edited by Dennis L. Largey, 277–78. Salt Lake City: Deseret Book, 2003.

G

Gaglardi, B. Maureen. *The Path of the Just: The Garments of the High Priest.* Dubuque, Iowa: Kendall/Hunt, 1971.

Garner, Bryan. *Garner's Dictionary of Modern Legal Usage.* 3rd ed. New York: Oxford University Press, 2011.

Garrard, LeMar E. *A Study of the Problem of a Personal Devil and Its Relationship to Latter-day Saint Beliefs.* Master's thesis, Brigham Young University, 1955.

Gaskell, G. A. *Dictionary of All Scriptures and Myths.* New York: Julian Press, 1960.

Gaskill, Alonzo L. *The Lost Language of Symbolism: An Essential Guide for Recognizing and Interpreting Symbols of the Gospel.* Salt Lake City: Deseret Book, 2003.

———. *Sacred Symbols: Finding Meaning in Rites, Rituals, & Ordinances.* Springville, Utah: Cedar Fort, 2011.

———. *The Truth About Eden: Understanding the Fall and Our Temple Experience.* Springville, Utah: Cedar Fort, 2013.

Gerritsen, Allen P. "The Hill Cumorah Monument: An Inspired Creation of Torleif S. Knaphus." In *Journal of Book of Mormon Studies* 13, no. 1–2 (2004): 124–35, 173.

Ginzberg, Louis. *The Legends of the Jews.* Philadelphia: The Jewish Publication Society of America, 1967–69.

Gnoli, Gherardo. "Zoroastrianism." In *The Encyclopedia of Religion*, edited by Mircea Eliade, 15:579–91. New York: Macmillian, 1987.

Godfrey, Kenneth W. "Freemasonry and the Temple." In *Encyclopedia of Mormonism*, edited by Daniel H. Ludlow, 2:528–29. New York: Macmillan, 1992.

Godfrey, Matthew C., Mark Ashurst-McGee, Grant Underwood, Robert J. Woodford, and William G. Hartley, eds. *Documents, Volume 2: July 1831–January 1833.* Edited by Dean C. Jessee, Ronald K. Esplin, Richard Lyman Bushman, and Matthew J. Grow. Salt Lake City: Church Historian's Press, 2013.

Goodenough, Erwin R. *Jewish Symbols in the Greco-Roman Period.* New York: Bollingren Foundation, 1964.

Gower, Ralph. *The New Manners and Customs of Bible Times.* Chicago: Moody Press, 1987.

Grandstaff, Mark R., and Milton V. Backman Jr. "The Social Origins of the Kirtland Mormons." *BYU Studies* 30, no. 2 (1990): 47–66.

Great People of the Bible and How They Lived. Pleasantville, New York: Readers Digest, 1974.

"The Great Temple." *The Boston Weekly Globe.* Boston, Massachusetts. April 12, 1892.

Greek Orthodox Church of the Annunciation. "Savanon." Kansas City, Missouri: Greek Orthodox Church of the Annunciation, 1987.

Greidanus, Sidney. *Preaching Christ from the Old Testament.* Grand Rapids, Michigan: William B. Eerdmans, 1999.

Griffin, Robert, and Donald A. Grinde Jr. *Apocalypse of Chiokoyhikoy, Chief of the Iroquois.* Quebec City, Canada: University of Laval Press, 1997.

Griggs, C. Wilfred, Marvin C. Kuchar, Scott R. Woodward, Mark J. Rowe, R. Paul Evans, Naguib Kanawati, and Nasry Iskander. "Evidences of a Christian Population in the Egyptian Fayum and Genetic and Textile Studies of the Akhmim Noble Mummies." *BYU Studies* 33, no. 2 (1993): 215–43.

H

Habershon, Ada R. *Study of the Types.* Grand Rapids, Michigan: Kregel, 1974.

Hafen, Bruce C. *The Broken Heart.* Salt Lake City: Deseret Book, 1989.

Hall, James. *Dictionary of Subjects and Symbols in Art.* Rev. ed. New York: Harper & Row, 1974.

Hamblin, William J., and David Rolph Seely. *Solomon's Temple: Myth and History.* London: Thames and Hudson, 2007.

Hamilton, C. Mark. *The Salt Lake Temple: A Monument to a People.* 5th ed. Salt Lake City: University Services Corporation, 1983.

Hamilton, Victor. *Handbook on the Pentateuch.* Grand Rapids, Michigan: Baker Book House, 1982.

Hamlin, John. *Surely There Is a Future: An International Theological Commentary on the Book of Ruth.* Grand Rapids, Michigan: Eerdmans, 1996.

Hancock, Levi. *Autobiography.* Provo, Utah: L. Tom Perry Special Collections, Harold B. Lee Library, BYU.

Hansen Jr., Gerald E. *Sacred Walls: Learning from Temple Symbols.* American Fork, Utah: Covenant Communications, 2009.

Hapgood, Isabel F. *Service Book of the Holy Orthodox-Catholic Apostolic Church.* New York: Association Press, 1922.

Harper, Steven C. "Endowed with Power." *The Religious Educator: Perspectives on the Restored Gospel*, 5, no. 2 (2004): 83–99.

Harrison, R. K. *Leviticus: An Introduction and Commentary.* Downers Grove, Illinois: InterVarsity Press, 1980.

Haymond, Bryce. "The Seal of Melchizedek Parts 1–4." *Temple Study: Sustaining and Defending the LDS Temple.* http://www.templestudy.com.

Hazlitt, W. C. *Dictionary of Faiths and Folklore: Beliefs, Superstitions and Popular Customs.* London: Bracken Books, 1995.

Hedges, Andrew H., Alex D. Smith, and Richard Lloyd Anderson, eds. *Journals, Volume 2: December 1841–April 1843.* Edited by Dean C. Jessee, Ronald K. Esplin, and Richard Lyman Bushman. Salt Lake City: Church Historian's Press, 2011.

Henry, Hugh T. *Catholic Customs and Symbols.* New York: Benziger Brothers, 1925.

The Herder Symbol Dictionary: Symbols from Art, Archaeology, Mythology, Literature, and Religion, Translated by Boris Matthews. Wilmette, Illinois: Chiron Publications, 1986.

Hertz, J. H. *The Pentateuch and Haftorahs.* 2nd ed. London: Soncino Press, 1962.

Hinckley, Gordon B. *Teachings of Gordon B. Hinckley.* Salt Lake City: Deseret Book, 1997.

————. "This Glorious Easter Morn." *Ensign*, May 1996, 65–67.

————. "We Bear Testimony to the World." *Ensign*, November 2006, 4–5.

————. "The Women in Our Lives." *Ensign*, November 2004, 82–85.

Hippolytus, "Apostolic Tradition." In *The Apostolic Tradition of Hippolytus*, translated by Burton Scott Easton, 33–61. Ann Arbor, Michigan: Archon Books, 1962.

Holland, Jeffrey R. *Christ and the New Covenant: The Messianic Message of the Book of Mormon.* Salt Lake City: Deseret Book, 1997.

————. "Israel, Israel, God is Calling." *CES Fireside for Young Adults.* September 9, 2012.

Holzapfel, Richard Neitzel. *Every Stone a Sermon.* Salt Lake City: Bookcraft, 1992.

Holzapfel, Richard Neitzel, and David Rolph Seely. *My Father's House: Temple Worship and Symbolism in the New Testament.* Salt Lake City: Bookcraft, 1994.

Hone, William, comp. *The Lost Books of the Bible.* Translated by Jeremiah Jones and William Wake. New York: Bell Publishing, 2004.

Hubbard, David Allan. *Tyndale Old Testament Commentary: Joel and Amos.* Downers Grove, Illinois: InterVarsity Press, 1989.

Hunter, Milton R. *Pearl of Great Price Commentary.* Salt Lake City: Steven & Wallis, Inc., 1951.

Hyatt, Philip J. "Dress." In *Dictionary of the Bible*, rev. ed., edited by James Hastings, 222–25. New York: Charles Scribner's Sons, 1963.

Hyde, Myrtle Stevens. *Orson Hyde: The Olive Branch of Israel.* Salt Lake City: Agreka Books, 2000.

I

Ivans, Anthony W. "Sealing Ordinance." In *The Development of LDS Temple Worship, 1846–2000: A Documentary History*, edited by Devery S. Anderson, 102. Salt Lake City: Smith-Pettit Foundation, 2011.

J

Jamieson, Robert, A. R. Fausset, and David Brown. *Jamieson, Fausset, and Brown One Volume Commentary.* Grand Rapids, Michigan: Associated Publishers.

Jarman, David Fenton. *The High Priest's Dress: Or, Christ Arrayed in Aaron's Robes.* London: W. F. Crofts, 1850.

Jerome. "Homilies." In *Ancient Christian Commentary on Scripture: Genesis 1–11*, edited by Andrew Louth, 70–71. Downers Grove, Illinois: InterVarsity Press, 2001.

Jessee, Dean C. *Personal Writings of Joseph Smith*, rev. ed. Salt Lake City: Deseret Book, 2002.

Johnston, Robert D. *Numbers in the Bible: God's Design in Biblical Numerology.* Grand Rapids, Michigan: Kregel Publications, 1990.

Josephus, Flavius. *The Complete Works of Josephus*, translated by William Whiston. Grand Rapids, Michigan: Kregel, 1981.

Journal of Discourses. Liverpool: Latter-day Saints' Book Depot, 1855–86.

"The Jubilee." *Deseret News.* Salt Lake City. July 28, 1875.

Julien, Nadia. *The Mammoth Dictionary of Symbols*, translated by Elfreda Powell. New York: Carroll and Graf Publishers, 1996.

K

Kaiser Jr., Walter C. "Exodus." In *The Expositor's Bible Commentary*, edited by Frank E. Gaebelein, 2:285–497. Grand Rapids, Michigan: Zondervan, 1976–92.

Kalmin, Richard. "Levirate Law." In *The Anchor Bible Dictionary*, edited by David Noel Freedman, 4:296–97. New York: Doubleday, 1992.

Kane, Nazneen. "'Priestesses Unto the Most High God': LDS Women's Temple Rituals and the Politics of Religious Identity." Doctrinal Dissertation, University of Maryland, 2011.

Keil, C. F., and F. Delitzsch. *Biblical Commentary on the Old Testament—Minor Prophets.* Grand Rapids, Michigan: Eerdmans, 1954.

Kennedy, A. R. A., and A. G. Macleod. "Kin (Next of), Kinsmand, Avenger of Blood, Go'el." In *Dictionary of the Bible*, rev. ed., edited by James Hastings, 550–51. New York: Charles Scribner's Sons, 1963.

Kertzer, Morris N. *What is a Jew?* Revised by Lawrence A. Hoffman. New York: Macmillan, 1993

Kiene, Paul F. *The Tabernacle of God in the Wilderness of Sinai.* Translated by John S. Crandall. Grand Rapids, Michigan: Zondervan, 1977.

Kimball, David P. "A Terrible Ordeal." In *Helpful Visions*, compiled by Orson F. Whitney, 9–17. Salt Lake City: Juvenile Instructor Office, 1887.

Kimball, Heber C. "A Letter From Heber C. Kimball to His Wife, Vilate Kimball." *Elders' Journal of The Church of Latter Day Saints* 1, no. 1 (October 1837): 4–7.

———. *Journal History of the Church of Jesus Christ of Latter-day Saints.* Salt Lake City: The Church of Jesus Christ of Latter-day Saints, 1860.

Kimball, Spencer W. *The Teachings of Spencer W. Kimball.* Edited by Edward L. Kimball. Salt Lake City: Bookcraft, 1998.

Kimball, Stanley B., ed. *On the Potter's Wheel: The Diaries of Heber C. Kimball.* Salt Lake City: Signature Books, 1987.

Klein, William W., Craig L. Blomberg, and Robert L. Hubbard Jr. *Introduction to Biblical Interpretation.* Dallas, Texas: Word Publishing, 1993.

Kotwal, Firoze M. "Ritual Aspects of the Gathas and Their Continuity in Later Tradition." *Iran & the Caucasus* 3 (1999/2000): 1–8.

L

Lacheman, Ernest R. "Note on Ruth 4:7–8." In *Journal of Biblical Literature* 56, no. 1 (1937): 53–56.

Laffey, Alice L. "Ruth." In *The New Jerome Biblical Commentary*, edited by Raymond E. Brown, Joseph A. Fitzmyer, and Roland E. Murphy, 553–57. Englewood Cliffs, New Jersey: Prentice Hall, 1990.

Larson, Anthony E. *Grand Paenoch* (blog). http://grandpaenoch.blogspot.com/2009/03 /artifacts-and-temple-3-cherubim.html.

LDS Bible Dictionary. Salt Lake City: The Church of Jesus Christ of Latter-day Saints, 2013.

Lee, Harold B. "Strengthen the Stakes of Zion." *Ensign*, July 1973, 2–6.

"Let the Holy Spirit Guide." *Hymns*, no. 143.

Levine, Baruch A. *The JPS Torah Commentary: Leviticus.* Philadelphia, Pennsylvania: The Jewish Publications Society, 1989.

Lewis, C. S. *The Problem of Pain.* New York: Simon & Schuster Touchstone Books, 1996.

"Life of Adam and Eve." In *The Old Testament Pseudepigrapha*, edited by James H. Charlesworth, 1:249–95. New York: Doubleday, 1983.

Louth, Andrew, ed. *Ancient Christian Commentary on Scripture: Genesis 1–11.* Downers Grove, Illinois: InterVarsity Press, 2001.

Ludlow, Daniel H. *A Companion to Your Study of the Old Testament.* Salt Lake City: Deseret Book, 1981.

Ludlow, Victor L. *Unlocking the Old Testament.* Salt Lake City: Deseret Book, 1981.

Luschin, Immo. "Temples: Latter-day Saint Temple Worship and Activity." In *Encyclopedia of Mormonism*, edited by Daniel H. Ludlow, 4:1447–50. New York: Macmillan, 1992.

M

Mace, David R. *Hebrew Marriage: A Sociological Study.* New York: Philosophical Library, 1953.

MacKay, Michael Hubbard, Gerrit J. Dirkmaat, Grant Underwood, Robert J. Woodford, and William G. Hartley, eds. *Documents, Volume 1: July 1828–June 1831.* Edited by Dean C. Jessee, Ronald K. Esplin, Richard Lyman Bushman, and Matthew J. Grow. Salt Lake City: Church Historian's Press, 2013.

Macoy, Robert. *A Dictionary of Freemasonry.* New York: Gramercy Books, 2000.

Madsen, Truman G. *Joseph Smith the Prophet.* Salt Lake City: Bookcraft, 1989.

———. "Zionism." In *Encyclopedia of Mormonism*, edited by Daniel H. Ludlow, 4:1626. New York: Macmillan, 1992.

Martin-Achard, Robert and S. Paul Re'emi. *God's People in Crisis: A Commentary on the Books of Amos and Lamentations.* Grand Rapids, Michigan: Eerdmans, 1984.

Matthews, Robert J. "Adam-ondi-Ahman." *BYU Studies* 13, no. 1 (1972): 27–35.

Maxwell, Neal A. *But for a Small Moment.* Salt Lake City: Bookcraft, 1986.

———. *Not My Will, But Thine.* Salt Lake City: Deseret Book, 1988.

———. "Swallowed Up in the Will of the Father." *Conference Report*, October 1995, 27–30.

———. *We will Prove Them Herewith.* Salt Lake City: Deseret Book, 1982.

Mayo, Janet. *A History of Ecclesiastical Dress.* London: B. T. Batsford, 1984.

McConkie, Bruce R. "Christ and the Creation." In *Doctrines of the Restorations: Sermons and Writing of Bruce R. McConkie*, edited by Mark L. McConkie. Salt Lake City: Bookcraft, 1989.

———. *Doctrinal New Testament Commentary.* Salt Lake City: Bookcraft, 1987–88.

———. *Doctrine New Testament Commentary Volume III: Colossians–Revelation.* Salt Lake City: Bookcraft, 1988.

———. "Eve and the Fall." In *Woman*, 57–68. Salt Lake City: Deseret Book, 1979.

———. "The Keys of the Kingdom." *Ensign*, May 1983, 21–23.

———. *Mormon Doctrine.* 2nd ed. Salt Lake City: Bookcraft, 1979.

———. *The Mortal Messiah.* Salt Lake City: Deseret Book, 1979–81.

———. *The Promised Messiah: The First Coming of Christ.* Salt Lake City: Deseret Book, 1981.

———. "What Think ye of Salvation by Grace." BYU Devotional. Provo, Utah. January 10, 1984.

McConkie, Joseph Fielding. *Gospel Symbolism.* Salt Lake City: Bookcraft, 1985.

———. "The Mystery of Eden." In *The Man Adam*, edited by Joseph Fielding McConkie and Robert L. Millet. Salt Lake City: Bookcraft, 1990.

McConkie, Joseph Fielding, and Craig J. Ostler. *Revelations of the Restoration.* Salt Lake City: Deseret Book, 2000.

McConkie, Joseph Fielding, and Donald W. Parry. *A Guide To Scriptural Symbols.* Salt Lake City: Bookcraft, 1990.

McGavin, E. Cecil. *Mormonism and Masonry.* Salt Lake City: Bookcraft, 1956.

McKenzie, John L. *Dictionary of the Bible.* Milwaukee, Wisconsin: The Bruce Publishing Company, 1965.

McLeod, Hew. "The Five Ks of the Khalsa Sikhs." *Journal of the American Oriental Society* 128, no. 2 (2008): 328–31.

Meyers, Carol. "Ephod." In *The Anchor Bible Dictionary,* edited by David Noel Freedman, 2:550. New York: Doubleday, 1992.

Meyers, Carol, and Eric M. Meyers. *Haggai, Zechariah, 1–8.* New York: Doubleday, 1987.

Mikita, Carol. "A look inside as City Creek Center's Completion Nears." March 1 2012. http://www.ksl.com/?nid=148&sid=19428181.

Milgrom, Jacob. *Leviticus 1–16.* New York: Doubleday, 1991.

Millet, Robert L. "Joseph Smith Among the Prophets." In *Ensign,* June 1994, 18–23.

———. "Joseph Smith Among the Prophets." In *Joseph Smith: The Prophet, The Man,* edited by Susan Easton Black and Charles D. Tate Jr., 15–31. Provo, Utah: Religious Studies Center, BYU, 1993.

———. "Zion." In *Encyclopedia of Latter-day Saint History,* edited by Arnold K. Garr, Donald Q. Cannon, and Richard O. Cowan, 1397–98. Salt Lake City: Deseret Book, 2000.

Millet, Robert L., and Joseph Fielding McConkie. *The Life Beyond.* Salt Lake City: Deseret Book, 1986.

Milton, John. *Paradise Lost.* London: Peter Parker, 1667.

Mitchell, Robert C. "DUP Receives Historic Gift." *Deseret News.* Salt Lake City. October 7, 1965.

Modi, Jivanji Jamshedji. *The Religious Ceremonies and Customs of the Parsees.* New York: Garland Publishing, 1979.

Moffatt, James, trans. *A New Translation of The Bible: Containing the Old and New Testaments.* New York: Harper & Brothers, 1950.

Molloy, Michael. *Experiencing The World's Religion's: Tradition, Challenge, and Change,* 5th ed. New York: McGraw-Hill, 2010.

Monson, Thomas S. "Welcome to Conference." *Ensign,* November 2012, 4–5.

Morley, Richard H. *A Scriptural Glossary of Manti Temple Terms.* Price, Utah: Wix Plaza Book Sales, 2004.

Morris, Leon. *Tyndale New Testament Commentaries: Revelation,* rev. ed. Grand Rapids, Michigan: Eerdmans, 1999.

Morris, Robert. *The Poetry of Freemasonry.* The Wrener Company, 1895.

Murphy, James C. *A Critical and Exegetical Commentary on the Book of Exodus, with a New Translation.* Boston, Massachusetts: Estes and Lauriat, 1874.

Myers, Allen C., ed. *The Eerdmans Bible Dictionary.* Grand Rapids, Michigan: Eerdmans, 1987.

N

Nachmanides, Ramban. *Commentary on the Torah.* Translated by Charles B. Chavel. New York: Shilo Publishing, 1973.

Nelson, Russell M. "Lessons From Eve" *Ensign,* November 1987, 86–89.

Neusner, Jacob, ed. *Dictionary of Judaism in the Biblical Period.* Peabody, Massachusetts: Hendrickson, 1999.

———. *The Enchantments of Judaism: Rites of Transformation from Birth Through Death.* Atlanta, Georgia: Scholars Press, 1991.

———. *The Genesis Rabbah: The Judaic Commentary to the Book of Genesis.* Atlanta, Georgia: Scholars Press, 1985.

Nibley, Hugh W. *An Approach to the Book of Abraham.* Provo, Utah: Foundation for Ancient Research and Mormon Studies, 2009.

———. *Approaching Zion.* Provo, Utah: Foundation for Ancient Research and Mormon Studies, 1989.

———. "The Facsimiles of the Book of Abraham: A Response by H. W. Nibley to E. H. Ashment." *Sunstone,* December 1979, 49–51.

———. *The Message of the Joseph Smith Papyri: An Egyptian Endowment,* 1st ed. Salt Lake City: Deseret Book, 1975.

———. *The Message of the Joseph Smith Papyri: An Egyptian Endowment,* 2nd ed. Provo, Utah: Foundation for Ancient Research and Mormon Studies, 2005.

———. *Mormonism and Early Christianity.* Provo, Utah: Foundation for Ancient Research and Mormon Studies, 1987.

———. "A New Look at the Pearl of Great Price: Part 3: Empaneling the Panel." *Improvement Era,* July 1968, 48–53.

———. *Old Testament and Related Studies.* Provo, Utah: Foundation for Ancient Research and Mormon Studies, 1986.

———. *Teachings of the Book of Mormon.* Provo, Utah: Foundation for Ancient Research and Mormon Studies, 2004.

———. *Temple and Cosmos: Beyond This Ignorant Present.* Salt Lake City: Foundation for Ancient Research and Mormon Studies, 1992.

———. *The World and the Prophets.* Provo, Utah: Foundation for Ancient Research and Mormon Studies, 1987.

Nicoll, W. Robertson. *Expositor's Greek Testament.* Grand Rapid, Michigan: Eerdmans, 1983.

Nyman, Monte S. *Doctrine and Covenants Commentary.* Orem, Utah: Granite Publishing, 2008–2009.

O

Oaks, Dallin H. "The Great Plan of Happiness." *Ensign*, November 1993, 72–75.

———. "Scripture Reading and Revelation." *Ensign*, January 1995, 6–9.

O'Collins, Gerald G. "Crucifixion." In *The Anchor Bible Dictionary*, edited by David Noel Freedman, 1:1207–10. New York: Doubleday, 1992.

Ogden, Kelly, and Andrew Skinner. *Verse by Verse: Acts Through Revelation.* Salt Lake City: Deseret Book, 1998.

Olderr, Steven. *Symbolism: A Comprehensive Dictionary.* Jefferson, North Carolina: McFarland & Company, 1986.

Old Testament: Genesis–2 Samuel (Religion 301) Student Manual, 2nd ed., rev. Salt Lake City: The Church of Jesus Christ of Latter-day Saints, 1981.

Olford, Stephen F. *The Tabernacle: Camping with God*, 2nd ed. Grand Rapids, Michigan: Kregel, 2004.

Oliver, George. *The Ancient Landmarks of Freemasonry.* Silver Springs, Maryland: The Masonic Service Association, 1932.

Olney, Oliver. *Oliver Olney Journal.* Unpublished Manuscript. New Haven, Connecticut: Yale University Beinecke Rare Book and Manuscript Library.

Ostler, Blake. "Clothed Upon: A Unique Aspect of Christian Antiquity." *BYU Studies* 22, no. 1 (1982): 31–45.

Otten, L. G., and C. M. Caldwell. *Sacred Truths of the Doctrine and Covenants.* Springville, Utah: LEMB, 1982.

The Oxford English Dictionary. New York: Oxford and Clarendon Press, 1991.

Oxtoby, William G., and Alan F. Segal, eds. *A Concise Introduction to World Religions.* New York: Oxford University, 2007.

P

Packer, Boyd K. *Eternal Love.* Salt Lake City: Deseret Book, 1973.

———. *Let Not Your Heart Be Troubled.* Salt Lake City: Bookcraft, 1991.

———. *Our Father's Plan*, rev. ed. Salt Lake City: Deseret Book, 1994.

Pagels, Elaine. *Adam, Eve, and the Serpent.* New York: Vintage Books, 1989.

Papanikolas, Helen. *An Amulet of Greek Earth.* Athens: Swallow Press/Ohio University Press, 2002.

Parry, Donald W., and Jay A. Parry. *Symbols and Shadows: Unlocking a Deeper Understanding of the Atonement.* Salt Lake City: Deseret Book, 2009.

———. *Understanding the Book of Revelation.* Salt Lake City: Deseret Book, 1998.

Parshall, Ardis E. "The Angel Moroni's Secret." *The Keepapitchinin,* April 2009. http://www.keepapitchinin.org/2009/04/30/the-angel-moronis-secret/.

Patrinacos, Nicon D. *A Dictionary of Greek Orthodoxy.* New York: Greek Orthodox Archdiocese of North and South America, Dept. of Education, 1984.

Peterson, H. Donl. *Moroni: Ancient Prophet, Modern Messenger.* Salt Lake City: Deseret Book, 2000.

———. "Moroni, the Last of the Nephite Prophets." In *The Book of Mormon: Fourth Nephi Through Moroni, From Zion to Destruction,* edited by Monte S. Nyman and Charles D. Tate Jr., 235–49. Provo, Utah: Religious Studies Center, BYU, 1995.

Pfeiffer, Charles F., and Everett F. Harrison, eds. *The Wycliffe Bible Commentary.* Chicago: Moody Press, 1975.

Plutarch. *Plutarch: The Lives of the Nobel Grecians and Romans.* Translated by Dryden. Chicago: Encyclopedia Britannica, 1982.

Port, M. H., ed. *The Houses of Parliament.* London: Yale University Press, 1976.

"Praise to the Man." *Hymns,* no. 27.

Pratt, Orson. "Celestial Marriage." *The Seer* 1, no. 2 (1853): 25–32.

———. *An Interesting Account of Several Remarkable Visions.* Edinburgh: Ballantyne & Hughes, 1840.

Pratt, Parley P. *The Autobiography of Parley Packer Pratt,* 5th ed. Edited by Parley P. Pratt Jr. Salt Lake City: Deseret Book, 1961.

Prince, Gregory A., and Wm. Robert Wright. *David O. McKay and the Rise of Modern Mormonism.* Salt Lake City: The University of Utah Press, 2005.

Q

"Questionable Spending." *The Salt Lake Tribune.* Salt Lake City, April 22, 2000.

Quodvultdeus. "Book of Promises and Predictions of God." In *Ancient Christian Commentary on Scripture: Genesis 1–11,* edited by Andrew Louth, 71. Downers Grove, Illinois: InterVarsity Press, 2001.

R

Rabinowicz, Tzvi M. *The Encyclopedia of Hasidism*. Maryland: Jason Aronson Publishers, 1977.

Rasmussen, Ellis T. *A Latter-day Saint Commentary on the Old Testament*. Salt Lake City: Deseret Book, 1993.

Rest, Friedrich. *Our Christian Symbols*. New York: Pilgrim Press, 1987.

Rhead, George Woolliscroft. *History of the Fan*. Philadelphia: J. B. Lippincott, 1910.

Rich, Ben E. *Scrapbook of Mormon Literature*. Chicago: Henry C. Etten & Co. 1913.

Richardson, Matthew O. "Voices of Warning: Ironies in the Life of Cyrus E. Dallin." In *Regional Studies in Latter-day Saint Church History: The New England States*, edited by Donald Q. Cannon, Arnold K. Garr, and Bruce A. Van Orden, 205–17. Provo, Utah: Religious Studies Center, BYU, 2004.

Ricks, Stephen D. "The Garment of Adam in Jewish, Muslim, and Christian Traditions." In *Temples of the Ancient World*, edited by Donald W. Parry, 705–39. Salt Lake City: Deseret Book, 1994.

"Revelation of Moses." In *Ante-Nicene Fathers: The Writings of the Fathers down to A.D. 325*, edited by Alexander Roberts and James Donaldson, 8:565–70. Peabody, Massachusetts: Hendrickson Publishers, 1994.

Roberts, B. H. *A Comprehensive History of the Church of Jesus Christ of Latter-day Saints*. Orem, Utah: Sonos Publishing, 1991.

Robinson, Stephen E. *Believing Christ*. Salt Lake City: Deseret Book, 1992.

———. "The Book of Adam in Judaism and Early Christianity." In *The Man Adam*, edited by Joseph Fielding McConkie and Robert L. Millet, 131–50. Salt Lake City: Bookcraft, 1990.

Robinson, Stephen E., and H. Dean Garrett. *A Commentary on the Doctrine and Covenants*. Salt Lake City: Deseret Book, 2000–2005.

Rockwood, Jolene Edmunds. "The Redemption of Eve." In *Sisters in Spirit*, edited by Maureen Usenbach Beecher and Lavina Fielding Anderson, 3–36. Chicago: University of Illinois Press, 1992.

Romig, Ronald E. "Temple Lot Discoveries and the RLDS Temple." In *Regional Studies in Latter-day Saint Church History: Missouri*, edited by Arnold K. Garr and Clark V. Johnson, 313–35. Provo, Utah: Department of Church History and Doctrine, Brigham Young University, 1994.

Romney, Marion G. "Mother Eve, A Worthy Exemplar." *Relief Society Magazine*, 55 (February 1968): 84–89.

Roth, Cecil, Geoffrey Wigoder, and Fred Skolnik, eds. *Encyclopaedia Judaica*. Jerusalem: Keter Publishing, 2007.

Rozsa, Allen Claire. "Temple Ordinances." In *Encyclopedia of Mormonism*, edited by Daniel H. Ludlow, 4:1444–45. New York: Macmillan, 1992.

Russell, Reed. "The Washington, D.C. Chapel." *The Keepapitchinin* (September 2012). http://www.keepapitchinin.org/2012/09/26/guest-post-the-washington-d-c-chapel/.

Ryken, Leland, James C. Wilhoit, and Tremper Longman III, eds. *Dictionary of Biblical Imagery*. Downers Grove, Illinois: InterVarsity Press, 1998.

S

Sailhamer, John. "Genesis." In *The Expositor's Bible Commentary*, edited by Frank E. Gaebelein, 2:1–284. Grand Rapids. Michigan: Zondervan, 1976–92.

Schaff, Philip, ed. *Nicene and Post-Nicene Fathers: First Series*. Peabody, Massachusetts: Hendrickson, 2004.

Scharfstein, Sol. *Torah and Commentary: The Five Books of Moses*. Jersey City, New Jersey: KTAV Publishing, 2008.

Scott, E. F. *The Moffatt New Testament Commentary: The Epistles of Paul to the Colossians, to Philemon, and to the Ephesians*. London: Hodder and Stoughton, 1952.

Searle, Don L. "The Conference Center: 'This New and Wonderful Hall.'" *Ensign*, October 2000, 32–41.

Sears, Jack. "A Sacred Witness to All Men." *The Instructor* 91, no. 3 (1956): 73–74.

Sessions, Perrigrine. *The Diary of Perrigrine Sessions*. Unpublished, owned by author.

Shipps, Jan. "The Scattering of the Gathered and the Gathering of the Scattered: The Mormon Diaspora in the Mid-Twentieth Century." In *The Juanita Brooks Lecture Series—Issue 3*, 1–21. St. George, Utah: Dixie College, 1991.

Sikh Religion. Detroit, Michigan: Sikh Missionary Center, 1990.

Singh, Nikky-Guninder Kaur. *Encyclopedia of Religion*, 2nd ed., edited by Lindsay Jones. New York: Macmillan Reference USA, 2005.

Skinner, Andrew C. "Savior, Satan, and Serpent: The Duality of a Symbol in the Scriptures." In *The Disciple as Scholar—Essays on Scripture and the Ancient World in Honor of Richard Lloyd Anderson*, edited by Stephen D. Ricks, Donald W. Parry, and Andrew H. Hedges, 359–84. Provo, Utah: Foundation for Ancient Research and Mormon Studies, 2000.

Slemming, Charles W. *These Are The Garments: A Study of the Garments of the High Priest of Israel*. London: Marshall, Morgan Scott, 1945.

Smith, Hyrum M., and Janne M. Sjodahl. *Doctrine and Covenants Commentary*, rev. ed. Salt Lake City: Deseret Book, 1978.

Smith, J. M. Powis, and Edgar J. Goodspeed, trans. *The Complete Bible: An American Translation*. Chicago: University of Chicago Press, 1949.

Smith, Joseph. "History of Joseph Smith." In *Times and Seasons*. Commerce and Nauvoo, Illinois: The Church of Jesus Christ of Latter-day Saints, 1839–46.

———. *Teachings of the Prophet Joseph Smith*. Compiled by Joseph Fielding Smith. Salt Lake City: Deseret Book, 1976.

———. *History of the Church*. Edited by B. H. Roberts, 2nd rev. ed. Salt Lake City: Deseret Book, 1978.

———. *Personal Writings of Joseph Smith*. Compiled by Dean C. Jessee, 2nd ed. Salt Lake City: Deseret Book, 2002.

Smith, Joseph F. "Opening Address." *Conference Report*, 1–6. Salt Lake City: The Church of Jesus Christ of Latter-day Saints, 1903.

Smith, Joseph Fielding. *Church History and Modern Revelation*. Salt Lake City: The Church of Jesus Christ of Latter-day Saints, 1946–49.

———. *Doctrine of Salvation*. Salt Lake City: Bookcraft, 1998.

———. *Man, His Origin and Destiny*. Salt Lake City: Deseret Book, 1954.

———. *The Way to Perfection*. Salt Lake City: Genealogical Society of Utah, 1949.

Smith, Lucy Mack. *History of Joseph Smith by His Mother*. Salt Lake City: Bookcraft.

Speiser, E. A. "Of Shoes and Shekels." *Bulletin of the American Schools of Oriental Research*, 77 (February 1940): 15–20.

Stevens, Edward L. *Reminiscences of Joseph, the Prophet, and the Coming Forth of the Book of Mormon*. Salt Lake City: Edward Stephens, 1893.

Strahan, James. "Ruth." In *A Commentary on the Bible*, edited by Arthur S. Peake. New York: Thomas Nelson and Sons, 1919.

Strausberg, Michael. "The Significance of the 'kusti': A History of Its Zoroastrian Interpretation." *East and West* 54, no. 1 (2004): 9–29.

T

Taxiarchae-Archangels Greek Orthodox Church. *The Consecration of Our Beloved Church*. Watertown, Massachusetts: Taxiarchae-Archangels Greek Orthodox Church, 2000.

Taylor, John. Discourse given October 8, 1871. In *Journal of Discourses*, 14:245–50.

Taylor, R. B. "Avenger of Blood." In *Dictionary of the Bible*, edited by James Hastings, rev. ed. New York: Charles Scribner's Sons, 1963.

Thayer, Joseph H. *Thayer's Greek-English Lexicon of the New Testament*. Peabody, Massachusetts: Hendrickson Publishers, 1999.

"The Temple." *The Salt Lake Herald*. Salt Lake City. October 4, 1891.

"The Temple." *The Salt Lake Herald*. Salt Lake City. April 3, 1892.

"Temple Souvenir Album." Salt Lake City: Magazine Printing Company, 1892.

Thomas, M. Catherine. "Hebrews: To Ascend the Holy Mount." In *Temples of the Ancient World*, edited by Donald W. Parry, 479–91. Salt Lake City: Deseret Book, 1994.

Thompson, Thomas, and Dorothy Thompson. "Some Legal Problems in the Book of Ruth." *Vetus Testamentum* 18 (1968): 79–99.

Todeschi, Kevin J. *The Encyclopedia of Symbolism*. New York: The Berkley Publishing Group, 1995.

Trent, Kenneth E. *Types of Christ in the Old Testament: A Conservative Approach to Old Testament Typology*. New York: Exposition Press, 1960.

Tresidder, Jack. *Symbols and Their Meanings: The Illustrated Guide to More than 1000 Symbols—Their Traditional and Contemporary Significance*. London: Duncan Baird Publications, 2000.

True to the Faith. Salt Lake City: The Church of Jesus Christ of Latter-day Saints, 2004.

Tucker, G. M. "Shorter Communications: Witnesses and 'Dates' in Israelite Contracts." *The Catholic Biblical Quarterly* 28 (1966): 42–45.

Tuveson, Earnest Lee. *Redeemer Nation: The Ideal of America's Millennial Role*. Chicago: University of Chicago Press, 1968.

Tvedtnes, John. "Priestly Clothing in Bible Times." In *Temples of the Ancient World*, edited by Donald W. Parry, 649–704. Provo, Utah: Foundation for Ancient Research and Mormon Studies, 1994.

Tvedtnes, John A. *The Church of the Old Testament*. Salt Lake City: Deseret Book, 1976.

U

Unger, Merrill F. *Unger's Bible Dictionary*. Chicago: Moody Press, 1975.

V

VanGemeren, Willem A., ed. *New International Dictionary of the Old Testament Theology and Exegesis*. Grand Rapids, Michigan: Zondervan, 1997.

Van Gennep, Arnold. *The Rites of Passage*. Translated by Monika B. Vizedom and Gabrielle L. Caffee. Chicago: The University of Chicago Press, 1960.

Van Orden, Bruce A. "Important Items of Instruction." In *Studies in Scripture: Volume One—The Doctrine and Covenants*, edited by Robert L. Millet and Kent P. Jackson, 497–511. Salt Lake City: Deseret Book, 1989.

Vawter, Bruce. *On Genesis: A New Reading*. New York: Doubleday, 1977.

Von Simson, Otto G. *Sacred Fortress: Byzantine Art and Statecraft in Ravenna*. New Jersey: Princeton University Press, 1987.

W

Ware, Timothy. *The Orthodox Church,* new ed. New York: Penguin Books, 1997.

Webster, Noah. *Noah Webster's First Edition (1828) of an American Dictionary of the English Language*. San Francisco, California: Foundation for American Christian Education, 1967.

Welch, John W., and Claire Foley. "Gammadia on Early Jewish and Christian Garments." In *Masada and the World of the New Testament*, 253–58. Provo, Utah: BYU Studies, 1997.

White, James F. "The Spatial Setting." In *The Oxford History of Christian Worship*, edited by Geoffrey Wainwright and Karen B. Westerfield Tucker, 791–816. New York: Oxford University Press, 2006.

Whitney, Orson F. *Life of Heber C. Kimball*, 4th ed. Salt Lake City: Bookcraft, 1973.

Widtsoe, John A. *Evidences and Reconciliations*. Salt Lake City: Bookcraft, 1960.

———. *Joseph Smith: Seeker after Truth, Prophet of God*. Salt Lake City: Bookcraft, 1951.

———. *Priesthood and Church Government in the Church of Jesus Christ of Latter-day Saints*. Salt Lake City: Bookcraft, 1994.

———. *A Rational Theology,* 7th ed. Salt Lake City: Deseret Book, 1966.

Wilcox, Keith W. *The Washington DC Temple—A Light to the World: A History of its Architectural Development*. Self-published by Keith W. Wilcox, 1995.

Wilson, Walter L. *A Dictionary of Bible Types*. Peabody, Massachusetts: Hendrickson Publishers, 1999.

Woodford, Robert J. *The Historical Development of the Doctrine and Covenants*. Provo, Utah: Brigham Young University, 1974.

Woodruff, Wilford. *Collected Discourses*. Compiled by Brian H. Stuy. B.H.S Publishing, 1999.

———. *The Discourses of Wilford Woodruff.* Compiled by G. Homer Durham. Salt Lake City: Bookcraft, 1964.

———. *Leaves from My Journal*. Salt Lake City: Juvenile Instructor Office, 1881.

———. *Wilford Woodruff's Journal*. Edited by Scott G. Kenney. Midvale, Utah: Signature Books, 1983.

Wright, R. Lane. *Testament in Stone: Symbols of the Nauvoo Temple and Their Meanings*. Nauvoo, Illinois: The Nauvoo Press, 2014.

Y

Young, Brigham. *The Complete Discourses of Brigham Young*. Edited by Richard S. Van Wagoner. Salt Lake City: The Smith-Pettit Foundation, 2009.

———. *Discourse of Brigham Young*. Compiled by John A. Widtsoe. Salt Lake City: Bookcraft, 1998.

Young, Edward J. *The Book of Isaiah*. Grand Rapids, Michigan: Eerdmans, 1997.

Young, Eugene. "Inside the New Mormon Temple." *Harper's Weekly*, 510. New York: May 27, 1893.

Young, George Cannon. *George C. Young Oral History*. Unpublished manuscript: 1980.

Young, Joseph Don Carlos. *Private Notebook*.

Young, Levi Edgar. "The Angel Moroni and Cyrus Dallin" *Improvement Era* 56, no. 4 (1953): 68, 234–35.

INDEX

M

N

O

P

ABOUT THE AUTHOR

Alonzo L. Gaskill is a professor of Church history and doctrine. He holds a bachelors degree in philosophy, a masters in theology, and a PhD in biblical studies. Brother Gaskill has taught at Brigham Young University since 2003. Prior to coming to BYU, he served in a variety of assignments within the Church Educational System—most recently as the director of the LDS Institute of Religion at Stanford University (1995–2003).